The Impact of the United States Supreme Court

SOME PERSPECTIVES

THE DORSEY SERIES IN POLITICAL SCIENCE

EDITOR Norton E. Long *University of Illinois*

AKE *A Theory of Political Integration*

BROWN & WAHLKE (eds.) *The American Political System: Notes and Readings*

DRAGNICH *Major European Governments* 3d ed.

EDELMANN *Latin American Government and Politics: The Dynamics of a Revolutionary Society* rev. ed.

FROHOCK *The Nature of Political Inquiry*

GRIPP *Patterns of Soviet Politics* rev. ed.

ISAAK *Scope and Methods of Political Science: An Introduction to the Methodology of Political Inquiry*

ISMAEL *Governments and Politics of the Contemporary Middle East*

JACOB & ATHERTON *The Dynamics of International Organization: The Making of World Order*

JACOBINI *International Law: A Text* rev. ed.

LUTTBEG (ed.) *Public Opinion and Public Policy: Models of Political Linkage*

MACRIDIS & BROWN *The De Gaulle Republic*

MACRIDIS & BROWN (eds.) *Comparative Politics: Notes and Readings* 3d ed.

MANGONE *The Elements of International Law* rev. ed.

MEEHAN *Contemporary Political Thought: A Critical Study*

MEEHAN *Explanation in Social Science: A System Paradigm*

MEEHAN *The Theory and Method of Political Analysis*

MEEHAN *Value Judgment and Social Science: Structures and Processes*

MINAR *Ideas and Politics: The American Experience*

MURPHY *Political Theory: A Conceptual Analysis*

NAGEL *The Legal Process from a Behavioral Perspective*

OSBORN *Soviet Social Policies: Welfare, Equality, and Community*

ROBINSON *Congress and Foreign Policy-Making: A Study in Legislative Influence and Initiative* rev. ed.

ROELOFS *The Language of Modern Politics: An Introduction to the Study of Government*

SARGENT *Contemporary Political Ideologies: A Comparative Analysis*

SIGLER *Courts and Public Policy: Cases and Essays*

SIGLER *An Introduction to the Legal System*

SPIRO *World Politics: The Global System*

WASBY *The Impact of the United States Supreme Court: Some Perspectives*

WESSON *Soviet Foreign Policy in Perspective*

The Impact of the United States Supreme Court

SOME PERSPECTIVES

STEPHEN L. WASBY
Associate Professor of Government
Southern Illinois University/Carbondale

1970
THE
DORSEY PRESS HOMEWOOD, ILLINOIS
IRWIN-DORSEY LIMITED, GEORGETOWN, ONTARIO

First Printing, July, 1970

Library of Congress Catalog Card No. 77-118193

Printed in the United States of America

This book is dedicated to
Former Chief Justice Earl Warren
and his colleagues of the "Warren Court"

Preface

There is a clear intent on which this volume is based: to attempt to pull together and begin to integrate the extant materials on the impact of the United States Supreme Court, so that they may be communicated to students and other political scientists, as well as to those with an interest in activities of the Supreme Court. If that purpose is achieved, the author will be satisfied.

While many political scientists still teach about the doctrine which the Court establishes, a rising proportion know they need to talk about what happens to those decisions after they have been handed down. The greater interest in the "judicial process" rather than in simply "constitutional law" reinforces this. Yet the extant materials on impact are not easily available for teaching purposes,[1] many of the more important items being in law reviews, generally inaccessible to both teachers and students.

Perhaps something more has also been accomplished within these pages. In the course of arranging the material available on a given subject, one has to face inevitable decisions as to what should go where and with what other material. The material seldom "falls into place" by itself without considerable nudging and sometimes even pulling and hauling. Odd items are forever jumping up and demanding recognition and a new place in one's scheme, or demanding that they be two (and three and four) places simultaneously. Through the arranging necessary for this volume, the author hopes he has contributed to further development of our thinking with respect to the impact of the Court and, as a result, to our knowledge about the place of the Supreme Court in the American political system. Let it be clear that no new field research was conducted for this volume; previously written materials—by lawyers, political scientists, sociologists, and journalists (including current newspaper items)—are the base on which this volume rests. To the extent that material is incomplete or otherwise weak, so will the volume be—but it is hoped the reader will interpret this as a statement about what we know concerning impact, not as a judgment about the author. There is no question that research is

[1] The reader edited by Theodore Becker, *The Impact of Supreme Court Decisions: Empirical Studies* (New York: Oxford University Press, 1969), is a major exception. Occasional items are included in collections of materials on the judicial process.

needed to flesh out what is found here. It simply has not been my purpose to do that research at this time, for this volume.

Much of what appears here is concerned with matters in the areas of civil liberties and civil rights. That may be a function of the author's interests. However, it is more likely a function of the thrust of existing impact literature which, starting with such subjects as school desegregation and church-state relations, has generally remained in the civil liberties area, although expanding to include obscenity, reapportionment, and criminal procedure, among others. An effort has been made to gather what could be found with respect to the impact of the Supreme Court on economic regulation, but here the materials are much skimpier. One wishes that impact scholars had been at work during the 1920's and early 1930's, as well as at earlier periods (like the late years of the 19th century) when economic concerns bulked larger in the Supreme Court's output.

Private law is not covered in this volume. There are two basic reasons for this. One is that the emphasis of the Supreme Court is on public law matters; while some Supreme Court decisions, such as the cases in which standards for libel are developed, relate to private law, most do not. The other reason is the unavailability of materials on the subject. An examination of the impact of court cases on private law will have to await studies of the impacts of lower courts and state high appellate courts.

The attention of the Supreme Court to civil rights and liberties in the post-1937 period, and particularly in the period of the Warren Court, has been reflected in the writing of those dealing with impact. In turn, it is reflected in the concentration on civil rights and liberties in this volume. To that extent, the volume is clearly time-bound, and might even be considered largely a study of the impact of the Warren Court, but it is not purposely so. However, we must recognize that the attention given to civil rights matters may mean concentration on one type of reception accorded the Court's decisions—a controversial reception, on the whole—and relative neglect of other types of receptions. To the extent the Warren Court has been an "activist" court, its reception (and the material reported here) may have been affected. In this connection, although the impact of the Warren Court is likely to continue far beyond the retirement of the Chief Justice, it is perhaps appropriate to be writing now, at the end of the Warren Court and before any possible changes in Court-enunciated doctrine come about.

Perhaps the author can be faulted for reinforcing the existing emphasis on civil rights and controversy instead of trying to correct it. To do so would be to write a different book, and the author feels that more thought needs to be given to concepts like "impact," "evasion," "compliance," and "aftermath" before further work—if it is to be fruitful—should be carried out. So perhaps the book some would like is not here. But also, hopefully, something which will help others write that other book may be somewhere within these covers.

The book is divided into two parts, each of which has its own introduction. The first part, comprising three chapters, deals with how we have studied impact and how we might look at the subject. It is here that those matters most important for developing a "theory of impact" appear, although work on the subject has not proceeded far enough for us to be able to present such a theory in well-developed form. In the second part, the thrust of the presentation is more substantive and description bulks larger, as we look at the Court's impacts in a variety of issue-areas and political arenas. In a final chapter, a set of hypotheses about impact is offered. The hypotheses, derived from the literature already discussed and arranged to parallel the presentation of an earlier chapter, serve as both a summary and a point of departure for further research and analysis.

* * *

This book has a long intellectual history, and an accumulation of debts to go with it. I first became interested in the problem of determining the Supreme Court's impact while examining the policy-making process concerning obscene literature in Oregon. James Klonoski and William Mitchell were major shapers of that effort. Hassan Mohammed-Nejad, formerly of Southern Illinois University, helped immensely by searching and summarizing much relevant journal literature. Members of my Winter, 1969, graduate seminar on the judicial process provided much useful feedback. To Donald Gregory, a member of that seminar and a subsequent associate, go special thanks for the important ideas he has contributed. Jeanne Hahn, Oberlin College, has generously shared her understanding of the group process and the NAACP. From those at the School of Law, University of Wisconsin, particularly Marygold Melli, Edward Kimball, and Frank Remington, I have obtained a greater understanding of the broader legal environment of which the Supreme Court is but a part. To the Russell Sage Foundation, I owe appreciation for the grant which allowed me to spend a year in Wisconsin.

All those mentioned here have contributed much to the book; some may be able to recognize their ideas, which I hope I have not pirated outrageously. Of course, they are not responsible in any way for errors of fact or misguided interpretation and judgments; I can only hope that, in the end, they do not wish they had nothing to do with the book.

* * *

Without further ado, having seen how the book came about and what the author intended, let the reader embark, remembering that, for authors as well as for others, the road to hell is often paved with good intentions.

Madison, Wisconsin
June, 1970

STEPHEN L. WASBY

Contents

Part I

THE "THEORY" OF IMPACT

The thrust of contemporary political science is toward the development of theory. This thrust requires that political scientists be self-conscious about what they are doing, that they be systematic, and that they begin at the beginning with the development of concepts which will be at the core of their work. Someone coming on the scene of work on impact may not find that those who have contributed to our "fund of knowledge" on the subject have fulfilled these criteria as well as one might wish—although, in any new area of study, much is to be understood as groping and exploratory. In this part of the book, an attempt is made to make a fresh start, without being particularly "original," using what has been done thus far and extrapolating from it.

In making that start, we begin with a chapter in which are discussed the views political scientists have taken toward the Supreme Court and the way the study of impact fits into the political perspective students of the Supreme Court have adopted in recent years. To provide an initial grasp of the subject of the volume, some initial examples of the effects of Supreme Court decisions are presented at the beginning of Chapter 1. The second chapter deals with the meaning of key concepts. It includes a discussion of types of impacts which goes beyond the more cursory treatment of the first chapter; an examination of variables relevant to the impact of decisions is undertaken here, also. Chapter 3 includes a number of frames of reference through which impact might profitably be examined. The emphasis is on impact as viewed through the perspective the frame of reference provides rather than on an exposition of the frame of reference itself. The Court as a legal institution is examined, as is its role in a network of interests and as an element in a communications system.

CHAPTER 1

Impact: A First Look

SOME EXAMPLES OF IMPACT

"Crime Rulings to be Reversed, M'Clellan Says"
"New Obscenity Ruling Draws Mixed Reaction"
"Illinois Bar Assails High Court Decisions"
"Bugging Decision Is a Concern"
"California Nude Dances Laid to Court Decisions"
"Drug Charges Dropped Under Spinelli Ruling"
"Railroad Setback in Court Decision"
"Ruling on Welfare Aid Meets Some Defiance"

The above headlines, culled from recent newspapers, indicate what at least some reporters consider newsworthy effects of Supreme Court decisions. To note some of the more visible and immediate types of impact here may help the reader to grasp some of the contours of the subject with which we are dealing. In looking at these examples, one should keep in mind that journalists and other observers do not write about a representative range of phenomena; they tend to emphasize the spectacular and what occurs counter to expectations. Just as there are relatively few stories about dogs biting people (unless it concerns a new method the mailman has for repelling canines) but people who bite dogs are newsworthy, so it is that noncompliance with court rulings gets more attention than compliance, even though the latter may be more frequent. Because political scientists share expectations with other members of the society, who expect compliance, we find that their work has emphasized noncompliance rather than compliance, and impacts in areas of controversy rather than routine activity.

Impacts occur with respect to many subject matters (Chapters 4 and 5) in many governmental and political arenas (Chapters 6 and 7) at national, state, and local levels. They even occur in other countries, although that is outside our focus of attention.

Some of the impacts of the Court have been quite evident, as attempts to overturn those decisions have been undertaken or as reactions to decisions have produced strong criticism of the Court or individual Justices. Thus, for several years the late Senator Dirksen (R–Ill.) attempted to overturn, by constitutional amendment, the decision requiring that both houses of state legislatures be apportioned on the basis of population. While he was not successful in obtaining the necessary two-thirds majority in the Senate, he achieved a majority vote in favor of his proposal on two occasions. Many national legislators, including Senator Dirksen, have also attempted to secure adoption of amendments permitting silent prayer in schools or prayer in public buildings, both aimed more or less directly at the Court's school prayer rulings; 115 congressmen introduced constitutional amendments dealing with those decisions.

These recent events have counterparts throughout our history. Constitutional amendments have been passed to overturn specific Supreme Court decisions. The earliest example is the passage of the Eleventh Amendment, preventing a citizen of a foreign country or of a state from suing another state, a direct result of *Chisholm* v. *Georgia.* The amendment was initiated in Congress the day following the decision. *Pollock* v. *Farmers' Loan & Trust Co.*, holding an income tax unconstitutional, led to the passage of the Sixteenth Amendment. And some historians say that the Fourteenth Amendment, particularly those portions dealing with citizenship, can be interpreted as an overruling of Justice Taney's opinion in *Dred Scott* v. *Sandford,* although the Civil War had in the meantime settled the matter of Negro citizenship politically.*

Statutes have resulted more often than have constitutional amendments. The prompt reenactment by Congress of the labor provisions (Sec. 7A) of the National Industrial Recovery Act after that law was invalidated is one example. Still another, with respect to procedure, is provided by the aftermath of *Carter* v. *Carter Coal Company,* in which the Court struck down the Guffey Bituminous Coal Act in a case brought by a corporation president against his own company. Congress promptly passed legislation to allow the government to become a party to any suit in which the constitutionality of a federal statute was called into question. When the Court held that the government must make available to the defense all records used by a witness (including, possibly, material identifying informers), the Congress modified and limited the decision by passing the Jencks Act, providing for production only of such records as a judge had determined relevant to the witness' testimony. In 1968, Congress limited the effect of the *Mallory* ruling on prompt arraignment by allowing up to six hours of prearraignment interrogation in the Omnibus Crime Control and Safe Streets Act.

---

* For citations to these and other cases mentioned in this volume, see the Table of Cases.

While perhaps only a small proportion of "reversal" bills introduced in Congress are enacted, virtually every Supreme Court decision on a major point of public law stimulates the introduction of several bills aimed at altering or overturning the ruling. Thus, when the Supreme Court invalidated arrangements whereby newspapers pooled advertising and business staffs but continued to publish separate papers, a number of senators and representatives immediately introduced the Newspaper Preservation Act of 1969, to allow the invalidated practices. In addition to legislation which is directed at overturning specific court decisions, statutes may simply be directed at a problem where pressure has built up because of earlier court decisions. Thus, the Court's invalidation of state regulation of railroads brought pressure resulting in the Interstate Commerce Commission Act. Sometimes collective action falling short of actual legislation is taken by some legislators. A prime example is the Southern Manifesto of March, 1956, signed by almost all U.S. senators and representatives from the southern states, severely taking the Supreme Court to task for its School Desegregation decisions.

Blaming the Court and its decisions for disliked social phenomena is a common sport, as shown by law enforcement officers attributing nude dancing to court decisions or claiming that crime rates have increased and criminals not brought to justice because of the decisions in the *Escobedo* and *Miranda* cases. Lawyers are not immune: we find the Illinois Bar Association's Board of Governors accusing the Court of " 'unsound' decisions" concerning group legal practice. Criticism of the Court's individual members is also not infrequent. We have seen members of the U.S. Senate, particularly Senators Thurmond (R–S.C.), Eastland and Stennis (D–Miss.), and Ervin (D–N.C.), berating then Justice Fortas, at the time of his nomination to be Chief Justice, for participating in decisions which overturned convictions of individuals for selling obscene literature. Thurmond said obscenity had mushroomed as a result of high court cases and added, "In the last two years it has grown much worse while Mr. Fortas has been on the Supreme Court." Senator Ervin had introduced an amendment to change the Constitution with respect to the appointing of Supreme Court Justices, a measure clearly aimed at the nomination by President Johnson of Justice Fortas to be Chief Justice. That the latter effort became entangled with partisan political considerations, such as the desire of Republicans to have Chief Justice Warren's successor named by the next President, suggests that impacts of Court activity are not always easily isolated from other chains of events. While the failure of the Senate to act on the Fortas nomination was the first time in the twentieth century a nominee for Chief Justice had not been confirmed, there have been other instances when senators have revolted against the actions of the Court when a nominee was before them, as in the instances of Charles Evans Hughes and John J. Parker (whose nomination was rejected) in the 1930's.

Not all activity in the aftermath of disliked decisions is in the forms of attacks and criticism. Outright refusal to comply, perhaps most clearly exemplified by "massive resistance" to school desegregation, which included nullification resolutions, cessation of state aid, repeal of compulsory attendance laws, and the closing down of all schools in some areas, occurs. Another example was the refusal in many school districts to discontinue classroom prayers after the *Schempp* decision. Decisions may be ignored, as some in the South ignored *Brown* v. *Board of Education,* feeling that the lack of enforcement of "but equal" in *Plessy* v. *Ferguson* ("separate but equal") meant that there was little need to comply.

Evasion of decisions is perhaps more common. In some states, when it has been felt that the Supreme Court's definition of obscenity has not been sufficiently restrictive, definitions of alternative concepts, such as "harmful materials," have been developed to allow suppression of material directed at youth. (Such laws were upheld.) After the Supreme Court, in *Buchanan* v. *Warley,* outlawed state statutes restricting ownership of property by Negroes, racial restrictive covenants were developed to achieve the same end, although their judicial enforcement was ultimately invalidated. Defense attorneys comment that police, in response to court decisions relating to standards of "probable cause" to make an arrest, simply change the formulae they utter when being questioned in court, in order to achieve the goal of conviction. For example, in drug cases, a policeman would say that a suspect dropped a foil package on the ground while the policeman was looking at him, thus establishing "probable cause," even though the event described is highly improbable. When the Court in the *Laub* case held the State Department without authority to bring criminal charges against those who had traveled to foreign countries on the Department's list of prohibited nations, the Department proceeded to revoke the passports of those who so traveled—until finally capitulating to an adverse Court of Appeals decision concerning that practice.

Another impact is a substantial rise in the level of political activity. Thus, in legislatures, not only do we find action directed against court decisions but we also find frantic activity directed at compliance, as often happened when the Supreme Court invalidated the apportionment of state legislative or congressional districts. In the two years after *Reynolds,* "thirty states had apportioned their entire legislatures; fifteen, their entire lower House; and thirteen, one-half of their Senates."[1*] Sometimes the activity which is stimulated results in overt political conflict. Even if one cannot say that the case caused the Civil War, some historians have argued that the *Dred Scott* decision nourished the conflict which led to the war. "The Supreme Court decision that the legal status of a slave who returned

* Numbered footnotes for each chapter will be found at the end of the text.

to a slave state after having left it was determinable by the courts of that state alone, might seem merely to settle a ticklish point of law, but it helped to precipitate the Civil War."[2]

Increased activity may occur within the court system itself. The questions asked in trials are affected. Thus, recent rulings on search and seizure have increased the number of motions to suppress and the number of arguments about the validity of warrants. The number of cases may increase, as others rush to see whether a recent decision applies to them or whether its boundaries can be stretched to include their slightly different circumstances. Within two hours of the decision in *Baker* v. *Carr* that reapportionment was a matter with which the courts would deal, suit was filed in Georgia testing that state's county-unit system of electing officials, which was declared invalid. And, as Robert Dixon has noted, "Under the impetus of *Baker*, reapportionment was on the agenda of most of the forty-seven state legislatures in session that year. Cases were before federal courts in thirty-one states, before state courts in nineteen states, and before both federal and state courts in eleven states."[3] Another reason for increased litigation in the wake of a decision is that the legal standards established require interpretation and elaboration. "Reasonable profits" in public utilities rate regulation cases and the "rule of reason" in antitrust cases are examples.

When the Court upholds a law, particularly one little used, lawyers may awaken to its possibilities. Thus, Dorsen writes, "The decision in *Hague* v. *CIO* . . . and the activities of the Department of Justice apparently awakened lawyers and litigants to the possibilities of the civil provisions of the Civil Rights Acts. In any event, the number of actions commended under these provisions began to increase rapidly."[4] When a particular approach has been validated by the Court, we find exhortations in other jurisdictions to adopt such tried and proven ways. Thus the state auditor in Illinois recently urged, after *Ginsberg* v. *New York*, in which New York's approach to the dissemination of "harmful material" to children had been upheld, that Illinois pass such a law. However, such efforts to extend the law are less likely to be highly motivated than efforts to respond when the Supreme Court has struck down an existing statute or regulation.

Cases have immediate impact for individuals. Some whose convictions of crimes rested on improper police procedures have become entitled to new trials and, when the prosecution preferred not to try again, to their freedom. Others found themselves still in jail, as occurred with Ernesto Miranda (the subject of *Miranda* v. *Arizona*), whose conviction was re-obtained without use of the confession the Supreme Court had held invalid; he remained in jail the whole time, because he was also serving a term for robbery. Miranda was not even able to benefit from the case bearing his name, because the Arizona Supreme Court held it nonretroactive when he later challenged the robbery conviction. Arthur Culombe, whose conviction was set aside on the grounds that his confession had been improperly obtained, was retried and was sentenced to life imprisonment after pleading guilty. Steve Nelson, whose conviction for violating the Pennsylvania antisubversion statute was set aside when the statute was invalidated on grounds that the federal government had preempted the field, similarly was never freed, because he was already in a federal penitentiary for a Smith Act violation. Just as prosecutors sometimes prefer not to try again when convictions have been reversed, so private parties may wish not to face further court action after the Supreme Court has decided a legal point in which they were interested. Thus, after *Jones* v. *Mayer*, the 1968 open-housing case testing the applicability of Reconstruction Era statutes, the company against whom the suit was brought settled out of court, paying all legal costs and making a $2,000 payment to Jones.

Cases also may affect individuals not directly involved. These individuals may simply share the characteristics of those who were parties. This is exemplified by the persecution of Jehovah's Witnesses unleashed after the Supreme Court upheld compulsory flag-salute statutes in cases involving members of that faith. Individuals in jail may find themselves freed, or at least able to challenge their convictions, on the basis of a case brought by someone else. Thus, in Florida in the first few months after *Gideon* v. *Wainwright*, requiring counsel for indigents in trials for major offenses, 1,000 prisoners were released because prosecutors could not or would not attempt to reprosecute. Of those 300 plus who were retried, most had their sentences reduced. Negroes may find that their children can attend a previously all-white school because of a case the NAACP has supported in another county or state. Those affected may be organized interests, like lawyers, as in the instance of the Illinois Bar's attack on the decision on group legal representation, or the NAACP, when its right to withhold membership lists from inquisitive government bodies was upheld. Large-scale economic interests may be involved, as when the Supreme Court upheld "full-crew" laws, thus "derailing" railroad efforts to reduce work forces. Governments as units may be affected, and Dolbeare suggests their greater reluctance to comply: "Participants may adjust their positions to court policies but . . . units of government are less likely to do this, to the point where they may on occasion act quite deliberately against known court standards."[5]

There is often an economic component to the impact, in addition to that on the policy preferences of groups or individuals. This is shown most clearly by *Shapiro* v. *Thompson*, the 1969 ruling invalidating residence requirements for welfare payment eligibility; this clearly increased the financial burden of states with high rates of in-migration of impoverished individuals. Thus, it was claimed immediately by California officials that

3,000–4,000 migrant poor would be added to the welfare rolls each month, with a resultant increase of $35 million in relief costs for federal, state, and county governments in California. Others stated that national welfare costs would be increased by $125 million to $175 million a year, with 100,000–200,000 people benefiting. This sort of fear led to or reinforced the push, by governors and others, for federal assumption of all welfare expenditures, somewhat ironic in that complaints by conservative governors should lead to an increased role for the federal government. Studies after several months suggested little evidence that the expected mass migration was occurring, although some experimental welfare programs at the local level had been abandoned for fear of movement from one county to a neighboring county.

Other economic costs also are imposed by court decisions. The aforementioned "full-crew" law decision will increase railroad labor costs, with the public eventually paying the bill through increased charges. After the portal-to-portal pay case, many suits for back pay were brought against companies. Even though Congress reversed the Court's ruling, clauses providing for such pay had been written into many collective bargaining agreements in the meantime and remained in effect. Requirements that indigent defendants be provided counsel at trial—and at earlier "critical stages" of proceedings—have brought the establishment of many publicly supported public defender systems or provisions for compensating court-appointed counsel, for example, in the Criminal Justice Act of 1964. In order to bring about compliance with Supreme Court decisions on police procedure, many local police departments will have to increase their budget allocations for training so that patrolmen will understand and be able to utilize proper procedures in making arrests. (Whether these procedures will be used is, of course, another matter.) To the extent that trials take longer because of the same rulings, as claimed by some federal judges, another cost to the taxpayer is added. The potential economic impact of court rulings is also shown by Martin Shapiro's suggestion that substantial enforcement of the *Plessy* v. *Ferguson* "separate but equal" rule in southern school districts would have "compelled many Southern states to double and triple their educational budgets and embark on enormous programs of school building and teacher training."[6]

Some of these last examples suggest that sometimes bureaucracies shift their patterns of activities in response to court decisions. Thus, despite disagreement on whether cases like *Miranda* have meant letting criminals loose, there is agreement that police procedures, or rather the law enforcement process more broadly, have changed. "The most fundamental change is not related to the incidence of crime but to the nature of the law enforcement process itself."[7] If police once relied on confessions, and defendants stop talking, as claimed by some noted prosecutors, then the police will have to work harder to secure evidence independent of what defendants say. (If, however, as some studies show, many defendants waive their rights and talk anyhow, this is less of a problem.) Police must be careful to provide warnings if convictions are not to be voided subsequently. (However, if the warnings are not presented and the defendants don't complain about this, again little effect will occur.)

The preceding examples may give an appalling impression to those who expect automatic and unswerving compliance with decisions of the highest court in the land or who expect the compliance process to be simple. The examples clearly indicate that 100 percent compliance does not exist. But what they indicate in addition is less clear, for, without extensive field research as yet not undertaken, it is difficult to judge the proportions of compliance and noncompliance occurring after decisions of the Supreme Court. Decisions do produce both support and opposition and may sooth as well as cause anger. Tempers may be calmed particularly when the Court's decision indicates it has backed off from an earlier decision which was intensely disliked. Thus, the ruling in *Barenblatt* that the questions asked of a House Un-American Activities Committee witness were made sufficiently pertinent and that the First Amendment could not be used as a reason for refusal to testify, soothed tempers frayed by *Watkins*, which had included a frontal attack on HUAC's charter and activities; similarly, the *Uphaus* case, allowing state action against subversion directed against state governments, calmed those unhappy about *Pennsylvania* v. *Nelson.* The rejoicing which occurs over some decisions is not related only to bad matters turning better—the individuals involved may simply be pleased with the decision, the more so if they are surprised at the outcome, as appears to have been the case when the Court invalidated the Keating-Owen Child Labor Law in *Hammer* v. *Dagenhart.*

Just as support for particularly criticized decisions exists (but tends to be underreported), there is much (although less well reported) compliance, which may exist alongside violent outbursts of criticism which may distract us. Thus, "Even in cases involving perhaps the most severely divisive issues in our society—racial integration and the church-state question—widespread compliance with the Court's determinations may be observed."[8] Changes in police practices have accompanied vitriolic comments about freed felons, and many school districts abandoned prayers and Bible reading at the same time we were hearing about the Godless Supreme Court. Schools have desegregated, legislatures have reapportioned, welfare residency rules have been eliminated, some within days of the relevant decisions—and sometimes even before, in anticipation of decisions not as yet handed down or before specific implementing directives are issued. As Johnson notes, "Court rulings have been implemented to a very great extent in the complete absence of specific legal obligations."[9] However, Dolbeare argues that "Governments do not appear anxious to have their policies gratuitously conform to court standards;

time enough for that when a decision is handed down and until then there are quite enough pressures to deal with."[10] Thus, the Illinois Supreme Court voluntarily reversed an earlier decision holding *Tropic of Cancer* obscene, without even being asked to do so, after the U.S. Supreme Court had held the book nonobscene. And the U.S. Department of the Interior restored a former employee to his job without awaiting a district court enforcement order after the Court had ruled, in *Vitarelli* v. *Seaton,* that proper procedures had not been followed in his discharge. The flurry of activity following court decisions is often a flurry of compliance-directed activity, and it is a flurry rather than isolated noises because many affected and potentially affected are moving to bring their policies in line with court directives.

In addition to situations where compliance and noncompliance clearly occur, we find instances, also little publicized, where little happens after a decision. If a decision reinforces expectations, instead of running counter to them, little immediate response may be evoked. Or what are later seen to have been implications of a decision may not be seen immediately, so a decision later judged to be important is greeted with indifference. If officials are already doing what the Court orders, as has been true with respect to certain criminal procedure matters, there will be little obvious effect. If the practice with which the Court has dealt exists in only a few places, uproar will be greatly limited.

Even though examples of constitutional amendments and bills overturning decisions were offered above, it needs to be stressed that much criticism, some of it based on people's imagining the worst and reacting promptly so that they will not appear to be approving, does not produce anti-Court actions and most of the bills introduced to overturn decisions remain just that—bills, not enacted into law. It may be that the newsworthy fact should be the vast amount of compliance rather than the lesser amount of noncomplying or evading action. Krislov remarks concerning the Steel Seizure Case of 1952 that "The most important fact . . . is that President Truman and his administrators accepted the decision without question."[11] And one could point to the issuance of a Presidential Executive Order to cure the defect in the coverage of the loyalty-security program which the Court pointed out in *Greene* v. *McElroy.* As Curtis remarks concerning the reaction to the number of federal and state statutes struck down by the Court in the 1865–1935 period, "One thing . . . these figures do prove, and that is the deference Congress and many of us paid the Court during this era, these seventy years."[12] Jacob adds that "Defiance of court orders occurs only in spectacular cases involving controversial policy decisions by the judiciary," and much less frequently with respect to state court decisions than U.S. Supreme Court rulings.[13]

The Court has had a considerable effect with respect to social change, instigating it in some cases, for example, desegregation, assisting it in other areas, as in culture change through freedom of speech cases, and serving as a drag or brake on the system, by striking down desired statutes. That the decisions of the Court clearly instigate and implement social, economic, and political change is confirmed by the virulence of much of the resistance to those decisions. At the least, those resisting feel they are being moved or forced to change. We have often lost sight of the impact on the economic system, or on government structure (the attention to the reapportionment cases is a notable contemporary exception), because of the great attention given in the post-1937 period to matters of civil rights and civil liberties, where the Court has clearly been a prime agent in broadening liberties throughout the nation. Yet the Supreme Court's decision in *Gibbons* v. *Ogden* aided in establishment of the first American common market; the Court assisted in the development of modern American capitalism by recognizing the corporation as a person; and, by striking down many state and federal regulatory statutes, it allowed the private sector of the economy full opportunities for growth and development. As Charles Warren argued some years ago, "To untrammeled intercourse between its parts, the American Union owes its preservation and its strength. Two factors have made such intercourse possible—the railroad, physically; the Supreme Court, legally." Or, as Warren argued more specifically, the Granger cases "permanently turned the economic and social development of the United States and . . . established forever the power of the States over the corporations and over monopolizing wealth."[14]

Warren's last point suggests the Court's relevance for the development not only of the economy but also our federal system. That the Court has served as a unifying force in the nation, and did so particularly in the early years of the United States, has been asserted by many. This effect can be crucial to the future development of any "new nation," and the United States was certainly in such a position in the late eighteenth and early nineteenth centuries. John Schmidhauser[15] reinforces the Court's role with respect to the development of federalism: "It is perhaps fair to say that the White-Taft Court, like its predecessor, did a great deal to accelerate the process [of centralization] not only by sustaining broad expansions of federal police power, but by frequently hampering state legislative activity and discouraging state legislative initiative." He comments later, "The Hughes Court, in the period after 1937 . . . contributed substantially to the continued vitality of both the states and the nation." And, to return to Warren: "No one can read the history of the Court's career without marveling at its potent effect upon the political development of the Nation, and without concluding that the Nation owes most of its strength to the determination of the judges to maintain the National supremacy."[16]

The Supreme Court's impact on political change occurs in a number of ways. One is the limit its decisions, at least occasionally, place on what majorities elsewhere in the system have enacted. This limiting effect has, according to Schmidhauser, led to "the probable weakening of democratic participation in meeting major social, economic, and political problems."[17] Others would argue the opposite—that the Court's actions stimulate, rather than suppress, political activity elsewhere. And if it neither limits nor stimulates, it may aid change by clearing away obstacles to developments in social and economic spheres.

It is clear that the Supreme Court's decisions help determine what the actors in other political arenas will deal with. Thus, Schmidhauser suggests that the Fuller Court reinforced proregulatory pressures "by imposing judicially created prohibitions on important state police power regulations and construing federal commerce power narrowly."[18] We have seen that politicians often feel compelled to react in some fashion to what the Court has done, particularly if an election in which they are candidates is fast approaching. If the Court has limited what the other actors can do by controlling possible solutions for a problem, the need to find ways around the restriction may be seen as great. If the Court instead upholds government action, the need to deal immediately with the Court's decisions is reduced.

However, some impact studies suggest that when the Supreme Court requires actions already followed in some jurisdictions, but prescribes additional specifics not being used, compliance may come harder in those jurisdictions than in ones not previously following even the general rule. Shapiro carries the argument further with the assertion that "patterns of judicial negatives . . . may become a crucial factor in determining what positive alternatives are available."[19] Not only may the possible alternative policies be limited, thus affecting the ability of other branches of the government in carrying out their functions, but participants are sometimes forced to shift the type of activities they carry out, and perhaps even to shift their activities from one political arena to another. Thus, in dealing with the economy, the executive, after the Steel Seizure Case, has been careful to take only those actions which cannot easily be challenged in the courts, which has meant principally dealing in terms of administrative regulations rather than utilizing more direct forms of action.

Furthermore, the Court itself is always there to be kept in mind by other political actors, which is perhaps the largest continuing meaning of *Marbury*. Even if some "pooh-poohed" the Court and insisted on their own determinations of propriety and constitutionality, someone else would (and generally does) invoke the Court's jurisdiction to seek the Justices' word on the matter. Even when courts merely reaffirm existing norms, demands for legislative action may arise—to change the rules or their application. Jacob, in arguing this position, says it is "most likely to occur when the norms originated under different social or economic circumstances, but courts continue to enforce them without significant changes."[20]

When we talk about the Court's reaffirmance of values or policies, we recognize another major function of the Court, and another impact: legitimation. As Dahl suggests, "At its best the Court operates to confer legitimacy, not simply on the particular and parochial policies of the dominant alliance, but upon the basic patterns of behavior required for the operation of a democracy."[21] In making the Constitution relevant to the present day through interpretation, the Court has helped keep the Constitution legitimate. Despite their initial strenuous resistance, the Justices' eventual validation of legislation regulating the economy assisted in giving the Positive State legitimacy. Both the corporation and the labor union have received the Court's stamp of approval, the former when it was recognized as a person for purposes of the Fourteenth Amendment, the latter when the Court upheld the National Labor Relations Act.

The Court is able to assist in granting legitimacy to policies and institutions because of the legitimacy attributed to it as an institution, a legitimacy perhaps greater than that of other institutions seen as more openly political. Tradition and its high place within government have over time given the Supreme Court an aura of sanctity. While the Justices have at times seemed to certain segments of the population to be unrestrained and overly and overtly "political" in their behavior, by and large they have been remembered most often as venerable figures in black often seemingly possessed of nonhuman qualities. This has contributed to the position of authority in which the Supreme Court finds itself today. While it is equipped with no army of soldiers to enforce its decisions, it finds that the decisions in most of the cases which come before it are accepted. The individual judges have not decided; the Court has spoken. That this feeling persists despite the often divided opinion among the judges is a tribute to both (*a*) the power of myth and (*b*) the willingness of citizens to submit to "law and order," without the overtones that phrase acquired in 1968. However, we must be careful not to confuse reverence for the Court with impact, or to presume that one follows directly from the other. The Court may simply be adored, without understanding. And, as some public opinion data show, Supreme Court decisions may have little actual effect on the public's view toward particular policies, thus casting some doubt on the Court's legitimizing function.

Many political actors feel that Court support for a position increases its legitimacy; at least the frequency with which Court statements are used to back up arguments in favor of particular positions makes it seem that way. "Political participants will utilize statements which favor their position, regardless of who makes them, as long as the source is generally considered legitimate."[22] And the actors go even further: they attempt to increase the strength of their arguments by predicting that the Court would support their position in the future. And both sides in a particular argument do not hesitate to draw on the same case in this process, suggesting that neither will allow the other to claim the Court all for itself, thus increasing the strength with which we can assert that the Court is felt to be legitimate.

When the Court has legitimized a given policy, one result may be more of the same type of policy. Thus, the Court's upholding of Granger laws was followed by passage of more state legislation regulating business. One must be careful here before asserting that the decisions "led to" the legislation, because it may be that the cause of the additional statutes was not the Court's approval but the social movement which gave rise to the initial legislation. Perhaps the most one could say is that the Court did not stand in the way (it was not negative) rather than that it assisted the legislation (was positive). However, if legislators in one state hold back to see whether the Court will sanction legislation passed elsewhere and, after the Court's approval, go ahead and pass similar statutes, we can say that the Court's legitimizing action had the impact of increasing the spread of the policy involved.

There is one last general or diffuse impact to be considered here: the opinions, attitudes, and expectations of members of the political system may be affected as a result of Court decisions, and these opinions may in turn affect later political action. These opinions, attitudes, and expectations affected may relate to the substance of policy involved in a Court pronouncement, to the Court, or to the political system. As early as Charles Warren, we heard the argument that "the impression made upon the public by the Court's decisions has often had as great an effect upon history as have the decisions themselves."[23] Murray Edelman, in writing about the effects of government actions generally, reinforces this point by asserting that government acts have their *greatest* impact not on the substantive demands held by individuals but rather by changing the demands and the expectations these people hold. He feels that "in the shaping of expectations of the future especially, the cues from government encounter few qualifying or competing cues from other sources; and this function of political activity is therefore an especially potent influence upon behavior."

Recently Jacob has argued that "Court actions . . . frequently strike at the core of people's personal behavior, their life-style or fortunes. Such contact with government about personally significant matters is likely to color people's impression of their government."[24] So *Brown* may have led blacks to feel that somewhere in the political system, "Someone up there liked them." However, as years dragged on, the decision was not implemented, and expectations with respect to the future for themselves and their children were not fulfilled, as "with all deliberate speed" meant more deliberation and less speed, the result may have been alienation from the system and even the Court. To the extent that rioting has resulted from such alienation, one might even say that urban ghetto riots were one impact of Court decisions. Similarly, those of extremely low income may have had their attitudes toward the law changed by the Supreme Court's rulings on criminal procedure, particularly those providing the right to counsel and to equal access to appeal for indigents. However, the extent to which those rulings are not implemented by local officials can have considerable importance in terms of expectations and attitudes toward the law by those affected.

Whether or not the impact of decisions on attitudes feeds back only on the Supreme Court, the legal system, or the larger political system is problematical. However, that the results are potentially crucial for the system is made clear by Jacob:

> Insofar as their impressions remain distinctive to the court, they may bear little relevance to their evaluation of the political regime in general. If their impression of the courts colors their perception of government or the political regime in general, such contacts with the courts may become highly significant elements in the generation of support for the regime or alienation from it.[25]

At this point in our examination and until more data are available, we cannot easily move beyond an evaluation shaped largely by our perspectives and expectations about compliance. We can, however, explore more thoroughly what "compliance" and "impact" mean, as a preliminary step toward collecting more data about actual impacts. First, we should, to provide some perspective, examine the ways in which political scientists have viewed the judicial system, particularly the Supreme Court, and the way they have come to and gone about the study of impact.

A POLITICAL PERSPECTIVE ON THE COURT

Only in recent years have those looking at the U.S. Supreme Court, or at the American judicial system more broadly, begun to see it in a political perspective. Even though the study of public law has not been monopolized by lawyers, those political scientists interested in constitutional law tended for many years to look at courts as *legal* institutions distinct from "political" bodies, for example, legislatures. Acceptance of the notion of separation of powers—that legislators make laws, administrators enforce them, and judges merely adjudicate disputes—supported a view of the courts as legal, not political, bodies. Even judges' function of interpreting the law was not viewed as political. Accepting courts as legal bodies was reinforced by the general concentration within political science on formal and institutional aspects of government.

Judges were seen not as making the law but as finding it. When scholars considered the traditional Anglo-American common-law system, in which judges, operating in the absence of statutes, were supposed to determine the rule of a case, they held that judges only found the law. This law was supplied by past precedents, which the judges were supposed to follow. That precedents were conflicting and might provide support for different views did not seem to change scholars' views. They presumed then that judges could still find "the law," as if it were, as Holmes put it, "a brooding omnipresence in the sky." The scholars took judges at their word concerning the process by which cases were decided: if the judges said they found the law, the scholars said the judges found the law.

When judges dealt with constitutions and statutes and their application, the law was to be found in the intent of the authors of the documents. If it could be said that the Founding Fathers had intended the Constitution to mean thus-and-such—a rather difficult assumption to accept—then one could legitimately say that judges could, with proper effort, determine that intent and thus find the law. Judicial decision would be the simple matter Justice Roberts said it was. In speaking of constitutional interpretation, he claimed that the Supreme Court placed a challenged law alongside the Constitution; if the two matched, the law was constitutional, and if they did not match, the law was invalid. The fact of dissent and disagreement within the U.S. Supreme Court and other collegial courts on matters of constitutional and statutory interpretation did not seem to disturb the scholars' view that the law was there to be found.

Eventually, however, it became recognized that when judges interpreted, they were making law, perhaps not in the same sense as legislators, but making law nonetheless. At least some judges conceded that "the law was what the judges say it is," instead of being predetermined. And the school of jurisprudence known as legal realism helped bring about a change in point of view by pointing to factors in judges' lives which affected the decisions they reached, thus indicating that the law was influenced by judges and not simply discovered by them. However, the legal realists have not convinced everyone, including lawyers. Thus, Edmond Cahn suggests, "There are countless lawyers who assume that if one does not mention the personal factor, it may become discouraged and go off and disappear somewhere."[26] And Shapiro suggests that the desire on the part of some constitutional law scholars for "neutral principles" of law is a direct carry-over from the idea of a law-*discovering* rather than a policy-*making* judiciary.

Assisting in the movement toward recognition that judges make law was political scientists' recognition that, despite the formal doctrine of separation of powers, all three branches of government shared power and each was, albeit in different ways, involved in making policy. The fact that we have always said that there were branches of government, one of which was the judiciary, placed it to some extent in the same category as two other institutions which were clearly political. "Thus the very Court that has always been preeminent in the American consciousness," Shapiro says, "has always been considered preeminently an agency of government."[27] In contemporary examinations of the operation of the separation of powers, differences in institutional frameworks were seen as imposing different types of constraints on legislators, administrators, and judges, but the similar contributions of each to the making of policy was recognized. The legal system was seen as being a variant of the political system instead of being totally *sui generis*. Some political scientists did move all the way from the position that the courts were purely legal to the position they were purely political, but the more balanced view held that they were political, or politically relevant, institutions affected by the special framework which our legal procedures imposed.

In studying the law, political scientists concentrated on public law matters to the virtual exclusion of private law. Perhaps close attention to private law, for example, the law of manufacturer's liability for negligence, would have more quickly disabused them of their notions that judicial interpretation involved no more than finding the law. But they did not study it, and instead dealt mostly with cases involving acts of governmental bodies and governmental rules. In studying these cases, their principal interest was in the doctrinal content of court decisions. There were, however, a number of other emphases which characterized the traditional study of public law. It was largely a study of constitutional law, because of the American practice of judicial review, which Shapiro defines as the channel through which "political considerations historically flowed into the study of law." But not even all cases involving constitutional law were examined. The approach of many political scientists, perhaps following from their use of the case method in the teaching of undergraduate constitutional law courses, was to concentrate on "leading cases," ones seen as particularly significant with respect to the development of constitutional doctrine on given subjects. And the "leading cases" studied were drawn almost entirely from the U.S. Supreme Court, making them even more unrepresentative of the output of the judicial system in the United States. The Supreme Court is less likely to follow precedent than are other (lower) courts, and unlike most other courts, it has considerable discretion as to whether to hear most of the cases brought to it; the Justices of the Supreme Court can therefore pick and choose most of what they decide. This discretion, coupled with the Supreme Court's position as the highest court in the land, has meant a much larger policy component to the Supreme Court's decisions than occurs in the mine run of decisions of lower courts. The emphasis on the

U.S. Supreme Court has also reinforced what Judge Jerome Frank called "the upper court myth," that is, that legal doctrine as stated by appellate judges is in fact the operative law. As the thrust of this volume suggests, one must go far beyond the Supreme Court, or even beyond courts in general, in order to ascertain operative legal doctrine or "law in action."

From this traditional perspective, still dominant in the undergraduate study of constitutional law, there has been a shift to the approach Glendon Schubert calls "conventionalist" because of its present dominance among scholars of the American judicial process, but better called "political." Included in the political analysis of the courts have been such subjects as the relations between interest groups and court cases, judicial selection, interaction among judges of collegial courts such as the Supreme Court, and the interactions between the Supreme Court, on the one hand, and Congress and/or the President, on the other. Traditional study of courts and their decisions undergirds political analysis. For a meaningful explanation of how the courts act, one must understand what judges have said and how that is related to what the courts have said previously. One must also understand the framework, including rules and procedure, within which those decisions were reached.

It is within the "conventionalist" or "political" view of the Court, just described, that the study of the Court's impact clearly fits. Such study is also related to sociological jurisprudence, in which scholars tried to determine what societal interests were being served by the law. While sociological jurisprudence may not have developed much beyond a set of categories of interests potentially affected, it did direct our attention away from sole concentration on doctrine. More recently, Arthur Miller has argued that judges should look to the impacts they have, and, in so doing, has moved from sociological jurisprudence to what we might call a "jurisprudence of consequences."

A still more recent approach to the courts is the behavioral, in which we find concentration on patterns of interaction among judges and on factors such as attitudes and ideologies affecting judges' decisions. One can become conversant with the techniques of the behavioral approach, such as bloc analysis, game theory, Guttmann scaling, and factor analysis, without a grounding in traditional constitutional law. However, studies about courts and judges utilizing those methods, like political analyses of the courts, will assist us in explaining effectively what occurs within courts if they are predicated upon an understanding of formal aspects of court procedure. Similarly, it is possible to study courts from a political perspective without attention to studies utilizing the behavioral approach, because judges' statements have political importance in their own right. However, consideration of the factors affecting judges' decisions may be necessary to a more complete understanding of political responses to those decisions, because the factors may influence the decisions or may be perceived by affected individuals, thus coloring the responses.

If we are to examine the Supreme Court, or courts, from a political perspective, what is involved? What do we mean when we talk about the Supreme Court as a political body? We mean that the courts' decisions involve policy, not only where other branches of government have refused or failed to act but also within the interstices of the policies adopted by those other branches. We also mean that the Supreme Court, the highest judicial body, which has the function of deciding what behavior is within the broad and vague limits established by the Constitution, is an integral part of the nation's political system and is, therefore, subject to many of the restraints imposed on other bodies within that system. The Court is in a very real sense, to use Lord Coke's term, a "supervisor of the realm"; however, supervisors are not autonomous with regard to the system they supervise. What is crucial is that the courts are *interdependent* with other elements in the system and in continuous interaction with them.

The courts sometimes are used at early stages of a controversy, sometimes at late stages, but they are always part of a continuing process, a "seamless web" by which policy is developed. For example, the development of antitrust policy is a story involving initial congressional action, passage of the Sherman Act, followed by the statute's judicial emasculation through the distinction, enunciated in *U.S.* v. *E.C. Knight Co.*, between manufacturing and commerce. These actions were followed by numerous judicial decisions *and* congressional statutes, such as the Clayton Act and the Robinson-Patman Act, which became thoroughly and inextricably intermixed. The question of whether labor should be included within the scope of the antitrust laws similarly involved legislative-judicial interaction. At first, the courts subjected the unions to the requirements of the statutes, in *Loewe* v. *Lawlor* (the Danbury Hatters' Case). This was followed by congressional exemption of labor in the Clayton Act, but the judges interpreted the statute to the contrary in *Duplex Printing Press* v. *Deering.* Only after the subsequent enactment of the Norris-LaGuardia Act, limiting the application of injunctions to labor unions, was the legislative policy accepted by the Court, both in letter and spirit.

We have generally tended to view the Supreme Court's participation in the policy process as coming late in that process, consonant with De-Tocqueville's famous assertion that all major social and economic questions in America became judicialized, and it may be that participants turn to other arenas to secure their goals before turning to the courts. As Vines notes:

> Supreme Court decisions often occur at or near the end of the political process. While events may continue after the Court's opinion . . . , often the action will bring an end to the dispute and resolve a controversy. Thus a Court decision may end a long and troublesome argument that has developed in the political system or may point the way to a settlement of a serious grievance.[28]

This view of the Court's late involvement has perhaps reinforced our view that court action is more final than that of other branches, that it is "the law." However, if we are serious when we talk of the Court and other agencies as interdependent, then we must recognize that political activity follows upon, and affects, Supreme Court decisions, just as it comes before and affects those decisions.

The Supreme Court legitimizes acts of other political agencies and resolves conflicts, but its "resolutions" are not final and may in fact initiate further action. Thus, as Schubert notes, "The decision of the Court is usually only one stage in a complex sequence of decisions and other events."[29] Or, as Shapiro comments, "When a judge makes law, his action is no more final than that of any other lawmaker. Our political system is marked by the constant communication, dissolution and recombination of various political forces in the process of continuously adjusting the law to changing social needs and political demands."[30] For one thing, political actors like to use court decisions for their own purposes. As Peltason has noted, "To win judicial support is a strategically important step for any interest."[31] And Schubert adds, "Decisions of the Court are themselves political data, and they provide strong ammunition for congressmen who would defend the status quo—as defined by the Court, of course—against proposals for legislative change."[32] Specific cases are cited in arguments both supporting and rejecting particular policies, and may be "used simply as symbols to validate any and all attempts" at legislation on a given subject. Thus, in the making of obscenity policy in Oregon, "Even when one participant in policy-making activity had cited a case to support an argument, other participants did not feel foreclosed from citing the opinions in the same case to support their differing positions."[33]

More important is the Court's dependence on other actors if the doctrine of its decisions is to become "living law." As Richard McCleery has phrased it, "A judicial decision is of no effect whatsoever as an instrument of social control until it is taken into hand and employed by some social group or political interest." We thus need to recognize that the aphorism that "the law is what the judges say it is" needs to be amended to "the law is what the judges say it is, after all others have had their say." Or, as Dahl states it, "What is legal at any given moment is what government officials enforce as legal with the sanctions officially available to them."[34] The rulings of the courts may very well be the *spoken* and *written* law of the land. But if what the judges say is not implemented, if it is resisted and evaded, then we "cannot accept as more than a passing polemical formula the aphorism that the law is what the judges say it is. Taken literally, this settles nothing . . . ."[35] The *effective* law of the land in any particular area of the country will be in part a result of the amount of compliance granted to judicial decisions. If that is true, power is less in the hands of the Supreme Court than it is in the hands of those who legitimate the courts' decisions: "The Supreme Court has power to the extent to which the avowedly political branches of government—Congress, the President, the state governments—affirmatively respond to the norm announced by the Court."[36] If this is the case, then it is certainly true that "the Supreme Court's most difficult function . . . is to attempt to legitimize its own acts."[37]

Despite all the foregoing, it is still possible that decisions of courts, or of the Supreme Court, are "accepted with greater finality than [are] decisions of the executive or legislative branches of government."[38] Courts, "particularly the less controversial state Supreme Courts, are held to have higher legitimacy than the more obviously 'political arms' of the government," despite the controversy in which the U.S. Supreme Court seems continually involved—controversy which, incidentally, makes us lose sight of the many decisions which are accepted without objection. In terms of the development of political science, the important point is that the question whether decisions of courts are accepted with greater finality is now treated as an empirical question—to be proved or disproved—rather than as an assumption not subject to examination. That change of focus is a significant indication of what taking a political perspective toward the Court entails.

THE STUDY OF IMPACT

The impact of what judges say is a crucial part of what is studied by those sharing a political perspective on the Court. It has become important as we have shifted our attention from "output, which is the decision of the Court including its orders and statement of policy," to consideration of "outcome, which is the final results or impact of output."[39] This development is much more recent than the beginnings of the political perspective on the courts. Explicit attention to impact, backed by studies of impacts of particular decisions, is less than twenty years old, dating from the aftermath of *Brown* v. *Board of Education*, which made political scientists aware that compliance with decisions of the Supreme Court was neither automatic, immediate, nor uniform. As Krislov has remarked, "From the standpoint of Court process, the decision in *Brown* v. *Board of Education* has had its greatest effect in educating students to the limits and operations of the court system generally."[40]

Much of the work on the impact of the *Brown* decision was narrowly descriptive, without much attempt at generalization, although some sociologists tried their hand at isolating the factors which explained resistance as against compliance within particular communities. Then came two studies on the impact of important Court decisions concerning church-state relations: Gordon Patric's study of the impact of the *McCollum* decision and Frank Sorauf's study of the aftermath of *Zorach* v. *Clauson.*[41] The volume of work on the subject has increased considerably since those two articles were published. During the entire period, principal attention has been devoted to problems in the civil liberties–civil rights areas.

While explicit attention to impact is recent, one can find earlier concern about the effects of decisions. Those who concentrated on the doctrine embodied in decisions often traced "lines" of cases, showing the history of particular ideas and thus the impact of one case on later cases. In addition, there has always been much speculation about the way in which doctrine might develop. The speculation has even extended to possible implications of a decision for the world outside the courts, as when writers talk of the possible reception a doctrine would receive, but writers seldom have checked out their speculations against actual events. This inattention is confirmed by a recent remark by a lawyer about an impact study: "So much legal research is done in libraries that it is pleasant to be reminded that there is a world outside of libraries in which the law also functions."[42]

The plethora of existing studies which has given rise to the present volume shows that inattention has changed to attention. One reason for the change, in addition to the shock of recognition caused by *Brown* v. *Board,* is a more general emphasis in the social sciences on the effect of legal decisions of any sort. "In recent years, a growing call has been heard for emphasis on the empirical consequences of legal decisions—not merely on the theoretical and logical aspects of a self-contained legal system, but also on the impact of the system on a broader society."[43] Thus, there is a relationship between studies of the impact of Supreme Court decisions and studies of the effect of statutes and regulations, within the rubric of sociology of law.

The emphasis of political scientists who have become involved in this endeavor has been limited largely to examination of impacts of the U.S. Supreme Court and, to a far smaller degree, of state supreme courts. While our look at impact shows that the "upper-court myth" has lessened its hold because it is no longer presumed that the only place to look for "the law" is in the doctrine of Supreme Court decisions, the concentration on high appellate bodies indicates that the myth has retained its hold on us; we are not concentrating on the decisions of lower courts where the bulk of cases are decided. Moreover, the appellate court emphasis has brought criticism, such as that "most impact analysis has been conducted as a 'top-down approach' which relies excessively on a hierarchical view of courts." As an alternative, we are told that our focus, like Cahn's "consumer perspective," should be on development of policy at the local level, "with Supreme Court decisions considered as one factor among many in that development,"[44] and that "only when we appreciate more fully the totality of the forces impinging on individuals at the level of implementation can we account for the varying responses made to Supreme Court policy and thus see this decisional structure in greater perspective."[45] In addition to attention to the impact of high appellate courts, or perhaps in part because of that emphasis, we have not studied impact with respect to a large range of law. The concentration has been on what Jacob has called "policy making" rather than on "norm enforcement," on large public policy issues rather than perhaps more numerous private law controversies, on impacts involving relationships between government agencies or between government agencies and individuals rather than between individuals and individuals.

In their initial work, those studying the effect of the Court's decisions tended to deal with compliance, or rather, noncompliance. Their initial attention was turned in this direction because they had assumed automatic compliance with the Court's decisions. To the extent the law is thought to be found and declared rather than the product of a political process, one gets the feeling that obedience should be forthcoming; after all, it is "the law" one is obeying, not nine men on the Supreme Court. If, however, one views the Court as part and parcel of the political process, one would be more likely to discount what the judges say. Work on noncompliance was a reflection of, and was reinforced by, values—values embodied, or thought to be embodied, in the American legal system, and values of those conducting the research. According to the "rule of law" supposedly prevailing in America, those affected by decisions of the courts, but most particularly by the decisions of the U.S. Supreme Court as the highest court of the land, are supposed to follow the Court's decisions even if they are unhappy with those decisions. They are, in other words, to comply at least until efforts have been made within other political arenas, such as the legislature, to reverse the decision, or within the judiciary itself to bring about reversal. That some individuals, including government officials, made no effort to comply with decisions even while seeking reversal through recognized channels brought attention to the matter of compliance and noncompliance. Because the decisions involved, like the School Desegregation Cases, were often liberal in thrust, and the values of those studying the court to a large extent were parallel, while the values of the noncompliers were clearly different, the researchers' values reinforced concern with noncompliance.

Their concern with noncompliance led to the study of areas where it seemed greatest. Those areas were ones, such as school desegregation, involving much social change; affecting large proportions of public officials, for example, police procedure; or directly involving important symbolic values, as with school prayer. As Barth has noted, "The opposition generated by unpopular decisions involving symbolic values, such as school prayers, is usually more diffuse and latent than the opposition generated by unpopular economic decisions like those of the 1930's."[46] Researchers thus probably found more, and more diffuse, noncompliance than if a fuller range of subject matter areas, including economic policy, had been examined. However, attention to areas of greater noncompliance allowed more ready identification of factors affecting impact, even if providing an incomplete picture of their relative weights.

Another limitation to what we have thus far done in impact analysis is our concentration on the effects of decisions without relating the results to the process by which they occur, even though one might classify impact studies as part of a "process approach" to public law matters. Thus, as Wells and Grossman comment, "The major emphasis [of impact studies] was upon the problem of implementation, rather than upon relating the process with the resultant policy."[47] We have concentrated on what comes out of the pipeline rather than dealing in addition with what goes on *in* the pipeline or how the pipeline affects the product, although process is recognized in that it is known that what the court does is followed by action elsewhere or that what the courts do follows action in other political arenas.

The study of impact can be aided by utilizing research in which impact was not a specific focus of attention. If we are to learn about the impact of Supreme Court decisions on, for example, police procedure, we need to know far more about the actual operation of police departments than we have in the past. Thus, the studies conducted by the American Bar Foundation in the 1950's before the major Supreme Court decisions on police practice are of considerable relevance for the impact scholar. Similarly, studies of community power structure can aid in examining the impact of decisions on school desegregation. There are also other types of studies helpful to us, including materials dealing with the history of our judicial institutions. Even if an historian intends to write only what we would now consider to be standard constitutional history, he may mention, for example, press reaction to nineteenth-century decisions on which we can draw, even if the data is incomplete. And our attention has recently been called to judicial biographies, "replete with the purported effects of jurists and decisions on public opinion, class interests, and institutional roles," although such studies "are simply outclassed by modern impact analysis."[48] What this suggests is that we may have far more material than that of which we are initially aware. For some time, each person has seemed to know only of the seminal articles, such as those by Patric and Sorauf, and of the general narrative material on the aftermath of *Brown*. Yet, when one starts looking, one finds much—both items which are directly studies of impact and other items quite relevant although not explicitly dealing with the subject.

Material on impact, explicit and implicit, needs to be pulled together and integrated. Much of what exists to be integrated, reported in the following pages (particularly in Chapters 4–7), is based on case studies of the effect of particular decisions in individual jurisdictions. Although we have been warned to concentrate on the process by which impact occurs and not just on the final result, we still need more case studies. But we need them concerning a wide range of subjects and variety of affected areas. We particularly need before-and-after studies and, as Milner has recommended, studies which examine the period *before* the decision, the time *during* which change is occurring, and the period *after* the event has passed from view. The fact that most impact studies have been carried out "after the fact" has contributed to our lack of understanding. If we could conduct before-and-after impact studies, we might be able to obtain a picture of change (or nonchange) less contaminated by reaction to a decision than is possible with after-only studies. Difficulties in carrying out before-and-after studies arise because one is not likely to know a priori where impact will take place, so that one could conduct a survey for the "before" part of a study. If one could find an area where it was not known what the Supreme Court was considering, and if one could determine that people in that area would react to the decision, one might be able to overcome this. Otherwise, some reconstruction is possible from newspapers, or from studies undertaken for other reasons, such as the American Bar Foundation studies just mentioned.

Although some volumes utilizing designs of vastly increased sophistication have recently appeared, we are not generally ready for studies based on elaborate, methodologically advanced research designs. The methodological difficulties confronting us are substantial, as we will see more clearly in the next chapter when we deal with the operationalization of such basic terms as *impact* and *compliance*. Before we become too pleased with ourselves for having come this far, we should note seriously Krislov's warning:

> Impact studies present grave problems in research and require vast resources seldom available. Even conceptually, the problem of impact measurement presents grave difficulties hardly resolved by the usual efforts at studying the immediate aftermath of some dramatic event or decision. (Even the most careful study cannot establish whether alleged changes were not merely coincidentally but actually consequentially related.) . . . Normal approaches [such as public opinion surveys], though excellent research strategies, not only provide limited information, but also require extensive and expensive efforts from researchers.[49]

Keeping this in mind, we should seek to improve the quality of our impact studies. But that goal exists primarily as a step toward another, more important, one—the building of theory concerning the judicial process and the role of courts and law in the political system.

CHAPTER 2

Impact and Compliance: What Do We Mean?

PROBLEMS OF CONCEPTUALIZATION AND MEASUREMENT*

Impact, compliance, effect, aftermath, evasion—all are words one hears in discussing the Supreme Court. We have seen examples of them in Chapter 1. However, we have left until now the matter of attempting to pin down what they mean. Despite the number of "impact studies" which have now been carried out, there has been insufficient grappling with the meaning of such concepts as *compliance* and *impact.* This lack of attention leads directly to confusion and to disagreement about the Supreme Court's place in the American political system.

When we begin to talk about what happens after the Supreme Court decides a case, we are initially talking about *aftermath,* that is, events which occur after the decision. However, we do not wish to examine the entire aftermath of Supreme Court decisions; many constitutional historians have already written on this subject, and their work need not be repeated. When we talk about aftermath, we are not necessarily talking about events affected by the decision, although we may leave the incorrect impression that the Supreme Court is in some way a cause of that aftermath, thus committing the fallacy of *post hoc ergo propter hoc.* We do not want to fall into the trap of claiming that because *B* follows *A, A* causes *B*. For example, after *Ex Parte Bakelite Corp.,* in which the Court declared that the Court of Customs Appeals was a legislative rather than a constitutional court, Congress declared it and other legislative courts to be constitutional courts (an action subsequently confirmed by the Supreme Court, in *Glidden* v. *Zdanok*). From that bare statement of facts alone, one could *not* assert that it was *because* of *Bakelite* that Congress

* An earlier version of this section appeared in *Law & Society Review.* The permission of the *Review* and of the Law and Society Association to use the material is gratefully acknowledged.

so acted, even though that might seem a likely inference. We need more evidence before *aftermath* becomes *impact*. For example, the lapse of time (more than twenty years) between *Bakelite* and congressional action would tend to negate our "likely inference."

If the term *aftermath* is too broad, what then? *Impact* and *compliance* are the two terms most important for our work; *evasion* is a special term subsidiary to the others. We may begin by asserting that there is a difference between *impact* and *compliance*. Political scientists' concern has been largely with the latter. Perhaps this was in part because some types of compliance, and particularly *non*compliance, could be seen easily, while to separate the impact or effect of a Supreme Court decision from other factors in the political milieu producing the same phenomena was a matter of considerable difficulty. By comparison with impact, compliance narrows our focus, restricting us to finding out to what degree a specific decision is obeyed. (*Decision* might mean the mandate of the Court with respect to specific named individuals, or it might mean the Court's holding in a case.) If we are interested in compliance, we would want to know, for example, whether the University of Florida Law School ever admitted Virgil Hawkins, or whether schools were desegregated after *Brown* or legislatures reapportioned on the basis of one man–one vote after *Reynolds*. In dealing with *compliance*, we are clearly interested in something narrower than the total impact of the decision, and to use one where we mean the other will not assist our work. "Supreme Court rulings . . . may invoke a range of responses. To use the term *compliance* to characterize this process is rather unfortunate, for this seems to suggest a single approved response to a court ruling. In certain instances, to be sure, such a view would be entirely satisfactory."[1]

Compliance brings a narrower focus than does *impact* but is not separate from it; compliance is a subset of impact. Using *compliance* does not, however, provide much relief from the measurement problems which afflict the determination of *impact*, which we shall discuss later. If, as Petrick argues, "The problem of non-compliance arises from the fact that human groups find it difficult to carry out effectively acts for which they have no underlying beliefs,"[2] then attitudes and beliefs, and particularly the matter of intent, must be taken into account in our examination of what happens with Court decisions after their issuance. In talking about impact, we can say that a decision had such-and-such an impact or effect, even on people who had no knowledge of or feeling about the decision; we can try to make judgments about impact on the basis of people's observable behavior. With compliance, however, we need to know whether or not they knew about the case and their intent with respect to it. "Whether the actions of other participants in the political process represent compliance with or evasion of Court decisions can only be determined after it is established that they were cognizant of the judicial policy."[3]

A person's behavior may be congruent with what the Court has ordered, but it may be that the person is operating parallel to the Court's line of action rather than operating *in order to* carry out that order. Perhaps he was going to do anyhow what the Court ordered. In these instances, the behavior is what the Court requires, but it is not carried out *because* the Court required it. Compliance requires the latter and implies a feeling that one ought to obey a decision. "An individual may sense that a law is just but violate it nonetheless (i.e., one should not confuse violation of a law with a 'rejection' of it); and individuals may conform to a law even though they view the law as unjust."[4] Or, as Feest argues with respect to other types of legal regulations:

> Compliance . . . is more than outward conformity with a regulation. Behavior which externally (objectively) conforms with a certain regulation may not coincide with internal (subjective) intention to conform. . . . The concept of compliance has . . . three essential elements: (*a*) norm-awareness, (*b*) intention to conform, and (*c*) conforming behavior.[5]

Compliance may thus exist even when disrespect for the law or the Court is being expressed, as was the case with most begrudging compliance with *Brown* v. *Board of Education.* In fact, the existence of complaints (except insofar as they are a coverup) coupled with behavior fitting the prescriptions of the Court might be taken as a clear indication that "compliance" is occurring. We might, however, want to give a specific title to situations where people obey a ruling while trying to change or reverse it; "reversal behavior" might be an appropriate label.

Why people comply raises the question of the Court's *authority,* the basis on which people accept its decisions as ones which the Court has a *right* to give, and which they, for that reason, ought to obey. Bases for that authority might include a formal allocation of power to the Court to decide constitutionality; the Court's expertise; the formal setting in which the Court operates, which evokes respect; charismatic leadership of some judges; and people's need for some body or institution which can confine conflict and thus fulfill security needs. The Court's authority is related to the *legitimacy* people grant it. But using compliance as a measure of legitimacy does not carry our analysis very far. Petrick has recently asserted that the final test of the Supreme Court's legitimacy is compliance with its decisions, particularly important because the Court lacks other legitimating devices such as the ballot box. He says that we measure state and local government reaction to Supreme Court decisions in terms of *behavioral* compliance or noncompliance. But how does one know from examining behavior to what extent the Court is considered legitimate? Perhaps a complete failure to attempt compliance would indicate nonlegitimacy, but what about token compliance? Petrick says it may indicate only nonapproval rather than nonlegitimacy. And if noncompliance does not necessarily mean nonlegitimacy, but perhaps only non-approval of a particular decision, has one gone very far?

Petrick also argues that if "compliance gradually and ultimately replaces non-compliance, it would appear that acceptance of the Court's authority is superseding disapproval of the decision."[6] Perhaps—but perhaps people's views toward the subject matter of the case itself have changed. Does increased compliance with *Brown* v. *Board of Education* mean that those people who first resisted the decision now love the Court? Not necessarily, any more than that the same compliance means greater feelings of brotherhood toward members of other races. Perhaps the compliers have accepted the necessity, for political reasons, for reasons of accepting federal funds, of allowing blacks to attend school with whites; perhaps they are just resigned to the situation. But neither of the latter alternatives means greater legitimacy would be granted the Court.

In suggesting that compliance occurs for political reasons, we recognize that some noncompliance is meant to be a grounds for bargaining within the larger political system, that is, it is *instrumental*. "The zone of acceptance is a consequence of either tacit or direct bargaining and thus is by no means an independent variable."[7] Political leaders may feel that if they refuse to grant immediate compliance to the Court's orders, they can gain some ends perhaps not related directly to the subject matter of the cases. The gains they seek may be within the states. Governor Faubus's attempt to prevent desegregation in Little Rock, coming as it did when he was about to face an election contest, may be explained in part as a maneuver for popularity among certain elements in the electorate. The gains may, on the other hand, be at the national level, particularly in Congress. When the national government does not present a united front, instrumental noncompliance is a temptation or meaningful alternative to the state politician. If the person with whom it is hoped a bargain can be struck realizes that the noncomplier must give in eventually, the attempt to bargain by delaying compliance may misfire. On the other hand, if the national official wishes to have the program implemented quickly, he may be willing to compromise or to make concessions in other areas to get his way.

When we talk about compliance, we know there is noncompliance. But there is also a shadowy something called "evasion," somewhere between outright acceptance and outright refusal to comply. How do we identify it? Some forms are relatively easy to distinguish. People attempt to limit the scope of the law, to avoid its full force, to make sure it doesn't apply to them. They do not say they will not conform or comply, but try to avoid a situation where that would become an issue. Sometimes this is made easy by the Court. If there has been a procedural defect which the Court has invalidated, it may be quite possible for affected individuals to achieve the same ends by altering their procedures only slightly, thus making the protection which the Court has appeared to give be meaningless, other than as a statement of principle.

This occurred in a number of the internal security cases of the 1950's. When the Court said that an inference could not be made that a person was a Communist, or was disloyal because he "took the Fifth," or refused to answer questions about his political affiliations, the hiring authorities then discharged, or refused to hire, individuals for failing to cooperate, unreliability, or failing to supply information—and, it should be added, the Court went along. More recently, in *Gardner* v. *Broderick*, the Court held that a policeman cannot be discharged for refusing to waive immunity. But if he can be discharged for refusal to answer questions concerning his official conduct, does this decision make much difference to him? It does preserve his Fifth Amendment rights, but it means being out of a job even without being prosecuted. Similarly, in the *Garrity* case, the Court held that testimony compelled under threat of loss of job was not admissible in criminal proceedings; thus an officer might testify and lose his job, with only the satisfaction, if it can be called that, of not being prosecuted. Again, in terms of employment, there is little difference in effect.

Some forms of evasion may not be easy to distinguish from compliance itself. In addition, if we look at the behavior of an affected individual not only with respect to a particular case in question but also his other behavior which might bear on the general subject, we can sometimes see that what appears at first to be compliance is coupled with other behavior which suggests a strong desire to evade the Court's rulings. Quiet acceptance may be only superficial, as the recipient attempts to bend the decision to his own needs. If, for example, a prosecutor said he would adhere to the *Roth* test of obscenity in dealing with "obscene" material, but then proposed new tests, for example, for "harmful materials" or "perversive" materials, which covered much more than fits within the *Roth* test, is he complying with the Court's decision or not? If a public official discontinues censorship knowing that "little old ladies in tennis shoes" will increase their activity to the same end, what can we say about his compliance?

What should we say when we find state officials persisting in trying to develop a statute or regulations which the Supreme Court will uphold, after the Court has struck down earlier regulations? After *Freedman* v. *Maryland*, procedures in a number of jurisdictions were revised to bring them under the Court's new requirements; not all such attempts were initially successful, but there were efforts made. Shall we say that this is evasion or avoidance, or that it is compliant behavior because the individuals involved were trying to mesh their interests/goals/values with what the Court will allow, and sincerely wanted to do something the Court would find acceptable? Or is the only action we can call compliance in such a situation the total absence of laws which do not exactly resemble the procedural requirements established by the Court in the

Freedman case? Certainly, even unsuccessful attempts to bring oneself within the rulings of the Court are different from the situation in which the Louisiana legislature, at the time of the New Orleans school desegregation crisis, modified statutes only slightly after they were struck down, as part of a continuing battle with the courts to avoid the force of school desegregation orders. But how do we judge, without examining motive and intent?

The difficulties in dealing with the conceptual boundaries of *compliance* and *evasion* have led to a search for other terms in which to cast analysis. Dolbeare and Hammond have recently suggested *response* as such a term. They argue, "There may be many forms of behavior short of tangible compliance. Formal, perfunctory, or rhetorical 'compliance' may be involved, as well as degrees of enthusiasm for the prescribed new behavior."[8] However, the term most frequently used is *impact,* and in recent years, we have seen a shift from concern with *compliance,* a narrower term, to the broader one; at least we find the latter studied in addition to the former. The shift in emphasis has not reduced the conceptualization or measurement problems facing students of the judicial process, as we shall soon see, nor has it meant that political scientists have changed their assumptions about what should happen after the Court decides a case. They are still affected by an expectation that decisions of the Supreme Court will have some effect and find it difficult to accept the possible irrelevance of decisions, or the relatively small role they may play in what occurs after the Court has spoken. If something like school desegregation depends heavily on the character and structure of the community and on the community's elites, the Court's decisions may not mean very much beyond having served as catalysts or sparks for action. Perhaps in some instances the Supreme Court is only hollering into an empty rain barrel; perhaps a decision never reaches the place at which it was aimed, such as the police in law enforcement cases. Perhaps, but this is a matter for research.

One of the prime difficulties in dealing with *impact* is that the decisions of the Supreme Court are part of a general milieu in which later events take place and part of a set of multiple causes of such events. If several factors are operating in the same direction, how does one "separate out" the impact the Court's decision has by comparison with other elements of the situation? If "the impact of a Supreme Court decision is measured not only in terms of its effects on the parties who actually win or lose the case, but by the manner in which it is reflected in the later conduct and thinking of society as a whole,"[9] how does one determine what other elements may have contributed to that "later conduct and thinking"? How does one, for example, separate the possible effect of the symbolic aspect of *Brown* v. *Board of Education* on (favorable) attitudes toward desegregation from the many other intervening variables which may have played a part in formation of that attitude? If the effects of criminal justice practices depend on such matters as evidentiary rules or the availability of resources, how do you determine the procedures' impact? How do you tell whether a particular case has had an impact on a lower-court judge, when a judge uses doctrine comparable to that of the Supreme Court but not exactly like it, or which might have been drawn from the Supreme Court's ruling, but which might also (or in addition) have been drawn from a ruling of some other court or from the judge's own ideology? How does one determine whether companies have taken the Supreme Court's cases on restraint of trade into consideration in determining trade practices, unless corporation officials will talk honestly about the subject? If a proposed merger takes a given form, how does one tell what role economic considerations played as contrasted with consideration of legal matters, including both Supreme Court decisions and advice of counsel as to the likelihood of action by the Department of Justice? When trying to judge the impact of the Court's decisions on government regulation of the economy, how does one separate the effects of those decisions from the "natural" growth of the economy and the existence of such economic forms as the corporation?

Arthur Miller, writing on the American economy, carries the point further and argues that the Court, "rather than being the *cause* of constitutional change, is the *instrument*" of such change by its updating of the Constitution, enabling the document "to remain relevant and current." Had the Court not done this, he asserts, the Court would have been swept aside, and thus he suggests that the Court's impact on the economy is "in the immortal words of Senator Everett McKinley Dirksen, about like that of a 'snowflake wafting down upon the bosom of the mighty Potomac.'"[10] There is, despite Miller's seeming clarity, considerable difficulty with what he says. How does one distinguish between the Court's being a *cause* and its being an *instrument* of social change? Even if one avoids one extreme, of assuming the Court to have a direct, unilateral, independent, and immediate effect, it is difficult to come to the opposite conclusion that the Court simply *reflects* what is going on in the society, economy, or polity. Miller himself says, "Doubtless [the Court] does have some power and does wield some influence over the shape of events." At a minimum, if the Court is in political interaction with other actors, the influence relationship is reciprocal, with the Court affecting others as well as others affecting the Court. Perhaps we can only arrive at the Scotch verdict, "Not Proved," rather than Miller's strong assertions about lack of impact.

While these comments have been directed to the problem of underestimating the Court's effect, we must keep in mind the more common difficulty into which writers about the Court have fallen, that of overestimating impact. This is what Schmidhauser means when he raises the question of how one avoids overstating the influence of a single institution like the Court upon federal centralization, which he claims grew "almost inevitably" from the structure of American society after the Civil War—and, one might add, prior to the Civil War as well. We would do well to keep this matter in mind.

But we must go beyond this general discussion to specifics. To turn to questions of measurement, in talking about *Brown* v. *Board of Education,* how much of what has happened with respect to school desegregation in the South does one attribute to the "changing South," to the economic and social changes which accompanied *Brown,* and how much to *Brown* itself? To pursue *Brown* a bit further, how can one determine if *Brown* has had an effect on movement of whites from the central cities of metropolitan areas to the suburbs? General population movement occurred during the period of *Brown* and its aftermath, even in southern cities where segregation in the schools continued. But can one infer from this that *Brown* did not have any impact on that movement? How is one to tell whether the movement might have been in anticipation of ultimate compliance with *Brown,* or whether *Brown* may have reinforced a preexisting desire to move to the suburbs? In order to provide even a preliminary test, one would need year-by-year mobility rates for the pre-*Brown* as well as the post-*Brown* years, with the latter divided into precompliance and postcompliance years by area, and one would also need data from some cities with long-standing desegregation (or at least pre-*Brown* desegregation) for control purposes. One can easily see that obtaining this data would pose considerable problems.

There are some questions of impact about which data may not be as difficult to obtain. For example, to test the effect of Supreme Court decisions on the level of litigation, one could examine lower-court dockets to determine how many cases have been filed dealing with the subject of a Supreme Court case. Or one could determine requests for certiorari dealing with a given subject. One could also look at the records of a particular organization, for example, the NAACP, to see if its activities in the field of litigation increased after a court victory. These would not provide perfect indicators of impact, but they would give substantial evidence on the matter.

Perhaps we can identify situations where the Court's actions have had no relevance and thus decrease the universe of phenomena at which we look. It is important to isolate the proportions of instances where cases do and do not have impact. This is one situation where negative findings, i.e., that there is no impact, are of extreme importance. Thus, to study an area in contemplation of possible impact and to find no impact is an important finding in itself. After this sorting-out process, we are, however, still left with situations in which it is unclear whether the Court's decisions did have an effect and with others where it is fairly clear that there was some effect but how much or of what kind is not certain. In this connection, it may help to look at the matter of relative rates: some activity may persist after a Supreme Court decision, seemingly indicating no impact, but the rate or intensity of activity may be slowed or advanced. The growth of the Positive State was not prevented by the Court's striking down attempts at economic regulation, but that does not mean the decisions were without effect, at least on the pace of that growth. To consider only instances where behavior or policy is completely reversed after a Court decision is to limit study of impact unnecessarily. But we must be careful, because of the discontinuous reception Supreme Court decisions receive, reducing the number of possible instances where we might find a test of impact.

FIGURE 2–1

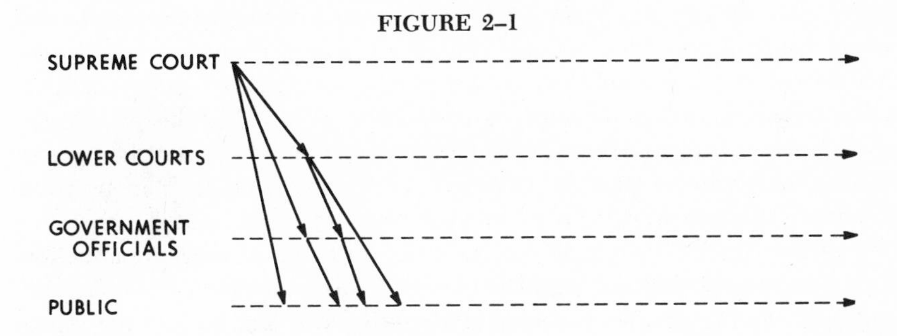

Not all impacts of court decisions are direct, as the diagram in Figure 2–1 shows. We may be able to talk about the direct effect a Supreme Court decision has on a lower-court judge. But if we are talking about the impact on government officials in local communities, or on "the public," we need to consider both direct impact and indirect impact. The indirect impact occurs when the Court's decision has an effect on some officials, who have an effect on others, who finally in turn have an effect on the local community. The community may not even realize that what is occurring is resulting from the Supreme Court's initial action. The second-order effects of a Court decision, that is, reaction of those affected by government agencies on which the Court's decision may first fall, may be greater or clearer than its direct effects. If an agency adjusts its policy or procedure to comply, some disfavored clients will complain; if an agency persists in the face of directives to change, as apparently has occurred with the Patent Office, those wishing the changes ordered by the Supreme Court will react negatively.

The difficulties of separating the impact of the Court's decisions from other factors influencing a given outcome may mean that we can isolate impact effectively only where there is direct and obvious (visible) resistance to a Court decision, and that the only impact we can study precisely is clear noncompliance. Part of the problem of determining impact is that we often do not have a test of whether the Court's decision is having an effect. For example, if the public holds parents to a higher standard with respect to the behavior of their children than does the law, how do we know that the law is even relevant? Would we have to say that the only impact in that situation would be a change in public attitude, so that only that which the law allowed was considered acceptable? If we note cases in which the Supreme Court has defined the jurisdiction of certain agencies broadly through statutory interpretation, what can we say when the agencies are cautious and do not utilize the full jurisdiction the Courts say they may use? Do we say there is no impact, or that the impact is that the decisions are irrelevant, or that the Court has not been successful in getting others to accept what it says is possible?

If we do try to go beyond obvious instances of direct noncompliance, we get into matters involving the concept *power*, a concept which, despite its centrality for political science, still lacks clear conceptualization. Power involves one actor moving another actor against his will, from passivity to an act or from one act already intended to another act; or it may also involve keeping a person from an intended shift in position. If *A* wants *X* done, and *B* does it, one is tempted to say that *A* has power with respect to *B*. But this is not really an adequate operationalization. If *A* wants something done and *B* may have done it anyhow, or may already be moving in the direction of doing it, we cannot say that *A* has power with respect to *B*.

On the other hand, it may not be necessary for *A* to want something done before we can talk about his having power; if *B* decided to do something because he *thought* *A* wanted it done, *A* might have power even if *A* had not communicated any orders or suggestions. We see this when actors comply with Court rulings before specific enforcement orders are issued or when they interpret a case as applying to them in advance of such application. Thus, "It is possible . . . that the mere presence and ready availability of the courts could influence behavior in such a way as to bring it into conformance with known court standards, and courts might then be said to have had a policy effect without a case ever being presented."[11]

This explains why Cardozo said that the power of the Supreme Court is not measured solely by the number of times it is exercised. However, it must be recognized that the power deriving from this anticipatory effect cannot exist perpetually without such specific action from the Court, at least occasionally, to serve to remind people that the institution was there and not moribund. The anticipatory effect can, however, also lead to restrictions upon or avoidance of the Court, as well as compliance. Thus, because of rumors the Court would strike down Reconstruction, the House Judiciary Committee reported a bill requiring two-thirds concurrence when a law of Congress was struck down. More recently, the Post Office often mooted cases involving restrictions on receipt of mail when an irate individual threatened to go to court, in order to avoid a court decision on its practices of holding mail.

Some feel we must include in a definition of power the communication of *A*'s desire to *B*, after which, for power to exist, *B* would have to do something he would not otherwise have done. However, *A* might engineer a situation so that *B* does *A*'s bidding without any direct communication or feeling of being coerced, implied in the term *manipulation*. However, the Supreme Court may be less able than other governmental bodies to structure situations in this fashion, because it is not able to retain continuous surveillance of cases once they leave the Court's hands. The foregoing implies that to obtain a clear measurement of power, one must know the intent of actors, at least the intent of those acted upon, just as one must know intent in order to measure compliance as some have defined it.

In measuring the Court's power, one may start with measures which utilize only visible activity.[12] However, even though relatively "hard," such measures are defective because they both go too far and are too limited. They go too far because they include situations in which an actor was already going to do what the Court requires, and they are too limited because they do not include situations in which no behavioral change occurs because the Court has prevented an individual from shifting his position. Therefore, measures of behavioral change or lack of change must be coupled with knowledge of intent, precisely the matter most difficult to uncover. With respect to historical examples, we obviously cannot find many of the actors so that we might inquire what their intent was. Even when actors are available, we would be likely to ask them only after a Court decision has occurred, thus allowing them to rationalize their acts and to adjust their responses to what they had already done. Even if we were to ask them before a relevant decision were handed down, their intent might be affected by the expectation of possible rulings and adjustment they had made in their behavior based on anticipation of the Court's ruling in a given direction.

If it is so difficult to ascertain intent, are we left without the possibility of studying impact? At least in the short run, the answer would appear to be no, because there is still much we can learn by depicting thoroughly what appears to have occurred in the aftermath of court decisions, in tracing out the consequences of Court action to the best of our ability in a far more systematic way than we have done heretofore. What can we use as measures? Where do we begin to look? For example, do we measure the impact of the School Desegregation decisions in terms of the percentage of Negro students attending classes in previously all-white schools? Or in terms of the percentage of school districts with some

Negroes in integrated classes? Or in terms of the movement of whites to the suburbs from the core cities of metropolitan areas?

In the area of criminal procedure, does one look at impact of decisions in terms of alleged increases in the crime rate? In terms of the number of cases which go to trial? In terms of increases in the length of time of trials? In terms of the number of cases lost at the trial stage (something far easier to measure than the number lost before they ever get to trial)? In terms of the frequency of guilty pleas, because defendants hope that a new Supreme Court ruling may save them? In terms of changes in police methods? In terms of the growth of interest groups, for example, of policemen, which arise in opposition to the decisions? Or in terms of the number of cases brought to the courts to test the applicability of what the Supreme Court has declared? An easy, but not satisfying, answer for the moment is that perhaps all of these, individually or in combination, might be legitimate operationalizations.

There are additional measures. One might be the frequency with which a court decision is mentioned:

> When the constitutionality of policy proposals is under discussion, one may expect frequent references to relevant Supreme Court cases. Most frequent mention can be expected from lawyers and in judicial proceedings. Less frequent mention would be likely by non-lawyer policy-makers, and by lay members of publics interested in policy outcomes. Infrequent mention would generally characterize non-judicial policy-making arenas . . . and non-governmental community action . . . .[13]

Thus, "A possible measure of the scope of the impact of Supreme Court opinions would be the frequency with which the opinions were mentioned outside courts and among non-lawyers, particularly by members of 'attentive publics.'" One type of mention received by certain Court opinions is that they do not provide enough guidance for lower-court judges or lawyers dealing with the subject. What such complaints mean is, however, not clear. It may be simply an escape or excuse for policy otherwise preferred, but it might mean that the complainers would comply if given the opportunity and the guidance; one simply cannot tell from the complaints themselves.

One can use numbers of those affected as a measure of impact. But if, with regard to school desegregation, one does use the percentage of black students attending classes in previously all-white schools, some questions are still unanswered. The percentage involved is usually quite small and is often cited with dismay by those who see it. But Robert Crain points out that those militating for school desegregation often cease their efforts when the numbers of black students added to previously all-white schools are quite small, perhaps indicating a preference for a symbolic rather than a "numbers" gain, thus suggesting a different basis for evaluation. One also has the difficulty of ascertaining how many black parents want their children going to school in previously all-white schools. Apart from the intimidation of those parents which occurs, there may be some who do not wish their children to be involved, or to be among the first. If one is to include them in figuring the base for percentage of black children in desegregated schools, one may not obtain a precise picture of impact—certainly one would not obtain the same picture as if they were excluded from one's count. To be sure, the percentage of all black students in desegregated schools (figured on the largest base) is quite important if one wants to know to what extent the *values* discussed by the Justices in *Brown* have been implemented, a matter crucial regardless of the wishes of the parents involved.[14] But even this suggests again that what one means by impact may require asking different questions in different circumstances.

Even if one solves the problem of calculating the percentage of students now in desegregated schools, one might want to know other items concerning compliance with *Brown*. What, for example, are the problems after desegregation occurs? Is there social segregation within the schools, or does desegregation occur there and perhaps extend to childrens' activities after school hours? Has there been restriction of faculty and student freedom of speech on the subject? The point is that it is important to know *where* to look in determining measurements.

To return to the matter of the proportionate amount of impact, one must recognize that there may be only a few jurisdictions in which a Court decision, even a doctrinally important one, can have a specific effect on individuals. We must keep in mind the difference between class actions, on behalf of the plaintiff "and all others similarly situated," and cases brought only on behalf of a single plaintiff. However, if a case rule can be used in only a small number of cases, the impact is limited. Examples include some of the Supreme Court's criminal procedure rulings of the 1960's, because the procedure involved occurred in only a single state, as was true with both right to jury (*Duncan* v. *Louisiana*) and courtroom television (*Estes* v. *Texas*), or because some states were already in compliance with rules the Supreme Court incorporated in the Fourteenth Amendment. Other cases with a limited effect include the *Penn-Central Merger* case, which immediately affected only the railroads involved in the merger. Although the case might also have a more diffuse effect of encouraging mergers, the number of corporations existing which could be covered by the case was relatively small. The Permian Basin Area Rate Cases directly affected only one major national government agency and a limited number of corporations involved in the rate-setting proceedings, although other possible effects, for example, on administrative proceedings generally, might have radiated from the cases.

In dealing with the measurement of impact, we must inject the notion of *time* into our study. Where in time does one look for impact? One must be careful. All impact is not immediate. There may be a lag before those affected even know about a decision, much less react to it or have time to react to it. Thus, Reich points out: "The 1963–1964 academic year was too close to the Lord's Prayer and Bible reading decisions, which came at the end of the Court's term the previous June, to permit school administrators not only to digest the meaning of the Court's words but to determine their own public reactions and establish policies that would fit their communities."[15] Officials may not know of a decision. In a recent situation in Little Rock, Arkansas, an interracial couple was denied a marriage license under the Arkansas antimiscegenation statute by a clerk who had not been informed (at least officially) of the Supreme Court invalidation of such laws. However, one must be careful to distinguish between resistance to the Supreme Court's rulings and the general slowness of the system to respond, and both were probably involved in that Arkansas situation.

Even when officials know of cases and agree that implementation should occur, it may be unrealistic to expect immediate full compliance, particularly where bureaucratic machinery must be altered. For example, after *In Re Gault*, providing fuller procedural protection in juvenile court proceedings, it would take much time to restructure the juvenile courts even if all had the will to do so. Some reforms required by the Court are more demanding than others, in both financial and psychic terms, the latter where there is considerable "investment" in the status quo, as juvenile officers had in the paternalistic philosophy underlying the older, more informal, juvenile court proceedings. And the speed of reaction may depend on how people feel about a decision. Thus, when people approve of a decision, there may be no immediate need for them to act. Follow-up action may be necessary to "nail down" a decision, but it may await possible voluntary compliance by others.

On the other hand, those opposed are more likely to feel compelled to react promptly rather than leave an impression of compliance by non-action. However, these individuals may change their minds later; that is, we can distinguish between immediate emotional opposition and "sober second thought," as in the case of the congressman who sponsored, but later withdrew, a bill opposing the prayer decisions. After time has passed following a decision, the "parade of horribles" which some have felt would come from the decision may not have occurred, and tempers may cool. Thus, Murphy noted, with respect to critics of the Supreme Court's decisions on internal security in the 1950's, that "after several years of living with decisions like *Mallory*, *Nelson*, *Yates*, and *Cole* v. *Young*, a crisis in law enforcement had not developed, nor had packs of Communists descended on the country or infested government employment."[16]

Just as all impact is not immediate, it may also continue for a long time. Thus, when the Supreme Court held that the 1952 *Doremus* challenge to Bible reading in public schools was not justiciable, the effect was not only on the taxpayer who had brought the suit, and lost, but on challenges to the practice, because it was a full decade before the Court dealt directly with the problem the case had posed. The long-run effects of many decisions may be nil, particularly in the economic area. Yet, because social forces outrun what the Court has done, long-run effects of a case may turn out to be greater than short-run effects. Kelly and Harbison have noted that *Marbury* v. *Madison*, which established judicial review, was an example of a case the implications of which were not clear at the time it was decided. "Marshall's argument in favor of the Court's power to declare an act of Congress void was not of major significance at the time he made it . . . ."[17] Similarly, the convictions upheld in *Gitlow* v. *New York* had far less immediate effect than did the ruling's incorporation of the First Amendment's protections for speech and press in the Fourteenth Amendment.

Time may be important because intervening events may be necessary before a decision is implemented, as when a particular murder may serve to make police officials aware of the implications of police procedure in cases such as *Miranda*. Another example is presented by the long lag between decision and action with respect to *U.S.* v. *Standard Oil Co.*, where the Court held there was no recovery by the government under the concept of allocating a cause of action to the master for injury to his servant. The government withdrew a number of suits similar to *Standard Oil* which were pending at the time of that decision, and Congress did not fill the statutory void the case left. Only after the General Accounting Office, in 1960, showed that substantial sums of money could be recovered —and were being recovered by those agencies, such as the Veterans' Administration, which were acting under their power to issue regulations to that effect—did Congress respond with the Federal Medical Care Recovery Act of 1963.

In dealing with impact in relation to time, one can designate an arbitrary cutoff point or talk in terms of immediate impact, that is, obvious changes clearly resulting from a decision or attributed to it, recognizing that the longer the time after a decision, the broader (in more areas) and thinner (less immediate and powerful) its impact. However, it is useful to consider long-run as well as short-run effects. The range of possible effects can be shown as in Figure 2–2.

There are immediate impacts, as of case X at point t_1, indicated by (1). Some decisions have no impact; they are never received or heard of, as

FIGURE 2–2

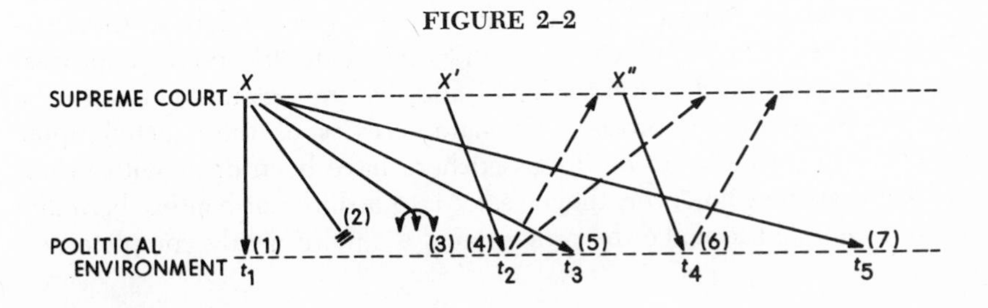

noted by (2), and as far as impact is concerned, we may say they have aborted. Some blend in with the political milieu, noted at (3). As we proceed through time, there are other decisions (X' and X'') which have their impacts, at points t_2 and t_4, noted at (4) and (6) respectively. Our initial case, X, has some long-range effects, for example, note points t_3 and t_5, at (5) and (7). The further one proceeds in time, the more one encounters a problem in distinguishing the impact of the case from other factors and from the impact of other cases on the political environment.

It should be stressed again that the relationship between the Supreme Court and the political environment is not unidirectional. Thus, Supreme Court cases lay the groundwork for later cases, in at least two senses: one, as noted earlier, a case will spawn additional cases aimed at clarification or extension; and, two, the impact of a case on the environment perhaps changes the environment in such a way that conflicts resulting in cases are produced. The Supreme Court receives feedback from its decisions (represented by the broken-line arrows), which may affect what the Court subsequently does. Thus the impact of the Court has an impact on the Court.

A LOOK AT RELEVANT VARIABLES

When we discuss factors or variables which affect or condition the implementation of Supreme Court decisions, we must realize that we do not have reliable data concerning the effect of those variables, because most impact studies have not been carried out with a careful prior specification of variables to be examined. However, on an ex post facto basis, we can identify and group a number of factors. We take the decision in a case as the independent variable and impact, however defined, as the dependent variable, with the items to be discussed here hypothesized to serve as intervening variables.

Under what conditions or "states of the system" do these variables intervene in the otherwise direct relationship between Court decision and impact? What might bring about a situation where all possible intervening factors are neutralized? Eventually one would like to know the full set of intervening variables and the relations among them, as well as their relative effect on impact. Such clearly is far beyond our grasp at the current time, but we can proceed to discuss the variables themselves. Some, nearest the initial (or "output") end of the impact process, relate to the characteristics of particular decisions. Others relate to the political process following upon the decision's release, and, as one extends closer to the "outcome" end of the process, to characteristics of those acted upon. (Some of the variables to be discussed here have been dealt with in our earlier discussion; however, they are set into a different context here and are also included to make the present analysis more nearly complete.)

One may start with the *case-by-case approach* utilized in the American legal system. The Supreme Court, while it may decide several cases on the same subject simultaneously, essentially works with one case at a time, utilizing the characteristics of the parties and their specific fact situation to cast light on "the law." This confining of the case to its facts may increase compliance by decreasing the number of broad decisions, an hypothesis parallel to the generalization that "the obstructional potential in legal matters . . . becomes greater when general policy is involved than when the ruling concerns a specific matter."[18] However, broad decisions, such as *Brown* v. *Board,* may absorb opposition, thus facilitating acceptance for other cases. Because decisions may be cumulative in their impact within the case-by-case approach, or may cancel out, offset, or soften the blow from earlier cases, one must note the relationship of a case to prior cases, or the *time sequence* of cases. With respect to the criminal procedure cases of the 1960's, the police and those supporting their position may have been particularly upset by a particular decision, for example, *Miranda,* but it is not that decision *by itself* which produced reaction so much as *Miranda* in relation to other, earlier decisions reaching in the same direction. In that set of cases, each reinforced the other, as far as the reaction of many law enforcement officials was concerned, and helped create a certain "climate" regarding "law and order."

Similarly, we can attribute President Franklin D. Roosevelt's attempt to "pack" the Supreme Court in 1937 to the large number of decisions striking down New Deal legislation rather than to a single decision. The action taken by Roosevelt may have been based less on the decisions themselves than on what people felt the attitude of judges to be toward the law, for example, whether it was an "activist" or "strict constructionist" Court. However, such an attitude would be detected from collections of cases more than from isolated decisions. In other instances, later decisions cancel out, offset, or soften the blow from earlier cases. For example, as already mentioned, "*Barenblatt* had soothed some of the institutional anger generated by *Watkins,* and *Uphaus* had eased resentment among local officials by acknowledging broad state authority to deal with internal subversion against a state . . . ."[19]

Juxtaposition of cases far more closely together may also have an impact. For example, Justice Marshall's decision in *Marbury* did not receive as much of a hostile reaction as it might have, because, only six days after the decision, the Court handed down a ruling sustaining the Circuit Court Act of 1802, thus pleasing the Republicans who had just been wounded by Marshall's attack on Jefferson. "The result was as pleasing to the Administration party as it was unexpected."[20] And anger caused by Marshall's decision in *The Antelope,* in which he said international law was not opposed to the slave trade, thus—in the eyes of his critics—missing an opportunity to strike at slavery, "was somewhat allayed by a simultaneous decision in . . . *The Plattsburgh* in which the Court held that an American ship was subject to condemnation where it was outfitted for the slave trade although a portion of its business was legal."[21]

We need to know if a case is one of "first impression," as when the Supreme Court began in 1957 to deal with the subject of obscene literature, or is a follow-up to earlier cases, as with the "freedom-of-choice" school desegregation cases. In Oregon, it was found that "at the beginning of a 'line' of Supreme Court cases, before the Court has clearly answered most questions concerning a subject, policy-makers have more freedom in claiming new policies to be constitutional or apparently constitutional than they do later,"[22] when elements in several opinions reinforce each other, and when loopholes in the earlier decisions are closed. As Cardozo remarked, "The implications of a decision may in the beginning be equivocal. New cases by commentary and exposition extract the essence. At last there emerges a rule or principle which becomes a datum, a point of departure, from which new lines will be run."[23] Important doctrinal developments may not be apparent except over the long run, until after several cases have been decided.

A number of factors relate to the characteristics of the case itself, without regard to content or context. Among these are the *relative unanimity* of the vote in the case and the existence of an "opinion of the Court" instead of a plurality opinion; whether statutory or constitutional *grounds* are used as the basis for the decision; the *completeness* of the decision in answering the questions put by the parties; and the *ambiguity* with which the questions are answered, one of the variables most frequently cited in impact studies.

Much attention is paid to the vote in a case. In order to appreciate this, one need note only the speculation about the likely reaction to *Brown* v. *Board* if the vote had not been nine-zero. An orthodox statement of the result of division within the Court is that by Barth: "A five-four vote is likely to increase the opportunity for attack upon the decision. Such a vote indicates a difference of opinion on the Court itself; if experts cannot agree on questions of the law, it is reasonable to assume others will also disagree."[24] And the vultures who would pick over the bones of the Court also use split decisions, particularly those which are five to four, as a grounds for delay, claiming that all that is needed to reverse a decision is for one judge to change his mind or be replaced on the Court. The orthodox statement of the effect of division is no more than an hypothesis, because we are not sure of a differential impact between cases with unanimous rulings and those with split decisions. Recently D'Amato has put forward a competing argument. He asserts, "It is not at all clear that a dissent or two will rally public opinion against the majority opinion. Psychologically, the precise opposite might result: readers of the case might feel that the contrary arguments had been clearly and effectively presented to the Court and decisively rejected by the majority." He goes on to argue that unanimity means a decision based on the lowest common denominator, thus a less strong opinion than one would otherwise have, with a resultant decrease in impact.[25]

Besides the actual vote in a case, the existence of concurring and dissenting opinions, or of several (rather than single) dissents or concurrences, is bound to have an effect. If a Justice can be as upset with his colleagues as was Justice Clark, in *Manual Enterprises* v. *Day* (an obscenity case), calling attention to the fact that "Those in the majority like ancient Gaul are split into three parts," it is likely that a decision will be robbed of much of its effect.

While the result of the case may be of more immediate importance than the grounds on which it is decided, the grounding of a decision in the Constitution rather than on a statutory base will be "tactically important in determining how to blunt or facilitate or change or eliminate the Court's intervention."[26] Decisions based on constitutional grounds may mean that victory in the legislature or executive branch by opponents of that decision will be less than complete victories, because the Court has reserved its power to declare statutes unconstitutional for use in such matters. Similarly, whether a constitutional basis or the Court's supervisory power over lower federal courts is used in criminal procedure cases can be important in determining whether state courts will follow the decision. That the Supreme Court rested its decisions in the *McNabb* and *Mallory* cases, concerning prompt arraignment of defendants, on the latter basis is one of the reasons why the states have generally refused to adopt the rules of those cases.

After the U.S. Supreme Court has spoken, the basis used by state courts interpreting the decision will also be relevant to the decision's impact. If state courts apply federal court rulings in their determinations, the content of those rulings may have sufficient impact on state policy makers to outweigh arguments based on the state constitution; this is particularly true if a case involving a state statute may be carried to the U.S. Supreme Court. The precedents used, or abandoned, will also be relevant grounds perhaps having an impact. The abandonment of the "separate but equal" doctrine of *Plessy* v. *Ferguson* in *Brown* v. *Board* made that decision particularly difficult for some to stomach, but such overruling was unavoidable. In other cases, where overruling has occurred *sub silentio,* the displeasure may be less great. Whether the Supreme Court has reversed or affirmed a lower court is a matter of related significance, as is the general question of whether government action has been upheld or overturned.

Competing possibilities have been suggested for the effect of lack of precision of statements. The first is that greater clarity would bring increased compliance. "When relevant court opinions are ambiguous . . . , the possibility of the adoption of legislation contrary to Supreme Court intent . . . increases."[27] Or, as Barth argues, "Ambiguity of a decision increases the likelihood that it will be misunderstood by the other actors in the political process and that the policies of the other participants will not be adjusted to conform to the decision."[28] Control of lower courts and public officers becomes more difficult. Attempts to use the opinion to support new policy will be greater than if the opinion had been precise, thus increasing the range of proposals considered.

"Conflict will be furthered by confusion and uncertainty about the modes of desegregation and the final outcome," some sociologists have argued. Although the Supreme Court made clear that it had no doubts as to what the final result of the School Desegregation Cases ought to be, the Court is alleged to have contributed to the conflict because of the variability in implementation it allowed. Several writers on the subject of authority and the removal of segregation have suggested that a clear and consistent statement of policy and the methods to be used in implementing it were necessary if such implementation was to follow without a high degree of conflict which might alter the course intended by the high-level policy makers. "Conflict over desegregation will be minimized: (1) the more clearly, legal procedures evolve for protecting the rights of minorities; (2) the more effective, well-disciplined and impartial are the law-enforcement agencies prepared to back desegregation and the more there is public expectation that such authority will act in case of violence . . . ."[29] Even if those affected by a decision have been presented with a clear policy statement, and know what is expected of them, they may be tempted to challenge the policy if they are not fully certain that it will be enforced or that noncompliance will be met only with a reprimand and no severe sanction. The energy which might be invested in evasive activity may be channeled into other, more peaceful forms of action if the "strong arm of the law" is highly visible and if the wielders of that power make clear that they will use it if necessary to bring about compliance. As these last statements suggest, more than clarity is involved, but clarity is quite important.

The second possible result of ambiguity is that it forces people to come back to the courts to ascertain what was meant, thus increasing the court's control over the policy making process. Thus, "The ambiguous parts of Supreme Court opinions 'invited' contestants to turn to lower courts for explication and elucidation of the high court's rulings. . . . Contestants might . . . have felt they could persuade lower courts to adopt new interpretations of higher court rulings."[30] The Court, Lowi writes, "can inundate itself in areas of 'hard law' where it cannot or will not enunciate a leading opinion expressing good governing rules," because "responsibility can be maintained only through regular, bureaucratic supervision" by the Court. On the other hand, "A strong and clear ruling . . . leads to significant decentralization of caseload and a good deal of self-administration by lower courts and counsel," yet "each decision in each lower judicial unit becomes more consistent with all other comparable decisions, because the clear rule is a good criterion, departures from which are easily detectible by higher courts and clients."[31]

One further effect of ambiguity in Court doctrine, an effect in the legislative arena, has recently been called to our attention. Pettit, writing about the problem of church-state relations and higher education, notes that "the centrifugal pull of localism and federalism would be offset when an overarching constitutional principle is unambiguous in its meaning and its application. . . . But when the constitutional principle is ambiguous, the patterns of constraints that are operative in the various regions of the country have a pronounced effect on senators' roll call positions."[32]

Once a decision is released by the Court, it enters the political milieu by means of a *communications process,* including both the mass media and an extended social communications network. Extremely important in that network are the members of the Court's attentive public, or attentive public*s* for particular issues. The *amount of knowledge* people have about the Court and its decisions has been held to be a variable relevant for impact, but it would seem that general awareness, rather than precise and accurate knowledge, may be enough to produce reaction. One might not even want to talk about compliance until the affected individuals are aware of what the Court had done. Relevant here is the fact that there are many jurisdictions in the country in which precedents are not known, even to lower-court judges, much less to legislators and administrators, or where they are known incorrectly because of inaccuracies in the way in which they have been reported.

The existing *political, economic, and social situation* into which a decision is injected has a number of relevant characteristics. Majorities, minorities, and factions are present. Parties and interest groups are also present in varying numbers and strengths. The diversity of interests in the social milieu and whether or not they can be focused nationally, or remain splintered at the state and local level, are important aspects of this factor. The relevance of political parties is clear, both historically and contemporaneously. In the very first years of the Court's existence, partisan battles had affected the Court. Warren suggests that "all the delicate questions" dividing Federalists from Anti-Federalists came before the Justices of the Supreme Court while they were sitting on circuit. The second instance of the use of judicial review, the famed *Dred Scott* decision, clearly had partisan impacts, in addition to its possible contribution to the Civil War. Kelly and Harbison write that both parties were embarrassed by the decision, because the Court's ruling "almost destroyed the supposed reasons for the Republican Party's existence" and "ultimately proved a major catastrophe to the Democrats" by causing a breach between the northern and southern wings of the party.[33]

Mendelson uses *Dred Scott* as an example to suggest that only when our party system is quite weak can the Supreme Court intrude upon national policy. It was a realignment of sectional forces coming from Lincoln's exploitation of the case in his debates with Stephen Douglas that elected Lincoln, Mendelson argues. He has been contradicted by Nagel, who argues, on the basis of congressional votes, that the period of highest judicial review was the one in which parties differed most. He concedes the relevance of party, however, by showing that when one party dominated Congress and the other the Court, friction was high, and that there was a relative absence of judicial review when Democrats controlled all three branches of government. He later argues that there is a "weak causal relation between Congress-Court party splits and an upsurge of Court-curbing bills," but notes that "all seven high-frequency periods [of Court-curbing attempts] involved party or factional differences between Congress and the Court."[34]

The reaction to the Granger Cases, decided a day before Congress elected Hayes President over Tilden, was conditioned largely by the conflict which had arisen in the Electoral Commission which resolved the disputed Hayes-Tilden contest; several Justices of the Supreme Court were members of that Commission. "The partisan excitement caused by this election and by the inauguration of Hayes led some newspapers to assert that public confidence in the Judges had been weakened, and that the country would be the less willing to accept the doctrines laid down by the Court."[35]

Coalitions between parties, between groups, and between each exist, and some of these coalitions are clearly activated by court decisions, as when the "Conservative Coalition" of southern Democrats and conservative Republicans operated to try to invalidate many of the Court's internal security decisions in the 1950's. Walter Murphy's description is worth quoting at length:

> Segregationists and the ultra-security-conscious had found a common foe in the Court and had found common ground for opposition in the concepts of states' rights and virulent anticommunism. In exchange for much needed aid in the fight for segregation as a way of life, Southern Democrats were willing to swallow their pride and to forget if not forgive the McCarthy wing of the Republican party for 1952 campaign charges of "twenty years of treason."[36]

Political and governmental units are in continuous interaction, sometimes in conflict, sometimes in consensus. This leads to the comment that "Supreme Court legislation has a great limitation—its effective authority is limited to doing those things which society is ready to do, but cannot accomplish in the elective arena,"[37] and to the hypothesis that Supreme

Court decisions can initiate social change only when other social agencies are in stasis. Similarly, if the Supreme Court is "ahead of the times" in its decisions, noncompliance bulks large, but if the Court is "behind the times" (but not too far), reactions to its decisions will be positive, and they will be both applauded and accepted.

The *geographical scope* of the effect of a decision is clearly one of the other environmental items which become relevant to a decision's effects. Thus, despite their extreme unhappiness with *Brown* v. *Board*, evinced by the Southern Manifesto, southern representatives were not able to take congressional action against the Court. Had northern cities, whose *de facto* segregation is only now beginning to be affected by the aftermath of *Brown*, been affected equally with the South at the time of the decision, reaction might have been more severe. *Per contra*, one can argue that if a problem with which the Court deals is concentrated in one region, the opposition to the Court's decision may be greater, because located in a more compact area, than if spread over a wider region. Another environmental factor is the *structure of the economy*, in which we might include patterns of industrial ownership and technology. Miller argues that changes in the economy are so swift and of such magnitude that they "wash out" the possible effects of decisions by the Supreme Court in the economic area. The technology which is part of our economic structure also has an effect on civil liberties, Miller argues, noting that it may make "the realization of those values unlikely at best, impossible in all probability," even though the Court's decisions on civil liberties and civil rights seem to be increasing the individual's freedom. Certainly the large impersonal organization and a large, computer-run economy appear to decrease an individual's freedoms in some respects, and technology has made it easier for some to invade the privacy of others.

If a decision is injected into a *crisis*, or is perceived as creating one, impact is likely to be immediate, as when the government has felt threatened with the loss of sources of information thought to be needed in pursuing alleged criminals. Crisis situations may also operate to vitiate the impact of a decision with which individuals had earlier begun to comply. While compliance with the Court's police procedure decisions had not been particularly high, there seems little doubt that riots caused a deterioration in the degree to which the rulings were followed.

While there are immediate reactions to the fact and content of Supreme Court decisions, much of the impact, both at the level of the local community and in "higher" political areas, is dependent on *whether the decision is followed up*, and on the number of people required for enforcement. There may be a considerable difference in the number of follow-up cases in the lower courts needed to achieve implementation. (Compare the myriad of cases post–*Brown* v. *Board* with the situation after *Freed-*

man v. *Maryland.* Only a few cases brought by the movie industry were necessary to eliminate censorship procedures offensive under that ruling.) If an interest group is present to bring cases in the lower courts and to press upon local officials the importance of the decision, as the NAACP did after *Brown,* then its impact will be felt more strongly than if one acts as "enforcer." There may also be a difference in follow-up depending on whether initial action in this direction is taken by public officials or by those without official authority. In considering follow-up, we must remember that there are some situations in which it is extremely difficult if not impossible for a follow-up to be initiated by those who would wish to do so. In explaining noncompliance with school prayer decisions, Dolbeare and Hammond indicate that one factor was that "there were no regular channels through which the issue could be raised to official visibility."[38]

The degree to which government authorities attempt to enforce a decision also helps determine the degree to which impact is felt. Because the Supreme Court is not able to exercise surveillance of its decisions, it is dependent on these other actors, governmental or private, to carry out this work. The Court cannot intervene in the life of the community to remedy situations it does not feel consistent with "the law" but must rely on other governmental organs to initiate independently such action as will ultimately bring issues before the Court for determination. For that reason, it cannot replace that which it declares must be eliminated. Such positive action must be taken by either the President, through Executive Orders or through his powers as Commander-in-Chief of the Armed Forces, or by Congress with the passage of legislation. The vacuum created by the Court's striking down of certain types of behavior or certain statutes will be filled either by the states or other federal government bodies. The degree to which that vacuum is filled may depend, however, on the degree to which responsibility to take action is focused on the officials mentioned. If no officials have "clear and unavoidable responsibility" to act, if none sees any gain from acting and does not see his self-interest negatively affected by inaction, then the vacuum may remain empty—at least empty of public officials.

For the effective removal of, for example, state discriminatory or segregatory action to occur, something more must be done beyond the Court's issuing a decision. There must be some way found by which the functions performed by segregation for the society in which it existed can be replaced, or the energy used in enforcing it channeled elsewhere; meaningful alternatives within the framework of what the Court will allow must be discovered.

> Any attempt to eliminate an existing social structure without providing adequate alternative structures for fulfilling the functions previously fulfilled by the abolished organization is doomed to failure . . . . To seek

> social change, without due recognition of the manifest and latent functions performed by the social organization undergoing change, is to indulge in social ritual rather than social engineering.[39]

If the Court cannot provide the alternatives and other branches of the government can, it should be clear how strongly the effect of Court decisions is related to the behavior of these other governmental bodies. Also, as Walter Murphy has suggested, the counterattack on desegregation (as well as segregation itself) fulfills a function, a fact which should be realized by those who look with horror on the pattern of noncompliance with the Court's rulings: "The counterattack is also serving to some degree as an escape valve for the disappointment and despair which the white South feels at the end of legalized public segregation . . . ."[40]

The *relative power and position of those responding* is a key variable to be examined. Thus, "counterstatement of constitutional principles—made by respected judicial authorities—nullify, to a certain extent, the effect on public opinion of the unanimous decisions of the Supreme Court."[41] Barth goes so far as to say, "Approval of a decision by the other decision-makers in the political process is probably more important than approval by the general public."[42] Although fairly regular support for the Court comes from the university community, there is no regular constituency operating on the Court's behalf. Even the organized bar often criticizes the Court, instead of taking the lead in seeing that its decisions are enforced. And Krislov notes, "When support for the Court has been forthcoming from the bar, it has characteristically been couched in the form of generalized appeals in the name of the rule of law."[43]

As not all impact is immediate, initial reaction to Court decisions, particularly by politically important and visible individuals, may condition much of what occurs later in the process. Krislov claims, "The appearance of support or opposition has significant consequences in both activating latent opinion and in converting mugwumps to one position or the other." He goes on to contrast the difference between President Eisenhower's "long-time equivocal stand on desegregation" with President Kennedy's "unqualified endorsement of the School Prayer decision," with the latter, but not the former, assisting in the formation of consensus.[44] The reaction of the immediate parties may have an effect on others affected or potentially affected by a decision. Thus, it is possible that the resistance to desegregation by Prince Edward County, Virginia, one of the school districts involved in the *Brown* decision, had a greater impact in terms of encouraging resistance than did comparable action of other units. In more general terms, the existence of statements in opposition to court decisions, made by public officials, may be essential if noncompliance is to occur, because "the tradition of compliance is so forceful that counterjustification must be formally created to sustain disobedience."[45] A spokesman for the "counterjustification" is needed, and the state or local public official is a logical spokesman, one whose visibility will be far more likely to attract support than would the words of most private citizens.

The *belief systems* or political culture of the nation or community must also be considered, as the "attitudinal environment" into which decisions of the Supreme Court come. More transient public opinion also is clearly relevant. People hold positive evaluations of the Court and negative views about particular decisions simultaneously; those positive valuations may cushion negative views about particular cases. Beliefs may be directly related to the content of relevant decisions, for example, school prayer or desegregation, but another set of attitudes and orientations, that is, attitudes toward the Supreme Court itself, is also crucial. Beliefs about the roles judges are supposed to play, that they are to be nonpartisan, impartial, and scrupulously honest are also relevant, and the extent to which it is believed that judges do act in that fashion will condition the reception accorded an opinion. The role played by individual judges, the charisma they radiate, or the hatred they stir ("Impeach Earl Warren!") also become relevant and are enhanced by people's tendencies to personalize events.

We have been told that the American citizenry reveres the Court, because that citizenry reveres the Constitution, with the judges being the "priests in the service of a godhead."[46] "Since the Supreme Court is popularly considered as exercising a guardianship over the Constitution, the result has been to invest the judges of the Court with all the panoply of sanctity with which the Constitution itself has been invested." This is reinforced by the observation that "The widespread adverse reaction to President Roosevelt's Court-packing plan showed that the charisma of the Court rested on a far more complex basis than the immediate popularity of its decisions."[47] The myth that judges are neutral and only discover law dies hard, despite observations such as that of Lerner, years ago, that "despite every proof to the contrary, we have persisted in attributing to them the objectivity and infallibility that are ultimately attributes only of godhead,"[48] and Murphy's more recent remark, "While the Court's sudden defection to the New Deal was perhaps the sharpest blow to the official myth since the McCardle case, belief in the distinction in judicial decision-making between will and judgment persisted, though now it became an ideal image of how judges had behaved in a lost and golden past."[49] Because the myth appears to some to facilitate compliance and increase impact, they have suggested that the Court, in order to preserve its stature and power, ought to maintain some vestige of the myth of judicial objectivity and the idea that law is only found, not made. However, it has recently been argued that "it is questionable whether a disbelief in the myth is necessarily incompatible with a belief in the Court's legitimacy and expertise."[50]

Much of the impact of Supreme Court decisions, particularly with respect to cases involving civil rights and civil liberties, takes place in the local community. Thus, the *characteristics of the community* become relevant factors. The *history* of the community with respect to the issue at hand (and its perceived importance to the community) are of much relevance. If local officials have had an established policy on a subject for some time prior to the announcement of the relevant Supreme Court decision, less is likely to happen than if they had no such policy. In this connection, Krislov notes "the relative ineffectuality of prescriptions in reversing actions of officials who had already established a policy based upon their own predilections and political vistas."[51] Just as past history is important, so is the community's *homogeneity*. Noncompliance with the Supreme Court's church-state rulings seems to have been greater in religiously homogeneous communities than in those heterogeneous communities with significant religious minorities, although, "Even in religiously homogeneous communities which project their intense religiosity into their school curricula, action by school officials under the aegis of Court policy may strike a responsive chord in the community or at least in a significant segment of it."[52]

The *size* of a community, while related to homogeneity, also had independent effects. Thus, in larger communities, elected officials may have greater discretion to ignore popular passions because of greater social distance from their constituents. In a small community typified by something approaching "mechanical solidarity," leaders and led are quite likely to be in frequent interaction concerning not only political matters for which the leaders are held responsible but concerning other matters of everyday living as well. More opportunities are created for "the led" to register opinions with the leaders and/or to apply pressure on the latter if an election is not at hand. In a large city, however, characterized by a high division of labor, leaders and led are in contact only infrequently and the former are less subject to the pressure which can be exercised in a situation of frequent and intimate contact. It is for this reason that the backing supplied by the Court's decision may be of more importance to leaders in a relatively small community than to leaders in a large city, providing both are equally willing to attempt to bring about integration:

> Judges, police officers, members of school boards and other representatives of governments are strangers to the people of the cities and it is seldom that the impersonal authority they represent is questioned. In the smaller communities, on the other hand, local officials are friends and neighbors whose judgment is frequently subject to challenge when it does not reflect community attitudes.[53]

The *dominant interests* in the community and the way in which they are structured would also seem to be relevant. This can work two ways;

not only can local interests restrict implementation if they oppose a decision but, "When . . . judicial decisions have been in harmony with the dominant interests of society, the justices have been the object of lavish praise, bordering on adulation."[54] At other times, their effect in support of compliance may be direct. For example, the "influentials" in "Eastville-Westville" supported the school superintendent's policy on school prayer; in so doing, they "reinforced his expertise power base and thus in turn reinforced the power base of the Supreme Court itself."[55] Particularly if legal specialists are part of the community power structure, the interpretation they give to the Supreme Court's decisions, conditioned by their attitude to the law itself and the Supreme Court, can be crucial. Thus, Reich has noted, "In some cases local counsels are, in effect, the medium by which the actual impact of a Supreme Court decision is determined."[56] Sometimes the effect of counsel is not seen by the public, in that he does not openly interpret the law to them, but the impact of that interpretation nevertheless clearly exists. The law of libel provides an example of this: the decisions of the Court have an impact on newspapers as they are interpreted to publishers by their counsel, who do not make public statements on what is acceptable to say and what is not. Gregory indicates that in Dallas, the city attorney advised a group developing a film classification ordinance that while the Dallas proposal involved classification and *Freedman* v. *Maryland* involved more direct censorship, a provision for prompt judicial review—required in *Freedman*—was necessary and should be included, and such a provision was incorporated in the Motion Picture Study Committee's recommendation to the City Council. Even when the "power elite" or the dominant interests of the community are not involved, the roles taken by the activists in the community are of considerable importance, particularly in view of findings that they are more tolerant of unorthodox minorities and more democratic in their outlook than those who tend not to participate in politics. Johnson also finds them to be more firmly supportive of "the Court and its Justices as part of the American political system."[57]

When we begin to talk about the characteristics of individuals, we need to note a set of social-psychological variables relevant to the responses to Supreme Court decisions. *Perceptions* of what the Court has said, as filtered by *attitudes*, lead to some basic questions about the study of impact, because one might wish to ask whether we should study the impact of a decision as announced by the Supreme Court or, taking our lead from Frank Sorauf, as perceived by those whose reaction we are examining. He wrote, "A Supreme Court precedent is in no sense an objective fact . . . . Its interpretations and application depend as much on the goals and involvement of the groups concerned as on the words of the decision itself."[58] Even though a researcher's perceptions of Court decisions, conditioned by his own values and training, affect his work, one can talk of a consensus among students of the Supreme Court which can be used as a base point for examining the impact of many cases, thus allowing us to treat a Court decision as an independent variable and perceptions as a variable intervening between decision and impact.

Expectations about what the Court will do can operate in a variety of ways. A lack of anticipation of a decision may lead to perceptions of greater change resulting from the decision than if the decision had been anticipated. The public may attribute more importance to a Court decision when the Court acts counter to expectations than when it decides a case in conformity with them. Even when decisions are negatively valued, public reaction may be quiet if the Court decides in accord with expectations. Another element of expectation concerns particular results expected. Thus, the strength of reaction to the Court's reapportionment decisions may have been a function of an expectation that a major shift in political power would occur, even though little hard evidence existed to support the expectation. The same phenomenon was exhibited with respect to certain criminal procedure cases, particularly *Miranda.* In both these situations, expected effects—at least not of the magnitude people had believed would occur—did not develop.

Although not a social-psychological item, *whether or not expected results develop* may have an effect on the way people view the Court's decisions. And that such results do not always develop is quite clear. A recently reported example concerns the effect of removing the state poll tax, as required by *Harper* v. *Virginia Board of Elections.* In a study of Houston registration and voting figures in 1966, Nimmo and McCleskey report that while people did register in the post-*Harper* period, the percentage of blacks registering was *less* than under the old system, although the percentage of Mexican-Americans registering was much higher. They note that "The racial, ethnic, and class response to the end of the poll-tax system apparently contemplated by its opponents did not materialize at the registration stage." While they were studying only the period immediately after the decision, they suggest that the "shape of the actual electorate in party primaries and the general election in 1966 was not greatly altered by the end of the poll tax," and that "among Negroes the advent of free registration brought a relative decrease in both registration and actual participation."[59]

We also find more inclusive *orientations* or *dispositions,* general outlooks toward objects in the world, which are of relevance. Orientation to authority and habit, a disposition to react in the same way one has reacted in the past, seem of particular importance. Dispositions to obey, if widely held, would make difficult arousing widespread opposition to Supreme Court decisions. "The inertial effects of public respect for the institution, fear of change, and the support of groups dependent upon the Court all have to be overcome in order to produce opposition."[60] Habit might mean a habit of compliance with Supreme Court decisions, perhaps leading by extension to anticipation of ways in which the Supreme Court will extend its rulings, or a habit of resistance, the hypothesis being that once one has resisted the Supreme Court, it is likely that one will do so again. Habit may also refer to the stability of patterns of social life, so that if the Court has commanded change, an inertia would exist which would have to be overcome if the intended social change were to be accomplished.

Individuals' motivations form another relevant social-psychological variable. Those seeking higher office within the judicial system might feel it appropriate to conform to the decisions of the higher courts. Those seeking elective nonjudicial office, on the other hand, might be motivated to "damn the Court" if the local electorate were unhappy with current Court decisions. Related to motivations, particularly for public officials, are *role conceptions.* Legislators, administrators, and lower-court judges have ideas about how they should behave toward the U.S. Supreme Court, conditioned by expectations (held by others) as to how they should behave. They share frames of reference as professionals, where their professional role may embody expectations about reaction to the Court. Particularly important is the question of the role to be played by legislators (and others) in determining constitutionality. The position that the Court shall be the sole judge of constitutionality may lead either to acquiesence in Supreme Court rulings or to legislative buck-passing of important issues to the courts. A lawyer's role conception of his place in the legal system is also of considerable importance. If he considers himself an "officer of the Court," then he is more likely to urge enforcement of Supreme Court mandates than if he looks upon himself as having sole or primary allegiance to his client's wishes.

* * * * *

Considered in this section have been a number of variables which may have an effect upon impact, and some of the ways in which those variables may operate. Among variables discussed have been characteristics of court cases and the process by which cases are decided; the political milieu into which the cases are injected; environmental factors; efforts made to follow up a decision; belief systems; community characteristics; and a set of social-psychological items. The reader will find these reappearing with regularity as he reads about specific instances of impact in later chapters. Before going on to that material, we shall make an excursion to examine possible frames of reference which might be applied in looking at the Supreme Court and its impact.

CHAPTER 3

Frames of Reference: Some Ways of Looking at Impact*

INTRODUCTION

Political scientists have developed a number of ways of looking at political phenomena. They utilize these frameworks to help them select and then organize data with which they work and to help explain (and perhaps predict) the political world. Eventually they hope that they will be able to develop these frames of reference into theories, collections of generalizations of considerable certainty and precision. Until that time, without probabilistic statements they can make with certainty, much less universal statements ("laws"), they must talk about quasi-theories, frameworks, or frames of reference.

No one frame of reference is dominant either in political science generally or in impact studies in particular. The competing frames of reference utilized contribute different perspectives by illuminating different aspects of what is examined. Some are broader in scope than others. Perhaps the most overarching is the idea of the "political system," developed most fully by David Easton, built around concepts of "inputs" from the environment, their conversion into "outputs," and "feedback."[1] Because it suggests possible linkages between various aspects (or subsystems) of politics and the larger political system or polity, it allows us to relate limited, specific studies to the more general theory we may be attempting to build. Other frames of reference are more limited.

In this chapter, we shall look at the impact of the Court, or matters relevant to that impact, through three frames of reference. The first

* A shorter and somewhat different version of this chapter was presented as a paper at the 1970 American Political Science Association meetings. Permission of the Association to utilize material from that version is gratefully acknowledged.

involves looking at the Court as part of our legal system, perhaps less a formal frame of reference than a point of view. Scholars in the field of public law have, historically, looked at the Supreme Court as a "legal institution." This entails examining some of the rules by which the Court operates, including the technical manner in which it determines cases, and canons for interpreting the rulings in those cases. We should be familiar with the perspective of lawyers and others looking at the Court as a legal institution, because the way in which a case is decided and the grounds on which a decision is based *may* affect what happens after the judges are done with it, even if all do not agree with lawyers as to what a case should mean or how it should be interpreted.

The second frame of reference discussed here involves looking at impact in terms of political interests, particularly as those interests are embodied in groups ("interest groups"). This "group theory," one of the first attempts at a general theory of politics, although now recognized to be limited by its emphasis on a single factor, requires shifting from looking at the Court as a legal institution to looking at it as part of the political system. Those who have used this frame of reference in political science have concerned themselves with courts for some time, but only as a matter subsidiary to their prime concern of explaining politics in group or interest terms. To examine the impact of decisions on groups, or to look at the relevance of groups for impact, is an extension of their work.

The third frame of reference involves seeing the Supreme Court as being a communicator connected to (and dependent upon) channels of communication. If decisions are to have an impact, they must reach an audience outside the Court. What happens to those decisions as they travel from the message giver, the Court, to message recipients such as attentive publics, and the way they are understood or perceived by the recipients, a concern of some journalists as well as communications theorists in recent years, will be discussed.

THE COURTS: SOME LEGAL ASPECTS

For some schools of jurisprudence, the matter of impact is for all practical purposes irrelevant. Those who feel that the law is found do not concern themselves with "the living law" after the judges have announced what they have found. Neither do advocates of the Austinian theory that law is the command of the sovereign: what the sovereign (perhaps the courts, by some formulations) declares is "the law," and that is that. At most, what follows is very automatic and mechanical: lower-court judges apply the law as discovered or commanded, and lawyers explain that same law to their clients, who presumably act upon it. Concerns revolve around constitutional or statutory exegesis and doctrinal matters. Once the law is ascertained, all is over.

There are, however, other schools of jurisprudence more directly concerned with matters external to or subsequent to the statement of doctrine. For adherents of sociological jurisprudence, law is to be developed in terms of social interests. Although said by some critics to be no more than a set of categories of interests, this "school" looks at the law in terms of how the law satisfies those interests, providing a jurisprudence which is to some extent result-oriented. The aspect of legal realism evident in Holmes's "bad man theory of the law," that the law is a prediction of what a judge will do in a particular case, and no more, is similarly result-oriented. So is the developing "political jurisprudence" which examines what judges do in terms of effects both for the judges themselves and the political system more broadly; this approach has clearly contributed to the study of impact of the Supreme Court.

Regardless of whether jurisprudes' concern has been an inward-looking one or one which also considered results, the rules judges followed in going about their work (whether discovering or commanding) have been of central importance to their work, as has the meaning to be attributed to a particular case. Both matters are of relevance to any examination of the impact of Supreme Court decisions. After examining these subjects, we shall look at a question drawn from the concerns of those who see the court as part of the legal system but who adhere to a political jurisprudence, that is, whether court action is planned and, by extension, whether impacts are planned.

Two central questions about the meaning of a decision are the breadth of reading to be accorded the holding or rule of the case, a matter of legal doctrine, and the inclusiveness of those bound by a decision. With respect to the former, the easiest thing to say is that the only consensus is that there is no consensus on how to determine the holding of a case. Even among lawyers, there is no clear and consistent feeling as to what the holding of a Supreme Court decision in fact is or should be. Sometimes a judge states clearly the holding of a case. In those instances, that would seem to be as far as we need to go. But some say that the judge's statement provides no more than a starting point. For example, they say that he may have dealt with matters not present in the case; to that extent, the stated holding is overbroad and must be limited. Or his statements of principle may have been gratuitous; he may have talked of how he would have decided other matters not before the Court *if* they had been. These remarks, called *obiter dicta,* are also to be excluded from the holding. The trouble is that one man's dictum is another man's holding. However, when the judge does state an explicit holding, we are in far less difficult straits than when provided a result with much discussion but no explicit statement of the principle on which the result is based or when judges simply provide a result in a case (judgment affirmed or judgment reversed), as when the Supreme Court issues a summary *per curiam* decision without opinion. Neither means that there is no holding; the difficulty becomes to ascertain what it is.

Without becoming involved in all the possible approaches which might be (and have been) used, we should point out that some argue that the principle of a case is to be developed in terms of all the elements present in that case and thus is qualified by all of them. This tends to narrow the scope and possible application of the holding. So does the technical legal view that the Court decides each case before it on the merits of that case and that any decision reached applies to that case, the facts raised by that case, and those facts only. However, if each case were limited to its facts, there would be little doctrine for lawyers to apply in any fashion. Others assert that the *ratio decidendi* (rule of the decision) may be limited to one specific aspect of the case, particularly if the judge concentrates on that aspect in writing his opinion; in this view, matters not discussed do not enter into the doctrinal principle developed.

Complicated as these matters are, they are not solely sterile philosophical (or jurisprudential) disquisitions. If a case is to be considered decided largely in terms of its facts, and thus a holding is grounded in that specific set of facts, the number of those to whom the decision might be applied is much less than if a holding can be developed in terms of broad categories and general principles. And arguments over these matters are clearly relevant to impact. For example, much of the controversy concerning the *Brown* decision concerned the scope to be accorded to the decision. Those in favor of desegregation and the removal of discrimination tended to feel that "even though the specific impact of the 1954 decision was directed at only a few school districts, the Court couched its holding in terms of unmistakable inclusiveness."[2] Those who supported programs like those declared unconstitutional and who disagreed with the position taken in the decision stated that the facts concerning their programs were different from the facts treated in *Brown* and that therefore the former were not struck down by that decision.

The Court has often tended, in exercising "judicial self-restraint," to decide cases solely on the basis of fact rather than on the basis of major constitutional principles which might be involved. However, at other times, it has felt compelled to deal with these constitutional issues, as it did in the *Brown* case and those decided simultaneously with it. When it does this, or makes broad statements of policy going beyond the facts involved in a given case, there is greater ground for feeling that the case is broadly applicable to the general subject matter under consideration. Some have gone so far as to suggest that *Brown* referred not only to all cases of school segregation but to all cases of segregation and discrimination in "public" facilities not already covered by previous cases, a position confirmed after *Brown* by "the various courts [which] . . . refused to limit the mandates of May 17, 1954, and May 31, 1955, to specific holdings and specific facts. Within two years after 'Black Monday,' a score and more of judicial decisions had recorded the wide swath which the *Brown* case had cut in other areas of racial segregation: in transportation, housing, parks and recreational facilities."[3]

Closely related to the scope of the legal principle in a case is the question of who is bound by a decision. For some, "One fact inherent in the nature of ordinary lawsuits is that they affect only the immediate parties. Thus an adjudication that one child is entitled to attend a certain school does not establish the rights of other children to attend it."[4] For this reason, "class actions" are brought on behalf of the specifically named plaintiffs and "all others similarly situated." However, it is not always clear who is "similarly situated." In school desegregation cases, it might be all those within a given district or all those within a state affected by laws being challenged. Thus, Leflar has argued, "Even this device . . . is available only for the benefit of other persons who reside in the same . . . district. Plaintiffs in a class suit can represent other parties only against the same defendant, and patrons of other . . . districts must file their suits against different defendants." The class suit, in other words, serves to cut down somewhat the number of cases that must be brought in attempts to bring about uniform interpretation, but they leave much to be desired. One is still left with the feeling that cases must be brought concerning each institutional sphere, as well as for each jurisdictional unit concerned with any one of these institutional areas.

If a decision is meant, at law, to affect only the parties to the case immediately before the court, then, with respect to the Supreme Court, we can talk only about the "law of the case" instead of the "law of the land." But while court decisions are, by comparison with legislative rulings, particular rather than general commands (compare even the broad *Brown* case with the 1964 Civil Rights Act), and while some claim that none other than the immediate parties is *bound* to obey a decision, clearly others do follow the rulings, at least as they interpret them.

Interesting in terms of *Brown* is whether one who participates as *amicus curiae* (friend of the court) in a case is bound by it. The southern states which were to be most obviously affected by *Brown* were invited to participate in argument concerning implementation and most refused, perhaps feeling that they could less well criticize (or refuse to comply with) a decision in the shaping of which they had participated. Oftentimes, the attorneys general of states having statutes similar to that before the Court in a case rush in to assert their interest in the statute and to argue for its validity. In so doing, they make it more difficult for themselves to claim later, after the Court has invalidated the statute, that the decision did not apply to them.

If no one took a decision as applying to more than himself, the courts would be flooded (or more flooded than they are now) with situations in which parties would want a specific ruling applied to their specific situation. It may be that, technically, "Neither the enterprise nor the government is necessarily bound by decisions to which they are not a party. . . . They continue on their practices until a specific judicial decree is aimed at them. The binding effect of law announced by the judiciary may well be minimal."[5] *Maybe*—but one can be fairly sure that corporation counsel and government attorneys as well are examining court decisions carefully to see what they can learn as a basis for their future behavior, whether that behavior be directed at complying with the Court's rulings or in some way circumventing them. We certainly find cases where lawyers have taken the doctrines used in one case and extended it to other areas: thus the distinction between manufacturing and commerce used by the Court to uphold state regulation of business was used later by corporation attorneys in their attempt to limit the thrust of national legislation, for example, by limiting the application of the Sherman Act. This has led to the statement that "the test of the quality of an opinion is the light it casts, outside the four corners of the particular lawsuit, in guiding the judgment of the hundreds of thousands of lawyers and government officials who have to deal at first hand with the problems of everyday life and of the thousands of judges who have to handle the great mass of the litigation which ultimately develops."[6] The importance of doctrine for the study of impact is shown by statements such as the foregoing and Shapiro's remark that "the overall impact of the Supreme Court on other political agencies is largely a matter of the verbal propositions of the law it advances . . . . For those propositions not only become part of the governing law that other agencies must at the very least appear to obey, but also determine what kinds of claims the justices themselves will subject to their attitudes in the future."[7]

If we restrict our discussion to the Supreme Court, the matter of the intended breadth of application of cases becomes at least somewhat clearer, although not completely without doubt. The Court is not compelled to hear all those cases which people wish to bring before it. By far the largest number of cases which people attempt to bring before the Court from the lower national courts or the highest courts in the states deal with subject matter such that Congress has decided that the Court should be able to decide, as a matter of discretion, whether or not it will hear them; these cases are brought up by means of a petition for certiorari. Over time, the Court has tended to accept for hearing only those certiorari cases which it considers crucial or which deal with facts differing considerably from those with which it has dealt before. It thus tends to leave in the hands of the lower courts the bulk of the cases, with the understanding that the lower courts will apply previous Supreme Court rulings to the material before them. This means that the Supreme Court limits its work load to those cases in which it can make major policy decisions, applicable to the infinite range of details brought before the lower courts in the course of their work. The cases which the Court accepts also tend to be representative of others. Sometimes several cases dealing with closely related aspects of the same subject will be accepted and decided simultaneously, using one decision to cover all the cases, which again stresses their representative aspects. Casper has suggested that this grouping of cases for argument and specification of questions in certiorari grants are the two most common ways in which the Court provides cues to lawyers to suggest that "their cases would be decided not on the basis of idiosyncratic considerations but would deal with broad policy issues."[8]

Pointing in the direction of generality of application for decided cases are statements of individual Justices, both on and off the bench, about reasons for the granting of certiorari. One reason for denial of the writ is that the Court thinks that the potential application of a case is quite limited. Thus, in *Rice* v. *Sioux City Cemetery,* involving a question of racial discrimination, the Court announced that its earlier grant of cer-unique in Iowa and the Court did not hear cases for individuals. And both uique in Iowa and the Court did not hear cases for individuals. And both Justices Frankfurter and Vinson have stressed the general application and broad significance of the cases which the Court is likely to choose to which to grant certiorari. Vinson went further, urging lawyers presenting petitions for review to stress their clients' specific cases less and principles more.

What potentially confuses the seemingly clear thrust of these statements is another set of statements, most clearly put by Justice Brandeis in *Ashwander* v. *Tennessee Valley Authority,* concerning rules of "judicial self-restraint." According to the "Ashwander rules," the Court will avoid making broad statements, will try to solve a case on its facts rather than on a constitutional issue if possible, will construe statutes so as to preserve their validity, and in general will avoid "reaching out" to decide matters not absolutely essential to the determination of a case. Where does this leave us? If the statements about judicial self-restraint are given greater weight, then rulings are to be read narrowly. Because Brandeis' statements are less rules for interpretation of cases than guidelines as to how the Court will try to operate in terms of its relations with other branches of government, the Court could accept the most significant cases from those offered to it and still limit what it does with them once it accepts them. If the statements about which cases the court is likely to accept are considered paramount, then the holdings—however determined—are to be read as applying broadly.

To some extent, discussion of how cases should be read is not particularly useful. This is because, even if one could establish that there is a definite way of determining breadth and scope of cases, there is no way of enforcing that reading on others. While we have tended to talk about the hierarchical federal court system, or of the hierarchical relations between the Supreme Court and state courts, the system is hierarchical in form only. Lower courts do not simply "follow orders" of the Supreme Court as a subordinate in a hierarchical organization is supposed to follow the orders of a superior. The Justices of the Supreme Court can, it is true, reverse decisions of the lower courts which clearly are in opposition to the Supreme Court's precedents, and, in fact, this is one stated ground for the granting of certiorari. However, not all violations of Supreme Court precedent are clear, and the judges have stated that they do not simply exist as a "court of error" to correct every mistake a lower court may make. In any case, the lower court judges have significant latitude in following the Supreme Court's directives, and different judges will find different ways of reading the cases, resulting in different applications in different places in the court system. The relationship between Supreme Court and lower courts is one of reciprocity and cooperation, not of command by the former of the latter, and, in such a situation, outright defiance may occur, as we shall see in Chapter 6.

Even when the lower courts are cooperating, only those instances specifically brought to court can be interpreted by the judges: they cannot go out and "make cases," even when they wish to correct noncompliance.

> The Court itself must necessarily operate within a rather rigid and narrow framework, having few alternative lines of action for dealing with the noncompliant. . . . It can only reasonably rely upon action supportive of its rulings from the inferior courts of the system, which, in turn, have a relatively meager arsenal of weapons at their command. The lower courts may ensure that the rulings of the high Court are implemented in those instances directly at suit, but they are otherwise limited only to the cases subsequently presented to them for litigation.[9]

This brings us to the question, often debated, as to whether the courts are active or passive bodies. The courts, and particularly the Supreme Court, have been criticized in recent years for "judicial activism" and for not using "judicial self-restraint." The issue of judicial activism, relating to the degree to which the courts should enter into questions presented to them or whether they should avoid matters and defer to other branches of government, is not, however, the same as the matter of courts' inherent passivity.

Regardless of their activity or restraint, it is argued that courts are *essentially* passive because they must wait until a case comes to them before they can act. The courts are placed in the position of deciding only those cases which come before them according to rules established by both Congress and themselves. It is also said that the courts are passive because they are only negative with respect to the formulation of policy, stating what litigants before them *cannot* do. The Supreme Court is generally being asked to determine solely whether a particular procedure is valid or invalid, and deciding that question does not require of the Court, even by way of explanation for its action, a program for replacement.

Even if one accepts that the Court must wait for cases to come to it and that it generally deals negatively with policy, one must also recognize that the Court's actions are in some measure purposive. When striking down a statute, the Court can, if it wants, specify some guidelines or principles by which other bodies can determine their behavior, although it does not always (or often) do so. Perhaps we should say that the Court is more likely to provide hints than directives. Even if the language is negative, the area of error can be so clearly spelled out that other governmental units have do doubt about what to do as far as correcting their actions is concerned.

Whether judges have planned their decisions to do more than resolve a dispute between the parties directly involved or, more broadly, to develop legal doctrine, is far from clear. Judges do not broadcast their intent, but it has been claimed that "judges were concerned with problems of implementation and compliance long before impact analysis became an important subject of judicial studies."[10] Moreover, from available materials, one can construct a set of rules of strategy which a "policy-oriented judge," that is, one who wishes to achieve certain results, might follow. Thus, one might put forth as an hypothesis not yet subject to confirmation or rejection on the basis of existing data that the goal of preserving the Court's autonomy and institutional strength might be forwarded by avoiding certain cases, or resolving them on other than constitutional grounds, in order to save the Court's ammunition for a later day. However, even if some judges are "policy-oriented," that does not indicate that judges make plans in common, although the decisions of the Court are reached collegially, through conference discussion and circulation of draft opinions.

There is clearly one sense in which decisions of the Supreme Court are planned: the Court is aware that it is handing down decisions, on particular days, on particular subjects. In other words, the existence of the decisions themselves is not fortuitous. There has been a conscious decision to accept a case for consideration, and the Justices have then voted on how to dispose of it. This sort of "planning" occurs because of what we might call bureaucratic constraints in any organization, particularly one with a large work load; for the work to be done, it must be arranged in some fashion. Moreover, because there is no rule which says the Justices must "vote a case up or down" within *X* days of receiving it, the Court controls when decisions are released to the public, although the opinion-writing speed of the Justice to whom the case has been assigned and the desire of his colleagues to write separate opinions may affect the "release date" of a case. However, the Court can act with considerable speed, as it did in both the Steel Seizure and Little Rock Cases; in the latter, the Court met in special session to hear and decide the case. Chief Justice Warren's 1965 announcement that decisions would be announced on days besides the traditional "Decision Monday," which would have the effect of giving better exposure to some cases, also indicates the way in which the Court can control the release of its output. The grouping of cases can also be planned; certainly, the way in which cases are grouped for decision is important in terms of effect. Announcing several related decisions on a single day may increase the impact of each of them, as appears to have been the case with *Ginzburg* and *Mishkin,* in both of which convictions for selling obscene materials were upheld. Likewise, decisions may be grouped in such a way that they balance each other; on the same day convictions were upheld in *Ginzburg* and *Mishkin,* the Supreme Court ruled that the book *Fanny Hill* was *not* obscene.

The Court can also control its own actions by avoiding major issues potentially available for decision in a case or by temporarily delaying reaching a decision. An example of the latter is *Brown* v. *Board of Education.* The case was originally argued during the Court's 1952 term. It was ordered reargued on the basis of several questions the Justices posed. In 1954, the Court decided only that segregation in schools was invalid, deferring until after further argument the matter of how that ruling should be enforced, after which came the 1955 decision that desegregation should take place "with all deliberate speed." In this instance, delay was allegedly utilized to allow a "massing" of the Supreme Court into a unanimous vote. It appears that sometimes the Justices are never able to reach the consensus they may desire before reaching a decision. This appears in badly divided courts, where the majority may be divided within itself into two or three segments, but also in continual postponement of reaching major issues. The latter is alleged to have happened with respect to the basic "sit-in" problem (a proprietor calling the police to enforce a trespass law against a would-be customer, in the absence of official segregation); the Court never decided the problem, and eventually was able to avoid it completely when the Civil Rights Act of 1964 with its public accommodations section was passed. The question then became, more simply, whether the act was a valid exercise of congressional power, and the Court so held. So anxious was it to avoid the sit-in question that it made the 1964 act effectively retroactive by abating sit-in prosecutions for incidents occurring before the passage of the legislation in *Hamm* v. *City of Rock Hill.*

Avoidance of decisions is avoidance of impacts. Thus, D'Amato argues that the Court avoided dealing with the issue of desegregation of cemeteries by deciding it had improvidently granted certiorari in *Rice* v. *Sioux City Cemetery,* and miscegenation, by finding grounds for not accepting appeals in 1942 and 1956 cases. The reason for this was, D'Amato imputes, to avoid "stirring up the troops" concerning matters which might interfere with the impact of *Brown*. However, while the Court may protect some of its goals by this avoidance, its failure to decide cases or to deal in particular areas may lead to the aggrandizement of power by other branches of government. Thus, there is an impact from indifference. Perhaps regulation of the economy is a relevant example; while the Court decides administrative law matters and antitrust policy, it is generally far less involved in the subject than it was before 1937. This ceasing to deal with an area with which it had dealt means greater growth for the other branches of government, in this case, particularly the executive.

Another type of "avoidance" occurs when the Court, having decided a major question of law, declines to accept further cases on the subject, thus "depressing the market" for them, as occurred after *Brown* v. *Board*, when the Court generally refused to grant certiorari to desegregation cases. An alternative is summary affirmance or reversal of cases, rather than subjecting them to the "full treatment" of oral argument and decisions with full opinion. These summary decisions are a necessary follow-through to confirm the fact that the Court is not willing to make new law on the subject, at least for the time being. That this latter device works may be shown from the unwillingness of people to try to file certain sorts of complaints, for example, concerning alleged obscene materials, because they see so many convictions reversed and cases thrown out.

The opposite of avoidance is encouragement. There are times when it appears that the Court—or at least some of the Justices—are inviting cases, perhaps so that they might intervene in the policy-making process. They may not seek out cases for review but can advertise their willingness to deal with them. This was clearly the case with reapportionment, when the Justices finally said, in *Baker* v. *Carr*, that the subject was justiciable and that federal courts could hear complaints about malapportionment. And it was also the case with *Flast* v. *Cohen*, when the Court said that federal taxpayers could bring suits to challenge federal government actions as being in violation of specific prohibitions of the Constitution. An example of a situation where the acceptance of a certain type of case was taken as an announcement that the court would accept more, even though the Justices did not specifically invite those cases, occurred with respect to sit-ins.

We find many instances where the judges, by calling attention to the fact they are *not* deciding certain points of law, may be suggesting to potential litigants that cases be brought to raise precisely those points. (An alternative inference which could be adduced here is that the judges don't know how to decide such cases and that they are expressing denials of a desire to act.) When Justice Brennan said in *Ginsberg* v. *New York* that provisions in thirty-five state obscenity statutes relating to minors were not "precise counterparts" of the New York law "and we imply no view whatever on questions of their constitutionality," one could be fairly sure some one would take this as a hint and test the variant provisions. Even if these are not intended as invitations to litigate, they clearly delineate areas for further cases. Sometimes judges go even further. Although they are supposed not to decide cases not before them, their *obiter dicta* sometimes suggest what they would do. Thus, when Justice Douglas suggested in *Freedman* v. *Maryland* that "the Chicago censorship system, upheld by the narrowest of margins in *Times Film Corp.* v. *Chicago* . . . could not survive under today's standards, for it provided not one of these safeguards, as the dissenters there pointed out," he was virtually asking for a challenge of the Chicago ordinance, which the Court did subsequently invalidate.

Beyond the question of avoiding or encouraging cases is the question of the judges' concern with the specific impact a case may have. One problem faced by an authoritative body, because it is in an interaction situation, is whether it should take into account the possible reactions of those who will be affected by its decisions, particularly when it believes that those reactions will be negative. The Court has the short-run job of saying what it feels the law to be, but it also has the long-range goal of preserving respect for the law; often these clash. Promulgation of a decision by a court when there is anticipation of a significant level of evasion or violation of that decision may do no good for respect for the law in general.

Chester Barnard is more direct: "Orders will not be issued that cannot or will not be obeyed. Executives and most persons of experience who have thought about it know that to do so destroys authority . . . ."[11] Barnard's statement refers basically to the behavior of executives within organizations, and the Court's position is in many respects different from that of the organization executive, because it is not in as constant interaction with those who feel it to be authoritative. It must be very careful that it does not too frequently *follow* anticipated reactions, or it will find that when it wants to *lead*, it will not be able to do so. It must hope that its position is such that enforcement will be granted to its decisions without much question, although at certain times it must temper its decisions and methods in an attempt to secure compliance. It will be noted that in the School Desegregation Cases, the Court, in ordering further argument concerning methods of compliance, invited the states which would be affected to become involved in the decision process by making suggestions about methods of implementation, with the hope that this might temper possible negative reaction to its decision. Only then did it hand down its ruling that the lower federal courts should be the bodies to make the final and specific decisions with regard to details of implementation.

The Court faces the difficult alternatives of (1) ceasing to be an authoritative body if it gauges its decisions solely or largely in terms of results it anticipates will occur or (2) being embarrassed if it does not take such anticipated results into consideration. The Court in the Desegregation

Cases solved the problem by making its major policy statement in a clear and authoritative fashion, leaving the fashioning of implementation (and therefore the initial exercise of sanctions) to the district courts. The Supreme Court's attempt to involve states other than those already immediate parties to the cases under consideration was not wholly successful, as several states with thoroughgoing segregation did not accept the invitation by the Court to play a part in the decision: "They wished to avoid the possible quasi-legal argument that they would be bound by the implementation decree issued in a case in which they had participated."[12]

We have further evidence, from papers left to posterity by deceased Justices, coupled with their other comments, both on and off the bench, that judges are concerned about the impact of their decisions and that they are aware that their decisions have impact. Some Justices predict the effects of the Court's decisions, as when Justice Black suggested that *Mishkin* v. *New York* would result in more lengthy sentences for obscenity convictions, or when Justice Marshall, in an income tax case, claimed, "The approach here adopted will affect only a few cases." In other cases, the lack of effect of decisions of other courts is used to buttress the Court's argument. Recently, Justice Marshall, holding in *Powell* v. *Texas* that jailing chronic alcoholics for public intoxication was not cruel and unusual punishment, cited the "inadequate response in the District of Columbia following [the Court of Appeals decision in] *Easter* v. *District of Columbia*," implying that a Supreme Court decision patterned on *Easter* would encounter the same problem. However, in *Cooper* v. *Aaron*, which arose because of the hostile reaction to desegregation attempts in Little Rock, the Court said that negative community reaction could not be used as a reason for refusing to desegregate or for delaying desegregation, thus holding that negative impact of one of its decisions could not be used to create further noncompliance.

Questions judges raise at oral argument of a case before them also reveal concern about impact. "The justices themselves, when the cases are argued before them, indicate by the questions they ask of counsel that they are more concerned with the strategic impact of possible alternative decisions than they are in finding convenient constitutional pegs upon which to hang a given result."[13] Of course, oral argument is only one part of a case, and the "convenient constitutional pegs" have probably been thoroughly provided in the briefs submitted to the judges. If judges have, for reasons of strategy, accepted on certiorari those cases that they are reasonably sure will produce the impact they want, they may use oral argument to assure themselves because the certiorari petitions do not provide them with the information they need; they may want to be more sure of what is involved.

That they have expected their decisions to have an impact is clear. Judges have from time to time indicated their clear expectation that public officials will know what the Court has said, and will operate on the basis of that knowledge. Thus, Justice Douglas has said, in the *Screws* case, that "He who defies a decision interpreting the Constitution knows precisely what he is doing." And the Court, when in the toils of statutory interpretation, presumes congressional silence or inaction following Court decisions to be knowing acquiescence in what the Court has done. That judges intend that their reasons for acting as they do be understood may also be inferred from a finding that there is a high rate of reversal in appeals from federal courts decided formally, but a high rate of affirmance in cases decided *per curiam.* The opinions written in the formal cases may have the purpose of providing "uniformity in the establishment and acceptance of the policy norms enunciated by the Court."[14]

Evidence even more confirmatory of the Supreme Court's awareness of and concern about the impact of its decisions is to be found, for example, in the criminal procedure decisions of the 1960's. Thus, Justice Stewart, writing for the Court in *Elkins* v. *U.S.*, holding inadmissible in federal court material seized by state officials in an unreasonable search, stated: "The federal courts themselves have operated under the exclusionary rule . . . for almost half a century, yet it has not been suggested either that the Federal Bureau of Investigation has thereby been rendered ineffective, or that the administration of criminal justice in the federal courts has thereby been disrupted." And Justice Harlan, concurring in *Sibron* v. *New York* (a "stop-and-frisk" case), noted that "the influence of a decision here on hundreds of courts and magistrates who have to decide whether there is probable cause for a real arrest or a full search will be large." The matter also arose often in the Court's frequent confrontation with the question of whether its procedural decisions were to be applied retroactively. Thus, Justice Clark in *Linkletter* v. *Walker:* "To make the rule of *Mapp* retroactive would tax the administration of justice to the utmost." And the Court, in the recent *Halliday per curiam* decision concerning the possible retroactive application of Rule 11 of the Federal Rules of Criminal Procedure (specifying questioning by the judge of a defendant concerning his understanding of a guilty plea), indicated explicitly that "the effect retroactive application would have upon the administration of justice" was one of several criteria the Justices were applying. In reaching their decision of nonretroactivity, they spelled out why they felt many cases would be affected. Prior to *McCarthy* v. *U.S.*, in which they had required full application of Rule 11, "the practice we were requiring had been previously followed by only one Circuit; . . . over 85% of all convictions in the federal courts are obtained pursuant to guilty pleas; and . . . prior to Rule 11's recent amendment, not all district judges personally questioned defendants before accepting their guilty pleas."

Criticism and limits to the Court's effectiveness are recognized by the judges themselves. Justice Clark acknowledged in a public speech a month after *Engel* that the Court had received more mail and telegrams of criticism over that decision than at any other recent time. The Court's rules recognize the existence of lack of compliance, at least by the lower courts; Rule 19 indicates that one ground for granting certiorari is a state court's deciding a case not in accord with decisions of the Supreme Court. Justices acknowledge that their decisions are not read with consummate care. Justice Stewart, concurring in the Court's *Giordano* remand of cases in connection with its 1969 eavesdropping cases, wrote, "One might suppose that all of this should be entirely clear to any careful reader of the Court's opinion. . . . Perhaps so . . . But 10 years of experience here have taught me that the most carefully written opinions are not always carefully read—even by those most directly concerned."

Sometimes justices are quite explicit about the lack of Court impact. Justice Warren, upholding the practice of "stop and frisk" in *Terry* v. *Ohio,* noted, in language confirmatory of some recent studies of police practices, that "the exclusionary rule has its limitations . . . as a tool of judicial control. . . . In some contexts the rule is ineffective as a deterrent, . . . [particularly] where the police either have no interest in prosecuting or are willing to forgo successful prosecution in the interest of serving some other goal." It has been noted that with this comment, "The Supreme Court, for the first time, expressly acknowledge[d] the practical limitations upon the ability of judicial review (through the exclusionary rule) to control police practices."[15] While this may have been the first time the Court had *expressly* acknowledged its lack of effectiveness in this area, a number of its criminal procedure decisions were in effect admissions of the limited effect had by earlier cases.

In many of the criminal procedure areas, the Court had dealt with matters on a case-by-case basis for many years, examining the facts of each situation to determine whether violations of due process had occurred. This happened with respect to right to counsel, utilizing the doctrine of *Betts* v. *Brady* and a distinction between capital and noncapital crimes developed in *Powell* v. *Alabama;* confessions; and search and seizure, particularly after *Wolf* v. *Colorado.* But the ills of which people were complaining and which resulted in attacks on specific convictions did not cease. It has apparently been too easy for those who would evade the thrust of the case-by-case rulings to confine those cases to their facts, not admitting the general principles underlying and implicit in them. This led (or forced) the Court, not unaware of what was happening, to make the sweeping decisions of *Gideon* v. *Wainwright* (right to counsel), *Miranda* v. *Arizona* (confessions), and *Mapp* v. *Ohio* (search and seizure).

Basing Court decisions on the practical needs of the police, or taking into account impact before it occurs, may have an effect beyond producing a more "moderate" opinion by the Court. Skolnick has suggested that such decisions encourage police to continue dubious practices they have found useful. Citing Justice Clark's references to the police's practical needs in *Ker* v. *California,* he remarks, "Every court ruling based upon the practical needs of the police as a working organization tends to reinforce —in the sense of the term as used by experimental psychologists—the tendency to continue every questionable practice that can be justified in the name of expediency, unless expressly forbidden."[16]

The evidence cited thus far does not enable us, except by extended inference, to make the jump to the position that because judges are aware of the impact their decisions have or are concerned about it, they plan to have some type of impact. However, some evidence adduced by Schubert supports the position that the judges do calculate carefully what they do, at least in terms of deciding what cases to hear. He suggests that the decision to grant certiorari in Federal Employers Liability Act (FELA) cases may be viewed in terms of game theory and that, when the cases are so viewed, blocs of Justices disposed to workmen's claims generally followed the strategies predicted by game theory for them, thus maximizing the judges' effectiveness.

When the Court refuses to hear a case, by denying certiorari or dismissing an appeal, there is an impact. The planned nature of these determinations, in terms of impact, is, however, subject to question. Just as the press and the public have generally viewed certiorari denial as approval of lower-court rulings, political scientists have come to disagree with the technical interpretation of this act, which is only that the necessary four judges did not vote to hear the case; the lower-court decision stands; and no approval of the lower-court decision is intended. Evidence has been presented which suggests that the Court's refusal to hear a case is not merely indifference but can easily be interpreted as intended approval of what is left undisturbed. Thus, Schubert shows consistent high reversal rates for cases accepted on certiorari in the 1948 through 1956 terms of the Court, and, in the 1953–56 terms, a high reversal rate for cases accepted on appeal from the state courts. Asserting that "the patterns of affirmances and reversals in the various types of cases are too definite to have arisen by sheer happenstance," Schubert concludes that "the Supreme Court's action in granting or denying access to petitioners must be informed not only by a judgment regarding jurisdiction . . . ; rather, the Court appears frequently to estimate what the outcome of a case would be if it were taken, i.e., to make a decision, in the psychological rather than the legal sense, on the merits."[17]

Our discussion of whether impacts are planned and the degree to which judges take impact into account brings us closer and closer to the political perspective on the courts. However, our concentration has been internal to the court and their principal inhabitants, the judges, as we have tried to look at certain aspects related to impact from a legal perspective.

THE COURT AND POLITICAL INTERESTS

Although political scientists studying interest groups have concentrated their attention on the relations between those groups and the legislature, they have been aware that the groups, although not operating in the same manner in the judicial system as elsewhere in the polity, have also taken cases to court. Murphy has said, "Court-congressional relations can be partly explained in terms of the judiciary's involvement in the struggle among competing groups to influence public policy. Groups which cannot achieve their goals in the legislative or administrative processes can often do so through the judicial process."[18] While some, such as Peltason, have viewed the entire judicial process in terms of the "group struggle" or the contest of interests, political scientists have generally concentrated on groups' rôle on the "input" side of the judicial process, on such items as the test case and the *amicus curiae* brief, rather than on the groups' participation in the aftermath of court decisions.

However, awareness of postdecision group involvement has become more common in the study of impact: "Groups whose interests have been frustrated by the courts can likewise seek redress from legislators or executive officials. This sort of group action has played an important role in most Court attacks . . ."[19] This activity of groups is also illustrated by Shapiro, in his discussion of the making of patent policy: "The propatent forces had done what many interest groups do when they lose with one set of politicians; they tried another, Congress. But the propatent forces anticipated that if they tried to get Congress to explicitly reverse the Supreme Court's opinions of the late 1930s and 1940s, they might run into substantial opposition." Therefore, patent interests tried to get enacted an ambiguous statute which would provoke opposition, and only partially succeeded in their goal of reversing the Court: "They ended up with a statute that did not clearly show a congressional intent to reverse the Supreme Court and thus one that could not be a very effective instrument in forcing the Court out of its position."[20]

Groups are often directly involved, in a number of ways, in what occurs after the Supreme Court decides a case. This involvement is sometimes crucial to the ultimate meaning of the decision: "What a decision means is determined by group conflict after the decision has been pronounced and the opinion read. All this activity . . . is part of the story of the group conflict." Ringing another change on the idea that "the law is what the judges say it is," Peltason goes on to add, "The Constitution, or anything else, is what the judges say it is only when the judges represent the dominant interest within the community."[21]

When a case does move out of the legal arena, activity often coalesces around particular interests, often organized as groups. Thus, Murphy's discussion of the conflict over bills to declare that federal preemption was not intended unless expressly stipulated (aimed at the *Nelson* case) is largely a recitation of which interests and groups favored the bill (including segregationists, the "ultra-security-conscious," the attorneys general of twenty-four states, the National Association of Manufacturers, and the U.S. Chamber of Commerce) and which opposed it (including the AFL–CIO, Americans for Democratic Action, and the NAACP).

Not only do groups get involved in activity relating to Court decisions when those decisions affect policy in which the groups are interested, but the groups and interests are also more directly affected, and sometimes their existence is the subject of court rulings. The NAACP was attacked through requirements that it produce membership lists as a condition of "doing business" in a state. While this was struck down in a number of cases, the refusal of the state courts to comply with the ruling in Alabama meant that the NAACP was out of business there for over a half-dozen years, "its state-wide organization . . . destroyed and its activities on behalf of the state's Negroes . . . completely disrupted."[22] This shows how lack of compliance with a decision can affect a group, the inverse of examples of groups helping to effect impact.

While the existence of the Jehovah's Witnesses was not directly involved in the Flag Salute Cases, a "reign of terror" was unleashed upon members of that sect after the Court had upheld the validity of the compulsory salute. While, as Manwaring suggests, "they probably faced a rough summer whichever way the decision went," the Court's "implied rebuke of the Witnesses aggravated the already charged situation."[23] Officials refused to prevent assaults upon members of the group or to deal with the assailants after the assaults; in some cases, police joined the mob attacks. The legal staff of the Witnesses had to put all its efforts into helping those against whom action had been taken in the aftermath of the decision. It is interesting to note, in terms of the group framework, that the act of another group led indirectly to the relieving of pressure on the Witnesses. The American Legion issued new rules of flag etiquette. The rules, subsequently adopted by Congress, provided that merely standing at attention in the presence of the flag was proper. Those supporting the Witnesses and opposed to the Court's *Gobitis* ruling used this rule to show that the pledge and salute were not essential to respect for the flag, and the Department of Justice's Civil Rights Section supported this interpretation. Manwaring suggests that it was the Justice Department's continuing pressure—coupled with public preoccupation with the war—which caused persecution of the Witnesses to abate and that the *Barnette* decision reversing *Gobitis* "had very little effect one way or another."

In the past, there has been talk of the Court's decisions in terms of who benefited from them, but it has been in gross or general terms, for example, in discussion of whether the nation or the states were advantaged when questions of federalism were decided by the Court. More recently, the talk has become more specific. Krislov, for example, presents a list of groups benefited by invalidations of legislation affecting political rights from 1789 to 1963. He finds that among those benefited have been Civil War Confederates, teachers, left-wing advocates and right-wing racists, circulators of leaflets, and religious dissenters. Groups frequently use decisions to support the positions they advocate on matters of policy. They may also utilize the decisions as defensive weapons. Thus, when one of the members of a state legislative interim committee asked the Illinois Division of the American Civil Liberties Union for a list of its membership, General Counsel of the organization responded in the negative, citing Supreme Court decisions to support his position: "I am certain that a Commission like yours . . . understands that the Supreme Court of the United States has ruled on at least two occasions that the First Amendment forbids governmental agencies to compel disclosure of the membership lists of private organizations like ours. See *NAACP* v. *Alabama* [and] *Dombrowski* v. *Pfister*."

Examples of effects of decisions on interests are numerous. The effect of *Hammer* v. *Dagenhart* on the leaders of the movement for child labor legislation has already been mentioned. When the Supreme Court struck down the Agricultural Adjustment Act, farm leaders, "at first stunned . . . soon sought other ways of continuing benefit payments" by shifting from acreage control to soil conservation.[24] In the nineteenth century, farm groups, for example, the Farmer's Alliance and the Granger movement, had shifted their focus from the state level to the national level when the Court invalidated their regulatory statutes and indicated that only national legislation would be proper with respect to the railroads. The *Danbury Hatters'* case, in which the Sherman Act was applied to unions, was seen by AFL officials as "a potential threat to the very existence of unions, which might become the objects of dissolution suits by hostile Attorneys General."[25] Even though this did not happen, the labor leaders immediately turned to Congress to try to abolish this threat. The effect of a decision may be less on a single interest than on the balance between interests, as when the railroads' bargaining position on the size of train crews was weakened by the invalidating of full-crew laws. In the area of patent law, Shapiro claims that the effect of Court decisions "is to create something so near to equality between the bargaining positions of the patentee and the infringer that the infringer need offer very little in return for using the patent," presuming both sides have equal financial resources.[26]

When groups are benefited or disadvantaged by the decisions of the Court, the attitude they maintain toward the Court may be affected, and they may either join or leave the ranks of those willing to give generalized support or opposition to what the Court does. On the positive side,

Shapiro suggests, "Judicial decisions negating various government and labor programs deemed inimical to business at one time created a strong business clientele for the courts."[27] On the other side, Warren notes the reaction of labor to both the *Debs* and *Income Tax* cases. With respect to the former, he said, "The decision gave great offense to certain labor elements in the community; and as it was rendered only a week after [the latter], it was criticized as an illustration of the prejudice of the Court in favor of capital."[28] Similarly, "The Supreme Court stimulated the strength of the Populist movement by convincing large segments of the nation that the entire government was in the hands of the 'plutocrats,' that they had no voice in their government, and that only a fundamental change in the relations of property to people could remedy the situation."[29]

Groups may be affected by being called on to follow up a decision, to "nail it down," particularly when the group has been involved in initiating the case or when the executive branch of government does not have provisions (either in terms of statutory authorization or the necessary manpower) for doing the follow-up work itself. Thus, "in certain highly controversial policy areas where supportive activity on the part of other political agencies is nonexistent or slow in coming, the burden of implementation of an initial Court decision and the expansion of its principles is placed upon the litigants and their success in the courts."[30]

Some follow-up activity involves serving as a watchdog, to see that affected agencies comply with the ruling. At other times, it involves direct requests that the agencies change their practices. The NAACP, after *Brown* v. *Board,* was actively involved in activity of this sort. Although the NAACP did bring court cases to enforce *Brown* in local jurisdictions, this did not come until after petitions had been presented to local school boards in the spring of 1955 after the second *Brown* decision; nothing had come of the petitions, and it became clear that such an approach was not going to be successful. (Little was done by the NAACP in the period between the first and second *Brown* rulings.) But this does not mean that the NAACP—or any organization in a comparable situation—brings cases in all locations. Only infrequently does one have a situation where a group can attack in all locations at once. Compliance with *Freedman* v. *Maryland* came about "because the chief benefactor—the American motion picture industry—was ready to take advantage of the gains in the decision and challenge all existing censorship laws which were being enforced," as well as lobby against any attempts to enact new censorship statutes.[31]

Considerations of strategy, based on limited resources, enter the picture, and where a group decides to follow up a decision may be a function of which cases it feels will have the largest "carry-over" into areas where cases are not brought. Thus, Berman suggests that the NAACP had, over time, shifted its approach from a "piecemeal" one "of merely providing legal aid to the individual Negroes who were receiving unfair treatment at the hands of the law" to the broader one of "challenging segregation where a victory in the individual case would also signify important progress for the whole group."[32] On occasion, situations pose challenges to organizations which cannot be ignored. Thus, when the schools were closed in Prince Edward County, Virginia—even after it became clear that this was not going to spread elsewhere in the South—the NAACP was faced with a situation which it had to attack in court, to "assure itself that this particular threat to integration and to public schools would never be posed again."[33] And the case of *Sweatt* v. *Painter,* in which the Court did everything but declare segregation in education unconstitutional per se, was interpreted clearly by the NAACP as a signal to shift emphasis in their strategy and attack segregation directly instead of continuing to bring "equalization" suits under *Plessy.* It should be recognized that, also for strategic considerations, some groups purposely do *not* follow up Supreme Court rulings. Thus, leaders of church groups in the state studied by Dolbeare and Hammond "perceived themselves and their groups as standing to lose much more from arousing public resentment than they could possibly gain from an effort to spur obedience" to the school prayer rulings, "and so they remained publicly silent."[34]

Implicit in the above is the suggestion that one effect of certain cases is to increase the litigation load of certain organizations, such as the NAACP or the Legal Defense Fund (officially, the NAACP Legal Defense and Educational Fund); the general level of litigation may increase as well, when other groups, seeing a first group being successful, decide to pursue similar litigation. If the government eventually begins to participate in the litigation which the group has been handling, the group's load can be reduced or at least shifted. After the passage of the Civil Rights Act of 1964, which gave the Department of Justice some power to act with respect to school desegregation, the LDF, while it still had many cases in progress, became more selective, taking cases which either interested it most or which could serve to prod the Department of Health, Education, and Welfare. This suggests that in considering interests and groups, we should be careful not to draw too firm a line between groups and the government. They interact, either by prodding or stimulating the other or even by working together. Thus, we find lawyers for the LDF and the government serving together in a recent case.

In the same connection, we may note a possible impact of *NAACP* v. *Button,* in which the Court invalidated a number of state antibarratry statutes aimed at organizations which were bringing cases to confirm the constitutional rights of members of the public. The ruling cleared away a major obstacle (or impediment) to the work of the NAACP and the Legal Defense Fund. (Another possibility, suggested by Hahn, is that such cases were "probably also the stimulus behind a number of other legal-aid-type outfits which got underway at this time," agencies which, but for the cases, might have had to fight the same battle themselves.) The antibarratry statutes, and the statutes showing general resistance to desegregation, illustrate something else about the involvement of groups in the impact process. Groups, in trying to enforce a decision, may set off resistance or further resistance by their activities. As noted above, the NAACP's litigation to enforce desegregation did not come until late 1955; while southern authorities were not complying with *Brown,* their noncompliance was relatively quiet. Perhaps they felt that, without suits, there would be no desegregation, and therefore, without the suits, there was no need for special laws to prevent desegregation. Many of the laws aimed at preventing the desegregation, or at making it ineffective as a practical matter, came after the NAACP began its substantial litigational activity.

We should note variable involvement of groups in the litigational and impact process. For some, such as the NAACP and LDF, the process is central; for others, like the AFL–CIO, it is important but not as central. Groups differ also in the frequency of their involvement. Some, with broad policy concerns, are often participants in the activity after court decisions. Others, not regularly involved, become activated to participate when "stung" by specific decisions. Thus, the Conference of State Chief Justices made a series of statements, first of concern, and then of outright criticism, after the Supreme Court decided cases dealing with the relationships between state and federal power. Other groups are born as a result of Court decisions. After *Brown,* a group called "Defenders of State Sovereignty and Individual Liberties" (the Defenders) was created in Virginia to try to preserve segregation in the schools. And we find a group entitled "Americans for Effective Law Enforcement" formed in June, 1967, to battle Supreme Court limitations on police. This group was headed by Professor Fred Inbau, who had written the manual on police interrogation specifically criticized by the Court in *Miranda;* he was joined by former Cook County (Illinois) Sheriff (now Governor) Richard Ogilvie; then Chicago Police Commissioner O. W. Wilson; and Harold Smith, former president of the Chicago Bar Association and Chicago Crime Commission. Perhaps one measure of the impact of a decision is the number of groups which are provoked to activity (or into existence) by that decision, or the level of activity of groups. Some of the activity may be directed at blocking the effects of the Court's decisions, but the activity itself is an impact even if it does not prevent implementation of the Court's policy.

The variable involvement of groups, particularly those opposed to the Court's actions, may limit the effectiveness of attacks on the Court. If all groups opposed to the Court (for whatever differing reasons) could be rallied to the cause simultaneously, successful attacks could be mounted more frequently. Stumpf, after examining "reversal bills" in Congress, concludes that the closer to unanimity is support of politically articulate groups concerned with a bill, the more likely it is to pass. However, he notes that when a reversal bill is grounded on anti-Court sentiment, support for passage can be found elsewhere than in groups, bringing passage without group unanimity.

In examination of interests, one set of individuals who merit specific consideration are lawyers. In their day-to-day work, they are affected—or potentially affected—by court decisions which alter the state of the law. As Miller notes, "Decisions . . . will be of importance to that segment of the legal profession, academic and practicing bar, that earns its livelihood following what the Court does."[35] Thus, after *Miranda,* the "criminal law bar" in some cities—characterized by criticism of upper-level police officials and defensive about their own law practice—worked particularly hard to adapt the *Miranda* rules to diverse new situations. But beyond that, they are organized into bar associations, which speak out on a variety of matters. Some of these are reasonably close to the concerns of lawyers as lawyers; thus we would expect some reaction when the Supreme Court deals with procedures for disbarring attorneys. The reaction to *Spevack* v. *Klein,* in which the Court held that a lawyer could not be disbarred for asserting the Fifth Amendment in an investigation into his behavior as a lawyer, was natural; many lawyers were unhappy, particularly with the implications of the case for situations broader than that involved in *Spevack,* where there was evidence independent of what the lawyer himself could have provided. In New York, from which the case had come, subsequent cases limited the possible thrust of the decision, leading to the observation that "whatever fangs *Spevack* might have had have been pulled."[36] But, beyond that, the Committee on Grievances of the Association of the Bar of the City of New York, in the statement it now sends to lawyers under investigation, asserts "that he is required to answer unless he claims that to do so would tend to incriminate him," and few have refused to respond.

Other matters involve lawyers only as citizens, but they react in organized fashion. Because the American Bar Association has been relatively conservative in its orientation, the ABA has clashed with the Supreme Court from time to time. An example of this conflict is the 1959 action of the ABA's House of Delegates, in which that group approved recommendations of the group's Committee on Communist Strategy, Tactics, and Objectives. The report of that committee "accused the High Bench of handing down decisions 'in such a manner as to encourage an increase in Communist activities in the United States' . . . ." The ABA adopted only the recommendations for legislative action to alter the Supreme Court's decisions, but, while the report (and its language) was not formally approved, "the intention of a large segment of the ABA to wound the prestige of the Warren Court was quite evident."[37]

Because the public may view the lawyers' opinions on Court decisions as of more value than opinions held by nonlawyers (because the Court deals with "law" and lawyers are experts in that same "law"), the statements of the bar may be particularly crucial in the development of public views about the Court. Well over one hundred years ago, the importance of the bar in supporting the position of judges was noted:

> Of all magistracies they are intrinsically the weakest. If they have been strong, it is because they had a hold on men's opinions. For that they are indebted chiefly to the legal profession. In a popular excitement, on occasions of the exercise of an unpopular judgement, where should they find their best support? Where they have always found it, in the lawyers themselves. . . . As yet the legal profession has formed a wall about [the judiciary] and protected it. If this wall were thrown down, the judicial establishment as it now stands, with its honor and its power, could not remain.[38]

However, there is no longer an identifiable "Supreme Court bar" arguing most of the cases before the Court and living in close physical proximity (and social proximity, as well) to the Justices, as there once was, which could serve as a source of support. Moreover, while not all lawyers (or even local bar associations) agree with the ABA's positions, there is no question that the bar in this country is *not* an adjunct of the Court, charged with or taking upon itself the task of explaining, interpreting, *and justifying* the Court's decisions to the public.

While lawyers do not fall all over themselves admiring the Court, they do on occasion move toward acceptance of the Court's rulings, even when those decisions strike close to home. Thus, although there is still much continuing controversy on the subject, the ABA has shifted from outright opposition to group legal practice to a consideration of protecting certain values within the framework of a group practice arrangement. At the 1968 ABA House of Delegates meeting, the chairman of the Committee on the Availability of Legal Services conceded Supreme Court protection for such programs and was reported as saying that the question was what specifics should be included in the programs: "The issue . . . is not whether group legal services should be permitted—the Supreme Court has ruled that, at least in certain circumstances, they are constitutionally protected."[39] Sometimes the acceptance is far less grudging. Thus, at the same meeting, an advisory committee of the Committee on Minimum Standards for the Administration of Criminal Justice reported that it had modified its standards to take into account the recently decided case of *Bruton* v. *U.S.*, which held that at a joint trial, a statement of one defendant implicating another codefendant could not be introduced.

Those who have studied interests and their organized version, interest groups, have often asserted that the internal politics of the groups are relevant to the groups' external activities. That is no less true of groups involved in the impact process. The dissent by local bar associations to stands taken by the ABA has already been noted. Murphy goes further and refers to the "schizophrenic contortions" on the part of ABA leadership caused by cross-pressures within the organization. When the organization's position drove important members—such as Justice Warren himself and Warren Olney, involved in administering the federal court system—out of the organization, pressures were built up for a change, even though the dissenting individuals were no longer members. "The ABA's public image was apparently hurt most when Chief Justice Warren resigned from the organization in 1959 in protest against attacks on the Court from bar leaders."[40] The Catholic church, Murphy also notes, was subjected to cross-pressures on the internal security issue. The church believed in racial equality, and the church hierarchy had supported the School Desegregation Cases, thus placing the church in opposition to those who would attack those cases—the same people attacking the Court for its internal security decisions; here the church's militant opposition to communism placed the church on the side of the attackers. Which way to go? What tended to happen is that "the church" spoke with several voices rather than only one.

The internal structure of groups is relevant, as well. Groups which have separately based state adjuncts, instead of only one national organization, are less likely to speak with a common tongue. The bar is a clear example. The ABA is structured independently of state (and city) bar associations, and what the former says does not control either the actions or public statements of the latter. Whether a group has a membership base at the local level, or whether it is simply run by leaders (and supported by contributions from nonmembers), is also quite relevant to what it can do. Thus, we find a difference in the litigation activities of the NAACP, which falls in the first category, and the Legal Defense Fund, which, since its ties with the NAACP were severed in 1956, falls in the second.[41] Because of its membership, the NAACP has had trouble finding litigants in areas where it may have wanted to bring cases, and pressure from parents in some areas to bring suits where the NAACP attorneys thought it disadvantageous in terms of developing the law. This occurred not only after *Brown* but before it as well. For example, because black students in Prince Edward County, Virginia, said they wouldn't go back to school until there was desegregation, the NAACP challenged the *Plessy* doctrine there, as well as at locations, such as Topeka and in Delaware, where it thought the situation more favorable.

The Legal Defense Fund, on the other hand, as a nonmembership organization, Hahn suggests, "was relatively free to pick and choose cases as it saw fit, thus perhaps easing somewhat, but not entirely, pressure from below." The LDF illustrates another point: just as the internal politics of groups affect what they do with respect to the Court, so do the relations of the group to other groups and to the social movements of which they may be a part. Thus, the LDF was drawn away from following up desegregation cases toward dealing with sit-ins by developments in the civil rights "movement." The LDF also moved into the area of "poverty law," when there seemed to be demands from its "social environment" to do so, as is evidenced from its recent broad-based attack on certain types of installment contracts and loan agreements after the Supreme Court struck down Wisconsin's wage garnishment statute in the *Sniadach* case.

Another relevant matter is the degree to which an organization is effectively organized and skillfully led. If the interests are highly organized and have resources, they will be in a better position to follow through to protect the advantages the Court has granted their cause or to fight to withstand disadvantages to which they have become subject. Labor-management relations is an area of this type, as we see in the immediate reaction to the full-crew-law decisions, as the unions began asking state legislatures to enact and strengthen minimum train-crew laws. A group with weak leadership cannot hope to accomplish as much as one with strong leadership, other things being equal. Thus, Murphy notes that those groups particularly successful in the lobbying against the Court in 1957–58 (the FBI, NAM, and AFL–CIO) were well organized and well led. That they participated actively is also in part explained by their "tangible and immediate" stake in the proposals aimed at the Court, which stimulated them to a higher level of activity, and, in the case of the FBI, to launch a campaign to change a Supreme Court decision (*Jencks*) seen as inimical to its interests. While the campaign was quiet and within Congress, House Judiciary Committee Chairman Celler had to reprimand the FBI for its activity.

Inclusion of the FBI in a discussion of organized interests is purposeful. Many group theorists, recognizing that government agencies—like private groups—lobby and have "organizational interests," include them. One could, from this perspective, also include the Court as itself an entity with an interest. Certainly, one can view some of the Court's activities as possessing characteristics similar to those of activities of interest groups. For example, Shapiro asserts, "Courts do in fact frequently lobby legislatures through opinions that point up the difficulties in administering provisions or their bad results."[42] He argues that the Court sometimes twists statutes more than is necessary while interpreting them, in order to prod the legislature into changing the statutes. However, while one can certainly look on the Court as an interest, most of those utilizing the group perspective have talked about groups in relation to the Court, treating the Court as a different sort of actor from the groups or interests.

In this section, we have tried to show the relevance of a group perspective for the study of impact, by examining how interests and groups are affected by Court decisions, how they react to them and participate in the aftermath of the decisions, and how their internal structure and operation affect that participation. Clearly, not all of the aftermath of Court decisions occurs in group terms, or even in terms of identifiable (but unorganized) interests. However, to look at the impact process without looking at groups is to provide an incomplete picture.

THE COURT AND COMMUNICATION

The communication of Court decisions to the ultimate consumer has become a subject of some prominence in recent years, as attacks have been made on the existing arrangements for the transmission of the content of those decisions and criticism has been heard of the distortions produced in the content. This criticism has been stimulated by the controversy in which the Court has been involved and by the demonstrated lack of knowledge held by the public about the Court. Newland's assertion is perhaps clearest: "Both the Court and the press need to improve their methods if essential public understanding and support of the Court and a dynamic legal system are to exist."[43] Concern with compliance has heightened interest in the subject, as Johnson notes: "Conceptualizing the judicial process as a communications process helps to understand the voluntary acceptance of and compliance with the Court's 'messages.'"[44]

There are a number of matters which must be examined in viewing the Court as part of a communications system or network. The character of the message transmitted into that network is one. What the "message" is can differ depending on what one is examining. Many studies of mass communications have treated the mass medium as the communicator and taken newspaper accounts as basic messages. That could be done in the study of impact; one could treat a newspaper report of Court decisions, however inaccurate, as the basic message and examine how people respond to it. While we will look at the effect of distortion of Court decisions by the media, we will instead treat decisions of the Court, or its orders without opinion, as the basic messages, with the accounts transmitted by the media as part of the subsequent process.

After looking at some characteristics of the initial message, we must examine the communicators of that message and some of the wide variety of formal methods aimed at getting the message "from here to there." The operation of those methods, in terms of their effects on distorting or otherwise affecting the message, will then be examined. The importance of individuals as intermediaries in the transmission of messages will be noted. Finally, while reserving for another chapter our discussion of public opinion about the Court, one of the end products of the communications process, we will look at a few of the relevant elements in the "receiving end" of the process.

We can look at individual messages or at collections of messages. The tendency thus far has been to examine specific decisions in terms of those aspects which might facilitate or inhibit understanding or acceptance. To do so is clearly important. However, each decision is not released completely separately from others, with the Court waiting until one message has been received, or at least transmitted, before releasing other messages. A great many messages are released simultaneously or nearly simultaneously. Because not all can be transmitted through existing clogged communications channels, some get greater attention than others, and some receive no attention at all.

To turn first to characteristics of individual messages (Supreme Court decisions), one continually stressed is the clarity or ambiguity of the decision. Johnson says, "A concern with message *clarity* by the Court improves the chances for adequate transmission," and notes, "If the message from above is ambiguous, district and state judges will find many convenient openings, allowing them to hand down decisions which will not fly in the face of local values."[45] Another matter is the relative technicality of the language, something different from ambiguity, because a message can be precise but so technical that the average layman cannot understand it. Here the question of the audience for which the judges write is important. They do not seem to be writing for the public. Perhaps they are writing for posterity, for lawyers (although there is no specific Supreme Court bar at which they can aim their comments), but: "Most judges do not expect to be read much by laymen and, therefore, do not think in terms of a lay audience in their writing styles."[46] Another analyst has suggested that the professional training of judges, as lawyers, and the fact that they are principally exposed to fellow judges outweigh audience concerns: "The time spent in law school, reading case after case, briefing, analyzing, and commenting on each one, and exposure to the literature of the law, to teachers, and to the shoptalk of colleagues probably are stronger formative causes in the design of a judge's rhetoric than is any sense of audience."[47] Because of this lack of concern for general audience, some individuals must interpret decisions for others, and the chances for misinterpretation (both purposeful and innocent) increase radically.

Not only are many decisions technical but judges differ in their views of what is constitutionally proper, or of the valid interpretation of a statute or regulation. Dissents to an opinion of the Court may help clarify but are likely to cause confusion—as well as giving those who disagree with the majority a handle on which to justify noncompliance. "The internal clash among the majority, concurring, and minority opinions sometimes helps to focus on the main issues; but just as likely, it causes confusion."[48] The "sharp crossfire" between judges also causes reporters to interpret cases in terms of battles between individual judges, and to lose sight of the legal issues involved. For this reason, Newland has called on the judges "to concentrate attention on the Court as an institution, or, when impelled to express separate opinions, to exercise individual restraint."[49] If they are not able to do so, "it may be equally impossible for the press and the people to understand this key political institution . . . and provide it with essential popular support and reasoned criticism." Not only do Justices on the Court differ concerning particular cases, but judges at one time differ with their predecessors and overturn precedents. This aspect of our legal process, based on our common-law tradition, is not understood and creates problems in understanding the Court's messages. The Court's ability to change its mind, however necessary to adapting the law to modern conditions, has as its price confusion and misunderstanding, which "brings on much of the heated criticism and unsophisticated praise of the Court."[50]

Other elements of the message are also important. Several analysts have suggested that "cues" as to the basis of the decision may help bring about acceptance. Johnson, comparing the New York Regents' Prayer decision (*Engel*) with the Lord's Prayer–Bible Reading Case (*Schempp*), attributed more sympathetic press treatment of the latter decision to the fact the Court made the limits of its decision quite explicit; in *Engel,* an important qualifier in which Justice Black pointed out that references to the Deity were not banned, was placed in a footnote. Earlier church-state decisions, he alleges, lacked cues related to the Court's base of power or cues as to why it was legitimate for the Court to handle such cases. He also feels that "symbolic rewards" should be distributed by the Court to the losing side to make less great their hurt and resulting unhappiness with the Court.

All of these items, taken together, affect what occurs later in the communication process. Because messages are not clear, succinct, and without contradictions, a situation is created in which "the task of understanding Supreme Court decisions has been made a struggle for both expert and lay consumer long before the Court's decision is even announced."[51]

As noted above, messages can be viewed individually, as we have just done, or collectively. The problems which the latter compounds can be seen in Newland's remark that on June 25, 1962, the day the *Engel* decision was handed down, the Court announced 16 cases with opinion in addition to 257 memorandum cases. Most were obscured, he notes, by the School Prayer Case, even though some, including an important antitrust ruling, were of "unusual significance." This situation is not without parallel. We find, at the end of the 1967 term, four separate days in which the Court deluged those interested with more than a half-dozen decisions decided with opinion. On May 20, 1968, fourteen such opinions were handed down; on May 27, seven; on June 10, twelve; and on June 17, nine. Thus, this was not a situation in which the Court retreated to handing down only three or four opinions per day after delivering a single heavy load; there was a steady heavy barrage for a period of more than a month at the end of the term. Nor were these minor cases. For example, the fourteen on May 20 included two cases from the private law area involving the right of illegitimate children to recover damages in wrongful death cases and, from the public law area, *Duncan* v. *Louisiana,* imposing the right to trial by jury on the states; *Bloom* v. *Illinois,* concerning the right to trial by jury in criminal contempt cases; two antitrust cases; and a case involving picketing on private property. May 27's offering included cases on draft-card burning, Indian fishing rights under various regulations and treaties, and the "freedom-of-choice" school desegregation cases.

As if this were not enough, on June 10 the Court "unloaded" on the public cases dealing with "stop-and-frisk" statutes, the right of federal taxpayers to bring suits to challenge statutes, the permissibility of supplying textbooks to parochial schools, and several cases dealing with public employees' refusal to answer questions and their resulting dismissals. The following week, the Court finished up its unloading by dealing with the "substitute father" rule for Aid to Dependent Children, a case involving community antenna television (CATV), the open housing case of *Jones* v. *Mayer,* and *Powell* v. *Texas,* concerning public intoxication resulting from chronic alcoholism.

What can happen as the result of such overload is shown by the initial reporting of the Court's decisions of March 10, 1969, when three cases dealing with demonstrations were decided. One, a certiorari denial, was incorrectly reported (see below); another, involving Dick Gregory, whose conviction was overturned on narrow grounds, was reported briefly; and a third, in which a Birmingham, Alabama, parade ordinance was overturned on constitutional grounds in a case involving Rev. Martin Luther King, Jr., and Rev. Fred Shuttlesworth, was simply not reported at all. A careful reading of some "in-depth" coverage several days later might have allowed the reader to figure this out, but the later story was not available to most of the American public.

In April, 1965, Chief Justice Warren had indicated that the Court would begin to use days in addition to Monday (the traditional "Decision Day") for the announcement of decisions. Presumably this was to help "spread the load," so that decisions could be better communicated and thus understood, so that fewer would be buried. The Court did initially make good on its word. The next week in which decisions were announced saw six full-opinion cases handed down on Monday, and four each on Tuesday, Wednesday, and Thursday. There were no more non-Monday decisions during that term except for a day in a week in which Monday was a holiday. During the 1965 term, the first full term after Warren's announcement, seventy of ninety-seven full opinions (72.1 percent) were handed down on Mondays, meaning that 27.9 percent (more than a quarter) were handed down on other days. However, after that term, the

Court's efforts to spread out the announcement of decisions nearly stopped. In the 1966 term, only 6 of 100 full opinions were handed down on days other than Mondays; in the 1967 term, 12.7 percent (14 of 110) of the full opinions were non-Monday issuances. And, of course, this leads up to the situation at the end of 1967 term just described. It should be noted that no effort has been made here to describe all the other orders handed down by the Court, almost all also on Monday. Certiorari denials alone often run over 100 on a single day, and on the first day of the term may exceed 400 or 500; to this, one might add denials of rehearings, *per curiam* opinions (both summary and those announcing points of law), grants of certiorari and notations of probable jurisdiction (in appeals), and miscellaneous orders.

It should be noted also that the decisions themselves are the only messages the Court transmits. There is little supplementary material provided by the Court, although there is some limited precedent for handing out more than copies of the decisions themselves. Because of the interest in *Chisholm* v. *Georgia,* the Clerk of the Supreme Court issued a summary to the newspapers. The "headnotes" which appear in the *United States Reports,* prepared by the Reporter of the Court, are not issued along with the opinion, and come only afterwards; the judges do not write their own headnotes. The newsman covering the Court, Grey points out, is left completely on his own. There is a press officer, but his task is to make the opinions available, not to discuss them. Summaries of the backgrounds of cases have been prepared in advance in recent years by law professors, under the aegis of the Association of American Law Schools, but they do not deal with the opinion itself. When being questioned by the Senate concerning his nomination to be Chief Justice, Justice Fortas suggested he would, if he could convince his brethren on the Court, make law professors provided by the AALS more available to newsmen to explain decisions immediately after they were handed down. He also suggested that he would supplement the existing "messages" by having prepared and released to the press some statistical analyses of the Supreme Court's work, such as percentages of criminal appeals affirmed and reversed, and that he would suggest some radio and TV coverage of delivery of judges' decisions from the bench.

The Means of Communication. While the Supreme Court releases texts of its opinions and orders as it hands them down, and while these are subsequently printed, most people do not hear about cases by reading those opinions. "The role of the press [is] . . . primary in the early flow of information and resulting opinion on what the Court has said."[52] This has generally been the case. In the very first years of the Court's existence, until 1816, "Except so far as the opinions were published in the newspapers, little was known of them by the general public or even by the bar. . . . Many years elapsed before the Supreme Court Reports obtained any wide sale or circulation among lawyers."[53] People may subsequently obtain copies of the opinion—for example, 13,500 copies of the *Engel* decision were sold by the U.S. Government Printing Office—but initial acquisition of information is through the press.

The principal disseminator of information about the Court's messages, in terms of the number of newspaper readers served, is the wire service. Even when a newspaper has its own Washington bureau, it often relies on the wire services for Court coverage: very few papers have their own reporters covering the Supreme Court. Looking at *Baker* v. *Carr* and the School Prayer Cases, Newland found, among the twenty-five evening papers he examined, that of twenty-three papers carrying reports of the reapportionment decision on the day it was announced, fourteen stories were from AP, five from UPI, one from the *Herald Tribune* News Service, and only two by staff writers for the papers. With respect to the prayer decision, ten "day one" stories came from AP, four from UPI, and two were put together from wire service reports. While the AP domination over UPI continued, Newland noticed a greater percentage of stories by staff writers starting on the second day after the decision.

Very few of the reporters who deal with the Court are properly trained. There are exceptions, like Anthony Lewis, who formerly covered the Court for *The New York Times;* the reporters who cover the Court for the Washington papers, the *Post* and the *Star;* and a few others. A few, following an example set by Lewis, have spent a year at law school to increase their familiarity with the legal process. But generally the reporters who write the stories for the wire services—and certainly the editors and rewrite men at the receiving end of the wire services—are not trained in the intricacies of judicial procedure. In addition, Grey notes that the reporters at the Court tend to be passive and to be quite deferential to the Court, quite a different attitude from that evinced by most other reporters toward the institutions they cover. A further note: in evaluating the coverage given to the Court, one must remember that the attention given by *The New York Times* (and the Washington papers, to a lesser extent) is not typical. "The *Times* . . . coverage," Grey writes, "attempts to meet the needs of the person with unusual degrees of interest and background in the law [and] the public official or private citizen who wants or needs to know what the Court is doing."[54] There may be citizens subscribing to other papers who *want,* if not need, to know—but they are likely to be out of luck.

Just as the *Times* coverage is specialized and performs a special function, coverage of the Court by magazines performs a function different from that of the daily press. Magazines are able to provide greater, more intensive coverage than the daily press; they are able to provide "in-depth" coverage where the daily media must be relatively superficial. Not as many people will be exposed to the magazines as will be exposed to the papers, but those who will, the "opinion leaders," are particularly important because they serve as a source of information and views for others.

The existence of official printed versions of the Court's decisions has been mentioned. This leads to another formal means of communication: the court system itself. In a particular case, the decision and accompanying orders of the Supreme Court are sent to a lower court for "proceedings not inconsistent with this opinion." "The formal judicial structure . . . provides an important channel through which a ruling is transmitted to those who are directly under obligation to act."[55] While there will be instances when a case pending before a lower court will be affected by a Supreme Court decision immediately, generally judges and the lawyers who practice before them can afford to wait until some official report reaches them. They are, therefore, generally not reliant on the mass media. However, judges' knowledge of cases is not automatic: they may not have time (or inclination) to read all that the Supreme Court decides. Therefore, lawyers become crucial in communicating cases to them, by citing them in the course of their arguments in specific cases. The lawyers are more likely to discover the relevant cases when doing their research in preparation for a case—"Perhaps the most substantial point of communication is through the prosecuting and defending attorneys in their preparations for cases and their resulting need to examine relevant decisions."[56]—and then to argue them to the judge who will be deciding their client's fate. "If counsel does not call such cases to the judge's attention, the latter might not know the relevant cases that exist."[57]

While Supreme Court decisions are printed, and thus available, many lower-court decisions—particularly rulings at the trial level—are not printed ("reported"), and thus are not available to local officials, such as law enforcement officers, who might want to determine the degree to which a particular Supreme Court ruling has been applied in their jurisdiction. Some confirmation of this comes from LaFave's observation that in the jurisdictions studied in the American Bar Foundation project, the police who were aware of local court decisions tended to be only those officers who appeared in court, with any further communication being by word of mouth.

Another device through which opinions reach lower levels of the government structure is the state attorney general's advisory opinion. While such opinions, issued upon request of a government official, are not binding on the courts, they are often followed as if they were so binding—and thus probably serve to depress the number of litigations commenced. Through them, relevant U.S. Supreme Court rulings may reach larger numbers of individuals, particularly local nonjudicial officials, than would be reached through the Court structure. The attorney general will not always agree with those decisions, and as his job is to interpret the application of a case to a state (or local) situation, his views may affect his interpretation. A number of attorneys general are initiating programs by which summaries of, and commentaries upon, Supreme Court decisions of relevance to law enforcement officers are regularly sent to the latter, by means of a series of "newsletters" or memoranda. These are not the same as the official Opinions of the Attorneys General, but may serve the same function. Some district attorneys, particularly in the largest jurisdictions, are also doing the same thing. Thus, after *Mapp,* the New York County District Attorney's office published a collection of federal cases dealing with search and seizure. In that same jurisdiction, the New York City Police Department's Legal Bureau serves as an advisor to interpret Court decisions to those involved in dealing with searches, for example, in preparation of applications for search warrants.

The role of lawyers and government officials in the communication of the Supreme Court's messages to others, particularly to the general public, is an example of a principle in communications theory known as the "two-step flow of communication." While there is direct communication from a message originator to the ultimate recipient, greater effects on the latter occur from communication originating with "opinion leaders," individuals who pay far more attention than the average citizen to the messages and who communicate them (relay them with greater or renewed signal strength) to individuals they know who rely on them for information and opinion guidance. Thus, if people do not understand or cannot follow Supreme Court opinions, and know little more than what they see about them in the headlines, they can follow what the "opinion leaders" or "knowledgeables" say about them. Those knowledgeables may be a school board lawyer talking about school prayer or a lawyer-legislator explaining the Supreme Court's obscenity decisions to fellow members of a legislative interim committee. If these "middle men" construe the Court's opinions accurately, then they may have the impact specified by the Court's language. If the opinion leaders misconstrue the opinions, intentionally or unintentionally, a distorting effect will occur. Their importance in either event is quite clear: "The public tends to take the word of lawyers, Senators, journalists, and other commentators who in fact do read opinions such as the *Brown* case. What the Court says in its opinions is extremely important for these informational middle-men, and the public inherits what the middle-men think."[58]

One other means of communication which should be noted is groups, both law groups and other interest groups or associations. The bar does not take upon itself the task of disseminating information about cases, although, as noted in the previous section of this chapter, opinions about cases may be spread by the ABA. A few, but only a few, lawyers do take it upon themselves to improve the knowledge and awareness of the public about Supreme Court decisions. It may be that the lawyers are not competent to do so. While the public may conceive of the law as generally composed of constitutional law (and criminal trials), most lawyers do not deal with constitutional law in general (and maybe even in particular). As a result, "Few members of the Bar are any more familiar with the work of the Supreme Court than are other semi-educated people in the community."[59] Grey suggests that when bar officials do speak about cases, they are being more careful than they were several years ago, so that, even if they do not add much to our knowledge, they do not add more to the confusion.

Specific groups do disseminate information about cases of particular interest to them, but only a limited number of cases are "spread to the winds" in this fashion. Thus, the Motion Picture Association of America (MPAA) sent a memorandum to "Counsel" (of various state and local groups) enclosing opinions plus a summary of major points made by the Court in striking down Dallas' film classification ordinance for vagueness; other relevant obscenity decisions were sent later. Because groups have a particular interest in decisions, they are likely to send along views with their reporting of the opinions. Thus, church groups, prior to the 1963 *Schempp* decision, had comments ready on the decision, many of them favorable; these had been developed in anticipation of the Court's handing down a ruling in the case. In addition to the church groups, the executive secretary of the American Association of School Administrators had sent a memorandum to that group's members before *Schempp*, predicting the decision. While this was "before" rather than "after" communication of a message, it apparently had an effect—of decreasing the confusion about the decision which might have occurred in the absence of the memorandum. This sort of communication "gets through" only with great difficulty, however, particularly when those on the receiving end do not wish to hear. Thus, Dolbeare and Hammond note that officials and attorneys at both state and local levels in "Midway" knew more about *Engel* than *Schempp*, interpreting the Court's doctrine as prohibiting only state-written prayers; in short, they knew about the decision which did not limit them but not about the one which would cause more "difficulties."

Police groups have also helped disseminate information. Thus, six months after *Miranda*, a regular column on important Supreme Court decisions, written by an attorney, was begun in *Police*, the publication of the International Association of Chiefs of Police. Earlier (a year prior to *Miranda*), the National District Attorneys Association had begun to publish a periodical containing the latest information on legal decisions on police behavior, including a review and analysis of the *Miranda* decision. This sort of activity stemmed from the need, mentioned earlier, to transmit decisions dealing with police procedure to the policemen themselves (and other law enforcement officials) if there was to be any chance the rulings would be followed.

Some efforts to give practical instruction in the ramifications of those decisions have been started, although most instruction the police receive in Supreme Court cases is limited to minute amounts (ten minutes at morning lineup, for example, in one large city) when it exists at all. Thus, Chicago-Kent Law School established in early 1968 an Institute for Criminal Justice, which was to begin giving police officials instruction in what they could and could not do under the Court's rulings, through seminars aimed at suburban, small-town, and rural police departments. This sort of communication is not the same as informing people of what the Court has said *and why,* but the police are less concerned with the Court's basic principles and more "with what it means in a concrete situation," something certainly necessary if compliance is to occur.

In his examination of the effect of the *Miranda* decision in four middle-sized Wisconsin cities (Green Bay, Kenosha, Madison, and Racine), Neal Milner has provided a basic picture of the ways in which police officers (patrolmen, their superior officers, and detectives) find out about Court decisions—and how they rate their sources. He suggests, "Because of the ambiguities in the communication process between police and court, no hierarchical channel of communication exists. Therefore, the impact of *Miranda* reflects peculiarly local patterns."[60] In Green Bay, which had the least professionalized police force, there was a wide variety of initial sources of information, including television and radio, magazines, superior police officers, and the attorney general. More than a third of the policemen (35.7 percent) found out about the decision from the newspaper, 12.9 percent directly from the Supreme Court opinion, and 10 percent from department training sessions.

The picture changes, however, when we look at *all* the sources from which policemen obtained information. Three quarters heard about the decision from a superior officer, with the same percentage reading about it in the newspaper, while 70 percent had some exposure via television and radio. Three fifths (61.4 percent) heard of the case in conferences and training, and 40 percent had direct exposure to the opinion. Other major sources were other police officers who were not superiors (one third), magazines, both specialized and nonspecialized (one third each), the district attorney (30 percent), the attorney general (22.9 percent), and the local judge (11.4 percent). Conferences and training, while not either the prime initial source or the one to which most men had been exposed, was rated the best source by far more men (37.1 percent) than named other sources as best. Newspapers were named the best source by 15.7 percent and superior officers, by 10 percent. Categorized differently, law enforcement sources were named by over half as the best source, 11.4

percent named outside specialized sources, 28.6 percent named outside nonspecialized sources, and 7.1 percent named local officials.

In Kenosha, the newspaper was not the major initial source of information, and no one initial source was dominant. Less than a fifth (18.8 percent) found out about the case initially from television and radio, 12.5 percent from the newspaper, 15.6 percent from a superior officer and slightly over 10 percent each from training sessions and the district attorney. There was, however, agreement that conferences and training were the best sources, with over one third so indicating. Another 17.2 percent thought that the attorney general, while almost 10 percent thought that the Supreme Court opinion itself, was the best source of information. Over half those getting information through conferences and training thought it the best source. While a strong majority of the Kenosha policemen perceived their sources of information as hostile to *Miranda,* those men more likely to rank as their best sources of information "outside" sources were more likely to see that information as being favorable to the decision.

In Racine, which has a relatively highly professionalized department, a high percentage of all policemen received the first information about *Miranda* from superior officers. Here the captain of detectives is relied upon for legal information; he prepared a *Miranda* memorandum after consultation with local judges and the district attorney. While two fifths indicated a superior officer as the first source of information, another one quarter indicated the newspaper. The superior officer was the source to which most men (84.5 percent) were exposed. Conferences and training sessions touched 69 percent; newspapers, 63.8 percent; the district attorney, 60 percent; the Supreme Court opinion itself, almost half; specialized magazines, 45 percent; and the attorney general, over one third. Again, conferences and training sessions were ranked as the best source by most men (one fourth), but one fifth each named a superior officer or the Supreme Court opinion itself. By category, over one half named a law enforcement source as the best source, as had been true in Green Bay; one quarter named outside specialized sources, and 17 percent named local officials.

In Madison, as in Green Bay, the most common initial source (for 40 percent of the men) was the newspaper. Fifteen percent found out about it through a superior officer, and somewhat over 10 percent each from television-radio and the opinion itself. Over 90 percent of the men were exposed to the decision in conferences and training sessions, by far the largest percentage in the four cities. Three quarters had some newspaper exposure to the case; 70 percent heard about it from a superior officer, with only slightly fewer hearing from the attorney general. About three fifths heard about it on television and radio, an almost equal number had seen the opinion, and only slightly fewer (57.7 percent) had some contact with the case through the district attorney. Magazines were the other major sources to which many Madison officers were exposed, 37.2 percent coming in contact with the case through nonspecialized magazines, and 30.8 percent through specialized magazines. Again, conference and training sessions rated the best source (45 percent). The attorney general was rated the best source by 20 percent, and the opinion was rated best by 15.4 percent of the men.

Looking at all four cities, Milner found little difference between those who approved of the decision and those who disapproved as to what they rated the best source of information, but the approvers were far more likely to have received information from training sessions than were the disapprovers. With respect to the relative professionalization of the departments, Milner found that formal law enforcement sources were emphasized as sources of information about the decision by those departments more professionalized. However, the more professionalized departments—like the less professionalized units—were relatively isolated from outside information which might have clarified some key elements with respect to interrogation techniques. He suggests, "Generally no department was amenable to advice from non-police groups."[61] While he had hypothesized that more professionalized groups would be more, rather than less, willing to listen to outside groups, he found that professionalization brought well-developed intradepartmental communication lines leading to a perception that outside information was not needed.

As discussion of the role of intermediaries in the two-step flow of communication may have suggested, messages do not pass through the channels of communication intact or without distortion. The channels are not "clean" and contain "static." "The formal legal channels through which decisions are transmitted are not necessarily neutral ones which would ensure the application of a rule substantially similar to that enunciated by the Supreme Court."[62] A number of those distortions need to be identified here.

In some instances, the reporting is simply inaccurate. Warren cites the example of Taney's opinion in *Dred Scott.* The press, he argues, spread "falsehoods" concerning that opinion, including a sentence that the Negro had no rights which the white man had to respect. Warren argues that Taney was merely stating existing law on the point rather than his own feelings and that the antagonism which developed against the Court "and the ensuing damage to its reputation"[63] came from the misunderstanding, rather than from the decision itself. Although Warren may have been trying to rehabilitate Taney,[64] his point about misinterpretation of Court opinions has been borne out in a number of subsequent instances.

For example, there is a recent incident involving a memorandum order of the Court, rather than a full opinion authored by one of the Justices. On April 24, 1956, the Court ruled: "*South Carolina Electric & Gas Com-*

pany v. *Fleming*. The appeal is dismissed. *Slaker* v. *O'Connor*. 278 U.S. 188." Papers carried a story that the Supreme Court had outlawed segregation on intrastate buses. However, the Court had not done that; *Slaker* v. *O'Connor* meant that the Court will dismiss the appeal where lower-court action is incomplete, and the case had come up to the Court from the Court of Appeals for the Fifth Circuit before certain district court proceedings were concluded. The papers corrected their story the next day, but the initial report caused considerable reaction, both in terms of criticism and compliance. The attorneys general of Virginia, South Carolina, and Texas called the decision an invasion of state and local rights, but officials of local bus lines in eleven cities (Richmond, Norfolk, Durham, Greensboro, Jackson [Mississippi], Mobile, Montgomery, Tampa, Wichita Falls [Texas], Beaumont, and El Paso) ordered an end to segregation.

In initial bulletins concerning *Engel* v. *Vitale*, UPI reported that the freedom-of-religion clause rather than the establishment clause was involved. The error remained in subsequent releases. Still more recent is a serious misinterpretation of *Barker* v. *Hardway*, a 1969 certiorari denial. On March 10, 1969, CBS News and other sources said, "The Supreme Court said that college demonstrators did not have to be given a hearing." Reading later, one might have found out that the Court said nothing to that effect but merely denied certiorari in a case involving a riot after a football game (not a demand for greater student rights or a protest against the Vietnam war) and that the students *had* been given a hearing, although not one of the students thought comported with "due process." While these examples involve stories misrepresenting decisions, there are other situations in which headlines are misleading, even when the stories following the headlines are accurate.

While a certain degree of inaccuracy in reporting may have to be accepted as a given, the effects of that misreporting when Supreme Court decisions are involved cannot be ignored. Perhaps because we expect the decisions of the Court to be final, to be "the law of the land," we are perhaps more likely to act upon the case as reported (or misreported) than we would be to act upon reports of actions by other branches of government, for example, Congress, about which reporting tends to be more accurate. Even if we concede that some misreporting will occur, it can be further argued that there is a distinct difference between errors we might consider basic, such as confusing a certiorari denial for a full opinion of the Court, and other mistakes perhaps less fundamental, such as a misinterpretation of the basis on which the Court has rested its decision, particularly where pressure does not allow enough time for a reporter to digest a case before he must file a story about it.

Another distortion which occurs is oversimplification. Johnson, amplifying the subject of headlines, notes that many headlines on the school prayer decision were "correct as far as they go, but they are obviously too brief to convey the full meaning of the ruling."[65] Thus, the fact that the prayer was state composed, a crucial element in *Engel*, was often omitted, nor did the headlines make clear that *only* that sort of prayer was banned; reaction to the case was based on the feeling that all prayer had been banned—which, of course, it was subsequently. Thus, the papers, and radio and TV as well, portrayed a decision far broader than what the Court had in fact issued. *Why* the Court decided a case is one of the matters often eliminated in basic reporting on Court decisions, in the drive for brevity and simplification. Johnson notes that reporting of *Engel* did not elaborate on the Court's reasoning, and it has elsewhere been noted that the emphasis on the reporting of *Miranda* was on what the Supreme Court said the police must do, but not on why this had been required. "The outcry that followed the Court's . . . ruling might have been less piercing if there had been more general public awareness of the nature of the interrogation evils the Court sought to combat and took the trouble to cite at length."[66]

Involved in the oversimplification process is an emphasis on individuals, rather than content. Thus, Grey remarks, "Often the names of individuals in Supreme Court cases get greater attention in headlines than the legal issues."[67] Analysts of the controversy over the famous Moynihan Report, in discussing press coverage of the report, put their finger on the central problem. While not writing about Supreme Court decisions, they make comments which are equally applicable. They note that the press handles reporting of social problems in terms of individuals rather than institutions and concentrates on personal experience. "The press treatment reflects the reductionist habits of journalists manifested in the dynamics of headline writing, the need for condensation of complex arguments (and the impatience with complexity because of this), the interest in 'human interest' handles, and the desire for reader identification based on sympathy rather than understanding."[68]

The same "compression" brings overattention to single cases decided on a given day, as noted earlier, and it is unlikely the press will go back several days later and pick up and report cases not initially covered, even when the Supreme Court is handing down decisions only (or largely) on Monday. Murphy noted that, among the important internal security cases decided by the Court, reaction (in congressional and executive circles as well as in the press, it must be added) focused on *Jencks* v. *U.S.* as the most dangerous of the cases, even though many other important cases had also been handed down. This emphasis on a single case occurs in part because of the use of a "roundup" story on what the Court has decided on a given day. The case featured in such articles by the wire services get "top billing" across the country, and the situation is reinforced by the tendency of copy men editing the wire service material to cut the last paragraphs of the wire service story (which might contain news of other cases) when in need of space.

While those reporting the cases tend to underemphasize the rationale behind Court decisions, immediate reaction to those decisions is quite heavily emphasized, particularly if "big names" have reacted. Newland has noted that reporting of the school prayer case, particularly starting with "day two," generally stressed reaction instead of the Court's decision. Even when the morning papers presented their first stories on the case Tuesday morning, they concentrated on reaction even though they had not reported the content of the decision itself. Concerning the reapportionment case, Newland says that people had been wating for the decision, it had wide ramifications, and the reaction was newsworthy, but the reaction did bury the decision itself. And some reaction, if not manufactured, is stimulated by the press itself. Many congressmen heard about the school prayer decision for the first time from reporters asking them their reaction. Because they did not know much about the decision (other than what the reporters told them briefly), their reactions to an oversimplified version of the decision compounded confusion, because those reactions were immediately reported and became part of the early information the general public had about the decision. The reaction which is reported, it should again be noted, is disproportionately negative. This occurs in part because defenders of the Court's decision speak up less, or certainly less quickly. However, even when they do speak out, their statements are not nearly as well covered as are the rantings of those complaining about the Court.

At the recipient end of the communications process, a number of items need to be noted. As we shall see in Chapter 7, many of the specific decisions of the Supreme Court never penetrate beyond the opinion leaders, never "get through" to the member of the general public. His views about the Supreme Court may, in other words, not be based on his particular reaction to specific messages communicated to him. Similarly, even if he does know of the Court's statements, his reaction is not likely to be determined solely by the message. His reaction to a decision may be a function of his acceptance of what the Court was going to say, before the Court said it, rather than to the statement of those views by the Court in a particular case.

Johnson's explanation of the less violent reaction to *Schempp* than to *Engel* is couched in these terms: "Newspaper and popular reaction—a more positive and less hostile reaction—may be due more to a gradual acceptance of the Court's position during the 1962–63 period than to any factor having to do with message characteristics."[69] Attitudes toward the communicator may be relevant; among these are the general aura of sanctity which the Court has for many people and the general reverence they express toward it. But these attitudes, like others, "are but one factor in the communication situation, and they interact with other factors important for opinion and behavior change."[70] Among the relevant attitudes toward the Supreme Court as a communicator of messages are one's role conceptions. One may perceive one's role as involving compliance with Supreme Court decisions, or one may feel that one's "constituents" expect one to comply.

One of the more useful concepts developed in recent years to explain people's response to communications has been the idea of "cognitive dissonance." As developed by Festinger, the concept suggests that an individual tries to reduce the amount of disparity between various stimuli affecting him and tries to bring his views and messages from outside into some sort of balance. This idea can be applied to the study of impact of Supreme Court decisions. A Supreme Court decision may not affect the existing balance in an individual's system negatively. If what the Court states is consonant with what an individual already believes, or with what is already occurring in his community, no imbalance, no dissonance, need arise. Thus, the banning of school prayer did not upset the balance of communities where the practice did not exist. But decisions striking down widespread existing practices often do upset the balance. When they do, the individuals affected resolve the dissonance in a number of ways, or at least they attempt to resolve it. One may reduce the dissonance by coming into compliance with the decision. Thus, one may begin to question the value of the practice which was struck down; if school prayer is at issue, one may begin to believe that such a practice really did not increase moral growth among school students.

Another common method is to attack the originator of the disturbance, in this case, the U.S. Supreme Court, either generally or specifically. In the latter instance, one might argue that the Court has gone beyond the power granted to it in deciding the particular case, or that its expertise does not extend to the subject matter in question, which should be better left in other hands. While to some this seems futile, because they feel that the Court will eventually triumph, this type of dissonance reduction may be an easier out for some groups, because it involves a lesser effort than does compliance. Thus, police complaints about the Supreme Court may be an easier way for the police to restore a balance that the Court has disturbed than to admit that there is much need for retraining and more professional conduct. Another method is to say that what the Supreme Court has struck down is not the same as practices in one's own community, and therefore the Supreme Court's decision doesn't apply. The justification of the released-time practice ultimately upheld in the *Zorach* case, after the decision striking down the practice of religious classes on school property in *McCollum,* is an example of such dissonance reduction. Other ways of avoiding compliance and of explaining away a disliked communication exist, including ignorance about local practices which may be not in compliance with the Court's decision.

* * * * *

In this section, utilizing the communications frame of reference, we have examined characteristics of messages originated by the Supreme

Court, some of the communicators and communications methods for those decisions, the distortions produced during transmission of the messages, and some other elements relevant to receipt of the messages. In so doing, it is hoped the usefulness of this perspective or frame of reference—as well as of the two discussed earlier in the chapter—have been itself communicated clearly.

Part II

THE SUBSTANCE OF IMPACT

Having explored impact through a variety of theoretical perspectives and having dealt with a variety of problems entailed in conceptualizing "impact," we now turn to more systematic examination of the actual impacts—of what has happened after the Supreme Court has ruled. While compliance with *Brown* v. *Board of Education,* the subject through which many became aware of the need to examine the subject of impact, has been mentioned, and while a variety of examples of impact have been used in an attempt to illuminate more general discussion, the "meat" of the subject has not yet been reached. This is particularly true if one is more interested in what has happened than in how one might view the happenings—although the author holds that the two cannot be separated without doing violence to the subject.

In attempting to portray the Supreme Court's impact, or at least to present what we know of that impact from the often vagrant sources in which we may find useful data, we can organize findings in several different ways. In the chapters which follow, two devices are used. One is to present material in terms of issue areas, to talk of the subject with which the Supreme Court has dealt and what has followed, treating each subject separately. The other is to look at the multiple arenas of politics in which the impacts of the Court's decisions take place.

We first turn to issue areas, starting with regulation of the economy. Here materials in the existing literature, on which this volume is based, are relatively sparse and, by comparison with other materials, disproportionately historical. The remaining areas all fall within the broad rubric of civil rights and civil liberties. The first, with its clear effect on the structure and process of government, is reapportionment. Then church-state relations are considered, through a look at released time and school prayer, and obscenity, as an example of the freedom-of-speech area. In Chapter 5, the crucial areas of criminal procedure—with a focus on right to counsel, the *Escobedo* and *Miranda* decisions, and search and seizure—and school desegregation are the subjects examined. In none of these areas, particularly the last named, is any attempt made to be complete or exhaustive, since histories and other descriptive presentations are available for the reader who would delve further. An attempt is made to arrange the material in such a way as to illustrate types of impact which have occurred and to present some of what appears to be the most valuable information thus far uncovered.

Because ours is a federal governmental system, with separation of powers, organizing an examination of impacts in political arenas is not without its difficulties. Undertaken first is discussion of what goes on in the lower judiciary, first the federal lower courts and then state courts. Then the other branches of the national government—Congress and the President and the accompanying administrative establishment—are covered. Moving downward in the federal system, reactions by state legislators and executives next come under scrutiny. Finally, we look at the effect which Supreme Court decisions may have had on public opinion. With the exception of the material on the lower courts and on Congress, the sections are not long. There are two reasons: we are simply not in possession of much source material discussing the matter directly, and the subject will have been touched upon earlier in the volume (in the examples of Chapter 1 and particularly in Chapters 4 and 5), so reference rather than repetition should suffice.

CHAPTER 4

Impacts in Issue-Areas: A

ECONOMIC REGULATION

The impact of the Supreme Court in the field of regulation of the economy covers a long historical span and a wide variety of subjects. While contemporary decisions of the Court continue to have an impact on the economy, or at least on certain aspects of it, the Court's attention has been turned, proportionately, away from matters of economic regulation in the period subsequent to 1937. The Court's involvement since then has been largely one of legitimation of federal legislation. Even when the Court has ruled on a subject before Congress has acted, as with offshore oil and regulation of insurance, it has generally upheld subsequently what Congress has done in reaction to the Court's initiative. New law with clear implications for regulation of the economy is being made by the Court in the area of administrative law, but the impacts appear not to be as substantial as were some of the Court's earliest decisions.

An area of law in which it is often speculated that considerable impact has occurred is antitrust, but much of what has been written *is* speculation; we are without studies to match the speculation. The earliest rulings of the Court, after the passage of the Sherman Act, are alleged to have had a noticeable effect, of producing uncertainty through adoption of the "rule of reason" for judging the legality of trusts. Later rulings by the Court limited the application of the act, causing the government to dismiss some appeals to the Supreme Court, and noticeably depressing the number of efforts made to dissolve industrial combinations until 1937. The government found itself forced to shift to a different remedy, that of obtaining injunctions against particular practices and seeking consent decrees which prohibited unfair competitive methods.

Beyond this, it is hard to tell how closely antitrust lawyers look at relevant court cases before considering mergers or whether they use those cases to determine what the rules are in dealing with other companies in trading arrangements. Even if the lawyers take the decisions seriously in the business collusion cases, they may not be able to convince others to change their behavior, for example, in talking informally after several drinks at a convention. It remains an open empirical question as to the possible effect of the decisions: when a merger is not consummated, we cannot tell whether economic reasons or a reading of the Court's decisions played a larger part, even if we assume both may have played *some* role. Similarly, to ascertain the gross effect of antitrust rulings on the structure of the economy is very difficult. Perhaps the Court has helped maintain the survival of small business enterprises. But has it simply extended their lives rather than guaranteeing them continuing existence? Again, on the basis of current evidence, one cannot say.

The economy of the United States in the early years of the Republic was clearly a developing one, in two senses: the economy was growing, and at the same time, it was being transformed from a series of state economies into a national economy. While one can argue that the first sort of growth would have resulted regardless of what the Court did, one can more persuasively assert that the Court's decisions concerning state economic regulation had a clear affect on the latter; at least, one can say the decisions made a contribution to the development of a national economy, although greater difficulty may exist in gaining more precision this many years after the decisions.

Nineteenth Century. Historians point to two decisions, both authored by John Marshall, which had particularly noticeable effects both in their time and over the long term. The decisions, *McCulloch* v. *Maryland* and *Gibbons* v. *Ogden,* also serve to illustrate that early decisions of the Court received the same wide variety of responses as more recent decisions of the Court in the area of civil liberties. Both decisions clearly involved what political scientists refer to as the "federalism variable"—matters of economic regulation could not be separated from questions of federal-state relations. In *McCulloch,* the state of Maryland had attempted to tax a branch of the Second Bank of the United States. After upholding the power of Congress to establish the bank (under the "necessary and proper" clause, thus giving a broad reading to congressional power), Marshall asserted that the state's power to tax would be power to destroy an instrumentality of the federal government, counter to the supremacy clause of the Constitution, and thus he invalidated the Maryland statute creating the tax. (The statement that "the power to tax is the power to destroy" was used for many years by lawyers and judges attacking specific taxes, particularly when they appeared to affect, directly or indirectly, government activities.)

That there would be some reaction to the decision was quite predictable, because the bank had been the subject of extended controversy between the political factions of the time. The reaction was essentially regional, with the decision being approved in the Northeast and denounced in the southern and western states. In the former, the bank had been generally approved and many in the business community felt that the powers of Congress should be broadly construed, while in the latter, where assertions of state sovereignty were regularly being made, the bank was already unpopular and growth of national government power was clearly not appreciated. "In Virginia in particular, Marshall's interpretation of the Constitution was challenged by a formidable array of states' rightists, led by Judge Roane of the Court of Appeals, and supported by the leading newspaper editors and by ex-Presidents Madison and Jefferson."[1]

Probably the clearest resistance—and a classic case of purposive noncompliance—occurred in Ohio. Resistance there, as elsewhere, was predicated in part on poor economic conditions, reinforced by the states' "policy of chartering State banks with an almost unlimited issue of paper currency," banks which "could not withstand the competition of a strong National banking institution."[2] Before *McCulloch*, Ohio had passed a law placing a tax on each branch of the national bank. After the decision, the bank sought and obtained an injunction against the state auditor. However, the auditor ignored the injunction; his assistant took the tax from the bank even after it was refused him, and the auditor took the money to the state capital. "Thus the State of Ohio was placed, through her high state officials, in direct contempt of an order of the Federal Circuit Court, as well as in a position of refusal to conform to the principles laid down in a decision of the Federal Supreme Court."[3] But Ohio was not content to rest with its own specific resistance; it was determined to go further. After adopting legislation outlawing the bank, the legislature passed resolutions to be circulated in other states protesting the decision of the Federal Circuit Court in granting the injunction and asserting the right of states to tax the bank because it was a "private corporation." This effort did not win many adherents, however, as only Virginia and Kentucky endorsed the resolutions, and Congress paid no attention to them. An effort to amend the Constitution to allow states to ban national bank branches from their jurisdictions was circulated among the states, and five states did formally ask Congress for such an amendment, but that move also died when nine states disapproved. The specific turmoil surrounding the decision died down, as economic conditions improved; later the bank itself died when President Jackson vetoed the renewal of its charter. But the long-term implications of the decision, in terms of asserting broad powers for Congress, still existed, and in the somewhat shorter run, the bank was able to contribute to economic stability.

Gibbons v. *Ogden* involved a monopoly granted by the state of New York to a steamship company for navigation rights in New York waters; this monopoly collided (figuratively, at least) with the asserted rights of others to operate boats under licenses granted by the federal government.

In this case, Justice Marshall, defining commerce in extremely broad terms (not again to be asserted for more than a hundred years after late nineteenth-century narrowing), asserted that interstate commerce did not stop at state boundary lines and that the monopoly clearly (and improperly) interfered with federal power over interstate commerce. However, Marshall did stop short of declaring Congress' power over interstate commerce to be exclusive, and that hesitation (if that is what it was) led to a variety of subsequent cases concerning the power of states to regulate commerce, particularly in the absence of conflicting federal regulation. An immediate impact of the case was on the steamboat trade in the area, which increased substantially, assisting in the commercial growth of New York City. The decision was popular, because monopolies were not well liked: "the chief importance of the case in the eyes of the public of that day was its effect in shattering the great monopoly against which they had been struggling for fifteen years."[4]

The decision was not, however, without its critics: some advocates of states' rights saw in Marshall's broad interpretation of interstate commerce that their position, particularly with respect to the slave trade, was to be weakened. However, the negative reaction was less great than it might have been because few recognized the nationalistic implications because of their attention to the monopoly aspect of the case. Also not immediately clear was the effect on transportation in general; steam railroad transportation was able to develop free from the restrictive effects of monopolies granted by legislatures. "Economic results of more far-reaching importance . . . were not appreciated until later years."[5]

Gibbons and *McCulloch* were cases in which interference with the extension of national power was defeated and national power with respect to the economy was broadly construed. The impact of those cases was substantial. Also having an impact on the growth of the economy were two cases dealing with the powers of state legislatures over corporations. Of particular note here are the *Dartmouth College* and *Charles River Bridge* cases, which did not involve conflict between national and state power but between vested interests and "popular sovereignty." The legislature of New Hampshire attempted to change the charter of Dartmouth College, originally bestowed by the English King, so as to make the institution public in character, at least in terms of control. The Court held that the legislature could not so alter the charter because of constitutional restrictions against the impairment of contracts. What happened as a result of the case was that legislatures altered the terms of new charters they were granting, either by placing time limits on them or by making the charters, by their own terms, subject to legislative alteration. Thus, business management could not proceed under a charter with the security of knowledge that no legislature could interfere with their plans, whatever they were. A case on its face limiting the power of the state over corporations and thus potentially increasing corporate power, thus may have had the opposite effect.

The immediate effects of the *Dartmouth College* case were somewhat muffled by another decision handed down two weeks later by the Court, a decision which received greater public attention. In *Sturgis* v. *Crowninshield,* the Court held certain state bankruptcy laws invalid, also under the obligation-of-contracts clause. However, the case was misinterpreted in the press, where there were reports that the Court had held that no state could ever release a person from his debts. The Court had, in fact, held only that debts contracted before the passage of such legislation could not be affected by the statutes. A number of other states passed laws based on this decision, applying only to debts occurring after passage of the laws. Both *Sturgis* and *Green* v. *Biddle* illustrate the point that decisions of greater lasting constitutional significance often are overshadowed in the short run by other decisions which have, or are felt to have, more immediate impact. The *Green* case dealt with Kentucky's statutes on land titles, which benefited Kentucky's own residents at the expense of absentee landowners; when these laws were struck down, the Kentuckians were so furious that they continued "for the most part to enforce [their] own laws, thereby virtually ignoring the Court's ruling."[6]

In the *Charles River Bridge* case, Massachusetts had affected the monopoly earlier granted to a bridge company by granting a charter to another company to locate a bridge a short way down the Charles River from the original grantee's location. The Court upheld this action in the face of a challenge from the original grantee. Such a decision might be thought to have limited business development, because no businessman could be sure of the competition he would have later. However, the effect appears to have been the opposite. Because of Justice Taney's strict construction of the initial bridge's charter, the case helped remove corporations from the monopolistic position they had held, and the unhappiness people had concerning corporations was reduced. Investors were also more willing to put money into ventures which were competing with existing projects, and so the end result was economic growth, not economic stagnation.

Child Labor. A twentieth-century case about whose impact we know is *Hammer* v. *Dagenhart,* one of a series of decisions dealing with a series of attempts to regulate child labor, ultimately successful only with the legitimation of the Fair Labor Standards Act of 1938. The initial effort, in the Keating-Owen Act, had been to prohibit the shipment in interstate commerce of goods produced by child labor. The Court held that there was a difference between *regulation* of commerce (acceptable) and outright *prohibition* (not acceptable) and that in earlier cases in which prohibitions of shipment of items in interstate commerce had been upheld, the items were themselves harmful, clearly not the case with goods produced by child labor. The initial reaction to the decision was surprise; the leaders of the child labor law movement must have presumed that their position would be upheld. The Court was held in generally high regard at the time, and few saw the decision as more than a temporary breach in decisions favorable to regulatory legislation; few saw it as they might see it several years later, as one of the first of a series of conservative decisions, although some did see the holding in the case as a warning that attempts to achieve social ends through Congress' power over commerce were to come to a halt. In any case, there was reluctance to attack the Court, and even those who were disappointed moved somewhat slowly to recover what had been lost. Part of this slowness was a result of the presumption of victory: no alternative plans in case of defeat at the hands of the Court had been set up.

In the reaction to the decision, newspaper editorial writers called upon Congress to enact another child labor law, but one which would be upheld by the Court. Some of the support behind the initial law appears to have fallen away, attesting to the power of the Court to legitimize a given position or to remove its legitimacy. While people were interested in the enactment of new legislation, they were for the time being occupied with the "Great War," and only as the Allies' victory neared did domestic considerations, child labor among them, grow to the prominence they had earlier had. In the fall of 1918, far more energy was devoted to enacting child labor legislation than was available in the spring of that same year, when the decision was handed down. As Wood has noted, "American humanitarianism and reform consciousness, although partially submerged by the military conflict in Europe, remained vital forces in national life and the masses of people willingly turned to the unfinished tasks in the quest for social justice and economic freedom."[7]

The idea of trying to secure child labor legislation in the individual states was rejected; concentration on new federal legislation was clear. Because the case had been decided by a close vote and because Holmes's dissent had been persuasive to many, it was felt that the Court might approve another effort. The closeness of the vote even led some to suggest leaving the Keating-Owen law alone until the Court's composition changed, but this position was not the prevailing one. Nor was the idea accepted that the law should be reenacted with minor changes relating to the intent of Congress not to interfere with local conditions and declaring that the states could not forbid the sale of products of child labor shipped into the state. The idea of a constitutional amendment was similarly disposed of. The Court was held in sufficient reverence that attacks on judicial review, such as the proposal that the law contain a provision that the Court could not review it, were rejected. The National Child Labor Committee, in its presentations to Congress, accepted the Supreme Court's holding as defining the area within which it could move, at least as to means if not as to ends.

The tack ultimately adopted was to utilize the taxing power, taking the lead in part from the Supreme Court's decisions upholding taxation of items like margarine and state bank notes and Congress' earlier action taxing white phosphorous matches. These precedents were reinforced later when the Court, in the *Doremus* case, upheld the Harrison Narcotic Drugs Act, which had a tax provision which clearly was aimed at eliminating drugs rather than simply raising revenue—the prime issue in the Court's handling of the second child labor law. The desire of supporters of child labor legislation to find a viable solution was strengthened by the actions of manufacturers in extending working hours for children and employing children not employable under the invalidated act. An immediate effort, while the war was still in progress, to reenact Keating-Owen under Congress' war power was not successful, although the War Production Board did order child labor clauses inserted in contracts with firms doing business with the government.

Successful in getting a child labor law based on the taxing power through the Congress, the proponents of the legislation quickly met another and more decisive defeat. The Court, in *Bailey* v. *Drexel Furniture Co.*, struck down the new statute, on the grounds that it interfered with a matter within the purview of the states—a ground common to the *Hammer* case—and that the tax was being used as a penalty (impermissible) rather than to raise revenue (permissible). While the leaders of the child labor law movement were less surprised at this defeat, having sustained defeat in *Hammer*, they were far more disappointed, because it became clear that the Court was not inclined to accept attempts to achieve the end they were attempting to reach. As a matter of fact, there was more severe criticism of the Court's *Hammer* decision after the *Drexel* case than after *Hammer* itself, as it became clear in retrospect what the Court had begun in the first decision. In addition, the Court's attack on the use of the taxing power in *Drexel*, combined with its attack on the use of the interstate commerce power in *Hammer*, left the Progressive movement without two key potential provisions on which to base its legislative program. The result was an attempt to pass an amendment to the Constitution, an amendment which was submitted by Congress to the states for ratification—and, because no cutoff period for its adoption was provided, the amendment is still awaiting ratification today, although not necessary in light of the FLSA and the Court's acceptance of its provisions in 1938.

Portal Pay and Tidelands Oil. Even though the Court turned away in part from the economic regulation area after 1937, and even though there are major areas, such as taxation, with which it deals only sporadically, it has continued to decide cases of considerable importance in some subfields in the area. Two cases the impact of which has been studied were decided in the mid-1940's; they are the portal-to-portal pay case, *Anderson* v. *Mt. Clemens Pottery Co.*, decided in 1946, and the offshore oil litigation, the initial case of which was *U.S.* v. *California*.[8] While most of the impact of the former was relatively short in duration, the impact of the latter is not yet complete, with the Court having handed down rulings and decrees in 1969, rulings which require still further action.

In the *Mt. Clemens* decision, the Court ruled that the time workers took to get ready for their jobs and in traveling from the plant gate to their place of work was to be compensated and thus included in calculations for hours of work (and overtime compensation). The decision followed two others providing portal-to-portal pay in mining situations. Labor divided on how to proceed after the *Mt. Clemens* decision. The AFL was cautious, arguing that the decision should be used as a basis for portal-to-portal pay provisions in future collective bargaining agreements, but that member unions ought not to file suit for back pay. However, the CIO leaders took a different position; they advised their members of their rights under the decision and urged the bringing of suits for back pay. Those suits were brought, in large numbers and for very substantial amounts—setting off a "second-order" reaction which led to congressional reversal of the Court's decision. "These hasty suits were to prove a major tactical blunder on the part of organized labor. The amounts demanded of employers were staggering. The huge sums . . . moved business opinion from unconcern . . . in June, 1946, to distress by September, and finally to something near hysteria by the end of the year."[9]

Hysteria led to several efforts in Congress to reverse *Mt. Clemens*. One was a broadside attack on the Fair Labor Standards Act itself, but the battle was lost because people were at the time more concerned over the Taft-Hartley Act, then in committee. An effort to remove federal and state court jurisdiction over FLSA overtime pay cases was also buried. The version which passed the House—and subsequently the Senate in only slightly different form—was more specific and more precisely directed at the Court's decision. Travel and makeready time were declared not to be work within the definitions of the FLSA, and no state or federal court was to entertain a suit for portal-to-portal pay, even if that suit had already been instituted. That the act reversed a Court decision seemed to bother few who supported the act, because of their feeling that it was the Court which had "subverted" Congress' original intent, which was now simply being restored. The Court received somewhat more support in the Senate than in the House, but the resulting Portal-to-Portal Pay Act, signed into law on May 14, 1947, was much like the bill which had cleared the House.

As noted by Morgan, Congress' statement in the bill "was one of the harshest statutory rebukes ever directed to the Court": "The Congress hereby finds that the Fair Labor Standards Act of 1938, as amended, has been interpreted judicially in disregard of long-established customs, practices, and contracts . . ."[10] It should be noted that not all of the impact of the decision was immediate, nor did the effect of the *Mt. Clemens* ruling end with the effective date of the new act. In the period between the announcement of the ruling and its reversal by Congress, many collective bargaining agreements containing portal-to-portal pay provisions were agreed upon; such provisions tended to remain in the agreements even after the new legislation. And some companies arrived at settlements with their employees, providing large sums to cover, retroactively, pay for the portal-to-portal activities.

Reaction to the initial offshore oil decisions was less great, and the overturning of the decision took far more time. At issue has been the ownership of the so-called "offshore lands" with their oil (and other mineral) deposits and the fees for the leases of such land. Opponents of state ownership claimed that the states would be more generous than the federal government with leases to oil companies and would be less likely to regulate them effectively. In *U.S.* v. *California,* the Court held that the lands belonged to the United States, not to the states. Editorial reaction was clearly negative, but the U.S. and California governments began to agree on the administration of the lands and the establishment of escrow funds. Little more seemed to happen immediately. The most pressing question seemed to be to determine the boundaries of the lands.

Pressure began to build up when the Supreme Court, in suits aimed at boundary definition, treated Louisiana and Texas as it treated California. "An overwhelming majority of those who expressed opinions stated that the Court had made fundamental errors in arriving at its decisions, particularly in the *Texas* case."[11] The National Association of Attorneys General, which led the fight for state control, was particularly stimulated to action by those cases. There were regional variations in reaction to the decisions, with the harshest criticism coming from the states primarily concerned. Congress received many requests for quitclaim legislation, whereby the federal government would have ceded title to the states, and the House of Representatives did pass a bill on the subject, but the Senate adjourned before acting on it.

While the subject was to be an issue in the Presidential election campaign of 1952, four years later, it was not a subject of controversy in the 1948 election. In 1951, those seeking quitclaim statutes were successful in getting legislation through the House, and, after the House agreed to the Senate version of the bill, it went to President Truman, who vetoed the bill in May, 1952. The issue had now become more clearly joined, as evidenced by the speech made by Democratic Presidential candidate Adlai Stevenson in Louisiana and Texas, hotbeds of proquitclaim strength: "I do not think it is wise policy for the Congress to institute a practice of giving away such national assets to individual states." Eisenhower endorsed state control and said he would approve quitclaim legislation; his victory made it only a matter of time before the lands were ceded to the states, and President Eisenhower did sign a quitclaim act on May 22, 1953, slightly less than a year after President Truman's veto.

While the question of where ownership lies, in the federal government or in the states, may have been settled by the President's signature, the matter of which lands are included within the "offshore oil lands" is by no means completed. The Supreme Court did uphold the quitclaim legislation in *Alabama* v. *Texas,* but it was not until 1960, in *U.S.* v. *Louisiana,* that it made the first of its major decisions about boundaries, holding Louisiana, Mississippi, and Alabama to a 3-mile limit, while permitting Texas and Florida, because of the conditions under which they entered the Union, to 3 leagues (closer to 9 miles). That decision itself set off reaction, determined in some measure by the financial implications. "Louisiana was by far the biggest loser. As a result of the decision, that state would have to surrender more than $308,000,000 which had been escrowed."[12] And the specific boundaries had not been measured.

In 1965, the Court held that Congress had left it to the courts to determine what inland waters were, and provided a definition for those waters. Two years later, the Justices decided that the 3 leagues of submerged lands to which Texas was entitled was not to be measured from artificial jetties but from Texas' 1845 coastline. This led to *U.S.* v. *Louisiana* (Texas Boundary Case), in which the Court held that the coastline to be used was the modern ambulatory one; in that case, the federal government's argument was based on the Court's 1965 *California* decision. As of this writing, the boundaries are still being measured. In early 1969, the Court decided *U.S.* v. *Louisiana* (Louisiana Boundary Case), further defining Louisiana's coastline but requiring naming of a Special Master to continue the work. Justice Black's tart remarks in dissent are appropriate:

> The doctrine [adopted by the Court] is tending to bring about interminable litigation. Passed 15 years ago, the Act has generated litigation that is not yet abating; we have another dispute similar to this one before us now, and neither the United States nor the State indicates that there is not far more time-consuming litigation still to come. . . . How many years the Master who must now be appointed will have to work, how many persons must be hired to help him, no one can predict.

Administrative Law. Two other subjects under the heading of economic regulation bear inspection in this section. One is the area of utilities regulation, which shows what amounts to a standoff between the Supreme Court and a major federal regulatory agency; the other is the field of patent law, a subject where the impact of Court decisions is extremely difficult to follow, in part because of the divergence of interpretation of decisions which has existed.

The case the aftermath of which we can examine in the area of regulation is *Interstate Natural Gas Co.* v. *Federal Power Commission.* The Supreme Court, in that case, read the FPC Act broadly and refused to extend an exemption of production and gathering activities to cover the sale by producers to interstate pipeline companies. The Court held that if natural gas were destined for ultimate transportation out-of-state, the price at which it was sold was subject to regulation by the FPC. Even before the Supreme Court ruled, efforts, stirred up by FPC action and lower-court affirmance, were being made to change the statute, so that it is difficult to state that legislative activity stemmed directly from the Supreme Court's ruling. When the Court did rule, Representative Ross Rizley of Oklahoma reacted by introducing legislation which would have exempted independent producers from price regulation. His bill passed the House, but did not come out of committee in the Senate. When another bill was introduced in 1948, there was somewhat more success, but the bill which passed in 1949 was vetoed without override. By this time, the FPC, which earlier had favored the extension of the exemption, was opposed to the Rizley bill, 3–2.

After the Supreme Court decision, the FPC itself had said it would not regulate independents. In August, 1951, in deciding the *Phillips* case, the FPC flew in the face of the Supreme Court's earlier holding by saying that production and gathering included sale of gas to interstate pipelines, making the sale exempt from regulation. This decision was taken to the Supreme Court which, in *Phillips Petroleum Co.* v. *State of Wisconsin,* reasserted the position it held in the *Interstate Natural Gas Co.* case and reversed the FPC. Action then shifted somewhat, as the FPC ordered a freeze on the wellhead price of natural gas, an action to which some states responded by announcing wellhead prices for gas in an attempt to prohibit the FPC from setting lower prices. However, the Supreme Court thwarted this effort by denying the states the power to set the prices. Gaining strength, the producers, "encouraged by President Eisenhower's announcement that he favored such legislation as a means of countering excessive centralization of government,"[13] again tried to gain a legislative exemption, and legislation passed both houses of Congress, only to be vetoed by President Eisenhower when it was discovered that gas interests had made a campaign contribution to Senator Case of South Dakota. The bill would have specifically overruled the Supreme Court decision, but the effort was lost because the producers overplayed their hand.

In the field of patent law, we are looking more at the impact of a collection of cases, or at a *pattern* of activity by the Supreme Court, than at isolated decisions. What occurred illustrates the diversity of interpretation of Supreme Court decisions which develops between the judicial circuits, and it points to some questions as to how the recipients of cases are supposed to interpret what they see and read. Shapiro points out that, during the 1930's, the Supreme Court, while not outwardly changing the doctrinal content of its patent decisions—in which the major question concerned whether an item was an "invention" (in addition to being novel and useful), changed its standards by invalidating a substantially higher proportion of patents coming before it. If one were looking at the language of the decisions, at the doctrine, little or no change would have been noticed; if one looked at *results,* a clear change in mood or attitude on the part of the Court would have been visible. By 1940, some people, particularly patent lawyers, began to be more aware that something might be happening. "A goodly number of them were saying openly that the Supreme Court was taking an 'antipatent' position, that is, raising the standard of invention . . . ."[14] The circuit courts did not, however, alter their positions on patent law in major fashion.

In 1941, the Court decided *Cuno Engineering Corp.* v. *Automatic Devices Corp.,* in which Justice Douglas used the phrase "flash of genius" to sum up what the Court had been talking about in terms of the invention standard. The phrase, not again used by the Court, was taken up by everyone else as a way of expressing what the Court was saying—and many took it to be an indication that the Court had now in fact changed its position. The *Cuno* case and the *Jungersen* and *A&P* cases, decided in 1949 and 1950, were the cases cited widely: "These three cases were a constant litany of citations chanted by courts and commentators to show that the Supreme Court had changed the level of invention."[15] As a result of those decisions, rather than the outcomes of the earlier rulings, some of the circuits began to change their position. The "deeds" of the 1930's, coupled with what many saw as a change in doctrine later, reinforced each other.

The Patent Office, faced by the invalidation of a large number of cases coming before the Court (although they actually involved only a small percentage of patents issued), tended to follow the Court's doctrine, which had changed little, and thus to alter its own policies very little. "The Office professed to see no change in the standard, and there was no observable tendency on the part of patent examiners to be less liberal in their treatment of patents."[16] If the Supreme Court was trying, through the results in its decisions, to tell the Patent Office to tighten up its standards, the message was ignored. Instead, the Patent Office relied on the unchanging doctrine the Court enunciated in its efforts to appear to be following precedent. Both the Court and the Office "had resolutely to continue saying that the legal doctrine had not changed and the old cases were good law."[17] If the Office admitted the Court had changed the doctrine, it would then have had to change its own approach or to explain why it was refusing to follow the Court.

While one cannot be sure that the ambiguity of the Court's messages in the patent field completely explains the divergence between circuits in their decisions, the ambiguity certainly played a part. As Shapiro notes,

> Caught in the midst of these messages some courts received the Court's new tone and ignored the doctrinal message, thus tightening their patent policies; others did the reverse. . . . Absent a single clear command, those of its subordinates who wished to disobey could do so by accepting the doctrinal message meant for outside consumption and screening out the tone that had actually been intended as an order to them.[18]

If the judges, like the men in the Patent Office, had followed what the Court did, not what it said, the Court's record in the 1930's (and later) would have been sufficient to achieve a consistent result. They did not, however, follow that record because they clung "to the traditional belief that, if the Supreme Court wishes to tell them something, it must tell them in the language of English, not statistics, and in the course of an opinion clearly setting out the doctrine to be followed, not in the pattern of who won and lost in the last twenty cases."[19] Some courts recognized that the Patent Office was not following the Supreme Court, and agreed with the latter's standards. Other courts invalidated patents, but without explicit recognition that the applied standard had changed. Some seemed to act as if nothing whatsoever had changed, doctrinally or otherwise. And still others, including the Court of Customs and Patent Appeals, recognized the change and indicated that they would fight that change.

Part of the aftermath of this confusion was an attempt to get Congress to change the patent statute. For fear of stirring up opposition, no frontal attack was made on the Court's rulings, and the statute passed was understood by most to be merely a codification of existing law. It was rather ambiguous; at least it did not clearly provide major changes. "The Congressional statute meant all things to all men."[20] Patent Office officials said that the statute merely confirmed the standard they had been following. Courts which had followed the Supreme Court's tone (rather than doctrine) "now read the new congressional statute as confirming their actions by confirming the standard under the banner of which the Supreme Court's tone and action marched."[21] And, because the statute was ambiguous, those which had not "heard" the Court's antipatent message still did not get the picture.

The Supreme Court did not reenter the controversy for some years after the passage of the statute in 1952, actually not granting certiorari in a patent case for fourteen years after the *A&P* decision. However, in 1966, the Court decided three cases.[22] The Court here adopted the position that the statute was merely codification and that decisions like *Cuno* were thus still the law. As a result, we find continuing divergence between the circuits in the patent law area, some stemming from the 1966 trilogy, some going back to the older cases before and including *Cuno* and *A&P*. Some circuits now apply the "nonobviousness" statutory standard of Section 103 of the Patent Act; other circuits apply nonstatutory standards; and still other circuits apply no consistent standard. At least one circuit explicitly requires a stricter standard than either Section 103 or the 1966 cases, while another, which purports to follow the 1966 rulings, in fact applies a harder standard, so that there "It appears that *Graham, Cook,* and *Adams* have had minimal effect." That there is continuing aftermath from the older cases is shown by the Eighth Circuit's reliance on the *A&P* and *Cuno* cases, which it holds that Section 103 merely codified, and the situation in the Ninth Circuit, where "the recent Supreme Court decisions have not altered its use of the severe A&P test."[23]

Patent law is only one area of administrative law, and a specialized one at that. Similarly, the Federal Power Commission is only one of the many federal regulatory commissions whose decisions the Court has reviewed. To present examples of the aftermath of decisions in those two instances is to do no more than suggest some possible effects of the Court in the area of administrative law. Other effects are clearly possible, but we do not know about them at the present time; they are an uncharted land, beckoning the researcher. For example, it can be argued that doctrines concerning rule making, notice, and hearing, developed in cases involving the regulatory commissions and in the broad area of economic regulation, laid the base for more recent rulings with respect to due process in the area of "poverty law," for example, those decisions requiring the following of certain procedures before a public housing tenant may be evicted. Initially, this impact is, however, from one area of the Court's own decisions to other decisions by the Court itself, rather than on external governmental agencies, but the lawyers who bring the cases challenging government practices on due process grounds may well be drawing on the Court's earlier decisions. In any event, after the Court has extended its rulings to the new areas, administrative agencies which comply are clearly affected, showing an impact of the earlier administrative law cases, albeit at second remove. The point with which to leave the reader is that further testing of this sort of speculation is necessary to fill in the holes in our knowledge.

REAPPORTIONMENT

There are several aspects of the impact of the Supreme Court's decisions on reapportionment which can be examined. The relatively immediate effects of particular major cases in terms of litigation and legislative activity are one; efforts aimed at blocking the "one man–one vote" doctrine are another. Also important, although more difficult to pin down, are effects on policy outcomes, on the form which political activity takes, and on beneficiaries of the policy. Our attention will be directed to the matter of state legislative apportionment rather than congressional apportionment because little was done to attempt to limit the *Wesberry* decision, although Congressmen reacted negatively to Justice Harlan's suggestion in dissent that the decision, requiring equalization of congressional districts, cast doubt on the constitutionality of the actions of the House of Representatives. The level of activity concerning congressional redistricting has been almost as high in some states as it has been concerning state legislative redistricting, so the *Wesberry* decision had an effect, with plans generally moving legislatures toward compliance. However, the aftermath of decisions dealing with state legislative apportionments is far more filled with activity and variegated results.

Major Cases. The first major Supreme Court decision on reapportionment to have an impact was *Colegrove* v. *Green.* That impact was essentially to delay efforts to change the apportionment of state legislatures and congressional districts to provide representation for those living in urban areas proportionate to their numbers. In *Colegrove,* which involved a challenge to Illinois congressional districts, Justice Frankfurter, in a plurality opinion, said that reapportionment was a "political thicket" into which judges should not wander, that the subject was inappropriate for judicial action. Even though Frankfurter's opinion was only a plurality opinion, "the Supreme Court's admonition . . . that courts should stay out of the 'political thicket' had obvious influence,"[24] as most plaintiffs bringing reapportionment litigation in state courts were turned away.

There were a few exceptions to this pattern, at first not significant, but in the late 1950's, several courts (one state, one federal, and one territorial) acted; the first two gave legislatures an opportunity to act, after accepting jurisdiction, and the legislatures "got the word" and did reapportion; the third (in Hawaii) brought about the same results by saying it would grant relief. Obviously, all three had to ignore the existence of *Colegrove,* indicating that case's fate: to be ignored rather than even distinguished.

The exceptions just mentioned were isolated cases. In 1962, however, the Supreme Court itself, in a major ruling, changed its mind and said, in *Baker* v. *Carr,* that reapportionment cases were justiciable—that the courts could listen and decide complaints about apportionment inequities. The Court did *not* decide in that case that apportionment should be on any particular basis; in fact, the Court did not even decide on its merits the Tennessee legislative redistricting case before it, but said complaints should be brought before federal district courts. *Baker* set off a wave of activity, perhaps in part because it was not properly understood. Many did think the Court had required population-only apportionment, even though it was to be two years before the Court actually required it for state legislatures.

The breadth of *Baker's* impact, whether or not based on a proper understanding of what the Court had decided, is shown in this summary by Dixon:

> Under the impetus of *Baker*, reapportionment was on the agenda of most of the forty-seven state legislatures in session [in 1963]. Cases were before federal courts in thirty-one states, before state courts in nineteen states, and before both federal and state courts in eleven states. At least one house of twenty-four state legislatures had either been declared unconstitutional, or declared suspect with the court reserving final judgment to allow time for legislative action. Twenty-six states had approved reapportionment plans or state constitutional amendments designed to reduce population disparities in legislative districts—some applying only to one house, some to both houses.[25]

Examples of what happened in two states suggest the variety of activity. In Tennessee, from which *Baker* had come, the legislature did make some minor changes in the apportionment arrangement, but a federal district court held this inadequate and invalid under the Fourteenth Amendment, although the court gave the legislature until June, 1963, to change the plan further. The legislature had, in addition to changing the apportionment, placed a constitutional convention call on the 1962 ballot, with the idea that such a convention would establish legislative representation on a so-called "federal plan" (one house based on area, the other on population); the call for the convention was approved, although other events intervened before it was to be held, leaving that part of the impact hanging.

In Washington, the suit of *Thigpen* v. *Meyers* was commenced immediately after *Baker* was decided, in order to challenge a 1957 apportionment. The legislature did not comply with an order to redistrict until February, 1965, although the suit had been brought in June, 1962. In December, 1962, the federal judges' order to the legislature was "relatively weak," in addition to which the Governor was unwilling to work toward compliance. The judges were unwilling to order at-large elections or weighted voting as remedies for legislative inaction. Compliance—with a later order—did come in 1965, when the legislature was dominated by one party rather than a coalition and when a new governor worked toward developing compromise. This led to an observation that compliance is encouraged when judges actively and directly promote redistricting and to a comment that judges' orders on reapportionment matters are necessary but not sufficient conditions for legislative compliance.

If we shift our attention from specific states to the general pattern, we find much variability, in part because the Fourteenth Amendment "equal protection" clause, the basis of malapportionment complaints, was ambiguous and because the Supreme Court had provided no rulings on the merits and, as a result, no guidelines. Dixon has, however, been able to identify a number of patterns of action which emerged after *Baker*. Some courts in effect passed the buck to other states by saying that they could not rule in the absence of standards, although a greater number were willing to say that existing apportionment plans were invalid, while disagreeing as to what degree they were invalid or how the invalidity was to be repaired. Another type of buck-passing was to the legislatures, as courts ordered them to reapportion, but often without providing guidelines within which they could work. Although "firm guidelines invariably produce speedier legislative action," the courts "split sharply . . . on the question whether a declaration of invalidity should be accompanied by specific directions to the legislatures."[26] Some courts increased the pressure, still without providing guidelines, by making clear that existing arrangements could no longer be used. Despite this, most suggestions for ordering at-large elections were rejected. Some courts did write apportionment plans, usually by combining parts of what the legislature had considered, but this affected only a small number of states.

While observers noted a wide variability in response to *Baker*, at least one hypothesized that federal judges would tend to treat post-*Baker* cases differently from the way state judges would treat them, for example, by being less likely to refuse to reach the merits in a case and by allowing less population inequality than would state judges, as well as being less critical of the Supreme Court's decision. In general, although some differences were found, the hypotheses were not confirmed. Both state and federal judges were unhappy at the lack of guidance provided them. "In their references to the Supreme Court's craftsmanship, the remonstrances of many federal judges were at least as strong as—if not stronger than—those of state judges." Both federal judges and state judges disagreed among themselves as to the meaning of *Baker*, with the patterns similar between the two groups.

In addition, "the state and federal courts did not differ significantly in their interpretations of the Supreme Court's mandate in *Baker*."[27] Ten of twenty-nine federal courts and six of nineteen state courts "ducked" cases by failing to reach the merits, contrary to the hypothesis but not a significant difference. Similarly, in seven of twenty-nine federal cases, the judges stayed their hands to allow the legislature to act, while state judges did this in only two of nineteen cases. Where state apportionment was held unconstitutional, delays to allow the legislature to act were granted in all five state cases, but in only nine of fourteen federal cases, a relationship in the hypothesized direction but not significant. These findings led to the conclusion: "These differences in the proclivity of state and federal judges to remedy malapportionment seem far too minor to confirm our hypothesis."[28]

In 1964, the Supreme Court—having decided congressional districting cases on their merits—"dropped the other shoe" hard by requiring, in *Reynolds* v. *Sims*, that "one man–one vote" apportionment was required in *both* houses of state legislatures. The "federal plan" or "federal analogy" was explicitly rejected. While mathematical exactness was not required, districts were to be as nearly equal in population size as possible, although no standard was established at which legislators might aim in trying to comply. One result of this was to increase the variation in what lower courts permitted. Dixon argues that change (from existing apportionment arrangements) would have been "just as dramatic" and treatment from state to state more equal "had the Court . . . indicated that by 'substantial equality' it was talking in terms of an absolute population variance ratio of 1.5 to 1 (or even 2 to 1) between the largest and smallest district, with most districts falling well within a 25 percent deviation from the average . . . ."[29]

It should be noted that another factor increasing variability existed: a communications problem. While we earlier discussed the communication of Supreme Court decisions to ultimate recipients, the matter of communication of decisions applying Supreme Court rulings to others who might be in comparable circumstances has not been mentioned. Dixon argues that, in the aftermath of *Reynolds*, "few judges knew what national pattern was being developed by the action of their brethren in other states . . . . As a consequence, parties in some states were denied apportionment features which were approved without question in some sister states,"[30] largely as a result of inadequate reporting of decisions or the unavailability of analysis of what was occurring.

The reapportionment cauldron, still bubbling with post-*Baker* activity, again was quickly brought to a boil by *Reynolds*. The existence of post-*Baker*/pre-*Reynolds* activity makes it harder to assess the specific impact of *Reynolds*, unless one is content to say that it acted as a reinforcing stimulus. Examination of what happened in several states illustrates this. In Oklahoma, a three-judge federal court had been dealing with reapportionment since 1962. The legislature reapportioned after having a grace period extended to March, 1963, but the court found this invalid shortly afterwards and undertook the apportionment itself, using a plan developed by the University of Oklahoma's Bureau of Government Research. That federal court order was stayed because the state supreme court modified the legislative plan, but the U.S. Supreme Court, in *Williams* v. *Moss*, affirmed the federal court action in June, 1964. This started things going again, with *Reynolds* now in the picture, leading the district court to find that the large multimember districts violated that decision (which had said nothing on the subject); finally subdistricts were worked out, and the plan was accepted. Tiredness may have explained eventual compliance: "Oklahoma was getting tired of its endless reapportionment struggle, which long antedated *Baker* v. *Carr*."[31] And the situation also suggests that the impact of *Reynolds* was largely anticlimactic, or at most to help the federal court administer the finishing touches to what it had already been doing.

The possibility of overestimating the impact of *Reynolds* is shown in Illinois, well known for its "bedsheet ballot" election of 1964, in which all 177 seats in the state house of representatives were filled in an at-large election. Because of the timing of the election, some have thought it resulted from *Reynolds*. Instead it resulted from a 1954 amendment to the Illinois Constitution, requiring population equality in house districts, coupled with an inability (and unwillingness) of Democrats and Republicans appointed to a redistricting commission to meet to agree on a plan before required deadlines expired. The Illinois senate's districting was under fire in 1964, but the three-judge court handling that case did not act, after a remand from the U.S. Supreme Court, in *Germano* v. *Kerner*, until after the 1964 election, perhaps because of the massive confusion caused by the at-large house election. The ultimate handling of the senate redistricting illustrates another point: the range of actors in reapportionment matters (and in impact generally) is very broad. "Events from remand in 1964 of the Illinois senate case to final accomplishment of reapportionment in late 1965 involved virtually every element of Illinois' legislative, executive, and judicial structure. It also involved the federal district court and, informally, the United States Supreme Court."[32]

One other state, Michigan, shows the speed with which compliance with a Supreme Court ruling can be required. When *Reynolds* was decided, the Michigan Supreme Court had just approved a reapportionment plan. It immediately reconvened (at its own call) and withdrew that approval, five days before the U.S. Supreme Court applied the *Reynolds* doctrine to the Michigan situation in *Beadle* v. *Hare*. The Michigan court gave an existing reapportionment commission only two days to adopt a new plan complying with *Reynolds*—a nearly impossible task because the standard to be applied was "spread through 233 pages of just-received United States Supreme Court opinions—as interpreted by the Michigan Supreme Court."[33] What happened illustrates that, at least in the short run, to the ready comes the victory. The Democratic members of the reapportionment commission had a plan ready, and it was that plan which was adopted. "The Austin-Kleiner Plan gave Michigan not only the earliest post-*Reynolds* v. *Sims* reapportionment in the nation, but also by far the tightest reapportionment in terms of the single consideration of mathematical equality."[34]

In addition to the activity by which *Reynolds* was applied to state legislatures, some courts went ahead and applied the one man–one vote principle to local units of government, thus anticipating the Supreme Court's 1968 ruling in *Avery* v. *Midland County*. For example, in 1964, a Michigan circuit court applied *Reynolds* to a county board of supervisors and a federal district court applied the case to Baltimore's City Council. And in Wisconsin, the same thing occurred. *Avery* itself is having a broad impact, although there have been some instances where the case has not been applied. Thus, the Missouri Supreme Court decided that one man–one vote apportionment did not apply to a junior college district, on the grounds that it was not a unit of local government with general government powers. The number of units covered is so great and the time since the decision so short that it is not possible to give a clear picture of what has happened in the aftermath of that ruling. However, the case has provided an answer to lower courts faced with numerous suits challenging local government apportionments. For example, the North Dakota Supreme Court waited from June, 1967, until one week after *Avery* to decide a suit by the City of Fargo against Cass County for redistricting of the county board. When it handed down its ruling, the court indicated it had been hopelessly divided but that *Avery* had provided the answer. More generally, compliance has been delayed for several reasons, one of the more important of which is that state legislation may be necessary to change the basis for local government organization before the local units may begin to come into compliance.

Anti-Court Activity. Thus far we have been examining activity dealing with the changing of existing apportionment plans. But that was only one part of the impact of the decisions in *Baker* and *Reynolds*, particularly the latter. There were many officials who were extremely displeased by both cases, although their reaction to *Baker* was mild by comparison to their later reaction to *Reynolds*, perhaps in part a function of the Court's not having reached the merits in the earlier case, leading some people to believe that if they were going to be affected, it would not be for some time. (We have, of course, seen that this was not to be the case.) Not all official reaction was negative, however, although those pleased with the decisions tended to be surprised. Even in 1964, when the reaction was more hostile than it had been in 1962, some members of both parties, for example, Democratic National Chairman John Bailey and Republican National Chairman (and later Vice-Presidential candidate) William Miller praised what the Court had done.

Some state legislative leaders, in the wake of *Baker*, did begin to move toward amending the federal Constitution to remove apportionment disputes from the jurisdiction of the courts. In December, 1962, the General Assembly of the States (part of the Council of State Governments) proposed several constitutional amendments, including one stripping the courts of jurisdiction over reapportionment matters; interestingly, the American Bar Association House of Delegates disapproved such a plan in mid-1963. The principal efforts to reverse the Supreme Court came, however, after *Reynolds* and took three forms. One was a congressional attempt to strip the courts of their jurisdiction over reapportionment cases, embodied in a bill introduced by Congressman William Tuck (D–Va.). The second was an effort, sponsored by Senator Dirksen of Illinois, to amend the Constitution to allow one house of a state legislature to be chosen on a basis other than population. The third was an effort, begun in the states, to request Congress to call a constitutional convention to consider the subject of reapportionment. None of the three has been successful, although, as of this writing, the last effort remains alive.

The Tuck bill was brought to the floor of the House directly from the Rules Committee after the Judiciary Committee had held eight days of hearings on 130 bills introduced by ninety-nine Members of Congress but had not reported a bill. The Tuck bill was passed, 218–175, on August 19, 1964, with Democrats opposed 96–140 (North: 12–124; South: 84–16), and Republicans favoring, 122–35, but failed to gain support in the Senate. Dirksen's efforts had the opposite difficulty—some (but more limited) success in the Senate, but not in the House. Before trying his constitutional amendment, the Senator tried a moratorium on litigation, brought before the Senate as a rider to a foreign aid bill. This was modified in consultation with Majority Leader Mansfield (D–Mont.), Deputy Attorney General Katzenbach, and Solicitor General Cox, but even this revision failed, and the most the Senate would pass was a "sense of Congress" resolution that the courts should "go slow." This failed when the House did not act upon it before adjournment. Part of the explanation for the failure of the clearly milder Senate proposals was the reaction *outside* of Congress to the Tuck bill. "The emotional reaction engendered by the extremism of the Tuck bill tended to spread without diminution to the moratorium proposal."[35] Timing was important here, as in other instances: the Congress recessed for the national party conventions, giving those opposed to attempts to tamper with the reapportionment rulings an opportunity to gain strength, as well as causing the drive by the proponents to lose some of its force.

Senator Dirksen, not to be daunted by one defeat, tried again in 1965, this time with the above-mentioned constitutional amendment. He did manage to achieve a majority vote in favor of his proposal (57–39), not sufficient under the requirement that constitutional amendments be submitted for ratification by a two-thirds vote. The pattern of voting on the amendment is worth noting. Senators from the North favored the proposal, 37–36, while those from the South favored it 20–3. Democrats were opposed, 28–36 (northern Democrats 10–33, southern Democrats 18–3), and Republicans favored, 29–3. Senators from states urbanized 60 percent plus were opposed to the amendment by a 4–14 margin, while those from rural states favored it, 53–25. While Dirksen again gained a majority (but not the two thirds necessary) the following year, his efforts were clearly not going to be successful. One difficulty was that Dirksen's efforts, as reported in the press, were perceived as an effort to eliminate one man–one vote completely, not simply, as the amendment proposed, to provide that one house of a state legislature could be apportioned on a basis other than population, if approved by the voters themselves. Even had Dirksen been successful in the Congress, time had been running against him. The courts did not cease ordering compliance with *Reynolds* simply because a constitutional amendment was being considered, and the legislatures did not stop redistricting, although some legislatures may have engaged in some considerable foot-dragging in the hopes the amendment would be submitted.

In addition to foot-dragging, a number of legislatures began to ask Congress to call a constitutional convention. At first this "campaign" was carried on at a low level of visibility, until some members of Congress discovered that only a few more states were necessary to achieve the required two thirds which the Constitution specifies is necessary to request a convention. At this writing, only one more state is necessary, but efforts have been made in some states to rescind earlier resolutions asking for the convention, and it is unclear what effect Congress will give to such actions. Also, much debate is likely over such matters as how long a resolution of a state legislature is effective, over what period of time may the resolutions from the two-thirds of the states be accumulated, and the effect which occurs when not all the resolutions request precisely the same amendment, even though all deal generally with the same subject. Even though the reapportionment amendment appears to have died with the death of Senator Dirksen in late 1969, what the continuing nature of this issue tends to do is to illustrate the never-ending character of the aftermath of Court decisions.

Political Process and Beneficiaries. Two other sorts of impacts need to be examined. One is on the political process. Was the process itself affected—over the long run—by the reapportionment decisions or, after the activity directed at reapportionment, did legislatures continue to operate in the same way? Because of almost continuous reapportionment activity, with three or four plans having been enacted in some states since *Baker* and the process not yet complete, to be added to by the post–1970 census reapportionment, it is difficult to give a conclusive answer. Certainly legislatures had proportionately less time to deal with other important matters, such as recurring financial crises, to the extent they dealt with reapportionment. Another effect was produced by the unsettled nature of district lines. A political scientist studying congressional election campaigns noted that "the changes of boundary lines unsettled political expectations sufficiently, so that there was more competition for office than normal,"[36] a remark broadly applicable.

One effect on the legislative process, an effect likely to remain when activity over reapportionment itself settles down, is a product of the reapportionment-induced shift from multimember districts to single-member districts in metropolitan areas. Jewell has noted a number of effects stemming from such shifts: (1) The strength of countywide parties decreases, while ward or precinct organizations carry more weight, and pockets of great strength for a single party may develop, making recruitment of minority party candidates quite difficult. "Where a minority party is just emerging . . . districting will encourage the party to concentrate its efforts in a few districts where it has a realistic chance."[37] In addition, both parties are now more likely to be represented within a metropolitan area than under the at-large multimember procedure, particularly noticeable in the case of Republicans in the South. (2) Cohesion within metropolitan legislative delegations is likely to decrease, in part because of the increase in minority party representation, but going beyond that factor alone. (3) Pressures on legislators from constituents may increase, because constituents may now turn to a single legislator rather than a number, no one of whom can serve easily as a point of reference for subsets of a large constituency. The style of representation may shift from that of "trustee" toward that of "delegate."

Another possible effect of the decisions on the political process is to limit gerrymandering by legislatures. While the Court has not dealt with the question of gerrymandering, there seems little question that the task of apportioning districts to benefit one party over the other has been made more difficult by requirements that districts be nearly equal in size. Strange-shaped districts may still result (although not all odd-shaped districts are gerrymanders), and minority groups may be carved up and distributed among various districts to dilute their potential legislative strength, but the Court's population-only requirements for districts—not previously part of the picture—will have to be dealt with.

As this analysis suggests, one can look at the effects of reapportionment in terms of beneficiaries. There tend to be more Negroes elected to the legislature in single-member metropolitan districts than from multimember districts, suggesting that their access to the legislative process is increased by the former arrangement and thus by reapportionment. Initially, after *Baker* and *Reynolds,* some thought that the principal benefit of the decisions would rest with residents of central cities, generally Democrats. This turned out to be a misreading; population shifts from 1950 to 1960 had been away from the central city and toward the suburbs. Thus, while one could talk of increased representation for metropolitan areas, often the suburbs (many of which, but clearly not all, were Republican) received as much additional representation as did the central city. In fact, Mitau argues, "Residents in suburban communities throughout the country fared much better than did those living in the core city."[38] Had the decisions been handed down prior to 1960, the principal initial advantage clearly would have rested with the central city residents, and resistance to the decisions might have been even greater than it has been.

People thought the city dwellers would benefit in part because they believed that the cities were being deprived of adequate financing for their projects by rural legislators, with the corollary that greater expenditures for health, education, and welfare programs would come from greater numbers of urban legislators. Such an assumption was not confirmed by studies carried out to examine the existence of rural-urban cleavage in the legislature. If a principal difficulty faced by cities or metropolitan areas in achieving their goals was that their own delegations were fragmented, reapportionment would not solve the problem and—as Jewell's findings cited above suggest—might only exacerbate it by increasing division within metropolitan area delegations.

Another set of studies also suggests that the effect of reapportionment on policy outcomes may turn out, for the states as a whole, to be minimal. Political scientists have related the degree of malapportionment in a state (the degree to which it deviated from population equality) to certain outcomes, such as the presence of an income tax, levels of expenditure for welfare functions, and the like. Generally, it was found that there was no significant relationship between malapportionment and policy outcomes, suggesting that bringing about population-only reapportionment might not mean major shifts in policy. While one certainly can find states where reapportionment has brought new faces in the legislature, new leadership, and a better "break" for the cities in terms of policies, one cannot as yet predict what the general pattern of impact with respect to policy will be, because of our lack of before-and-after studies, forcing us to make inferences from other data, such as the malapportionment studies just cited.

CHURCH-STATE RELATIONS

That impact studies deal with instances of greatest controversy concerning Supreme Court cases is perhaps nowhere clearer than with respect to the subject of the relations between church and state. Recent writing on the subject has been almost totally in terms of the school prayer decisions of the 1960's: *Engel* v. *Vitale,* outlawing a state-written prayer, and *Abington School District* v. *Schempp,* striking down the practices of Bible reading and recitation of the Lord's Prayer. That concentration has some advantage, in that it allows us to see broadly what the impacts of the cases are, whereas isolated case studies about a variety of different decisions might not be as easily comparable. In addition to school prayer, we find studies in the area of released time, involving the two earliest important contributions by political scientists to impact study, the already-cited articles by Patric and Sorauf.

Released Time. We turn first to released time. The first case was *McCollum* v. *Board of Education of Champaign,* involving the practice of releasing children from class, upon parents' consent, for a short period one day each week for the purpose of religious instruction conducted on school property and taught by clergy. The Supreme Court struck down the practice as a violation of the establishment-of-religion clause of the First Amendment. The impact of the decision was affected by the fact that there were many programs of religious instruction connected with the public schools, clearly not all of which involved precisely the same procedures as did the program involved in *McCollum.* This provided an open invitation to those running different programs to justify them by differentiating theirs from the invalidated one, perhaps carried to greatest length in the item-by-item comparison of the Champaign and New York programs when the latter was challenged.

Most program discontinuances or changes revolved around the on-premises aspect of the *McCollum* situation. As Patric noted, "The week-day programs which entailed the simultaneous use of public school time and property were the only ones severely modified or completely abolished." For example, "almost all on-premises weekday programs in Illinois, Michigan and North Dakota were dissolved or radically changed."[39] The magnitude of the drop-off may have been on the order of 20 percent in terms of programs, about 10 percent in terms of pupils. Much of this loss was regained later. However, not all on-premises programs were discontinued. Sorauf suggests that up to 40–50 percent of programs of religious education in school buildings continued after *McCollum* and despite it. Virginia's Attorney General Almond ruled that they might continue, and state education officials as well as church leaders agreed with him. This "massive resistance" to the *McCollum* decision is interesting in light of Virginia's later "Massive Resistance" to school desegregation, providing evidence for the hypothesis that resistance to one decision predisposes one to comparable reaction toward others. Churchmen and public officials tended to be the principals involved in decisions both to continue and to terminate practices, elsewhere as well as in Virginia. Sometimes the initiative to resolve matters was taken by the school officials or other public officials, sometimes by the churchmen.

Where the matter of on-premise classes was not involved, far fewer programs were discontinued or changed. Programs in Chicago and New York (the *Zorach* situation) were among these. What appears to have been an important variable here is the existence of long-standing legislation permitting religious instruction on public school time. On the basis of

Patric's findings, we might hypothesize that the longer a law has been in effect, the more unwilling legislators will be to discard the practice it embodies. Thus, in Indiana, Minnesota, and California, where this situation obtained, the states' attorneys general held no action in compliance to be necessary. In addition, we find those favoring continuation of the practice appearing to have carried generally more weight in the resolution of the compliance question than did those who opposed continuation (and favored strict compliance). "In only a few instances . . . were local opponents of religious instruction able to secure enforcement of the *McCollum* decision with regard to other than on-premises programs." In some jurisdictions, where there may not have been pressure from either side, the officials (state and public school) and those affiliated with the church groups which had set up the programs tended to be the ones who "interpreted the Court's ruling and were usually responsible for putting it into effect."[40]

One further point might be made here. If one reads *McCollum* strictly, as applying only to situations where the religious instruction was "on premises," then instances where off-premises religious instruction were discontinued show how broad the effects of a specific decision may be. In these same terms, the fact that relatively few off-premises programs were dissolved should not necessarily be taken as instances of noncompliance, because the *McCollum* case was not directed at them.

Where *McCollum* had struck down a program and been prohibitory, *Zorach* upheld a program (of religious education off school grounds, but on school time while nonparticipating children remained in school) and was legitimizing. Where *McCollum* had reduced the number of programs and the amount of attendence, *Zorach* did not seem to increase them. Sorauf suggests that by 1953 the attendance in such religious education programs was back at the pre-*McCollum* total, and notes that those running the programs showed over 3,000 communities with programs and an enrollment of 3 million (up from 2 million–2.5 million about five years earlier). He talks of an all-time high in enrollments but subsequently mentions modest over-all growth. Perhaps, in absolute figures, there was growth, but if one takes into account expanding school population with the post–World War II baby boom, would the advocates of released-time religious education have recouped their losses or still be suffering a proportionate loss? Again the measuring problems involved in determining impact show themselves.

Another measure of the impact of *Zorach* is that no new programs of released time were enacted in the states, despite the enthusiasm and rejoicing by the programs' sponsors in the wake of the decision. Perhaps the principal impact was to increase the faith of the leaders of the movement, or to provide "a tonic to the movement." The legitimizing effect of a Supreme Court decision seen here can also be seen in the calm which came upon the released time scene after the decision, with the opponents of the policy, although unhappy, recognizing that the constitutional issue was settled and not bringing more litigation. What may also have contributed to that result, as well, was the tightening up by school officials in the way they administered the program, at least in New York.

While the decision had legitimized a program of released time off school property, this did not appear to affect the continuing noncompliance with *McCollum*. Perhaps after *McCollum*, the resistance of those who thought that the Court had struck down all school-time religious education programs might have been easy to understand, where there was strong desire for such programs; however, even after *Zorach* provided a viable alternative, the programs in defiance of the Court continued. And as Sorauf discovered, this was clearly noncompliance, not a failure to follow because the Court was not understood; he found the most noncomplaint school superintendents in Pennsylvania to be *best* versed on the law.

Two "spin-offs" from the *Zorach* decision might be noted. One was that some interpreted the case as *requiring* rather than *permitting* released time programs, when the latter was clearly all that the Supreme Court had dealt with. The other was the dictum of Justice Douglas that "we are a religious people whose institutions presuppose a Supreme Being." The case has in some sense perhaps had a greater continuing impact in terms of that now oft-quoted dictum than in terms of the substance of the decision itself. Certainly, when Sorauf writes that the case "has created a symbol and an endorsement . . . that is at the moment reshaping and molding the very values which the Court will have to attend to in later decisions,"[41] that dictum is very much a part of the symbol.

School Prayer. We find reaction to the school prayer decisions at national, state, and local levels from officials, individual teachers, and religious groups. We also have studies of states which differed in their approach to school prayer prior to the decisions, providing still another dimension to the impact picture.

Reaction to the school prayer decisions in Congress was perhaps as strong as to *Reynolds* v. *Sims*. Over one hundred Congressmen (more Republicans than Democrats, with most of the latter being from the South and from rural constituencies) introduced amendments to the Constitution on the subject. As Katz has noted, "Political leaders and a number of spontaneous citizen's organizations opposed the decision so strongly that they were willing to alter the words of the First Amendment to gain a reversal."[42] It should be noted that the reaction to *Engel*, involving a state-written prayer in one state, was far greater, at least in terms of immediate emotional outburst, than to *Schempp*, affecting a majority of states. This may have occurred because the first decision was read to be far broader than it was, as saying what the second actually did, and because people were prepared for (or resigned to) the *Schempp* ruling.

While the Tuck bill on reapportionment had at least cleared the House, the Becker amendment on school prayer failed in the House when Becker could muster only 167 of the necessary 218 signatures for a discharge petition to get the bill out of the Judiciary Committee, where it was opposed by Committee Chairman Emanuel Celler, who had also vehemently opposed the Tuck Bill. Reich notes, "Three heavy volumes of testimony and statements produced by the House Judiciary Committee from its hearings on the . . . Becker Amendment in April-June, 1964, are, in effect, documentary evidence of the massive political activity indirectly stimulated by the Court."[43] Also, just as had been the case with reapportionment, Senator Dirksen introduced a constitutional amendment, although one more limited than that pressed by Representative Becker. Again Dirksen could not muster a two-thirds vote in favor of his proposal.

The campaign for the amendment to the constitution came to an end far more quickly than it had with reapportionment. One key reason may be that there was not the mass of follow-up litigation which had characterized the reapportionment impact, and resistance tended to be a local or community-by-community matter. To be sure, national leaders spoke out. Within the churches, "The Jewish community welcomed [*Schempp*], Protestant leaders were divided but the overwhelming majority of the national leaders approved the decision, and the Catholic Church was firmly opposed to the decisions."[44] Particular groups of clergymen and other church leaders in particular places made statements and passed resolutions on both sides of the decision. Some Catholic theologians were among the most articulate of those attacking Senator Dirksen for trying to be "more religious than the Pope" by pressing his amendment.

The Governors Conference in 1962 called for a constitutional amendment allowing Bible reading in the schools. And there was some litigation: Mitau notes that lower courts struck down Bible reading in five states shortly after *Schempp,* although the Florida Supreme Court upheld practices conflicting with the ruling. Some attempts by parents to evade the ruling, by substituting voluntary prayers, ended up in court. When prayers occurred before and after the school day in one town, the judge only prohibited the ringing of the school bell to designate the period, while upholding the prayer itself. When parents in a New York community wanted a prayer with the milk and cookies, the practice was blocked, with the judges holding that the state is not required to permit student-initiated prayers.

On the whole, however, the battle was fought out elsewhere than in the courts. And not all noncompliance was resisted, by any means. Where one religion predominated in an area, or where religious sentiment was relatively homogeneous, those in the minority may have been unwilling to subject themselves to obloquy by attacking the practices, particularly as their children may have been ostracized at school. The school officials whose responsibility it might be considered to comply with "the law" may have been hesitant to move against practices firmly supported by the school boards to which they were directly responsible, or by interests in the community to whom they looked for approval. However, Dolbeare and Hammond show that continuing noncompliance may occur without being a result of strong school office preference or strong feelings by community elites, and is not necessarily deliberate defiance of the federal high tribunal. The critical nature of the role played by local officials is shown in "Eastville-Westville," the school district whose reaction to the decisions is portrayed by Johnson. There the superintendent (rather than the principal, because the former had more "social distance" from the teachers) was able to use the Supreme Court's policy to change local practices; he felt he needed those decisions even though he himself opposed the practices. "Because of the Court's *Engel* and *Schempp* rulings, the superintendent was able to carry out a policy which flew in the face of the dominant values of the community as well as those held by many in the educational system itself, without a word of criticism reaching his ears."[45]

We do have a relatively broad picture of compliance and noncompliance with the school prayer rulings as a result of several surveys, both national and within particular states. Surveys by the State Superintendent of Education in Kentucky, and by the Indiana School Board Association, both showed low compliance; only 61 of 204 school districts in Kentucky had discontinued prayers and Bible reading, and 121 superintendents had unwritten policies permitting both, while in Indiana fewer than 6 percent of the boards had changed policies to come into compliance with the Court. In Texas, in a survey conducted by the Council of Churches, the change was negligible, and few responding said they agreed in principle with the decisions, relevant to Johnson's observation, "Those who personally agree with the substance of Supreme Court policy also acknowledge to a greater extent the Court's legitimacy and expert bases than do those who are displeased with the substantive ruling."[46]

In line with other research, Dierenfield found major regional differences both in frequency of the practice and degree of compliance. Thus, in comparing the responses he found in 1960 with those in 1966 concerning regular devotional services, he found 8 percent of the reporting districts in 1966 showed all schools in the system with such services, where the comparable figure in 1960 had been over 33 percent; the drop for districts reporting some schools having services was from 17 percent to 10.7 percent. With respect to devotional Bible reading in the schools, we find a shift nationally from almost 42 percent Yes (have the practice) to just below 14 percent. However, the 42 percent figure (1960) covers up vast regional differences—from 11 percent in the western states and 18 percent in the Midwest to more than 75 percent in the South and more than two thirds in the East. By 1966, except for the South, the regional variation had decreased; western, midwestern, and eastern were all below 5 percent, although the South still showed more than half retaining the practices. Dierenfield's work also shows variation by size of unit, but the spread is not as great as for regions. In 1960, almost 31 percent of communities from 500 to 2,500 had the practices, as did 54 percent of the largest communities (100,000+). In 1966, the largest units still were the ones where the practice would be most frequently found (almost 30 percent), but existence of the Bible reading had dropped to under 10 percent in the smallest communities.

Dolbeare and Hammond, exploring regional variations in compliance, suggest that eastern and southern states had had requirements of a constitutional or statutory variety concerning religious observances, thus explaining in part the earlier high level of religious observances in the schools. In the western United States, such practices were explicitly prohibited, with resulting low rates of occurrence. In the Midwest, by contrast, there were neither requirements for nor prohibitions against, and the rate of occurrence was in-between, with about half the districts having some religious exercises. After the Court's decisions, eastern states, the authors note, removed their requirements, and compliance followed the legislative or court action. In the South, on the other hand, requirements were not removed, and were supplemented in some cases, with resulting low decreases in the incidence of services.

If we shift from the units involved to teachers, we can find out other factors relevant to compliance with the school prayer cases. To test the impact of the *Schempp* and *Murray* decisions, Way conducted a national survey, using a random sample of 2,320 public elementary schoolteachers (in 464 schools). He found noticeable shifts in classroom practices concerning prayers and Bible reading. Whereas more than 60 percent of the teachers had had classroom prayers at the time of the decisions, by 1964–65, this had dropped to 28 percent, most of whom were involved in daily prayer practices; with respect to Bible reading, the percentage dropped from 48 percent to 22 percent. "The average teacher," Way asserts, "did feel the impact of the Supreme Court's decisions."[47] While teachers did have much discretion in what they did and while their personal religious views had an effect on their compliance, the policy under which they operated also had a marked effect. When asked about school policy on prayers, 155 said that some prayers were favored, 494 said they were opposed, and by far the largest number, 1,011, said there was no policy, that it was left to the teacher's discretion, or that they did not know of a policy. The figures for Bible reading are much the same. The effect is shown by the fact that only 4 percent of the teachers in schools opposing the prayers did say them, while 43 percent of those in schools favoring the prayers did so. Having no policy or teacher discretion was equivalent to having a policy in favor of prayer, as 40 percent of the "others" had prayer exercises in their classrooms. For Bible reading, 91 percent of those in schools favoring the policy had the practice, but only 3 percent of those in schools opposed did; here, only 25 percent of the "others" had the practice.

Frequency of church attendance by the teacher was found to be relevant: "The more frequently a teacher attended church the more likely she was to have prayers and Bible readings in her classroom before the Court decisions and to continue them after the decisions were announced."[48] The matter of habit also showed up in Way's finding that the more years of experience a teacher had, the more likely the teacher was to continue the practice after the decision. Religion of the teacher was related both to participation in the practices before the Supreme Court decided the cases and to compliance as well, but members of different religious groups did not react in the same way. Thus, Way found that Jews, Roman Catholics, and liberal Protestants participated in the exercises at about equal rates before the decisions (around 40 percent for Bible reading, 55 percent for prayer), with conservative Protestants participating at much higher rates (over 70 percent for both practices). After the decisions, the compliance of Jews and Roman Catholics was quite similar, but liberal Protestants did not comply as much and continued the practice at rates higher than the new rates for Jews and Catholics. Many conservative Protestants complied, but their participation in the exercises remained extremely high (around 50 percent) after the decision.

If we turn to two states where compliance with school prayer decisions has been examined, we find that the stance of the state toward the issue *before* the decision is extremely important in what happens *after* the decision, although the predecision state of affairs is clearly not totally determinative of postdecision aftermath. Reich, who examined California, notes, "By the time of the Supreme Court's decisions in the prayer cases, law and policy in California probably were as firmly committed to the principle of church-state separation as they were in any state."[49] Thus, the decisions of the U.S. Supreme Court reinforced a policy going back over fifty years. That meant that the impact of the decision in California may have been less with respect to school prayer or Bible reading than with respect to other issues, such as celebration of religious holidays, graduation ceremonies, and the use of school property by religious organizations. As Reich notes, the "really important effects may come in the radiation of sanctions beyond the original boundaries of the decisions . . . ."[50]

Of particular importance in this respect is the language in the Court's decision about permissibility of studying religion or the Bible in school, that because one could not have Bible reading as a devotional exercise, a "religion of secularism" need not be established. While perhaps a more solid comment than Justice Douglas' *Zorach* dictum, the remark may, like it, have had more impact, in California and comparable states, than the basic holding of the decision. Certainly, the language was used often by school officials in applying the decisions, and Reich has observed, "Without the prayer decisions it is unlikely that there would have been the strong emphasis by school administrators, school boards, and their legal counsel on the important place that they say religion and the Bible can and should have in the curriculum."[51]

There was some activity after the decisions; many inquiries were made to the Attorney General's office, but he did not make new policy, instead referring most items to the attorneys for the counties. However, three days after the decision was announced, he did write a letter to the state's Superintendent of Public Instruction. He used this as a vehicle to criticize those who had been criticizing for some time an earlier Attorney General's opinion; his emphasis was that a religion of secularism would not be established by eliminating certain practices, and he asserted that *Schempp* supported California's policy.

However, on the whole, activity was not great. Education officials Reich interviewed said that they thought the impact of both *Engel* and *Schempp* was not great in California, but he notes that "the prayer decisions do not imply massive administrative and physical changes in school systems. The effects of the prayer decisions are more subtle and less visible, and thus more difficult to measure . . . ,"[52] perhaps implying that the impact may have been underestimated. Perhaps there *was* little negative impact, but Reich makes clear, as noted above, that the decision clearly served a legitimizing function, for example, by "provid[ing] highly visible support for current policies. This reinforcement effect has permitted some school administrators to reiterate standing policies and has given others the occasion to establish them."[53]

In Tennessee, state law required Bible reading, thus clearly distinguishing that state from California. When *Schempp* was handed down, the State Commissioner of Education, while formally leaving the matter to local officials, "was reported as saying that it was permissible to read the Bible in public schools despite *Schempp*."[54] The change which resulted from this was minimal. Of the 121 of the state's 152 districts for which policy was ascertained, 51 did change their policy somewhat, but *only one* eliminated devotional exercises; the others made student participation voluntary and left matters to the individual teacher as to whether the exercises should be held. What individual teachers did is less clear, but the state continued to print the requirement of the state law in the teachers' regulations handbook, something certainly not likely to bring about movement away from the practice.

Even though the change was minimal, Birkby tried to ascertain correlates of such change as did occur. He found no difference between urban areas and rural areas, and only a slight relationship between a tendency to change and the existence of religious pluralism or heterogeneity in a community. Nor did socioeconomic characteristics serve to distinguish changing from nonchanging boards. Going beyond his data, he suggests that in changing districts "a perception of the Court as an authoritative body exercising legitimate power was strong enough to override any commitment to devotional exercises . . . . Public opinion in changing districts probably was perceived by the board as favoring or at least not opposing compliance with *Schempp* and strengthened the board's desire to comply."[55] But does shifting to a "voluntary" arrangement (in which students may feel social pressure which serves to vitiate the voluntariness) mean compliance with *Schempp?* Apparently the people of Tennessee were confused as to what the Court had meant, because the Court had not spoken about programs with the "voluntariness" aspect to which Tennessee's changing districts moved. If one takes movement away from school prayer required by state law, then the districts found in Tennessee to change were complying; if one takes the decision as prohibiting prayer directed by the teacher, even with students' participation not legally mandatory, then clearly the change was not enough to bring compliance.

In examining a third state, which they call "Midway," Dolbeare and Hammond provide a somewhat different perspective. Despite reporting in questionnaires by school officials that their schools were complying with the Court's rulings, "schools regularly engaged in every form of religious observance known to the fertile imagination of generations of teachers,"[56] six years after *Engel* and five years after *Schempp.* This occurred despite knowledge by most teachers that the Court had ruled concerning school prayer, and in part because of a feeling by school principals "that teachers legally could, and generally that they should, engage in some form of religious observances." Even superintendents, who knew the cases more clearly, felt that as long as state and local school agencies were not requiring prayer, teachers could do as they pleased—but they went further; "Lest they [the teachers] feel too much pressure to conform to the Court's rulings, the superintendents took care to convey notice of the nature of their freedom to them."[57]

One of the striking findings made by Dolbeare and Hammond was the lack of controversy at the local level concerning school prayer, a lack particularly noticeable by contrast to the controversy mentioned earlier at the national level. "There is a wide bifurcation between a national issue and its local application," they note. "The national issue never linked in and made contact with the local public schools. It remained one of the abstracts about which people feel deeply, but it never aroused conflict over the actual local practice."[58]

OBSCENITY*

By far one of the most controversial issues of our times is that of obscenity. Closely connected with sexual aspects of our morality, discussion of the subject tends to produce considerable emotion. The political power of the topic has been seen often, from instances when district attorneys conduct "campaigns against smut" to the attack by several senators on Mr. Justice Fortas for having participated in a series of decisions which the senators alleged contributed to the sale of pornography and thus, it was claimed, to the erosion of our national morals. The attack on Fortas was not, however, fortuitous. It stemmed from a widely held feeling that, first, obscenity was increasing; second, that little can be regulated with respect to obscenity; and, third, that the Supreme Court had played a large role in this state of affairs.

There is little question that the Supreme Court's decisions on obscene materials have restricted what may be suppressed. In the only slightly more than ten years since the Court began to consider substantive tests for obscenity, in the *Roth* and *Alberts* cases in 1957, the Court has struck down convictions for the sale of obscenity far more than it has upheld them and, in so doing, has added elements to its 1957 definition which are felt by many to limit what those who wish to proceed against alleged obscenity could eliminate from their communities. However, even though the Court has generally *limited* what may be done, it should be noted that some recent decisions, at least within the framework created by the earlier cases, permit some restrictions, when purveyors of obscene materials aim at particular groups (*Mishkin*), including children (*Ginsberg*), or when they go out of their way to titillate or to "pander" to the "prurient interest" of members of the community (*Ginzburg*). Another way in which the Court has limited what might be done to obscenity, and that appears more noticeably in the area of movie regulation than in the regulation of printed matter, concerns procedures. The Supreme Court has been dealing with the law of movie censorship for far longer than with definitions of obscenity, within a legal framework which permitted movies to be treated differently from other "speech," particularly printed speech. Recently, however, the Court has been setting procedural standards for film censorship, in decisions which have had a clear-cut effect on attempts to control what is shown in movie theaters.

We turn first to movies, both because the effects of Court decisions seem clear-cut and impact appears to have been great and because the effects have been studied more systematically than have the effects of the Supreme Court's general obscenity decisions. Studying the former is

---

* I wish to express my appreciation to my fellow "obscenitarian" (he says it should be "dirtymovieologist"), Donald Gregory, for his comments on this segment.

also easier because there are fewer jurisdictions which have tried to limit film showing than have tried to limit books (potentially all jurisdictions in the country, as all states, have general obscenity laws); while general obscenity statutes may be (and are) applied to movies as well as books, special methods have been developed to deal with films in advance of their being shown.

Before embarking on a discussion of the limitations on film censorship imposed by recent decisions, we must recognize that an early decision of the Court helped to encourage, and legitimize, efforts at film control. In 1915, the Justices ruled that films were principally entertainment, and thus not entitled to be treated in the same manner as other speech with respect to the protections of the First Amendment. This decision, the *Mutual Films* case, brought about considerable censorship of films—censorship in the sense of "prior restraint," that is, requiring that films be shown to officials before being viewed by the public, with the possibility that the films would be banned or would be cut before display would be allowed. "Unlimited censorship or something very close to it actually did come about in the years following the decision. It came about in large measure because the courts, including the Supreme Court, allowed it to come about."[59] Judges did not review censors' judgments closely, and no effective limitations were applied in interpreting the *Mutual Films* ruling. Distributors and exhibitors generally lost in the courts in the years following *Mutual Films*.

However, the standards, or rather the lack of precise standards, used by the censors, led to cases which brought a shift in the 1950's in which the Supreme Court, followed up by the lower courts and some legislatures, severely restricted the restrictors, although not forbidding outright some form of prior restraint in the film area. The first case was *Burstyn* v. *Wilson*, involving the film *The Miracle* in which a peasant woman is seduced by a man she believes to be St. Joseph, later giving birth to what she thinks is the Christ child. The censors in New York State, after protests from religious groups, banned the movie as "sacrilegious," a term the Court found excessively vague. Although the case had an effect in terms of eliminating a reason which the censors might use to suppress films, the case had another aspect, more important in long-run terms. The Court recognized that films were not to be considered simply entertainment (as they might legitimately have been in 1915, at the beginning of their development) but that they were also important communicators of speech, of ideas, and thus were within the scope of the First Amendment. However, the Court did not strike down prior restraint as used with respect to films, although one outcome of the case was the invalidation, by the Kansas legislature, of the state censorship law, because the legislators believed the Court had done exactly that. (Their action was later set aside.)

The effects of *Burstyn* were far-reaching. State supreme courts in Ohio, Massachusetts, and Pennsylvania struck down the film censorship laws of their states. In *Superior Films,* the U.S. Supreme Court had reversed the banning of a movie by the Ohio film censorship unit, but the agency had continued to operate in much the same manner; when some of its subsequent orders were appealed to the Ohio Supreme Court, that court held that exhibition of any film could no longer be banned by the group. The New York censors were to find that *Burstyn* was not to be their only difficulty, and, although it may be marked as the "beginning of the end" for the agency, the end did not come until the mid-1960's. When a license was not granted a film because it showed a human birth, claimed to be "indecent," a lower New York court reversed. In a case involving a movie showing nudist camp activities, the New York Appeals Court determined that no standard had been left to the New York censors besides "obscenity," as a result of the U.S. Supreme Court rulings.

Carmen notes, "On only two occasions since the Supreme Court began to encroach upon state and local movie censorship authority have the courts of New York upheld an agency ruling against a film."[60] Further adding to New York's grief was *Kingsley Pictures* v. *Regents;* involving the movie version of *Lady Chatterley's Lover,* which had been proscribed on the grounds it portrayed adultery in a favorable light. Portrayal is not advocacy, said the U.S. Supreme Court, and advocacy of unpopular ideas as well as acceptable ones is allowed under the First Amendment, and the censors were reversed again.

The collective impact of these decisions, not only in New York but elsewhere, was twofold. The number of cities and towns involved in movie censorship "decreased appreciably."[61] And there was an effect on film content as well. Randall argues, "The new freedom [*Burstyn*] provided helped to stimulate a maturity in the medium that eventually saw greater sophistication of subject and treatment and less dependence on the 'family' film."[62] This trend in the content of movies had begun earlier, in part in response to decreasing attendance at movies resulting from the pull of television. The *Burstyn* ruling reinforced the impact of an earlier decision, the *Paramount Pictures* case, in which the movie companies had been forced, in an antitrust action, to divest themselves of the movie theaters they owned. Through that ownership, they had been able to make effective the decisions of the Production Code Authority (the "Hays Office") regarding content; after *Paramount,* independent movie producers, who did not always feel bound by the code, were able to market their product far more easily, and they were more willing to deal with controversial subjects.

Thus far the Court had been dealing with the standards used by censors. The basic framework of censorship was still untouched. Then the Court decided two cases dealing with procedures. In the first, *Times Film*

v. *City of Chicago,* the permissibility of requiring a movie exhibitor to submit films to the censor for viewing—at the core of prior restraint—was upheld. However, the decision did not serve to reinforce censorship, and the aftermath shows a continued weakening of film censorship efforts. In the second, *Freedman* v. *Maryland,* the Court surrounded the film censorship process with a series of procedural requirements—prompt action by the censor, the availability of prompt judicial review, and the censor's having to bear the burden in court of supporting his action in cutting or banning a film.

In examining the aftermath of *Times Film,* it is difficult to tell whether the case had much impact. The fact of continuing invalidation by lower courts of censors' rulings might simply have been a continuation and extension of trends which had been developing before *Times Film.* Thus, we see that in eleven appellate decisions between the decision and the *Freedman* ruling four years later, the censors won no cases on the merits (although they did win three cases on other grounds), and in some instances licensing itself was overturned on state constitutional or statutory grounds. *Times Film* seems to have been irrelevant. A considerable reduction in the number of film censorship agencies from two years before the decision to two years after it, coupled with the fact that many new agencies did not come into existence after the Court's legitimation of the core of film censorship, suggest the same thing. Despite this evidence, an argument has been made for the relevance of *Times Film* for these events and its impact on them. Randall asserts that Chief Justice Warren's dissent carried much weight with those affected, and that his statement reinforced the "considerable antilicensing swell that had been mounting in the American courts"[63] since *Burstyn* v. *Wilson.* Some state courts drew their rationale from Warren's statement, one going so far as to quote only from it (a dissent) while not mentioning the *Times Film* majority opinion.

Freedman's impact was and is perhaps more obvious. Carmen notes that the case "had the effect of throwing the entire censorship operation into a state of turmoil"[64] in Maryland, from which the case had come. Four state censorship boards existed at the time of the ruling; in less than a year, all—plus those in a number of cities—were taken to court on the grounds that their procedures did not conform to the ruling. Thus, in New York, whose censorship operation was perhaps the best known, the Board of Regents changed its procedures after *Freedman,* as supplemented by the *Trans-Lux per curiam* ruling of the high court, but these changes were overturned by the New York courts, utilizing the *Freedman* test. The remaining, older provisions of the state statute were then struck down in a remand of the U.S. Supreme Court's New York ruling. Three state legislatures ended film censorship by not renewing their relevant state statutes. Thus, censorship existed in principle after *Freedman* but in highly circumscribed form and had life in only a few locations. Efforts were made in some jurisdictions to comply, as in Chicago, where the city ordinance was amended, but the procedural requirements of the new ordinance were found to be unsatisfactory when challenged: the Supreme Court, in *Teitel* v. *Cusack*, struck down the ordinance, on the grounds that the review procedure still took far too long.

Thus far, in talking about the effects of the film regulation decisions, we have been talking mostly about impacts on public agencies, although the effect of *Burstyn* on film content has been noted. Another potential impact of *Freedman* should be raised here: Randall argues that there is an inverse relationship between informal censorship (that carried out, often on an *ad hoc* basis, by individual or private groups) and the existence of prior restraint. He suggests that where prior restraint exists with adequate procedural safeguards, of the sort required by the Court in *Freedman*, there may be less restriction on the availability of films than if no prior restraint whatsoever exists (the goal of many civil libertarians). This occurs in part because a film proprietor, even if he stood to win in the courts, may be unwilling to go to court to defend his interests. In these terms, *Freedman* provides the basis for protection, but the decrease in the number of units regulating films—a decrease resulting in part because of the invalidation of arrangements for failure to meet *Freedman* standards and their not being replaced by units satisfactory under the ruling —may mean that *Freedman* will contribute, along with other Supreme Court rulings, to an increase in informal censorship.

The effect of the Court's movie censorship rulings, Randall argues, shows that legal doctrine affected the censors, although many are unsympathetic with the Court's substantive rulings and may not know the law perfectly. However, they do not operate in a world of their own: they are affected by two important sets of actors. One set, despite the above comment about reluctance to litigate, is made up of the persons who wish to show a film. Thus, "the film proprietor enforces the doctrine on the censors."[65] In the four instances from April, 1968, to January, 1969, where the Dallas film board disagreed with the distributor about a film's classification, threat of court suit made the board back down. Included along with the exhibitors should be the distributors, either regional or national. As Justice Marshall has noted, they must be permitted to participate and often are the prime participants in a case when the exhibitor, perhaps for local reasons, doesn't want to go to court, but the distributor, perhaps to avoid difficulty with his film elsewhere, wants its showing permitted. The distributor may also be involved "behind the scenes" even when the exhibitor is the ostensible moving party; the former may provide counsel or financing for cases.

The other set of actors consists of the prosecutors who must proceed with censorship cases after the censor has made his decision. "An attorney general or a corporation counsel, though usually critical of the film proprietor, has no desire to undertake an unsuccessful legal defense of a censorship order. In effect, then, legal departments exercise a continuing check on censorial authority."[66]

That government attorneys are not the only ones who follow the law, even though they may be less than pleased with the Court's doctrine, is shown by the actions of some lower courts. While we do not have enough information to provide a broad, nationwide picture, we do know what has gone on in some states. One is Illinois, which provides some examples of courts' voluntary adherence to the Supreme Court's doctrine. The Illinois Supreme Court's self-initiated reversal of its decision that Henry Miller's book, *Tropic of Cancer,* was obscene, after the federal high court's application of the *Jacobellis* national community standard ruling to that same book in *Grove Press* v. *Gerstein,* has been noted earlier. Another example of the same type of action occurred when the state high court reversed its affirmance of the obscenity conviction of Lenny Bruce for a nightclub act because it felt the U.S. Supreme Court, also in *Jacobellis,* had said one could not convict for obscenity if the obscenity outweighs the social importance of the item (or act) in question. An analyst of the Illinois court's actions has noted, "The state's highest court . . . has been forced to follow, reluctantly in recent cases, the mandatory guidelines of the United States Supreme Court." The former court "has been increasingly frustrated in its attempt to conform its concept of obscenity with that of the nation's highest tribunal,"[67] he adds, because the U.S. Supreme Court has not provided adequate guidelines for others and because it does not share the view of those in state legislatures that "obscenity" is an evil which must be within the power of the state to restrict more than the Court now permits.

The frustration of lower courts does not always result in voluntary withdrawal of decisions already rendered or in following, even begrudgingly, the high court's doctrine. Instead, the frustration often spills over in criticism of the Court and resistance to its rulings. One example is the ruling of Kentucky Court of Appeals Judge Osborne, in *Cain* v. *Commonwealth,* where that court sustained Kentucky's obscenity statute. Confirming our earlier observation that splits in the court are a variable relevant to impact, the judge held that two Supreme Court decisions were not controlling because the Court had not arrived at an "opinion of the Court": "We do not interpret the *Redrup* v. *New York* opinion as being controlling upon the issue here before us for the simple reason that there was no clear majority of the Court in support of any of the numerous principles set out therein." (What makes this particularly interesting is that the Court was *not* split, but had issued a *per curiam* opinion, with two Justices dissenting. Perhaps because the Court had split badly on other cases, Judge Osborne saw them as without a majority opinion here.)

With respect to the argument that *Memoirs* v. *Massachusetts* had added to the definition of obscenity the test that an item must not be declared obscene unless it were "utterly without redeeming social importance," Judge Osborne made the same contention, and said that the test, while agreed to by three Justices, was not law because the other Justices had not agreed. But he was not content to rest there, lashing out at Justice Douglas, who, he said, "has never purported to follow the law established by his court or any other court where matters of obscenity are involved." He then broadened his attack: "While the courts have vacillated and overexplained, divided and fought, the sentiments of the people of this country have been clear and unassailable. . . . It seems to be universally believed everywhere, except in the halls of the judiciary, that obscenity as such is not entitled to the constitutional protection awarded free speech."

Frustration may also explain in part why jurisdictions continue with statutes very much like those long since rejected by the Supreme Court. A review of existing statutes after *Ginsberg* v. *New York* produced the finding that there were still nine statutes modeled after the *old* New York statute, dealing with the portrayal of crimes of violence and bloodshed (the obscenity of violence rather than of sex), even though that statute had been thrown out years before in *Winters* v. *New York* on grounds of vagueness, and seven statutes limiting available material to that acceptable to youth, resoundingly rejected by the Court in 1957 in *Butler* v. *Michigan*. The same review also revealed how quickly communities pounce on a procedure when the Court upholds one which may serve to restrict material (although, as noted, this did not occur with *Times Film*); at least twenty city councils across the country were found to have passed statutes like that validated in *Ginsberg* in less than a year from the time of the decision. Additional impact of *Ginsberg* is shown by the numerous state statutes passed in 1969 legislative sessions, with language closely tracking that of the New York statute, and in the language of proposed federal legislation dealing with the mailing of obscene material or advertising to minors.

While frustration and resistance have occurred and continue to occur, resulting from disagreement with the Court's limitation on what can be included within the definition of obscenity and unhappiness with the Court's ambiguity, one can talk more specifically about the matters which the Court did settle in the series of decisions starting with *Roth* and which were left unsettled. As noted in a study of Oregon obscenity policy, "The court *did* settle one problem by saying that obscenity statutes *were* constitutionally permissible."[68] That the court included a definition of obscenity appeared to many to indicate that statutes should no longer rely on the standard list of words (*obscene, lewd, indecent*, and so on) without definition. And legislatures did work to change their definitions to include new Court standards. In a number of jurisdictions, the politics of obscenity was the politics of a search for a definition. However, when the Court kept changing standards by adding elements to the definition, some began to argue that no legislature could keep up with the Court's twists and turns and that it ought to be left to the courts to read into the statutes whatever the Supreme Court had most recently decided. That legislatures did have difficulty was acknowledged by a state court judge: "It is obvious that the legislature has experienced some difficulty in keeping up with the rapidly changing United States constitutional concept of what constitutes obscenity."[69]

With respect to particular parts of the Supreme Court's standard, there seemed to be little disagreement at first that the local community was involved, although how the community standard was to be ascertained was often thought to be far more difficult. Resistance developed to the idea of a national standard propounded in *Jacobellis,* particularly because of the plurality opinion in that case. That an item should be judged in terms of the "average man" was resisted by those who felt that the obscenity "problem" concerned dissemination of material to children and therefore one should be able to judge material with reference to them. However, what the "average man" was did not seem to pose problems. One court doubted whether anyone could deal with the concept "prurient interest" without resorting to a dictionary. That the standard appeared to have been restricted to "hard-core pornography" seems to have been understood, because it led to attempts to develop alternative definitions of other material so that the latter could be controlled. The definition of "harmful materials" in terms of "utterly without redeeming social importance for minors" in New York was, as noted earlier, accepted by the Court.

The conflict which can occur in the application of the standards of the Court's rulings to a given item is shown by a recent Oregon incident. The Oregon Supreme Court upheld an obscenity conviction based on the sale of a book entitled *Lesbian Roommate,* holding that the book's purpose was to incite lascivious thoughts and that it was patently offensive with respect to representation of sexual matters. The bookseller sought habeas corpus relief in the federal district court. There Judge Solomon not only found that the book was not patently offensive, but he also held that inciting lascivious thoughts did not satisfy the Supreme Court's standards concerning appeal to prurient interest. In reaching his conclusion, he cited from *Memoirs* that several tests must be met *together* before an item could be declared obscene, and then proceeded to compare the book in question with others held not obscene by the Supreme Court (U.S.); thus he was directly applying specific Supreme Court decisions to reach his result.

Censors' knowledge of the law of censorship has been seen to be "imperfect." The degree of lack of knowledge, confirmation of the greater amount of heat than light in the obscenity area, is thoroughly portrayed in a study by Thomas Barth of the impact of obscenity cases in several

Wisconsin communities and throughout that state. He put a series of factual questions relating to Supreme Court obscenity cases to district attorneys and local policy makers. With the former, he found only 32.7 percent of the responses correct, and almost one fifth incorrect, with a third indicating not sure and the remainder not responding to the questions. No district attorney answered correctly all six questions asked, and Barth was able to rate only 20 percent as having high perception of Court policy (medium perception: 42 percent, low: 20 percent). Full-time district attorneys did rate somewhat higher than part-time prosecutors. What is particularly striking about Barth's findings is that prosecutors involved in obscenity cases, and who therefore one might presume would have examined the law, still felt some books to be obscene the Supreme Court had said were not so. "If such was the situation with three men who had presumably prepared cases in this area, one can assume the lack of perception of Supreme Court policy to be even greater among others." More broadly, with respect to magazines, "The highest number of responses which indicated that the material was legally obscene came in the three categories of magazines which had been specifically considered by the Supreme Court and found not to be so."[70] Results for local policy makers were much the same.

Barth also studied another group of individuals particularly relevant to the existence of printed matter in any community: the booksellers. He found that they were no less ignorant of the Supreme Court decisions than were prosecutors and other local officials, a finding confirmed by Levine, who found, "Only a small minority of booksellers are enlightened about the supposedly momentous decisions of the United States Supreme Court,"[71] and that only 3 percent of those he studied sought, on a regular basis, legal advice about the books they sold. One might explain the "ignorance" of the public officials as resulting from conflict between the thrust of their jobs, to control or limit obscenity, and the Supreme Court's rulings. However, this is difficult with booksellers, who have been beneficiaries of most Supreme Court decisions. Lack of knowledge, and failure to act on that knowledge, would not be in their interest, if one defines that interest as a desire to be able to make available the broadest possible range of material. But many booksellers apparently do not define their interests that way, particularly if they are not sole or major wholesalers/distributors in large cities. However, they also do not respond to decisions which suggest they should tighten up what they do. Thus, few appear to have altered their practices in the light of *Ginzburg,* which allowed conviction for "pandering," and allowed methods of distribution and sale to be taken into account in obscenity prosecutions. Only 5 percent of the booksellers studied by Levine had "consciously instigated" changes in the way they operated as a direct result of *Ginzburg* in the year subsequent to that decision.

The booksellers not only know little about relevant law but appear to be quite willing to comply with requests of local officials to eliminate items the officials find distasteful or claim to be obscene, even when the officials may not be making judgments which comport with Supreme Court decisions. Private suggestions by officials are included in the "informal censorship" of which Randall writes. Barth notes that when officials suggest removal of an item of printed matter, "dealers and distributors are highly susceptible . . ., especially in the smaller and medium-sized counties and cities."[72] The booksellers are very much aware of norms within their communities, and they do not wish to handle material which might offend their clients. This may explain why many booksellers and distributors favor statutes which provide for proceedings against books before individuals are prosecuted for sale of the materials; they wish to be warned by the courts before being treated like "common criminals." They would prefer to be on the "safe side." Therefore, they "operate under a set of assumptions that is undoubtedly more restrictive than the Court's,"[73] and a community will end up having available as reading matter what the dealers themselves, through a combination of personal views and perceptions of what the community will tolerate, determine. "To a great extent, public access to books about sex is dependent upon the openmindedness and the moral irresponsibility of individuals who comprise the bookselling profession."[74]

CHAPTER 5

Impacts in Issue-Areas:B

CRIMINAL PROCEDURE

Introduction. Nowhere is it as clear as in the area of criminal procedure how much we are victims, and have been victims, of the "upper-court myth." Our attention has been drawn largely to the decisions of the Supreme Court establishing new rules of criminal procedure, and attacks made on the decisions have continued to focus our attention on them. To be sure, many of the rulings have been dramatic, as in the case of *Gideon* v. *Wainwright,* initiated by a Florida prisoner writing directly to the Chief Justice of the United States and represented, once the Court decided to hear his case, by Abe Fortas, later himself a Justice. And certainly there have been so many important decisions in this area that one may have little time available for more than simply digesting what the Court has said. Because the Court has continued to insist on incorporating the Bill of Rights into the Fourteenth Amendment Due Process clause on a piecemeal basis ("selective incorporation"), and has now incorporated much of the Bill of Rights, one is inundated with cases. To name just a few, one has *Mapp* v. *Ohio,* applying to the states the exclusionary rule with respect to illegally seized evidence; *Gideon* v. *Wainwright,* on right to counsel; *Pointer* v. *Texas,* on the right to confrontation of witnesses; *Malloy* v. *Hogan,* concerning the right not to have to incriminate oneself; and *Miranda* v. *Arizona,* excluding from trial all confessions obtained when the defendant has not been warned of his rights when taken into custody. In addition, one has other cases in which the content of the incorporated provision is developed and explicated, and still others where points of federal criminal procedure are developed, absent the question of application to the states.

Whatever the reason for the attention to the Supreme Court's rulings, such attention is both incomplete and somewhat misguided. It is incomplete because the entire law enforcement process outside the courts is ignored; it is perhaps misguided because the decisions of the Court may mean little or have little impact on the law enforcement world or perhaps even an impact rather different from what the Justices may have intended. Over thirty years ago, Thurman Arnold argued, "The temper of the police commissioner is of much more significance on governmental interference with rights of respectable citizens [one might say: any citizens, particularly the downtrodden] than appellate-court utterances."[1]

More recently, it has been suggested that there is a considerable difference between what Herbert Packer calls the Due Process Model of law enforcement, involving an adversary approach, and utilized by the courts in considering most criminal procedure questions, and the Crime Control Model, in which managerial considerations of law enforcement and order maintenance are paramount. Lack of congruence between the two models, or between the views of (appellate) judges and law enforcement personnel, helps explain lack of impact of court decisions in this area. So does the general organization of police departments, which are often quite decentralized, and the fact that, of everyone on the force, the policeman on the beat has the greatest individual discretion to act. To obtain due process of law, Wilson writes, "requires administrative regularity, strongly enforced department rules, and central authority. These are weakened, and thus regard for the rule of law is weakened, by decentralization." Where a police department is most concerned about order maintenance (rather than law enforcement), "central command [is necessary] to insure a reasonably common definition of appropriate order . . . and the protection of the civil liberties of suspects and witnesses."[2]

That results of decisions may be different from what we might presume the Justices intended, when looked at from the point of view of the accused, is somewhat chilling. If the Court intended to produce more protections and fewer occur, is there not something seriously wrong? One cannot show empirically that the reverse of intended action occurs, but a recent finding supports the general assertion and should be kept in mind. Oaks and Lehman, in a study of the administration of criminal justice in Illinois, found that prosecutors were trying harder to obtain guilty pleas because they had found lower rates of findings of guilty by judges. These lower rates stemmed from "the imperatives of the due process revolution, and especially the right to appeal."[3] The prosecutor was able to bargain with the accused because of the long sentences which might be handed down at trial if the defendant pleaded not guilty and was found guilty. The increased use of plea-bargaining by the prosecution, to the extent effective and thus resulting in higher rates of guility pleas, led Oaks and Lehman to comment: "The due process revolution can be said to have produced its antithesis if the increment in persons convicted . . . was drawn from those who would not have been convicted if they had chanced trial or who would have been dismissed had they not pleaded guilty before making motions that would have resulted in dismissal." Thus, "the prosecutor [may] be able partially to neutralize *Escobedo* and *Miranda* by offering yet more radical charge and sentence reductions."[4] While Oaks and Lehman are only hypothesizing, the possible effect of the Supreme Court decisions—once we look at the place where the ultimate impact occurs—should make us think carefully in this area.

Right to Counsel. We have little systematic evidence, of a before-and-after sort, on the effect of the Supreme Court's key right-to-counsel cases, most particularly *Gideon* v. *Wainwright,* providing for representation of indigents at trial when a serious penalty is involved, thus covering felonies and major misdemeanors but also including the extensions of right to counsel—both forward (to appeals) and backwards (to earlier "critical stages of the proceeding"). Most of what we know is spotty. Part of this may be explained by the fact that compliance of one sort or another with *Gideon* and its progeny was generally forthcoming. This area may be one where the court says something and, lo and behold, that "something" appears. To be sure, there were arguments after *Gideon,* but they tended to be over whether assigned counsel or public defender systems were better and over at what time in the proceedings defendants should be represented.

Part of the compliance with *Gideon* may have been the result of the earlier indirect impact of another Supreme Court ruling. In *Johnson* v. *Zerbst,* the Court had required counsel for indigents in *federal* felony trials and held that counsel could be waived only if that waiver were intelligent. The case clearly involved only federal jurisdiction, yet, after a provision embodying the rationale of the case was inserted in the Federal Rules of Criminal Procedure in 1946, more than twenty states adopted the rule *before Gideon* was decided. Nonetheless, after *Gideon,* many legislatures acted quickly to do something about the case: "To facilitate compliance with *Gideon* (and other subsequent implementing cases), legislatures and courts in twenty-three states took specific actions within twenty-four months to expand or improve their assigned counsel or public defender systems in varying degrees."[5]

The first issue of the *Defender Newsletter,* published by the Defender Project of the National Legal Aid and Defender Association, also asserted, "Whatever the exact legal import of the *Gideon* decision and the others handed down recently, it is clear that they have been taken as a call to action by many attorneys, judges, and legislators." Noted in the *Newsletter* were new public defender laws, statutes authorizing units of government to compensate attorneys, increases in compensation for both assigned attorneys and public defenders, and extension by some states of appointment of counsel to periods before trial. The U.S. Congress, in the Criminal Justice Act of 1964, provided compensated counsel in federal criminal cases, as the result of *Gideon,* and, later, when the Supreme Court in *Mempa* v. *Rhay,* had extended the right to situations before trial and to probation revocation hearings, amendments were introduced by conservative Republican Senator Hruska of Nebraska to bring the act in line with the newer decisions, and eliminate the "gap between the point at which the defendant is now entitled to counsel and the point at which counsel may receive a fee under the act."

An example of the way compliance can come about is provided by the experience in Pittsburgh after the decisions in the *Wade* and *Gilbert* cases, providing a right to representation at police "lineups." Prior to the decisions, there had been no standing police regulation on the conduct of such proceedings. Within days after the decision, an applicable directive was published. The public defender, the county bar association, and legal aid all looked at the practice. Legal aid agreed to provide, initially and temporarily, counsel for those in lineup; the bar association trial committee provided police with a list of volunteers to serve as counsel (these were experienced defense attorneys). What is interesting is that police initiated meetings with bar officials and other interested persons, rather than waiting until pressed by someone to comply with the decision. "The *Wade* decision has stimulated a beneficial review of lineup procedures by the Pittsburgh police in an effort to improve techniques and meet constitutional standards."[6] While this may sound like a "fairy story" in comparison with the "horror stories" often recounted about police practices or resistance to change in general and to Supreme Court decisions in particular, it does illustrate that an "era of good feeling" can exist and may have characterized much of the aftermath of the right-to-counsel decisions, at least those providing the right at trial, even if police were not happy about the presence of counsel at interrogation.

The states from which both *Gideon* and *Douglas* v. *California* (the latter providing for right to counsel on first appeal) had come were clearly affected by the rulings. In Florida, the Florida Supreme Court, anticipating the U.S. Supreme Court's decision, adopted a rule at the suggestion of the Judicial Council that a prisoner could move, before the court that sentenced him, that his sentence be vacated on the grounds that it was imposed in violation of the laws or Constitution of Florida or the United States; this was potentially applicable to 4,500 prisoners. And, as we have seen, many prisoners were released after *Gideon* when prosecutors would not retry them. Florida also adopted a new statewide public defender system; this was also initiated by the Judicial Council in anticipation of the decision. It became effective July 1, 1963, quite soon after *Gideon* was handed down. In California, the results of *Douglas* were varied. Courts which had appointed counsel in appeals only after a conviction following a plea of not guilty began to appoint them as well in appeals following guilty pleas. Public defender offices were requested to handle appeals of indigents. A "marked increase" in appointment of private counsel immediately after *Douglas* was noted in Los Angeles County, also.

The reactions mentioned thus far have been fairly specific. There are two other matters, both more general and more speculative, which should also be mentioned. One points in the direction of broader ramifications for *Gideon* and other right-to-counsel decisions. The other suggests that the gains already mentioned may be in large measure illusory. As to the first, Casper argues that the establishment of agencies the specific function of which is to provide attorneys to serve as counsel for a particular class of individuals will result in more litigation on behalf of these people *as a group* than was the case when they were being represented by "private" counsel primarily involved in other matters. Just as the Supreme Court, to the extent it has diverged from the case-by-case approach, has paid more attention to the broader aspects of the litigation before it, so lawyers, whose employment is a result of the right-to-counsel cases, will pay more attention to the broader aspects of the cases with which they deal. The "lobbying" function of this group of lawyers will be noticeable, and this leads Casper to say, "The use of litigation for 'political' ends is on the increase." Thus, "The decisions of the Warren Court have not only affected political and social policy in the areas they have touched, but they have also contributed both directly . . . and indirectly to the development of a segment of the bar much more attuned to and concerned with the use of litigation for 'activist' goals."[7] This effect is somewhat like that of decisions which "gave increasing freedom and opportunities to civil rights organizations to press [the Court] . . . for ever widening reforms."[8]

On the other hand, we find the argument raised by Blumberg, who, while not explicitly dealing with impact, explores the environment into which Court decisions would be injected. Looking at the practice of law in the high-volume criminal court setting, he suggests that constraints imposed by the daily working relationships of defense attorneys and by the organizational situation in which they find themselves tend to undercut or negate any benefits which high-sounding appellate court rulings might bring. Commitment to client shifts to (at least an unstated) commitment to keep things going in the court structure. The lawyer's chief function may become that of getting the client to plead guilty, to get the matter over with. Blumberg observes, "It is popularly assumed that the police, through forced confessions, and the district attorney, employing still other pressures, are most instrumental in the inducement of an accused to plead guilty. . . . It is actually the defendant's own counsel who is most effective in this role."[9] While a defendant in some cases may be better off pleading guilty to a reduced charge, Blumberg's suggestion is that the thrust of the lawyer's immediate work situation and his concern for such matters as being paid tend to supersede the adversary role the higher courts see for him when they decide cases increasing rights to assigned counsel. This gives importance to his observation, "A particular decision may rest upon a legally impeccable rationale; at the same time it may be rendered nugatory or self-defeating by contingencies imposed by aspects of social reality of which the lawmakers are themselves unaware."[10]

An extension of right to counsel which has begun to receive much attention, because of its effect on a specialized subsystem of the judicial system and on those connected with it, is its extension to juvenile court proceedings, in the case of *In Re Gault*. More than right to counsel was involved in *Gault*, but that aspect has received particular attention, and it might be argued that the other rights provided (including the right to confront witnesses) cannot easily be enforced without implementation of the counsel right. American Bar Association President William T. Gossett recently urged additional work by lawyers to implement the decision. The decision, coupled with the report of the President's Commission on Law Enforcement and the Administration of Justice, he said:

> seem to me to have offered to lawyers a second chance to form the lead battalion in a new line of march against juvenile delinquency. . . . Rarely has there been greater opportunity to help fashion new law and related processes in a more challenging or critical field. There has been a loud, clear call for help that reaffirms the imperatives of our traditional public responsibility; and more of us should be responding. . . .[11]

In a survey of juvenile judges about developments after the decision, Monrad Paulsen found that the use of defender systems had been extended to juvenile courts after *Gault*, at least in large cities. New legislation had been introduced and passed in several states extending compensation to appointed attorneys in juvenile court appearances. Some jurisdictions had devised forms to tell parents of their children's rights (not unlike "*Miranda* cards"), but he felt that it was unclear how well juveniles' right to counsel was being made known. Paulsen did feel, "Whatever the scheme for providing counsel, lawyers are generally being made available to juveniles in serious delinquency cases,"[12] and some states were making the decision retroactive in effect.

Observations carried out in three large cities make one hesitate about accepting Paulsen's generalization. Failure to provide the rights indicated in *Gault* was noted, and notification of rights to parents or minors was generally only partial or prejudicial. In two cities, notice about the right to be represented was mailed to parents, but there was no mention of the right to have a lawyer appointed, and the mailed notice was considered adequate by the judges, who did not again raise the question at hearings before them. In one city, "In not 1 case among 59 were the parents and minor adequately advised on their right to counsel."[13] The observers also asserted that if the judges had been required to say that no inference would be drawn from a juvenile's failure to speak on his own behalf—part of the right not to incriminate himself—"there would not have been any case in the three cities where the privilege was fully implemented."[14] In one city, to avoid the thrust of *Gault*, separate "formal" and "informal" calendars for juvenile cases were created. In the former, where the possibility of commitment was involved, a lawyer was appointed, but those in the latter category were "declared not subject to commitment, and Gault's requirements are not implemented."[15]

It should also be recognized that appointment of counsel in juvenile cases may not bring the same results as appointment in adult criminal cases. As noted, not all the full panoply of rights accompany the juvenile "defendants" to which his adult counterpart is entitled. A study of the public defender's role in juvenile court proceedings in "Metro" after *Gault* revealed that more findings of guilty resulted when public defenders represented juveniles than when they represented adults in other courts in the same jurisdiction; there were also fewer guilty pleas in the juvenile courts and fewer acquittals by motion of the state. The observers concluded, "Juvenile clients do not get the same standard of representation that is accorded to adult defendants,"[16] but they indicated that a lesser standard for guilt than the "beyond a reasonable doubt" standard of "adult" courts is used in juvenile proceedings and asserted that their evidence did not show the public defender had "sold out"; he can and did help in getting dismissals and lighter sentences for his clients.

It should be noted that, in part as a result of *Gault,* the "beyond a reasonable doubt" standard, as well as other protections from the criminal justice system, are being "imported" into the juvenile system. Thus, in the case of *In Re Urbasek,* Justice Underwood argued that the reasons which produced the *Gault* ruling "logically require that a finding of delinquency for misconduct, which would be criminal if charged against an adult, is valid only when the acts of delinquency are proved beyond a reasonable doubt to have been committed by the juvenile charged. . . . The language of that opinion exhibits a spirit that transcends the specific issues there involved." The impact of *Gault* was carried further as a result of *Urbasek,* which was cited by a Rhode Island judge who held, "*All* of the safeguards that are afforded to an adult criminal trial should be, and constitutionally must be applied to a juvenile case"; to be included were a right to jury trial and guilt beyond a reasonable doubt. "To interpret otherwise," Judge DeCiantis wrote in the *Rindell* case, "is tantamount to rendering Gault a mere exercise in rhetoric rather than [a] bold and eloquent decision." While these decisions may at the present time be isolated, they suggest some possible impacts of *Gault,* whether directly, or with the impact of cases utilizing *Gault,* at second remove.

That those involved in the bureaucracy handling juvenile delinquents have been less affected may be the case. At least this is the impression one gets from a report of the effect of *Gault* on those administering juvenile training schools. A number of such administrators reported little direct impact of the case, although this was true in some instances because the states (New York and Illinois) had already enacted *Gault*-type statutory protections. It is claimed, however, that "some superintendents are observing their training school children are being taught not to admit any of their actions and are looking to attorneys to speak for them," and that the number of juveniles in training schools released on or requesting *habeas corpus* hearings increased as a result of the decision. A work load increase on training school staff is also claimed: "Throughout the nation, the number of court hearings involving training school staff is increasing and staff are expected to prove their allegations within a legal framework."[17] The unhappiness at having to work in an "alien" framework, albeit one the Court has decided is necessary to protect the rights of juveniles, seems clear from the last statement.

Before *Gault*, and foreshadowing it, the Supreme Court had decided a case involving the rights of juveniles which has also had an effect on both those rights and on juvenile court procedures. That case is *Kent* v. *U.S.*, in which the Court declared that a juvenile was entitled to be represented by an attorney at a hearing at which it would be determined if he should be waived over to adult court for criminal trial there. Some states promptly distinguished the case, saying it applied only to the District of Columbia, where it had arisen, or that Kent had a lawyer—the same basis on which some distinguished away *Escobedo*. The New Mexico Supreme Court did this in ruling that certification of an indigent juvenile to the criminal court, where he received a two- to ten-year sentence for aggravated battery, was not a critical stage of the proceeding requiring appointment of counsel. Courts in Virginia and Maryland did the same thing, but were more tentative, and used the nonretroactivity of *Kent* (and *Gault*) to justify their decisions.

In Texas, we find a situation where the legislature was more willing to comply than were the courts. There the practice had been to judge a juvenile's age at the time of trial, not time of offense, unlike many other jurisdictions, which use the latter. The legislature changed this, in a statute an observer has called "a model for compliance with *Kent*."[18] The changed rule was held unconstitutional by the Texas court, which, even after *Kent*, upheld murder convictions where no notation about a murder charge had been made in the juvenile court record.

In Indiana, after a short delay, the *Kent* procedural safeguards were made mandatory for all Indiana juvenile courts, in *Summers* v. *State*, where the matter was raised by the Indiana Supreme Court on its own. However, *Summers* to some extent involves less than *Kent*, in that there is no requirement that counsel have access to a child's social history records, on which the state might base its decision to request trial as an adult; in other respects, the decision requires more than did the U.S. Supreme Court in specific criteria set and in the provision that an improper waiver deprives the district court of jurisdiction over the juvenile.

***Right to Counsel Plus:* Escobedo *and* Miranda.** Continuing our discussion of cases with a right-to-counsel element, we turn to perhaps the most controversial of the Supreme Court's 1960's criminal procedure cases,

Escobedo v. *Illinois* and *Miranda* v. *Arizona.* These cases, because of their broad sweep, were particularly important for law enforcement agencies. Prior to the cases, High Court rulings on interrogation matters had not posed much problem for many police departments, because, decided on a case-by-case basis and limited to a certain set of facts, they did not deal with common situations. *Escobedo* and *Miranda,* and particularly the latter, did deal with more common situations.

While usually discussed together, the doctrinal thrust of the two cases differs. *Escobedo* is essentially a right-to-counsel case, deriving from a situation in which someone in custody was denied opportunity to see his attorney while he was being questioned by police. *Miranda* is basically a confession case, with the Court holding that confessions obtained when a suspect has not been informed of his rights when taken into custody are inherently invalid. *One* of the *Miranda* rights is the right to be represented by an attorney, and another is to have an attorney appointed if one cannot afford one's own. The two cases are grouped together because of the feeling that the presence of a lawyer will make it more difficult for the police to enforce the law and convict criminals, just as right to counsel is perhaps the most basic right provided in *Gault.*

Views of the effects of the cases clearly differ. District attorneys testifying before a Senate subcommittee disagreed: one said that there was too little information to determine the effect of *Miranda* on the crime rate, while his colleague from another city said the case had had a "frightful impact" and a "damaging effect" on law enforcement, and had caused crime to increase. Both did agree that fewer suspects had talked, but were clearly in disagreement in going beyond that. Members of the President's Crime Commission also disagreed. The majority, in the report published in February, 1967, felt it too early to determine the case's effect, but four members (Jaworski, Malone, Powell, and Storey) asserted in their "Additional Views," "If the majority opinion in *Miranda* is implemented in its full sweep, it could mean the virtual elimination of pretrial interrogation of suspects . . . . Few can doubt the adverse effect of *Miranda* upon the law enforcement process."[19]

It should be noted that, despite specific objections raised to it and cries of "Horror!" *Miranda* may have received greater immediate acceptance—at least of the fact of its existence—than had *Escobedo,* because "more key police officials seemed to have anticipated this change than they had in regard to *Escobedo.*"[20] Here we find a parallel to the situation in the school prayer cases, where *Engel,* though less far-reaching than *Schempp,* provoked greater negative feedback because less expected, while the latter, more far-reaching, decision stirred up less hotheaded reaction because people were ready for it.

One effect of the case was to shift the focus of those examining the criminal law process away from the trial itself and toward the period between arrest and trial. Another effect was the increased recognition that court decisions would not by themselves change police behavior; attitudes of the public about what the police should do (maintain order or enforce the law, for example) were also important. When one researcher wrote, "With some exceptions, recent Supreme Court decisions involving [procedural] rights provide a relatively strong measure of protection against abuses, particularly when interpreted carefully by an enlightened police administration, conscientious prosecutors and cautious judges,"[21] his use of the words *enlightened, conscientious,* and *cautious* suggest that the protections will not automatically be forthcoming.

Just as the views of the effects of the cases differed from individual to individual, surveys which were conducted in individual jurisdictions did not produce identical results, although their thrust was generally in one direction. For example, a Los Angeles County survey by District Attorney Evelle Younger showed confessions essential to successful prosecution in only a small percentage of cases. In St. Louis, it was found, "Only one-tenth of 1 per cent of those arrested were released as a direct result of the *Miranda* decision."[22] Earlier surveys after *Escobedo* add something. A Brooklyn judge studied 1,000 indictments occurring after that case, and found incriminating confessions involved in only 86 cases. In more than a third of those cases (30), the defendant said his confession was voluntary; in 42 of the other cases, an initial challenge to the voluntariness of the confession was withdrawn and the defendant pled guilty. In only one of the remaining fourteen cases was a confession ruled inadmissible.

After *Miranda,* a similar study by the same judge produced comparable results (275 confession issues in 2,000 felony cases, with only 22 contests at trial about admissibility of the confession and only two motions to suppress granted). In Detroit, in a study covering periods in 1961 and 1965, it was found that confessions were crucial in a smaller percentage of the cases in the period after *Miranda* than before. A thorough study from California also suggests that the cases may not adversely affect rates of conviction. In that state, one was dealing not only with *Escobedo* but with its application by the California courts, in *People* v. *Dorado;* the California judges held that *as the result of Escobedo* police had to advise an accused of his right to remain silent and to consult with counsel prior to interrogation, basic parts of what the U.S. Supreme Court was to decide in *Miranda.* In a thirteen-month period (1965–66), there were 134 cases in the *Escobedo-Dorado* category in the appellate courts; affirmances of trial court convictions rose, not decreased, during the period studied, and occurred at the rate of 65–70 percent. In one county where police had been giving the warnings even before *Dorado,* the felony conviction rate was *higher* than the statewide average, leading an observer to assert, "In California a successful conviction rate does not appear to depend on avoidance of the requirement of *Escobedo.*"[23]

All of these studies, however, raise questions of measurement. While the last-cited California study involved appellate court decisions, the other studies involve trial courts. None so far cited involve the "intake" process, that is, they do not deal with effects on arrests (as opposed to convictions), on refusals to indict, or on the behavior of law enforcement officers generally. Thus, "Statistics derived from convictions and affirmances are misleading when they are used to show that a ruling like *Miranda* had had little impact on the balancing of the rights of the individual with the rights of society. . . . . What would be far more material . . . would be studies to establish the frequency of nonarrests and of dismissals at preliminary stages of the judicial process . . . ."[24] Police may continue to want to interrogate, for reasons other than producing convictions; they may not want to give up the interrogation. What many consider to be abuses in the law enforcement process may continue to exist if outside the purview of the courts.

Certainly, what we have mentioned so far has not told very much about actual police behavior in response to *Miranda*. If *Miranda* potentially affects police more than the prosecutor, except with respect to cases already prepared for trial when the ruling was handed down, then knowing about the latter's response is not enough. Available studies of police responses, like those mentioned below, are concentrated upon the detective bureau and perhaps also upon superior officers. Perhaps the discretion such officers have as interrogators limits the amount of change produced by the decision, and perhaps *Miranda's* effects do not extend further down in the police department. However, Milner's data that, in the four Wisconsin cities he studied, almost four fifths of all police officers *dis*approved of *Miranda,* while only one fifth approved, suggests the importance of examining how police react *behaviorally* to *Miranda*. Milner found little relationship between attitude and amount of formal education. Those newest to the police forces had the lowest rates of approval.

Before turning to some surveys more systematic than those mentioned above, we might note a few other radiations of the impact of *Miranda*. For one thing, the authors of the interrogation volume cited by the Court updated and changed their book. The thrust of the authors' new argument is that confessions can still be obtained and suspects want to talk. Material from earlier editions clearly conflicting with *Miranda* has been deleted, and material on how to comply with both the spirit and letter of the case has been added. Military law was also affected by *Miranda*. Counsel—to all servicemen, not just indigents—had been available since before *Gideon,* although the Court of Military Appeals had held in the *Wimberly* case that counsel was not denied when it was not requested by a defendant. Military departments, upon hearing of the *Miranda* ruling, "advised their law enforcement personnel of the decision and issued instructions calculated to require compliance."[25]

The case in which the application of *Miranda* was recognized by the Court of Military Appeals had been tried the day after *Miranda* was decided, with the military lawyers in the case working from *The New*

York Times account of the case in applying it to the situation with which they were working. When that case was appealed, it was held, in the *Tempia* case, that *Wimberly* was inapplicable for cases tried on or after the *Miranda* decision date. Notice of this decision was promptly circulated to judge advocates so that they would know "that the military requirement for full compliance with *Miranda* had been confirmed."[26] It has been argued that the effects of *Miranda* on the military (through the *Tempia* ruling) will be greater than the effects of *Miranda* in civilian life, because "the controlled military atmosphere has invited circumvention" of the right to counsel upon request: "The rules found in *Tempia* have offset the psychological advantages of the controlled military atmosphere."[27]

If we return to the appellate court level, we can see that there have been a number of instances in which *Miranda* was held not to apply to the facts of cases before those courts and thus its effect blunted. While a Virginia court held that *Miranda* did apply when a defendant was requested to answer questions at the jailhouse and would not have been permitted to leave (thus the questioning was custodial) and while questioning about cigarette papers during a warrant-based search of a college room, absent *Miranda* warnings, led to a voiding of a conviction, one finds, on the other hand, situations such as the following where *Miranda* was distinguished:

1. Detention and interrogation at the Mexican border leading to a seizure of heroin and cocaine held not custodial.
2. A request for proof of ownership of a car on the street held not custodial.
3. Questioning of an erratic driver at roadside, with lack of *Miranda* warnings, did not void a conviction, although the policeman did intend to arrest, because he had not told driver he was not free to go.
4. Questioning of the wife of a stabbing victim at the station house, when the interrogation had not focused on her, held noncustodial.

The most systematic surveys available on the effect of *Miranda* are, with the exception of Milner's Wisconsin study, station house studies, based on observation and interviews. Carried out in New Haven, Connecticut, Pittsburgh, and Washington, D.C., they provide much useful information about the types of impact the *Miranda* case had. In the first place, there was generally an effort made by police officials to inform their subordinates of the decision and how it might be complied with. In Washington, D.C., General Order No. 9–c was issued a month after *Miranda.* It set out in elaborate fashion both the requirements *and reasoning* of the decision, and it required warning of rights prior to any custodial interrogation.

In New Haven, detectives were told of the decision by their superiors but seemed not to understand; they did increase their understanding as a result of more complete lectures on the case included in in-service training courses. "As the detectives learned more of what *Miranda* required through the summer, they increasingly informed suspects of their rights. They were markedly more likely to give some advice when the suspect was accused of a serious crime."[28] "*Miranda* cards" (with lists of the rights specified by the Supreme Court in its decision) were given to detectives and patrolmen in New Haven, with instructions that they be read to the suspect at the time of his arrest. And in Pittsburgh, where some aspects of the *Miranda* rules had been part of departmental policy (right to remain silent, and, post-*Escobedo,* right to counsel), the additional aspects were communicated.

While superiors made efforts to disseminate information about the case, the rates at which the warnings were given was not high, although it was found to improve as detectives and patrolmen became more accustomed to the ruling. In Washington, the warning rate went from somewhat over 50 percent to 75 percent after the decision, as far as station house warnings were concerned, and interrogations decreased somewhat. A separate field study—of on-the-street situations—suggested an extremely low rate of warning giving. When we say that the warning rate increased, we do not mean that all four warnings were given to everyone. Only 30 percent of post-*Miranda* defendants interviewed in Washington said they had received all four warnings. Of 41 post-*Miranda* defendants who had been interrogated, almost one third said they had not been given a single one of the *Miranda* warnings; the rest said they had received *some,* with well more than half of that group claiming to have been given all four warnings. Thus, while "*Miranda* clearly affected the giving of specific warnings by the police, the police fell far short of the standards set by the court."[29]

In New Haven, all the advice required by the decision was given to only 25 of 118 individuals. Most did receive some advice: right to silence (90), warning that what they said could be used against them (51), right to counsel (81), and right to appointed counsel (27). Improvement as a result of the decision, as well as the time it may take for adaptation to occur, is shown by the fact that in the two weeks after the ruling was handed down, less than one half received warnings including more than half of the *Miranda* elements; by the end of the summer observation period, more than two thirds were receiving such a warning. The number of *full Miranda* statements increased "dramatically" during the same period, from none in June to over one third in August.

Beyond knowing how frequently the warnings are given, we would like to know the effect of such warnings on those to whom they are given. In general, the picture is one suggesting that the effect is *not* to make defendants/suspects quiet in a large number of instances. In Pittsburgh, where detectives make an effort to obtain a confession from all suspects, the confession rate did drop. Before complying with *Miranda,* the Detective Branch was successful in getting confessions in more than half of the cases (54.4 percent); this dropped to 37.5 percent after compliance, and this drop is attributed by observers to *Miranda* itself. To put this in perspective, however, the observers pointed out that of seventy-four suspects who did not talk, seventy-three were held over for trial, which they say suggests the police do not need confessions to justify arrests in a large proportion of cases.

In New Haven, where the detectives had not made a practice of obtaining statements from all suspects, figures are somewhat harder to interpret, in part because: "The *Miranda* rules may have provided the detectives with an excuse for avoiding the laborious process of statement-taking when they felt it unnecessary for obtaining a conviction."[30] Observers felt that warnings reduced the success of interrogation in only eight of eighty-one cases. Where confessions did not take place during interrogation, they often took place later, at the plea-bargaining stage, thus merely postponing rather than eliminating their existence. Even in the situation where the police gave more adequate advice of rights—in difficult cases where they needed information (where, for example, they had enough to go to trial but not enough for a conviction without a confession)—the police were quite successful ("disproportionately successful") in their interrogations, perhaps because in these same cases they put together most of the elements of psychological interrogation (isolating the suspect from friends, disregarding his right to end questioning). The failure to end questioning when it is requested or when the suspect wants it ended is one of the principal violations of the *Miranda* doctrine. However, even if the violation did not occur, continuing confessions would occur in many cases. If suspects, told of their right to counsel, "usually neglect the offer and let the interrogation proceed,"[31] the *Miranda* rule does not affect the law enforcement process in a negative way to a noticeable extent.

It is interesting to note that the New Haven and Pittsburgh *Miranda* studies were brought to the attention of the U.S. Senate when it was debating the Crime Control Act of 1968, by those opposing limitations on *Miranda*. The arguments based on those studies clearly had little effect. "Congressional reaction to the *Miranda* decision and related holdings seem to have been based not so much on conclusions regarding their impact on law enforcement as on the human tendency—particularly compelling in an election year—to find scapegoats, to assign responsibility or blame for complex and baffling social problems."[32] Despite vigorous assertions of the unconstitutionality of Congress' action, Congress passed the Crime Control Act with provisions that judges were to allow confessions if they were found to be "voluntary," a provision clearly aimed at *Miranda*. Subsequently, Attorney General Mitchell ordered U.S. attorneys to present at trial confessions obtained in the absence of the *Miranda* warnings, thus reversing Department of Justice policy. (It is interesting to note that at the same time they were rejecting *Miranda*, congressmen followed *Jackson* v. *Denno* by requiring an away-from-the-jury screening of the confession by the judge.)

The Washington, D.C., study found that even relatively quick availability of station house counsel did not prevent suspects from talking, even after they knew a lawyer was coming to the station house. Sometimes this occurred because the police persisted with interrogation even when they knew the lawyer was coming. And only a few ("an astonishly small number") requested counsel even when they were available around the clock. Those analyzing the Precinct Representation Project concluded that only 13 percent of the defendants who should have requested counsel did so. That this is important is seen in the fact that only about half of those who obtained counsel were interrogated, a lower figure than for those without counsel. The observers conclude, on this point:

> A definite relationship existed between the giving of the warning of the right to station-house counsel and the . . . defendants' decision to obtain counsel: close to two thirds of those . . . who reported receiving this warning did request counsel. Yet the fact remains that over one third of these defendants receiving the warning did not request counsel. Moreover, when no warnings were given or when warnings other than the right to station-house counsel were given, the overwhelming response of well over three quarters of the remaining "post-*Miranda* defendants" was not to request counsel.[33]

The warnings may not be understood, which appears to have been the case in a large number of instances. For example, in Washington, "15 per cent of the eighty-five 'post-*Miranda* defendants' failed to understand the right-to-silence warning, 18 per cent failed to understand the warning of the right to the presence of counsel, and 24 per cent failed to understand the warning of the right to appointed counsel."[34] In addition, police may not offer to help call counsel, or to inform defendants how they may start to find a lawyer. At times it has been suggested that counsel is needed by those who become entangled in the criminal process because they tend to be disproportionately undereducated and less sure of how to handle themselves vis-à-vis authority. The information cited above about lack of understanding of the warnings would tend to confirm this. But we must be careful not to assume that simply because someone is educated (or well educated) he also knows his rights. A large number of years of formal education is not the same as knowledge of the criminal process.

The general finding of the principal New Haven study, that "the *Miranda* warnings are no substitute for the close knowledge of the institutions and personalities of the criminal process that the suspect will never have,"[35] may apply to the well educated as well as the not so well educated. This is shown in a follow-up New Haven study, involving Yale University graduate students interrogated by the FBI after the October, 1967, depositing of draft cards at the Department of Justice in Washington. Of about twenty persons interviewed in that study, only two mentioned either *Miranda* or *Escobedo* spontaneously, and none seemed to know what was involved in a waiver of rights or how evidence obtained could be used. The FBI had advised people of their rights, but like the New Haven police, had done so with little explanation, with a terse tone, with comments about what lack of response or refusal to respond meant, and without always giving the warnings before beginning questioning. (Compare this with the content of FBI lectures on *Miranda:* professionalization was urged upon local police, who were asked to obey decisions even if they were not clear; however, the emphasis was on ways of keeping old procedures and of not having to give the warnings.)

After a meeting was held in which law professors explained rights under *Miranda,* those interrogated generally answered nothing, but many did go through the charade of the interrogation (answering background questions, if not substantive ones). Their nervousness appears to have interfered with their applying what they had heard from the law professors: "Our interviews reinforce the conclusions of the Miranda Project that the psychological interaction between the interrogator and the suspect in an interrogation is extremely subtle, and the interrogator has most of the advantages."[36] Those informed extensively about their rights still felt they should answer at least some questions. The analysts concluded that "if the high purposes of *Miranda* are to be effected, the warnings alone are insufficient even in the extremely favorable situation. . . . For full achievement of *Miranda's* values, a suspect needs even more than a sympathetic explanation before his interrogation—he needs a sympathetic advocate during the interrogation. Only in this way will most suspects be able to assert a measure of control over the situation . . . ."[37]

Search and Seizure. Some of the aftermath of *Mapp* v. *Ohio,* applying to the states the exclusionary rule concerning improperly seized evidence, is not unlike the aftermath of *Escobedo* and *Miranda.* Perhaps the reaction to the latter cases was greater because they came later and people—often the same people—were already "worked up" over the alleged effect of *Mapp* on police practices and law enforcement.

While the doctrine of *Miranda* could be expressed in some short statements which could be put on a "*Miranda* card," the rules relating to search and seizure were clearly not so easily reducible to a few sentences. Thus, the ruling by the Supreme Court that improperly seized evidence could not be admitted in state courts did not solve the problems of the policeman who, when making an arrest, had to decide what he could look for and what he could not. As LaFave has noted:

> For the exclusionary rule to be completely effective, it would appear that (1) the requirements of the law on search and seizure and related practices must be developed in some detail and in a manner sufficiently responsive

> to both the practical needs of enforcement and the individual rights of privacy; (2) these requirements must be set forth in a manner that can be understood and applied by the front-line lower-echelon police officer and must be effectively communicated to him; and (3) the police desire to obtain convictions must be sufficiently great to induce them to comply with these requirements.[38]

As we have seen with respect to interrogation, there are times when the police wish to use it, regardless of *Miranda,* not to obtain evidence for conviction of the person interrogated, but for other reasons, such as to obtain leads about other people. So it is with search and seizure, where the practice may be used for imposition of informal sanctions or, less delicately put, harassment. However, that the exclusionary rule is not without effect is shown by compliance when police do seriously want conviction: "The exclusionary principle puts pressure on the police to work within the rules in those cases where prosecution is contemplated."[39]

While LaFave argues that there are deficiencies in the exclusionary rule in all three matters about which he writes, there is little question that the *Mapp* decision had noticeable effects. LaFave himself cites the increase in training in several previously nonexclusionary states and an increase in training of state and local law enforcement officials by the FBI, although he says that competing demands for local resources and competing demands on available training time, coupled with a lack of effective training materials and the personnel qualified to give the training, has made the improvement in training far less than it might otherwise be.

Former New York City police official Michael Murphy also argues the difficulties of training, both in large police departments (27,000 men in New York), where there is a "problem of dissemination of this information down through a chain of command so that it is thoroughly understood,"[40] and in smaller jurisdictions where reliance must be on prosecutors who have little time or where the police departments must, completely unequipped for the purpose, rely on themselves. With regard to smaller jurisdictions, failure to have problems of search and seizure after *Mapp,* as indicated by most county prosecutors at the July, 1962, meeting of the Pennsylvania District Attorneys Association Conference, does not mean the same issues did not arise. It *may* be that the law enforcement officials were so poorly trained that they went ahead and seized material and no one knew the difference.

As Philadelphia District Attorney Arlen Specter has claimed, "Police practices and prosecution procedures were revolutionized in many states"[41] by *Mapp.* He also says that the effects of the case have been felt particularly in states which did not previously have an exclusionary rule. He is echoed by Murphy, who says, "I can think of no decision in recent times in the field of law enforcement which had such a dramatic and traumatic effect as [*Mapp*]."[42] Specter cites substantial increases in warrants required and a 35 percent decrease in gambling cases in the New York City Magistrate Courts as being the results of *Mapp*. In addition to this drop in arraignments, Manwaring mentions a drop in convictions on illegal weapons charges of 19 percent and a similar drop in obscenity cases of 46 percent during 1961. Narcotics convictions and guilty pleas also dropped off, "accounted for by an approximate 21% drop in arrests and a 32% drop in defendants held for trial after preliminary hearing—a total decline of some 41% in the number of suspects actually reaching trial."[43] Even though the police made fewer arrests, perhaps because they were unsure of what to do, they also made, as Manwaring points out, many mistakes which showed up in preliminary hearings and trials. That this may have been transitional is shown by New York officials' later comments suggesting that the rate of prosecutions completed successfully rose after the first year post-*Mapp*, "as police became accustomed to their new procedures and aware of their precise powers."[44]

According to Murphy, while search warrants were rarely used prior to *Mapp*, almost 18,000 had been obtained from mid-1961 until 1965. Murphy claims that the effect of *Mapp* is far greater than even these figures show, because of the amount of time needed to draft applications for the warrants, persuading the magistrate of the need for the warrant, and opposing motions to suppress evidence. In Philadelphia, trial and magistrate courts were "inundated by the flood of problems" concerning warrants and motions to suppress; Specter characterizes the initial court reaction in Pennsylvania as one of dismay, and one court called it a hurricane sweeping over the land. One police official, playing on *Dred Scott*, referred to it as the "dread *Mapp* decision." However, Specter stops short of saying that the decision was detrimental to the conviction of criminals. He does assert that the ability of police to get evidence on which to base convictions had been impaired, but he says that it is impossible to determine whether this had been detrimental in a broader sense. He does point out that because of police confusion on the detailed application of search-and-seizure rules, the right to privacy, intended by the Court to be protected, was not better observed in the post-*Mapp* period.

Within several months of the decision, Specter's office circulated a 25-page memorandum on the law of search and seizure, but Specter concedes that this was too long for policemen and too short for the trial courts. Another device used to clarify the law was the appealing of two cases carefully chosen for the purpose, and Specter feels the resulting rulings were helpful. The courts in Pennsylvania appear to have shared the views of law enforcement personnel about *Mapp*, at least according to Specter's view. He notes their limitation of the application of *Mapp* in a number of instances and their broad interpretation of reasonableness (on the side of the police). "The state courts' reluctance to honor *Mapp* fully," he also writes, "also stems from the deepseated conviction that the arguments against the exclusionary rule are still compelling, notwithstanding the

Supreme Court's contrary conclusion."[45] This suggests again that courts are not in a hierarchical relationship to each other, except on paper; for the lower courts to follow a Supreme Court ruling, more is necessary than the utterance of the ruling itself; the values in the ruling must be understood and internalized, and then operated upon, by those judges below.

More systematic information bearing on the impact of *Mapp* is available to us through two studies, one by Nagel based on questionnaires, the other, by Manwaring, an examination of appellate court rulings. Both found differences between states which had had an exclusionary rule prior to 1961 and those which had to initiate it after 1961. Respondents to Nagel's questionnaire (police chiefs, prosecutors, ACLU officials, defense attorneys, judges) from the noninitiating (pre-1961) states were more favorable toward the rule than those from the post-1961 states. It is interesting to note that many did not know accurately whether or not the exclusionary rule had existed in their states prior to 1961. "The errors of the police chiefs tended to be in the direction of thinking the exclusionary rule did not exist in their states prior to 1961 when it did, whereas most of the errors of the other groups were in the direction of thinking that the exclusionary rule had always existed."[46] In a study of North Carolina police chiefs, sheriffs, prosecutors, defense attorneys, and trial judges, Katz found that 18 percent of the judges questioned thought there was no exclusionary rule before 1961, although the state had had a pre-*Mapp* exclusionary rule enacted by statute in 1951. Similarly, 29 percent of the defense attorneys were not aware of the statutory exclusionary rule, so *Mapp* led to an increase in their knowledge.

In a recent broad statement about the effects of the *Mapp* rule, Nagel has said:

> If the policy is "no admissibility of illegally seized evidence," then the most relevant policy appliers would be police, prosecutors, and trial court judges, while criminals and law-abiding citizens would be the main policy recipients. The desired goals of such a policy would probably be a decrease in illegal searches (a behavioral effect) and thus an increase in public attitudes of security from arbitrary search (an attitudinal effect), without substantially increasing criminality (a behavioral effect) or lowering police morale (an attitudinal effect). Possible side effects (not likely to be mentioned as part of the goals of the policy) might include the simplification of search warrant procedures, the broadening of the concept of legal search, and perhaps increased friction between prosecutors and police over police tactics.[47]

Findings from the above-mentioned study he conducted earlier cast light on many of these points.

Nagel found that police adherence to legality in searches did increase between 1960 and 1963—at least his respondents reported that it had—and that there was a positive correlation (+.56) between increased police education on the subject and increased adherence to legality. No change in police effectiveness in search was reported overall, although a decrease for the "new" states was noted. The *Mapp* case did bring about an increased raising of search and seizure issues, for example, at trial, particularly in the "new" states but not only there. "No change" was the response most frequently reported with respect to searches declared illegal, although respondents in "new" states were more likely to report increases. However, Nagel also reports a correlation between increased raising of search issues in court and an increase in their being declared illegal. There is also little relationship between the exclusionary rule and crime rates, when states in the same region are compared.

Nagel also attempted to find out the direction in which attitudes had changed since before the adoption of *Mapp*. He noted movement in the direction of agreement with statements that the same rules should exist for federal and state police; that the legality of search should be broadened; that more flexible search warrants were needed; and that safety should be emphasized more and liberty less. However, ACLU officials disagreed on all except the first item, defense attorneys split on the second and disagreed on the last two, and judges split on the last. There was movement toward disagreement with the statement that reliable evidence should be admitted regardless of its source (police chiefs split here). There was no clear direction of change on other items, such as that exclusion reduces illegal searches, that exclusion is socially desirable—on both of which there is present agreement—that exclusion increases crime (the police chiefs agree, the others disagree), and that exclusion hinders the police (defense attorneys and ACLU officials disagree, the other officials agree).

In North Carolina, Katz found that the ruling had "passed into the collective consciousness of the participants concerned" with great rapidity,[48] but differences between the categories questioned did appear. Thus, while 59 percent of the prosecutors felt reliable evidence should be introduced regardless of how obtained, only 8 percent of the judges and 10 percent of the defense lawyers agreed. There was somewhat more consensus on having the same standards for federal and state courts, with two thirds of defense lawyers, three fifths of the judges, and two fifths of the prosecutors agreeing that the standards should be the same. Greater consensus occurred on the question of whether exclusion of evidence was effective in limiting improper searches: 78 percent of the judges thought so, as did 64 percent of the prosecutors and 62 percent of the defense attorneys. Police and prosecutors generally felt that effective law enforcement had been hindered and morale lowered, and that the number of guilty going free had increased along with an increase in the number of improper search defenses raised. Defense attorneys, while sympathetic to the prosecutor's viewpoint, felt that police attempts to comply had increased, as had the education of the police on the subject of proper searches. Only a small percentage felt that more defendants were going free.

In examining the effect of *Mapp* on state court decisions, Manwaring found that those states which did not utilize the exclusionary rule prior to *Mapp* adopted it after that ruling. However, the impact of *Mapp* in terms of getting states to adopt federal precedents on specifics of search and seizure was far less great, with considerable resistance being shown, particularly by those states which already had begun to develop law relating to the exclusionary rule. Some states denied that the Supreme Court had said that federal search precedents should be applied by the states. California, which had adopted the exclusionary rule in 1955, was one such state. While noting, "It is ironic that the nation's largest single compliance problem under *Mapp* should come from a highly distinguished judiciary already applying the exclusionary rule on its own," Manwaring states, "Where a state judiciary *anticipates* a federal rule, but with variations of its own, those variations are going to prove very hard to kill."[49]

Other states tried to limit *Mapp* to the fact situation involved in the case, while some judges argued that the Court's rulings on search and seizure had been based on its power to supervise the lower federal courts, and were thus inapplicable to the states. Other excuses were developed; in a commonly used one, the Supreme Court itself was cited. In the earlier *Rabinowitz* case, the use of a fixed formula to decide the validity of searches had been criticized; that critical language became "one of the most widely and indiscriminately used of all federal rulings in state search and seizure litigation." Even after *Mapp,* some state judges continued to cite *Rabinowitz,* not *Mapp;* this went on in California at least until 1963, and in that state, "Not till 1964 was a conviction reversed in substantial reliance on federal search law."[50]

Failure to cite federal precedent, however, did not mean nonadherence to those precedents. New York provides an example. Because that state, which was a pre-*Mapp* nonexclusionary state, has such a volume of search-and-seizure cases, it quickly developed, post-*Mapp,* a large number of its own precedents on the subject. It is those state precedents which are often cited; however, the original cases were based on federal precedents, and Manwaring argues that New York law on the subject "is a well-nigh perfect reproduction of the federal model."[51] He concludes from his examination of state decisions that the Court was successful in getting the exclusionary rule adopted, but far less so in getting federal search precedents applied by state judges. He explains this phenomenon as partly the fault of the Court itself, claiming the Court could have been clear on this point in *Mapp,* that it lost valuable opportunities to clarify the situation by denying certiorari in search cases for two years after *Mapp,* and that there was no clear majority opinion when the matter was reached in *Ker* v. *California.* On the point of the judges' reluctance to deal with the matter after *Mapp,* he argues, "Whatever say the canons of self-restraint, judicial reticence is no service where it simply encourages the lower courts to fool around."[52] If, however, certiorari was denied because the judges knew they were in disagreement—witness the split in the Court in *Ker* even after the two-year wait—abstention may have avoided even further confusion. The "stray language" in both *Rabinowitz* and *Ker* is also criticized by Manwaring, although he concedes that "judges are likely to find in any binding precedent just about what they want to find there." However, he feels that "the Court could have done much more than it did to make evasion difficult."

Another aspect of the search-and-seizure question is wiretapping. Until recently, the impact of decisions in this area has been largely at the national level, because restrictions on wiretapping were not clearly extended to the states by the U.S. Supreme Court until *Berger* v. *New York,* which establishes strict procedures to be followed if wiretapping is to be permitted. While the impact of *Mapp* concerned the degree to which states would adopt the exclusionary rule and federal search precedents, the aftermath of the wiretapping cases has been within the federal government, where the ball has been passed back and forth between the Supreme Court and the Congress. In the first important case on the subject, *Olmstead* v. *U.S.*, decided in 1928, the Supreme Court upheld the practice on the grounds that nothing had been "seized" and there was no invasion of a person's quarters; however, the practice was illegal in the state of Washington, where the federal agents had performed the wiretaps, and Holmes in dissent referred to the government's action in violating the law to catch criminals as "dirty business."

Olmstead had been a prohibition case; those involved in dealing with similar cases continued to wiretap after the decision, feeling it to be constitutional, although the FBI disapproved of the idea and, at the time, did not use wiretapping to obtain evidence, although subsequently Attorney General Mitchell authorized FBI and prohibition agents to wiretap, after receiving permission from superiors.[53] Congressional reaction was slow in coming, because Congress was not in session when the decision was handed down, and the stock market crash was in progress when Congress next met in late 1928 and early 1929. A year later, however, Congressional interest was aroused. Although defeated, an amendment to an appropriations bill, to forbid spending of money in connection with wiretapping, sparked debate over the subject. The Attorney General swept aside arguments against wiretapping based on the fact that it was illegal in many states, asserting that such state statutes were aimed at police, not federal agents. However, the Attorney General also claimed not to be aware that any judges had talked about wiretapping being reprehensible, when Representative Tinkham, the leader of the antiwiretapping campaign, asked him to justify what Tinkham said four justices had called "more or less despicable."

While Tinkham was unsuccessful with his amendment the first time, Congress did pass one in 1933, aimed only at the Bureau of Prohibition. More important by far, however, was the passage of the Federal Communications Commission Act, Section 605 of which made it illegal to intercept and divulge communications by wire. Section 605, incidentally, was not specifically aimed at *Olmstead,* as it appears the entire bill was offered as a revision and codification of existing law, with wiretapping mentioned neither in committee nor in floor debate. The Supreme Court's subsequent actions on the subject, at least at the federal level, became a matter of statutory interpretation. Of these, the most important were the *Nardone* cases. In the first *Nardone* case, the Court held that wiretap evidence could not be used in federal courts and, in *Nardone II,* that evidence obtained through leads secured by wiretapping was also barred. The *Nardone* rulings received initial executive compliance and legislative resistance. Attorney General Jackson issued an order forbidding prosecution of cases after April 1, 1940, where wiretap evidence was involved. However, President Roosevelt wrote to Jackson saying he thought the Court did not mean to include "national security" cases within its ban, and he made it clear that he wanted wiretapping continued in such instances—which it has been allegedly only on approval of the FBI Director and the Attorney General.

In Congress, those favoring wiretapping tried to get *Olmstead* legislatively reinstated. After the first *Nardone* case, both houses passed bills to permit wiretapping by federal agents, but compromise between the two houses was not reached before adjournment. By the next year, when the effort was made again, FBI Director J. Edgar Hoover was opposing change in the law. At this point, one could talk of the "relative inactivity of Congress . . . locked on dead center."[54] In a situation in which Congress ostensibly forbids wiretapping and the Court has reinforced the policy by its rulings, but where considerable pressure and desire for wiretapping exists, then, as Murphy has noted, "Orders of the President, the Attorney General, and the Director of the FBI, [and] decisions of U.S. Attorneys not to prosecute local police for violations of Section 605," as well as congressional debate, "have had as much to do as court decisions with whether or not wiretapping will be used as a standard technique in criminal investigations."[55] The controversy in 1969 after the Supreme Court's decision in the *Alderman* case continues to give credence to Murphy's observation.

SCHOOL DESEGREGATION

Introduction. In 1969, the Department of Health, Education, and Welfare released figures showing that about 20 percent of Negro students in the southern states were in desegregated situations. The variation from state to state was, however, quite substantial, ranging from 7 percent in Alabama and Mississippi to around one quarter in Arkansas, Florida, North Carolina, Tennessee, and Virginia, and almost 40 percent in Texas. Changes from 1966 to 1968 shown by HEW to have taken place in school districts which had submitted plans for voluntary compliance were also substantial; for example, the percentage of Negro students in desegregated situations rose from 8.2 percent in 1966 to 21.8 percent in 1968 in Arkansas; in Mississippi the jump was from 4 percent to 12 percent; overall, the increase was from 14.1 percent (1966) to 18.9 percent (1967) to 25.6 percent (1968). While the increases are substantial, particularly if one looks at percentage increases, one has to remember that, as Senator Hart (D–Mich.) recently argued in the Senate, "In 1963, 9 years after the Supreme Court had declared that dual, racially-segregated school systems were unconstitutional, 1 percent of the Negro students in the Southern States attended school with whites." Thus, compliance with *Brown* v. *Board* had been slow.

The above-cited figures may not tell us all we need to know, or may not provide the only picture in which we might have an interest. If we are interested in postdesegregation effects, for example on attitudes, to see whether "the attitudinal goal of the school desegregation policy [which] was to lessen the feelings of Negro inferiority"[56] has been effective, we might carry out psychological depth studies before and after desegregation occurs in particular communities. While discussing measures of the impact of decisions in this area, we might note that expenditures for education might also be relevant; at least, they have been held to be for the belated impact of *Plessy* v. *Ferguson,* before *Brown* was decided. Anthony Lewis has argued that compliance with *Plessy,* in terms of providing educational facilities that were equal as well as separate, did not come until after the Supreme Court "beginning in the 1930's and 1940's made it clear that the legal basis of segregation was threatened"[57] in cases from postsecondary education and that average per pupil expenditures in six southeastern states in 1944 were less than onehalf for Negroes what they were for whites. Only after the late cases did the expenditures of "those vast sums on Negro education that we now hear so much about" take place. That the South had, even if belatedly, begun to comply with *Plessy,* is reinforced by D'Amato's comment, "The *Brown* decision wiped out the motive for constructing new all-Negro school facilities, and created instead widespread apathy on the part of school boards throughout the South."[58]

In talking about *Plessy,* however, we must remember the broad effects of that decision—particularly in connection with the Supreme Court's other decisions of the late 1800's dealing with the rights of Negroes. Those decisions provided the frame of reference within which segregation was developed in the first half of the twentieth century and served to reinforce some practices which were only beginning to develop in the last years of the nineteenth century. Thus, Loren Miller declares that, as of the early 1900's:

> The Negro, under the Court's guardianship, was reduced to a despairing second-class citizenship: voteless in the South; helpless in the face of constant and brutal aggression; indicted by all-white grand juries and convicted by all-white trial juries; denied access to places of public accommodation; represented in public office by those whose very elections were dependent on their promise to white voters to double and redouble his disabilities; forced to scrounge and cadge for an education; segregated in every phase of his life; condemned to separate and unequal schools and public facilities of every kind; and with no place to turn for redress of his grievances except to the Court that had approved the devices used to reduce him to his helpless and almost hopeless degradation.[59]

The Civil Rights Cases, in which the Court had invalidated Congress' attempts at a public accommodations statute by saying that, under the Fourteenth Amendment, Congress could only prohibit *state*, not private, action, had led to increased racial discrimination. Negroes had been left without a vote as a result of a number of factors, among them "Supreme Court decisions sapping the vitality of equalitarian legislation enacted by Congress."[60] *Plessy* sanctioned the drawing of racial classifications by the states. This case, after which racial segregation increased radically, and *Berea College* v. *Kentucky*, in which the Court upheld Kentucky's statute prohibiting the voluntary commingling of the races, led to officially directed segregation of all kinds. As Berman has argued with respect to *Plessy*, "What the Court had done was not so much to sanction an existing practice as to put forth the idea for a new one. The result was that under the protective umbrella of the Plessy doctrine racial segregation came to dominate virtually all areas of Southern life."[61] The importance of this is that, in *Brown*, the Supreme Court may have been doing little more than beginning to undo that for which it may in large measure have been responsible—at least in connection with indifferent officials of the executive branch and a complacent Congress.

To return to *Brown*, even if one were not sure precisely what measure to use in ascertaining impact, for some years after the ruling one was dealing with the impact of court decisions—the *Brown* decisions of the Supreme Court and various decisions of lower federal courts and state courts, particularly the latter. To be sure, there was legislative action in the states, aimed at blocking the effect of *Brown*, but the stimulus was judicial. This had occurred in part because the phrase "with all deliberate speed" gave lower courts far more discretion than they normally have. And some judges used the discretion in such a way that *Brown* might never have existed. Thus, in Dallas, "Flying directly in the face of the desegregation ruling, and even after one reversal by the Court of Appeals,

District Judge William H. Atwell declined to order Dallas, Texas, to set a date for integration because this would cause 'civil wrongs.'"[62]

Judges opposed to the decision did not need to go as far as Judge Atwell; they could say that *Brown* was the law of the land but that they could do little to stop the states' efforts at noncompliance. Murphy and Pritchett note that while southern state judges "criticized the school desegregation decisions on and off the bench [and] were among the leaders of the movement in the 1958 Conference of State Chief Justices to reprimand the Supreme Court," in addition to giving "moral support and perhaps, one may guess, legal advice to southern political leaders, . . . no state supreme court has yet failed to concede that the school segregation cases are the law of the land and binding on lower courts." Murphy and Pritchett found that state supreme court resistance came through "(1) refusing to expand the school decision to other areas; (2) upholding the constitutionality of state efforts to evade compliance; and (3), in line with the state chief justices' censure, balking at Supreme Court decisions in related areas of race and of federal-state relations."[63] Thus, we must note that "with all deliberate speed" is "a rule which causes decisions to vary from court to court and from case to case."[64] This was something which showed up clearly in the different amounts of time allowed by judges before desegregation had to begin or be complete and in the amount of the school system in which desegregation had to be initiated, such as first grade, several grades at once, or only high school. Thus, in Little Rock, where major conflict was to develop, the first step was to occur in the senior high schools in 1957, more than two years after the *Brown* implementation case, and the entire school system would not be covered for an additional six years.

The executive branch of the federal government did little at first, and was not a party to school cases, although the Department of Justice did help secure compliance in some instances, as in cases at Clinton, Tennessee, and Hoxie, Arkansas. President Eisenhower never supported the decision while he was in office. "At no time while he was President did Eisenhower express any personal opinion about the correctness of the Supreme Court decision, and he made it clear that he thought it would be improper for him to do so."[65] His only direct action was to issue an executive order ending segregation in schools on military bases. The Department of Justice's court participation was only at the request of the courts, as a result of administration policy. When the President was criticized for his nonaction, his response was, "The President would not make any assumption that the judicial branch of the Government is incapable of implementing the Supreme Court's decision."[66]

Congress also stayed largely out of the picture. Certainly, it did not explicitly support desegregation for ten years. However, it did support related measures, such as the provisions in the Civil Rights Act of 1960 making it a crime to interfere with court-ordered desegregation or to cross state lines to avoid prosecution for school bombings, and measures facilitating change, such as the establishment of the Civil Rights Commission and the Community Relations Service. It was not until 1964, with the passage of the Civil Rights Act of that year, that Congress firmly supported desegregation by providing that funds could be cut off from school districts which did not desegregate. That action shifted the attention of many to the executive branch, where the Department of Health, Education, and Welfare works out the guidelines which are to be applied to school districts to see whether or not they are in compliance. By 1969, fifteen years after *Brown*, it has become difficult to separate the effects of the case itself from the effects of the 1964 statute and its administrative implementation.

It is, however, clear that the aftermath of *Brown* is still in progress. For example, when Berkeley, California, adopted bussing to end *de facto* segregation in the schools, School Superintendent Neil Sullivan claimed that it was the first real compliance with *Brown*. Clearly the effects of *Brown* are being felt in the North, where cases are now being brought to eliminate *de facto* segregation and segregation of faculties. The famous New Rochelle, New York, case is an illustration; there the district court held that the school board had gerrymandered school district lines in violation of the Fourteenth Amendment as construed in *Brown;* the judge said there was no difference between gerrymandering and the formality of a dual system like those in the South. That the issue has been so long in coming to the North may be explained in part by the fact it has taken so long to "clean up" in the South—not yet completed—and because of the different stance of northern officials. Joining those who claim that *de facto* segregation is really largely *de jure,* through official drawing of district lines to keep the races separate, Rainwater and Yancey contend, for example: "Supporters of white supremacy in the South had proved themselves to be considerably less skillful than the northern functionaries and power figures who support *de facto* segregation and discrimination. . . . The northerners avoided or minimized open confrontations."[67]

"The basic conflict between the litigants as to the meaning of the *Brown* decision clearly illustrates the confusion which surrounds the case," wrote one observer of the New Rochelle litigation.[68] There *is* no clear agreement, even in the 1960's, about the meaning of *Brown*—as to whether it requires only elimination of separate school systems or more positive action to alleviate racial imbalances. At the beginning of the Nixon administration, Secretary of Health, Education, and Welfare Finch argued that the Supreme Court had only outlawed deliberate racial discrimination but not segregation as such: "'If you look at the Supreme Court decision, segregation, in fact, is not prohibited by law,' said Finch. 'What is prohibited is deliberate discrimination,' he said." King sums up the situation in the mid-1960's by saying, "The majority of courts have found that racial imbalance per se presents no question of constitutional deprivation."[69] But he notes that exceptions exist.

With respect to the South, we find the Court having now to deal with "feedback" from its earlier decisions. The plans which some jurisdictions adopted—in large measure to slow down or spread out desegregation—have now been challenged in the Court, and we are getting "second-generation" impact as the Court now strikes down many of those arrangements. This is true, for example, with "freedom-of-choice" plans. The Supreme Court said that these, and "free transfer" plans (where transfer to other schools is allowed once attendance zones are established), are invalid where they have not been effective in effectuating *Brown* v. *Board.* In the *Green* ruling, the Court noted that *Brown* was no longer new doctrine and that much time had been allowed for the resolution of problems of maintaining dual systems; it also held it relevant in judging "freedom-of-choice" plans as to when the plan had been adopted. If it had not even been adopted until ten years after *Brown,* as was the case in *Green,* that raised questions about the compliance intentions of the plan's authors. It may be that the "freedom-of-choice" plans, or at least their widespread use, were the result of earlier Supreme Court action. It has been argued that when the Supreme Court held, in *Goss* v. *Board of Education,* that "minority transfer" plans—allowing those in a racial minority, but not majority, to transfer to other schools—were invalid as perpetuating segregation, it "gave a critically important shot in the arm to experiments just getting under way with giving pupils a 'free choice' of schools." The "minority transfer" arrangements, keeping whites in integrated schools when they were in a majority but not when they were in the minority, might have provided a "transitional device essential in many cases to the initial establishment of unitary zoning."[70]

When the Court did invalidate freedom-of-choice plans, a number of changes did result. "The Court's ruling and similar mandates have produced various arrangements, including the establishment of firm biracial attendance zones, pairing, and the wholesale closing of Negro schools."[71] In addition, the resistance which we shall see characterized the earlier post-*Brown* period continued. The Columbia, South Carolina school board abandoned a plan to pair four schools when whites objected. Schools opened under freedom-of-choice even after a three-judge court stayed a district court order requiring maintenance of freedom-of-choice. In Cameron, South Carolina, when the court ordered more integration, the white faculty resigned and no students appeared for classes. In Mobile, Alabama, thousands of whites protested when the school board offered a plan of biracial attendance zones with no transfer to satisfy a Court of Appeals order; a federal district judge eliminated the high schools from the order. When the Court of Appeals for the Fifth Circuit ordered elimination of freedom-of-choice arrangements in Louisiana, the Chief Judge of the federal District Court for the Eastern District of Louisiana, while he relayed the appellate court's orders to the school boards, urged the school boards to appeal to the Supreme Court, and severely criticized both the Court of Appeals and the Supreme Court. In Gould, Arkansas, also involved in a freedom-of-choice ruling, white students stayed away from schools, and a month later began attending an academy set up for them, reminiscent of the direct aftermath of *Brown* in some communities. We also find congressional attempts, as in appropriations legislation for fiscal year 1970, to stop the administration from refusing to accept "freedom-of-choice" plans. And we find the first key ruling of the Burger Court holding against the federal government in its request for a delay of desegregation in Mississippi school districts.

Post-*Brown* History. Because several histories of the "ordeal of desegregation" have been written, there is no need to repeat a chronology of events after either the 1954 or 1955 Supreme Court rulings. What can be done is to pull together materials to present a number of themes which recur in the writings on the subject.

Despite some people's perception of considerable violence in connection with desegregation, a perception perhaps reinforced by the violence in northern ghettos in the last five years, most of the action in resistance to *Brown* v. *Board* took place not on the streets but in state legislatures and governors' offices. In fact, one might say that the initial reaction to both rulings was calm. Thus, Sarratt notes, "In the spring of 1954 the people of the South showed no great concern about the Court's opinion."[72] This was in part because there had been little enforcement of *Plessy* v. *Ferguson*. Newspapers certainly paid much attention to the decision, but "editorial reaction in the South was cautious or aggrieved," with editors not yet aroused to "frank hostility" stressing difficulties in compliance. "Many Southern editors at this stage urged a calm, constructive approach to the problem." When the "with all deliberate speed" pronouncement was handed down in 1955, "the South reacted to this second ruling generally with a feeling of relief,"[73] apparently recognizing what has in fact come to pass: that it would be a long time before the doctrine of *Brown I* would be enforced in most school districts.

While the image of governors' reactions is perhaps colored by George Wallace's "stand in the schoolhouse door" and Ross Barnett's defiance of federal court orders concerning the admission of James Meredith to the University of Mississippi, not all governors reacted in a similar manner. The governors in the southern states clearly did not advocate compliance, unlike the border state governors, who did (with the exception of Oklahoma), but they "adopted a 'wait and see' attitude" between *Brown I* and *Brown II*. "During this interim their reactions in most instances were restrained when related to their later behavior."[74] Generally the governors wished to keep segregation but did not want to run afoul of the Supreme Court; included in this number was Governor Byrnes of South Carolina, himself a former U.S. Supreme Court Justice.

While this position may seem illogical, many government officials, no matter how badly they want a goal, would prefer to achieve it without deliberately crossing the Supreme Court if the goal can be so achieved; even leaving the impression that the Court is not being disobeyed may be important, additional testimony to the Court's charisma. Peltason argues, however, that the segregationists did not hesitate to attack the Court; what they hesitated to attack was the Constitution. Had the Justices, he asserts, written an opinion more heavily laden with precedent and more heavily quoting the Founding Fathers, and had they not cited the work of sociologists and psychologists (even in a footnote), perhaps it would have been more difficult for attacks to be made on the Court itself.

After *Brown II,* there was an intensification of resistance, a more heated rhetoric, a polarization of viewpoints, and a situation of overwhelming public unanimity against the Supreme Court, particularly in the states of the Deep South. Although some did realize that it would delay desegregation, the 1955 ruling "reinvigorated the defense of Southern customs and traditions."[75] Where at first there had been minorities in the state legislatures opposing the most "far-out" measures of resistance, and where votes were cast against such measures, after a period of time, the opposition vanished. "Potentially far-reaching enactments were adopted swiftly by a vote which, if not unanimous, was less than half-a-dozen votes short of that goal. The stampede sometimes began before a bill was introduced."[76] Thus, interposition resolutions against the Supreme Court's decisions passed the senates of Alabama and North Carolina, and both houses in Louisiana and South Carolina, unanimously. Federal judges who shortly after *Brown* had been saying in their communities that communities would have to desegregate, "in the face of segregationist onslaught, . . . backed down."[77] Southern members of Congress put forth the Southern Manifesto in March, 1956, strongly attacking the Court's decision:

> We regard the decision of the Supreme Court in the school cases as a clear abuse of judicial power. It climaxes a trend in the federal judiciary undertaking to legislate, in derogation of the authority of Congress, and to encroach upon the reserved rights of the people. . . . The Supreme Court . . . undertook to exercise their naked judicial power and substituted their personal political and social ideas for the established law of the land.

While some southern senators apparently hesitated to sign, in the end nineteen of twenty-two did so under pressure from the Manifesto's sponsors. The House delegations from Alabama, Arkansas, Georgia, Louisiana, Mississippi, South Carolina, and Virginia *all* signed; only twenty-four representatives did not, including three from North Carolina, two of whom were defeated for reelection.

Those whites opposed to the decision began to gravitate toward groups connected with the Citizens Councils of America. Racial estrangement began to occur; reasonable relations between the races which had existed prior to *Brown* became severed. Muse writes:

> Choruses from Negro colleges ceased to be invited, as they had often been invited in the past, to sing for white audiences; Negro groups were excluded from holiday parades and festivities in which they had formerly taken part; and many white community leaders who had been conspicuously active in aiding and advising Negroes abandoned this activity . . . . Even the Urban League, a long-respected Negro assistance organization, not involved in the school-integration controversy, was deserted by many of its white friends and supporters; . . . Urban Leagues . . . were excluded from local Community Chests . . . .[78]

Negroes' reaction to the decision also clearly played a part in what happened. The activity of the NAACP in petitioning school boards for desegregation, and then bringing court cases when the petitions were unsuccessful, has been mentioned. On the other hand, one can argue, "The attitudes of Negroes partially accounted for the gradualness with which desegregation spread."[79] Some Negroes simply did nothing to bring about compliance. "The vast majority of Negroes in the South made no attempt to exercise the right to a desegregated education that the *Brown* decision gave them." In some cases, this was because the significance of the decision was not at first clear—something which happens with many Supreme Court decisions and many people—but, in others, some who knew what the decision meant "feared that efforts to secure its enforcement would lead only to grief. . . . The statements of Negro 'segregationists' were so widely quoted by white propagandists as to give an impression that these Negroes were prominent and substantial in number, but they were in fact rare and generally little-known individuals."[80]

State legislatures tried a variety of different techniques in their desire to avoid compliance with the Court's ruling. The summary by Blaustein and Ferguson is worth quoting at length:

> The various legal attempts to avoid the consequences of desegregation fall into four categories. Many of the Southern states have reintroduced into the legal scene one or more of the multiple variations of the pre-Civil War doctrines of interposition and nullification. Other states have entered upon a course of legislative action designed to disqualify potential plaintiffs and the NAACP from bringing court actions to end segregation. Still other states have sought to retain separate school systems by changing the theoretical basis of the separation from a classification explicitly based upon race to a classification based upon such factors as "scholastic

> aptitude," "psychological aptitude," and "free choice." In the fourth category are the various ways and means which have been devised to separate the operation of the schools from the state.[81]

Pupil placement acts, generally vesting power in the local school boards to assign pupils, were perhaps the most popular legislative devices. By the end of the decade, all the southern states had them. They were generally effective: "Without ever referring to the subject of race or color they did much to block the impact of *Brown*."[82] The device of tuition grants for use in private schools was also quite popular, although not all the states which enacted enabling legislation paid out money.

The stiffest resistance, short of violence, came in Virginia's "Massive Resistance," ending in school closings in several jurisdictions. "Massive Resistance," in terms of specific plans aimed at noncompliance with *Brown*, did not develop immediately after the decision, although activity concerning the resistance problem did begin quite soon after *Brown I* was decided. Governor Stanley invited Negro leaders to meet with him and urged them not to press for implementation of the decision; that request was refused, and it took almost two years (until 1956) before some other method for circumvention was developed. A Commission on Public Education was formed to develop plans, but it did not have the scene to itself, for the "Defenders of State Sovereignty and Individual Liberties" (the Defenders) were started in Prince Edward County. That Prince Edward County was involved helps explain why resistance was as strong as it was in Virginia. Prince Edward was a "Black Belt" county where resistance to Negro participation in politics (as, for example, by voting) or school attendance was greatest. Muse argues, "Initial resistance to the Supreme Court's school desegregation order in Virginia, and in the South, was undoubtedly encouraged by the fact that the only strictly Southern localities involved in the original litigation were two rural Black Belt counties in which any degree of racial integration would be most difficult to bring about." He asserts that if desegregation had been attempted first in counties with small Negro populations, "it would have moved faster and with less convulsion."[83]

The conflict over what strategy Virginia should adopt was not between whites and blacks; the latter had pressed for compliance and were ignored. It was between whites and whites, between those who were more segregationist and those who were less so. Thus, there were those, although not many, who were pleased that the Supreme Court had disposed of a practice they had come to feel was unconstitutional. "There emerged *degrees* of white segregationists and integrationists where there had once appeared the illusion of total agreement."[84] The desire to develop a specific technique which would work to prevent desegregation was strengthened when federal judges ordered desegregation at both

Alexandria and Charlottesville. The plan ultimately adopted involved removing state aid from schools which desegregated, and providing tuition grants to students. Thus, if local school boards under desegregation order should continue to run their schools, they would have to do so without any state funds. That the state meant business was shown by the fact that 12,000 students were locked out of school in the fall of 1958 at Norfolk, Charlottesville, and Front Royal. However, the plan was in continual difficulty, because the federal government—including federal judges—would not "cave in" in the face of Senator Byrd's strategy. The Massive Resistance laws were struck down by the federal courts in early 1959, and the state backed off from its adamant position. As Muse has noted, armed rebellion was not in the minds of the Virginians who did not want to comply with *Brown*. And the substitution of private schools for public ones had proved "egregiously impracticable."[85]

Although Prince Edward had been directly affected as one of the specific cases involved in *Brown*, the closing of schools there did not, it should be stressed, occur until after the failure of Massive Resistance throughout the state. In June, 1959, after a federal district court order to desegregate, the Board of Supervisors of the county simply said they would appropriate no money for the schools for the coming year. A system of schools for whites was established in the community. No schools were established by Negroes until one year before the reopening of the public school system, in part because Negro leaders felt that such a move would be acquiesence in a system of segregated (private) education. The public schools in the county remained closed for *five* years, producing what has come to be known as the "crippled generation," the black students who had no schools at all for four of those five years. And the public schools reopened only after the U.S. Supreme Court decided in the *Griffin* case that schools could not be closed in one county while open elsewhere. The white students generally, after *Griffin*, remained in the private schools, drawing their tuition grants, because "the Supreme Court had not ruled on whether the grants were permissible where public schools were open."[86]

While Massive Resistance—at least in the specific form described—occurred only in Virginia, observers suggest that it had a clear impact on what went on elsewhere in the South. That effect was of two types. Ultimately, other states could see that defiance of the federal government was not likely to be successful. "The truth came quietly home to many Southern politicians that 'you can't win' against the Supreme Court and the government of the United States." However, before Massive Resistance collapsed, others may have been encouraged to "take on" the government. "Virginia's posture had dignified and encouraged resistance to the desegregation rulings in all her sister Southern states."[87] At least some in Arkansas seem to believe that Governor Faubus may have been strengthened in his resistance at Little Rock by what his confreres in Virginia had done.

Before turning to look at Little Rock, a brief look at the New Orleans crisis is appropriate. Here one had a situation in which a local school board, although not wholeheartedly, was attempting to comply with federal court orders to desegregate the schools; the school was thus unlike the officials of Prince Edward County. Action in New Orleans also was belated, not really heating up until 1959, although the legislature had passed a series of bills in 1956 and 1958 intended to impede desegregation by providing, *inter alia,* for removal of officials who assisted in desegregation. When the school board acted as if it might comply with federal court orders, the attorney general of the state went to court against the school board, and the court obliged by issuing an injunction to prevent it from integrating.

The primary battle was, however, between the federal district court of Judge J. Skelly Wright and the legislature. "The summer of 1960 consisted of a running battle between the federal courts and the state of Louisiana. . . . As Judge Wright put pressure on the school board to comply with his desegregation order, the legislature stepped up its own campaign at its regular session in 1960."[88] Regular sessions were not enough, however, as Governor Davis kept calling special sessions—five in all through 1961, even after the battle was for all practical purposes lost—to pass new bills which the courts almost as promptly struck down. For example, in one instance, Judge Wright issued a restraining order against the entire legislature based on his notes from a television showing of legislative action aimed at the school board. Some of the judicial action against the governor came as a result of a suit filed by thirty white parents who were afraid the governor, in control of the schools, would shut them down. In *Williams* v. *Davis,* the federal judges struck down the legislature's acts, nullified the governor's seizure of the school board, and ordered the board to move along with desegregation. However, the decision, in late August, 1960, did little to dispose of the situation, because of the persistence of both the governor and the legislature and the fact that the school board had ceased to fight back at the state officials' action. The legislature went so far, in mid-November, as to declare all acts of the school board illegal and to warn banks not to honor the board's checks or to do business with it. While legislative resistance continued, with much heated oratory, even after the U.S. Supreme Court upheld district court action in striking down the remaining legislative acts and enjoining officials from interfering with desegregation, the Supreme Court's ruling at least ended the legal battle. The well-known boycott was still to follow.

While we noted earlier that the impression of widespread violence in connection with desegregation is incorrect, there is no question that violence occurred. Disorder was at its height from August, 1956, through

September, 1957; although a school was bombed in Nashville, most incidents occurred in small rural communities. Clinton, in eastern Tennessee, was one of the better-known instances; that town "represented the southernmost attempt at integration up to that time in the Old South east of the Mississippi River."[89] In Mansfield, Texas, the court action to which people reacted was the first in east Texas, where most of the state's Negroes were located. It was instances like these, coupled with Little Rock, that "gave a widespread impression of rebellious violence, approaching anarchy . . . and aroused the deepest pessimism."[90]

Much has been said about Little Rock, which is particularly interesting because of the self-fulfilling nature of Governor Faubus' prophecy. After the Arkansas legislature had "nullified" *Brown* in the state in 1956 and had passed a number of statutes to avoid integration, the governor, claiming that violence would result from desegregation, called out the National Guard to prevent black children from attending Central High School in Little Rock. The presence of the National Guard itself produced a mob and a generally ugly situation. The school board, which had initially proceeded with plans for desegregation, then turned to the federal district judge to find out what the board should do, asking that it be allowed to postpone desegregation; the judge refused, and, in addition, asked the U.S. Attorney General to enter the case to proceed against Governor Faubus and the National Guard commanders.

The governor removed the troops on September 20, 1957, as a result of Judge Davies' order. The governor had met with President Eisenhower on September 14, before the court order. When a mob gathered, on the 23rd, again to prevent the children from entering, the President issued an obstruction-of-justice proclamation, and on the 24th federalized the National Guard and sent in paratroopers to keep order. What would have happened had the governor neither called out the Guard nor made his "statements of doom" is unclear. What is clear is that the coming of the 101st Airborne Division did not end matters. The following year the schools were closed after action by the state legislature. At the end of that year, 1958–59, the private schools which had been set up for the white children were in serious financial difficulty. Another court order requiring that public schools be opened ended that battle, but the continuing effect on Little Rock itself—in terms, for example, of attracting industry—were to be long lasting.

What factors influence desegregation compliance? While no definitive answer can be given, a number of factors may be mentioned. One key one was geography. One finds repeated references in the literature to greater compliance in the border states than in the Deep South. As Sarratt noted, "Compliance . . . began in the border area, usually in the larger cities." The difference can be noted both with respect to local school officials and to legislators. "By contrast to their counterparts in the former

Confederate states, the legislators of the six border states accepted the *Brown* decision from the outset. . . . Their first and continuing reaction was to comply."[91] In fact, if one looks at the first years after *Brown*, there was almost no compliance *except* in the Border states. Related to the geographical factor, and confusing us as to its effect, was the extent to which desegregation had begun to disappear before *Brown* and without the stimulus of that case. This appears to have been the situation in Washington, D.C., and such states as Delaware, Kentucky, Maryland, Missouri, and West Virginia.

Economics was also involved, particularly given the attempts by some jurisdictions to comply belatedly with *Plessy*. Blaustein and Ferguson cite economic reasons to explain compliance in the large cities: "Cheap labor —which in the South means Negro labor—is far more important in rural regions than in urban centers where skilled labor is at a premium. The demand for skilled labor automatically creates a demand for better educated labor, regardless of race or color."[92] Nagel mentions the expense of duplicate facilities and the loss of industrial development where substantial resistance to the decision occurred, although he mentions as an inhibiting factor economic competition between Negroes and whites. However, in terms of economics, Negroes could not bring economic pressure to bear in the area of school desegregation that they could, for example, with bus segregation, where a boycott would directly and quickly hurt a municipal transportation system financially.

A reason not relating to economics but to the legal system is offered by Blaustein and Ferguson. They say that judges in applying *Brown* seldom if ever explained the basis for the decision. They "parroted" *Brown* or rephrased it but did not explain the basis for the decision. The commentators argue that for *Brown II* to be effective, one needs two kinds of decisions: "The first type . . . requires an express statement of the federal district courts as to the actual basis of their decisions . . . The second type of decision . . . would make federal district court decrees directly binding upon school boards which were not parties to the litigation . . . ."[93] With respect to the first, if a judge did not personally agree with the Supreme Court ruling he was being asked to enforce, perhaps the most which could have been expected of him was a paraphrase of what his judicial superiors had said; perhaps—given the fact that some of his brethren had refused to comply at all—to ask him to have justified a decision he did not accept was asking too much.

Many of the factors adduced as explanations for compliance or noncompliance with *Brown* come from studies of different types of communities. One finding of interest is that there may be less conflict if elementary instead of high schools are desegregated first, particularly in larger communities. In the past, one has heard that resistance to desegregation is greater if it occurs in the early grades, because of white parents' resistance to having their children in contact with black children with whom they might become friends. If the children are kept separate until high school, it is argued, there will be less "mixing." In small communities, with few elementary schools, this "mixing" might well take place in desegregated elementary schools. However, in large cities, with at least a modicum of residential concentration by race, desegregation of elementary schools, with the "neighborhood school" concept kept intact, will mean little actual biracial school attendance. As Lasch has noted, "In some communities a declaration of desegregation at the elementary level meant the least upheaval in attendance patterns, since residential concentration assured predominantly white or Negro enrollments in any case."[94] Peltason also argues that residential separation may help bring about desegregation, in that community leaders who live in situations such that "schools where their children go will hardly be altered by the abolition of legal segregation"[95] are willing to help bring about compliance.

While we have suggested that groups help bring about desegregation, Crain argues that what is primarily operating is the ideology of the school board members involved in the controversy: desegregation is not, he says, basically a bargaining and negotiating problem. The "overall tone" of a school board's reaction, and certainly its initial response, is a function of the board's predispositions. But ideology in turn is related to a number of items which clearly influence the general situation. For example, a board's failure to prepare for the inevitability of desegregation, or to see that it is inevitable, will condition the level of conflict which arises when, for example, a court finally orders the board to desegregate. In writing about New Orleans, Crain points out: "The school board waited until the last possible moment to begin a campaign to keep the schools open, and even then they were hesitant to commit themselves."[96] Without this "head-in-the-sand" attitude which the board maintained for over four years, a way of dealing with the governor, short of the board's actual pledges of cooperation to him if he would keep schools open and segregated, might have been developed.

This hesitation is related to a larger syndrome Crain calls "conflict-tolerance." Unless a board is willing to depart from the wishes of its constituents, he says, desegregation is often unlikely to come about. A board "must take considerable risk; it must be willing to alienate the 'rednecks,' to run the danger of social danger or even physical attack."[97] If a school board recognizes that conflict is legitimate (and many in their views of politics in this country do not so recognize) and that one must make unpopular decisions, it will be more likely to proceed with desegregation. Thus, as Tumin writes, "Silence and inactivity favor the existing traditions and bold public affirmations of the importance of social change are almost always required if that change is to come about."[98] In this respect, the member of an urban school board may find it easier to proceed with desegregation than his rural colleagues, because the former "may be far less vulnerable to adverse public reaction than the rural member . . . ."[99] And school boards may find they have less to lose in forging ahead with desegregation than a mayor might: because the latter is involved in a wide range of decisions, what he does with respect to one has an effect on what he is able to do with the others. The school board, on the other hand, deals only with schools and doesn't have to worry about bargaining on other matters. However, because the school boards do not run the schools on a day-to-day basis, their members view desegregation as a policy or ideological matter, thus perhaps making it less easy for them to accept desegregation than if they also saw pragmatic aspects of the decision, as would a full-time administrator. And, in such situations, as Tumin sums it up, "It is the rare moment in human history when an otherwise respectable, law-abiding and community-rooted leader can successfully confront and turn back a group of men who have been incited to act violently their sense of bitterness and frustration."[100]

Even though federal judges clearly deal with other members of the community in a different setting from that in which the school board member or city councilman sees them, the judge is also subject to the same pressures, although his position as an officer of the federal government may "reinforce his backbone." While it may be a measure of the judge's competence "to avoid reversals of his rulings by a higher court," and while "the living traditions of the law oblige the district judge, whatever his own views and however strong local pressures, to follow the rulings of his judicial superiors," the "obligations" are often not sufficient to keep the judge on the path, particularly where the issue is as emotional as desegregation. Thus one finds that "A judge who violates local beliefs may indeed—despite his constitutional independence—find his position so uncomfortable that he is forced to retire."[101]

So far we have been talking primarily about school board members. One should, in addition, look at community elites—which may or may not include school board members—and other leaders. Thus, statements by antisegregationist ministers may "put a damper on any attempt to give a religio-moral tone to the segregationist position."[102] Those who arise in crisis situations, often not part of the regular community elite, can be crucial to what happens in the community. These people have often not been active participants before the crisis; they "come up suddenly from no one knows where, to fill in the vacuum of leadership and power which is created when either the respectable leadership fails to exercise power, or when, . . . the respectable leadership is rendered virtually powerless by the executive withdrawal of public power and supervision . . . ."[103] Crain stresses that in New Orleans the elite's nonparticipation helped exacerbate matters, and the legislature's commendation of those parents who had removed their children from the schools is not unlike the situation described by Tumin, when "an invitation is extended to the population to come and do as it sees fit with the events of the day."[104] The elite's participation can be important because it generally need not be responsive to public opinion, as elected officials often must be. However, their effect may be less a matter of directly influencing the decision to desegregate or remain segregated and more a function of the political system they set for the city. If the elites are active, then a vacuum of the sort mentioned above, into which unknown and untrained leaders might move, is less likely to come about. Particularly where potential lawlessness (of the mob action sort) may be involved, "The assurance that any acts of violence will be met by the full force of the law and other instruments of community restraint is a major preventive of lawlessness."[105]

CHAPTER 6

Impacts in Political Arenas: A

THE LOWER JUDICIARY: FEDERAL AND STATE

When the Supreme Court decides a case, the case is often remanded to the court from which the case came, for "proceedings not inconsistent with this opinion." The very language of the remand order suggests the amount of flexibility available to the lower courts. One might argue that, in many cases, the amount of discretion afforded the lower court when the Supreme Court has decisively decided an important matter of law is quite small. That may be true, although even in such situations, lower courts are found to have ignored the Supreme Court. But because of the breadth of some Court rulings in deciding such matters of law, and because "general principles do not decide specific cases," the remand process is not always a matter of simple application by the lower court of the Supreme Court mandate to the fact situation before it. In addition, in major areas such as school desegregation and reapportionment, the Supreme Court has left it to lower courts to develop the law in the first instance before the Supreme Court will itself deal with the matter.

The relationship between the Supreme Court, as the highest court in the land, and lower courts, whether federal or state, is not a strictly hierarchical bureaucratic one where orders go forth and are quickly and promptly obeyed—something which may not happen in real-life administrative bureaucracies, either, but which is supposed to be the case. This is true even with the lower federal courts, part of the national court system, over which the Supreme Court is supposed to have some degree of authority. It is perhaps more obvious that it is true with the state courts, because the highest state courts, while supposedly subordinate to the U.S. Supreme Court because of the "supremacy clause" of the Constitution, are the highest courts in their own jurisdictions, with greater expertise in understanding and interpreting the laws of the state or the state constitution; lower state courts, as part of the state court system, may feel that state high courts have more authority over them than does the U.S. Supreme Court. In the discussion which follows, we will deal first with lower federal courts, and then with state courts.

Federal Courts. When the Supreme Court precedents applying to a case before lower federal judges are clear, those judges know what is expected of them—that they should follow the precedents. Whether they *will* follow them may be another matter. But what is not clear is what they should do when the precedents are not clear or, even when the precedents are clear, it might appear that the Supreme Court is going to change its mind on a subject. In other words, the lower federal judges (and, to some extent, state judges as well) must face the question, "Should we anticipate what the Supreme Court might do?" One noted judge has argued that even though the lower court may be overruled for doing so, it should follow clear precedent. Judge Calvert Magruder criticized judges in another circuit for "counting noses" after the first flag salute case and deciding that the Court was going to change its mind, thus relieving them of the obligation of following that earlier ruling. But where no controlling precedent exists, matters are less clear. Magruder suggests that judges can examine earlier Supreme Court cases to see what their logical consequences might be, and can utilize dicta in earlier cases in an effort to divine what the Supreme Court would have done or would do in dealing with the problem. On the other hand, the lower-court judges can assume that the Supreme Court would find it more useful to have the lower court deal with the case fully, to provide the Supreme Court with the benefit of its thinking, regardless of past Supreme Court dicta. But there is no rule to tell a lower-court judge which strategy to use.

There is also the question of the Supreme Court opinion which lower-court judges feel to be unhelpful. Magruder speaks of situations where courts of appeals have devoted much time to writing an opinion, only to be reversed in superficial and hastily prepared opinions. This the lower-court judges would be less inclined to follow, even if they could, despite their awareness of the pressures under which the Supreme Court operates. Similarly, when the Supreme Court reverses without opinion after the lower courts have devoted much thought to a subject, the judge may be tempted to act as if the reversal hadn't occurred.

Serving to point up the effects of these situations is Sanders' comment: "If the edict itself is uncertain, or if there is a question as to whether the high court would itself now follow it, the possibility of variation and flexibility in lower court action is multiplied tremendously."[1] To Sanders' comment, Shapiro adds, in explaining differences in interpretation which arise between lower-court judges dealing with the same Supreme Court opinion, "The less clear and direct the policy communication from the Supreme Court the more likely are the resisting circuit judges to 'misunderstand' it and continue along their own path."[2] And he goes on to say, reinforcing earlier discussion of the effects of ambiguity, "The clearer the message, the higher the cost in ignoring or misunderstanding it."

As this may suggest, the Supreme Court's rulings are only *part* of the "generalized tensions" felt by the lower-court judge, not the whole directing force behind his work. The rulings create pressure in one direction, but "much more specific pressure" may derive from the emotions of the area to be affected by a decision. The federal judge, particularly the district judge, is open to those pressures because he is a resident of the district, responsive to the social, economic, and political values of the area, and a product in part of political party machinery (even if not active in the party, his selection involved the party). As Krislov notes, "The federal district judge is . . . likely to have been the product of a routine political career."[3] While the Supreme Court "represents" a national constituency, the federal judge represents a quite local one. In addition, when the President or particular executive branch agencies, for example, the FBI, appear to wish to avoid following up a Supreme Court ruling, pressure from "above" is minimized (even though the judge is not part of the executive branch).

Lest we leave the opinion that all pressures are centrifugal and lead the lower-court judge away from the Supreme Court's rulings, and that, other things being equal, lower-court judges will *not* follow the High Court's rulings, we should make clear that this is not the case, although our attention has been drawn to instances of noncompliance and nonhierarchical behavior. Hamilton, writing about judicial performance in the voting rights area, where judges were following statute rather than Supreme Court ruling, suggests that there are judges who do in fact decide cases counter to their personal views, even when the subject matter involves race and the location is the South. He notes the objection to using the judicial approach to enforce civil rights, that community pressures will negatively influence federal district judges. "The fact of hostile local opinion," it is asserted, "coupled with, in some instances a judge's personal segregationist bias, likely contributes to making the inherently slow and cumbersome judicial process even more slow and therefore even less effective. . . ."[4]

However, Hamilton goes on to distinguish between three types of judicial performance—those of judicial aggressiveness, resistance, and gradualism. The first type is characterized by active enforcement of the rights involved, while the resistant judge imposes light if any penalties for violation of rights. The gradualist judge may, like the resister, fear the consequences of enforcing Negro rights, but does so anyhow, and he may become an aggressor if particularly clear cases of rights violations come before him. "He will do so not so much to protect Negroes, but to maintain and protect the integrity of the law he is called upon to apply." Finding examples of all three types throughout the South, Hamilton concludes, "While it may be true that community pressures buttress some judges' segregationist attitudes, it is not true that community pressures will control the result of the litigation. The judicial aggressor, and to a lesser degree the judicial gradualist, are examples of the invalidity of this objection."[5] While judges may in some sense be politicians, they are *judges,* with roles which differ from those of "normal" politicians.

It has generally been held that a lower-court judge's unwillingness to be reversed (or dislike of being reversed) by his judicial superiors was an important motive in keeping him from departing from the higher court's rulings. And we find that many judges have in fact followed Supreme Court precedents religiously. A recent study of Circuit Judge John J. Parker, whose nomination to the Supreme Court was rejected by the Senate, showed that in sixty-four of seventy-two cases, Parker was consistent with the Supreme Court. In the eight cases where he was not, seven had no controlling Supreme Court precedent, leaving only *one* case of seventy-two in which he conflicted with the High Court. In his situation, compliance had high costs, because labor unions attacked his nomination because he had written a decision upholding "yellow dog" contracts (in which workers agree not to join a union), on the authority of the Supreme Court's ruling in *Hitchman Coal Co.* v. *Mitchell.*

However, some judges are willing to absorb the costs of being reversed. Magruder obviously felt that reversal should be accepted as a cost of following past cases. If the judge has intensely held policy preferences which run counter to those embodied in the Supreme Court's rulings, "he may sometimes be willing to incur these costs . . . but . . . the question is one of degree."[6] Peltason's study of southern federal judges in the aftermath of *Brown* also shows that while "judges will do what they are told by the United States Supreme Court . . . none of them . . . is particularly anxious to attack strongly entrenched local institutions," and that "the ambiguity of the Supreme Court's instructions has been resolved to conform to the dominant political forces in the South."[7]

In examining what does happen in the lower federal courts, we can look at a number of matters. One is the degree to which Supreme Court decisions are cited by the lower courts and the reasons for citation. It becomes clear that mention of a case does not mean it is being directly followed, and, alternatively, a case may be followed but accompanied by judicial criticism. We can also look at instances of cases which "float around" in and between the lower courts before finally being disposed of, and other instances of conflicts between the circuits in interpretation of Supreme Court rulings.

Turning first to the matter of citations, we can draw on studies by Krislov and Sanders. Krislov examined the frequency of citations of various Supreme Court cases where laws had been invalidated in the free-speech area during the period, 1867–1958. The Supreme Court itself had cited the cases anywhere from two to 144 times, with a mean figure of 41.[8] Other federal courts had a mean citation figure of 37, and the state courts, where the range was from 6 to 370, had a mean figure of 74. What is more important is to see the use to which lower federal courts put those cases. By far the largest category was the one in which the court simply cited a case as a sample or explained the case; this accounted for over three quarters of the citations. In another 12 percent of the citations, judges went beyond mere citation to justify the cases. In only 44 of 1,465 instances (3.0 percent) were the cases held to be controlling. In over 100 instances (7.3 percent), the cases were distinguished, questioned, or overruled—more than twice the percentage of instances where the cases were followed. From this, Krislov rightly concludes, "It appears there has been a tendency to overemphasize the precedent value of cases."[9]

Sanders' exploration provides more detailed information for specific cases in the civil liberties area. Concerning *Mallory* v. *U.S.*, in which the Court held that a defendant had to be arraigned before a magistrate as soon as possible after arrest, Sanders found fifty-eight citations through August, 1959, where federal district courts or courts of appeals discussed the case. The lower courts distinguished the case twenty-three times, holding it to be different from the cases then before them. By contrast, the lower courts followed it as controlling authority only three times, although it was explained in some detail in eight other cases. "On the whole," Sanders concludes, "the lower federal courts have not received favorably the *Mallory* precedent."[10] Murphy suggests that the lower federal judges, particularly in the District of Columbia, from which *Mallory* came, had been able to permit the use of confessions obtained during delays in arraignment by explaining, limiting, and distinguishing *Mallory* itself, which, he says, "provides a classic example of the power of inferior judges to reshape legal doctrine expounded by the Supreme Court." After the search and seizure case of *Rea* v. *U.S.*, in which it had been held to be error for a federal court not to enjoin use in a state criminal case of evidence illegally obtained by a federal official, Sanders found sixteen citations, none of which indicated that the case was followed.

With respect to the *Yates* case, involving Smith Act prosecutions and in which the Court limited its earlier *Dennis* holding, Sanders finds results different from those just mentioned. In ten references to the case, he finds no instances of the case being distinguished, and finds, as well, a number of citations to cases where the case was followed as controlling. He argues that this sort of reception is more typical of what occurs with Supreme Court rulings than was the case with the aftermath of *Mallory*:

> The overall judgment as to the functioning of the lower federal courts in relationship to the Supreme Court has been favorable in terms of the implementation of the Supreme Court's pronouncement. . . . The fact of

> normal acceptance of the principle and the normal absence of a grudging approach to its implementation brings into even greater prominence the two or three instances in which federal district courts have seemed to engage in undue delaying tactics in the implementation of the Supreme Court's pronouncement.[11]

He shows that judges often are sufficiently willing to apply a court precedent that they extend it to areas other than the one from which the precedent originally derived. In this connection, he cites the "rather generous acceptance" of the basic principle of *Brown* v. *Board,* and shows its extension by three courts of appeals to such matters as recreation, restaurants in county courthouses, and allocation of public housing units. (However, in Topeka, directly involved in *Brown,* a three-judge federal court accepted a plan which did not accomplish desegregation for the 1955–56 school year. The Virginia and South Carolina federal courts involved in dases decided with *Brown* issued injunctions against segregation, but which were to go into effect only after school boards had made "necessary arrangements.")

Another example of the extension of a decision has occurred more recently with *Baxstrom* v. *Herold,* in which the Court held that keeping a mentally ill prisoner in a prison hospital after the expiration of his term, without a special hearing, was impermissible. Other courts, basing decisions at least in part on *Baxstrom,* extended the requirement of a separate hearing to mental hospital commitment after a finding of not guilty because of insanity and to commitment after a defendant's plea of not guilty by reason of insanity—both on the grounds that there was no justification for a lack of procedures available to those involved in voluntary commitments—and to the transfer of a juvenile from a boy's training center to a men's correctional center after an administrative determination of incorrigibility.

Conflict between the circuits is at least in part a function of the ambiguity of Supreme Court opinions which we have been discussing. We see that this occurs not only in the civil liberties–civil rights areas, where personal philosophical preferences are likely to come to the fore, but in less controversial areas as well. For example, the Supreme Court decided in 1963, in *U.S.* v. *Muniz,* that a federal prisoner could recover under the Federal Tort Claims Act for the negligent acts of employees which cause personal injury to federal prisoners; this made the Prison Industries Fund not the exclusive source of compensation. Following the Supreme Court's ruling, the Third Circuit held that the Prison Industries Fund was not the exclusive remedy, thus following the Supreme Court, but the Second Circuit held for exclusivity of the Prison Fund. A comparable conflict has developed over certain procedural rules dealing with the initiation of suits. In 1965, the Supreme Court held, in *Hanna* v. *Plumer,* that the "outcome-determinative" test in diversity-of-citizenship cases could not be invoked to invalidate application of appropriate Federal Rules of Civil Procedure. Earlier the Court had applied a state rule of personal service rather than the federal rule. After *Hanna,* "conflict and uncertainty concerning Rule 3 have not completely abated," wrote a commentator.[12] He found that the Courts of Appeals in the Sixth and Eighth Circuits had continued to hold that state law controls (in situations involving state statutes of limitations), with the circuits drawing on the Court's 1949 ruling, while district judges in New York had put aside the earlier case in order to follow the 1965 ruling, in cases quite similar to those in the Sixth and Eighth Circuits. The substantial divergence between circuits in the patent law area, both before and after the Supreme Court's recent rulings, has already been dealt with at length.

Cases involving the Smith Act of 1940, outlawing overthrow of the government by force and violence, provide another example of diversity in the follow-through by lower courts after Supreme Court rulings. However, the divergence here was mostly in the rationale put forth by the lower courts in upholding Smith Act convictions rather than in the results or outcomes of the cases. In 1951, the U.S. Supreme Court decided the *Dennis* case, involving some of the top Communist leaders in the United States. The Court upheld the constitutionality of the Smith Act and the convictions of the Communist leaders for conspiring to teach and advocate the overthrow of the government by force and violence and for conspiring to organize the Communist party. The Court used the "clear-and-present-danger" test in arriving at its conclusion, although it was made clear that the government did not have to wait until a group was ready to take over the government before the latter could act to protect itself.

In the period following *Dennis,* "The lower federal courts . . . evolved a bewildering variety of interpretations."[13] The lower courts were at least in agreement in rejecting objections under the First Amendment to either the Smith Act or specific prosecutions, and all convictions appealed were affirmed, in the period between *Dennis* and the 1957 *Yates* case, in which the Court restricted Smith Act convictions to situations involving specific incitation to violence and not simply abstract discussion of overthrow of the government. However, in these cases, "although [lower-court judges] avowedly followed the guidelines laid down in *Dennis,* their interpretations showed little resemblance to *Dennis.*"[14] One court upheld a Smith Act conviction as a straight criminal conspiracy, while another completely ignored the clear-and-present-danger test and dealt instead with the subjective intent of the conspirators. Another court used a version of clear and present danger, but a weakened one.

After *Yates,* we find somewhat more divergence in one sense but less in another. As applied to prosecution for membership in the Communist party, "the diversity of federal court interpretation of *Yates* . . . left the whole matter in an ambiguous state."[15] In interpreting *Yates,* at least one court seemed to be relying more on the substance of *Dennis* by stressing advocacy rather than incitement, an indication of the difficulty of finding compliance when there are earlier cases to which the lower courts can retreat and from which they can draw for their opinions. Some convictions were affirmed at the court of appeals level and some were reversed—a divergence not found with respect to *Dennis*—and some trials were never held. With respect to the more central part of the *Yates* decision, "There was . . . wide variation in the circuit courts' understanding of *Yates*," but "most courts applied the new doctrine without extraneous comment." "There was far less variation in lower court applications of *Yates* than there had been previously in the application of *Dennis*."[16] Again the variation occurred in the way the courts stated the basis on which their decisions rested. What this suggests is that Supreme Court decisions may be followed in terms of results, even though it appears from the language of the opinions that there is divergence between the lower courts and the Supreme Court, just as the language can be followed but the results differ.

While we have talked about divergence between circuits, we have not mentioned repeated failure by lower courts to follow Supreme Court rulings. This has occurred in the relationship between the courts of appeals and the federal district courts, where the former have applied Supreme Court rulings to fact situations which have come up from the district courts and where the latter refuse to follow the appeals courts' mandates—despite Shapiro's comment: "There are certain mechanisms built into the district-circuit relation that enforce a far higher level of loyalty by the districts to the circuits than necessarily exists, except on a voluntary basis, between the circuits and the Supreme Court."[17] The most extreme examples come from the school desegregation area, and involve Prince Edward County, Virginia, and Dallas, Texas.

In Prince Edward County, after *Brown,* a three-judge court required admission of Negro children. After the plaintiffs asked for a definite time for such admission to be fixed, the three-judge court turned the matter over to a single judge, who ordered deferral of the desegregation order on the basis of current conditions, including public opinion. When the Court of Appeals for the Fourth Circuit reversed and remanded with an order to the judge to abolish discrimination in school admission immediately, the judge fixed ten years after *Brown II* as the compliance date, although he did reserve power to order acceleration. Again, the Court of Appeals reversed and remanded, and directed the district judge to enjoin the defendants from action regulating admission on the basis of color and to require applications of Negro children for admission to the high school for September, 1959. As we have seen earlier, the schools were ultimately closed.

In Dallas, the federal district judge refused to convene a three-judge court, found the facilities in the schools substantially equal, and held that *Brown II* required integration on the basis of planning by local school officials and local judges. With no such plan available, he dismissed plaintiffs' suit. When the Court of Appeals for the Fifth Circuit reversed, the district judge declined to issue an injunction on the grounds it would harm whites to admit Negroes to already crowded white schools, and again dismissed the case, to give the school board time to act. Again the Court of Appeals reversed, and directed the judge to enter a decree requiring desegregation; in addition, the appeals court denied rehearing requested on the grounds that Texas law barred a district from receiving state funds if integration had proceeded without an election. Upon remand, the district court finally ordered integration for the midwinter term (January, 1958). This time, the Court of Appeals reversed at the defendants' request, on the grounds the judge had not complied with prior orders and had left inadequate time for planning the transition. In July, 1959, the district judge again declined to order immediate desegregation, indicating he would hold further hearings later. More compliant action did come at a later date.

All such difficulties are not in the civil rights area, however. One which was recently again before the Court involved the divestiture by El Paso Natural Gas Company of Pacific Northwest Pipeline Company, which the Court had held, in a Clayton Act case, it improperly acquired. After the first Supreme Court decision, the government and El Paso entered a consent decree, accepted by the lower court, transferring the illegally acquired assets to New Company. The Supreme Court set aside the decree. On remand from this case, the district court chose the Colorado Interstate Gas Company as the best qualified applicant for making the New Company a serious competitor in the California market. Under the district court's order, El Paso would have had considerable stock in New Company—clearly not divestiture. Thus, in *Utah Public Service Commission* v. *El Paso Natural Gas Co.,* with the matter before it for the third time, the Court had to hold that complete divestiture, as originally ordered, still was not brought about and had to order that all managerial and financial ties be severed between El Paso and New Company.

Thus far we have been talking about whether lower federal courts followed or did not follow Supreme Court rulings. Another category of impact contains those instances where judges follow a case but add criticism of the Supreme Court's rulings to their opinions. Thus, when the Court of Appeals for the Ninth Circuit reversed a conviction of a pair of Communist leaders after *Yates,* Judge Chambers "remarked tartly that the court would have upheld the validity of the convictions on the basis of past practice had not the Supreme Court changed the law,"[18] and showed his displeasure that the Communists couldn't be prosecuted under the Smith Act's organizing provisions unless they set up the CP–USA as a new organization. Mollan notes additional instances of "personal dissatisfaction" with that decision. A federal district judge in Arkansas recently complained about the amount of freedom the U.S. Supreme Court had left him in school desegregation suits. He said "that the United States Supreme Court decision in a similar case involving the Gould School District, which borders the Grady District on the South, left 'little room for maneuvering.' . . . 'Counsel knows the very limited, if any, discretion the federal courts have left under the decisions of the Supreme Court of the United States.'"[19] It is doubtful that Judge Young would have made these remarks if he supported the Supreme Court's ruling.

Sometimes the displeasure of lower federal judges with Supreme Court decisions is found beyond the boundaries of the cases they decide. Thus, when *U.S. News and World Report* conducted a poll of all district and circuit judges concerning the reaction to the 1958 statement by the state chief justices criticizing the Court, 59 (of the 128 answering) expressed approval, and 50 disapproval. The Judicial Conference of the United States, containing the federal circuit and district judges, has endorsed bills to reverse Supreme Court decisions, including *Mallory,* and federal judges have testified before Congress on such matters. Recently, a Court of Appeals judge, in giving some law school lectures, went so far as to propose reversing Supreme Court decisions by constitutional amendment. Judge Henry Friendly was particularly critical of decisions concerning the right not to incriminate oneself. Such statements of criticism, whether from on the bench or off, can have important "second-order" effects by giving support to congressmen, the President, state legislators, governors, and local officials who are interested in undoing or not following Supreme Court rulings.

State Courts. The resistance of state court judges to Supreme Court decisions has already been noted, as has its most obvious manifestation in recent years, the 1958 statement by the Conference of Chief Justices. After calling attention to the influence of Supreme Court decisions, the justices decried a "continuing and . . . an accelerating trend towards increasing power of the national government and correspondingly contracted power of the state governments," much of which, they felt "comes from the extent of the control over the action of the states which the Supreme Court exercises under its views of the Fourteenth Amendment." While one can argue that the charges made cannot be supported, the fact of the statement itself is important. It is important even if it does not represent the views of all state judges, for example those who, as Peltason notes, sometimes represent interests which would expand, not limit, Supreme Court rulings. But very clearly state court judges do not follow the U.S. Supreme Court's rulings automatically, regardless of the existence of the supremacy clause. They do so in part because of their position in a court system which, while in some measure integrated into the national court system through the role of the U.S. Supreme Court in reviewing state court decisions, is essentially independent from the federal courts; because of the differences in recruitment between them and Supreme Court Justices, an even greater difference than between lower federal judges and U.S. Supreme Court Justices; and because they feel they must (or may) base their decisions at least in part on the constitutions of their states. They may also be more willing to criticize as they become aware of their lesser chances of appointment to the U.S. Supreme Court.

The U.S. Supreme Court may, on very rare occasions, attempt to discipline a state judge. Thus, in 1969, a motion was made to hold in contempt of the Supreme Court an Alabama judge who disobeyed an order against officials to prevent them from using ballots without the names of candidates of the National Democratic Party of Alabama. Judge Herndon left the NDPA candidates off the ballot in Greene County. The Supreme Court, in dealing with the substantive matters concerning the ballot, in *Hadnott* v. *Amos,* ordered a new election for Greene County, in which the black candidates won control of the county board and school board. The Court, in *In Re Herndon,* delayed disposition of the contempt motion until there could be a disposition in federal district court of contempt proceedings there. While not taking action, the Supreme Court was clearly indicating it could do so. Despite this incident, the Court usually relies on other methods, particularly reversal of lower-court rulings, to secure compliance with its decisions. Sometimes that compliance is not easily obtained, as we see not only from contemporary examples but from our past constitutional history as well. "Whether or not the higher court can . . . effect its will regardless of the lower court depends upon the timing of subsequent cases on the same question and the intensity of feeling in the high court. If cases develop at a pace commensurate with that of the flow of events the upper court may in fact be effective."[20]

Before turning to historical examples, we might look at two situations of repeated interchanges between the U.S. Supreme Court and state courts which occurred since World War II. The first, *Florida ex rel. Hawkins* v. *Board of Control,* involves the application by Virgil Hawkins for admission to the Law School at the University of Florida. In 1949, Hawkins, a black, asked the Florida courts for a mandamus order for admission. In 1952, the Florida Supreme Court dismissed the suit. The U.S. Supreme Court, in 1954, remanded the case to the Florida courts for consideration in light of the first *Brown* decision. The Florida Supreme Court appointed a master to take testimony as to when Hawkins should be admitted. After a Supreme Court denial of certiorari, the Court later, in a new *per curiam* ruling, said that no reason for delay existed. The Florida Supreme Court refused admission, this time on grounds Hawkins didn't seriously want to go to law school and that violence would result from his admission. Certiorari was denied again, but without prejudice to Hawkins' seeking relief in district court. The federal district judge refused to let him present evidence and denied him an injunction against the university. The circuit court remanded to the district court for a hearing on the merits. At that point, the district court judge held Hawkins had established no right to enter the law school, but held in a class action that Florida should not limit admission to graduate schools to whites only. It should be noted that, despite the intransigence of both the state courts and the federal district court, some state judges did dissent to the rulings of their brethren, indicating that they had no choice but to put the *Brown* decision into effect as the law of the land.

The second situation involves the state of Georgia. After the Supreme Court, in the *Avery* case, had struck down Georgia's jury selection plan in 1953, there was a challenge to a conviction and a death sentence obtained after that case was decided, in *Williams* v. *Georgia*. Georgia conceded the invalidity of the jury selection process but said that the challenge was not timely. The Supreme Court remanded for further consideration by the Georgia courts in view of the state's concession, but the Georgia Supreme Court refused to reverse, with Chief Judge Duckworth asserting, "This court bows to the Supreme Court on all federal questions of law but we will not supinely surrender sovereign powers of this State." This time, the Supreme Court denied certiorari, and Williams was executed.

While there are a number of important historical examples of state court resistance to U.S. Supreme Court rulings, perhaps the earliest famous incident was the case of *Martin* v. *Hunter's Lessee*. The Supreme Court had invalidated Virginia's confiscation of land belonging to an enemy alien. The Virginia courts refused to honor the Supreme Court's order, giving rise to another case, in which Justice Story made clear that the Supreme Court had the right (which it had exercised for some years, anyhow) to review (and reverse) the judgments of state courts. Virginia Judge Spencer Roane took considerable issue with Story. His reply was that there was no authorization for the central government to be the final judge of the extent of its own power; there was no clause forbidding state courts to pass finally on their own acts; and the supremacy clause was binding on state judges only as state judges, so their decisions were not reviewable by a court of another jurisdiction (meaning any federal court). This was one of the most comprehensive and clearly stated views voiced against the Court's powers of review. The conflict between the Supreme Court and Virginia continued with the case of *Cohens* v. *Virginia*, involving a conviction in Virginia for the sale of District of Columbia municipal lottery tickets. When the case came before the Supreme Court, the

Virginia legislature passed a resolution protesting the Supreme Court's assumption of jurisdiction. The Supreme Court did take jurisdiction, but affirmed the convictions, thus quieting the controversy, at least for the time being.

The decision in *McCulloch* v. *Maryland*, upholding the United States Bank against state attempts to tax that institution, brought forth much resistance, including statements by Virginia Judge Spencer Roane attacking the ruling. In Ohio, the supreme court there refused for two years to enter the Supreme Court's mandate in the related case involving Ohio's attempt to tax the bank. "Finally, late in 1826, three Judges of the State Supreme Court decided to conform to the mandate which had been issued to it, stating that they were 'not prepared to adopt the theory' on which a denial of the jurisdiction of the Supreme Court under the Judiciary Act was based,"[21] although the chief justice of the state supreme court in another case clearly did hold to that position and refused to prepare the record of a case so that it could be appealed. Resistance by state court judges was so widespread at this time that when judges in Kentucky indicated they were bound to follow the Supreme Court's ruling in *Sturgis* v. *Crowninshield*, involving Kentucky's land laws, Warren refers to their "courage, integrity and independence," although nowadays one might *expect* that following the Supreme Court's word would be normal and not "courageous" action.

The Civil War, or rather the period immediately before it, produced the next resistance to the U.S. Supreme Court. Much of this revolved around enforcement of the Fugitive Slave Acts, to which many Northerners were strongly opposed. After the state courts in Wisconsin had released, on habeas corpus, a prisoner being held for violating those laws, the U.S. Supreme Court reversed in *Ableman* v. *Booth*, indicating that the state courts could not interfere with federal law enforcement. The Wisconsin Supreme Court refused to comply with the mandate. Six months after the decision, the United States attorney moved to file with the state supreme court clerk the two mandates from the U.S. Supreme Court, but his motion was not granted. When Booth was again arrested, again he was released by the Wisconsin Supreme Court on habeas corpus. When the Civil War began, the deadlock between the two courts was broken, with the state court holding that the U.S. district court had jurisdiction of the suit against Booth by the owner of the slave Booth had rescued and that the judgment against Booth's printing press by a federal marshal was valid and not open to collateral attack in state court. However, the state court had held the U.S. Supreme Court "at bay" for over two years. A comparable situation almost developed in Ohio, when the Ohio Supreme Court, after *Booth*, asserted the right to decide whether or not the Fugitive Slave Acts were constitutional, in connection with habeas corpus writs for prisoners in federal custody for violation of the acts. However, the state court decided that the law was constitutional, thus eliminating conflict.

That the refusal to implement a Supreme Court order is not simply a matter of ancient American history is shown not only by the *Hawkins* situation but also by the litigation involving the NAACP in its attempts to strike down Alabama's statute requiring the production of membership lists as a prerequisite to "doing business" in the state. After the Supreme Court held that the state could not require membership lists, and could not hold the NAACP in contempt for refusing to turn them over, the Supreme Court mandate, sent down on August 1, 1958, did not go very far. Three months later, the Alabama Supreme Court had done nothing with it, although the NAACP moved that the mandate be forwarded to the circuit court, and renewed the motion several times. The state attorney general filed a brief with the Alabama Supreme Court in mid-December showing alternatives available to that court in dealing with the matter, none of which entailed following the mandate. On February 12, 1959, six months after the Supreme Court's mandate was issued, the Alabama Supreme Court denied a motion to send the case to the circuit court, affirmed the contempt adjudication against the NAACP, and reinstituted the $100,000 fine against the organization. The state court claimed that the U.S. Supreme Court was mistaken in resting its decision on the idea that refusal to produce membership lists was the sole reason for holding the organization in contempt.

When the U.S. Supreme Court again reversed the Alabama Supreme Court, in *NAACP* v. *Alabama,* the state supreme court indicated it was waiting for a U.S. Supreme Court decision on the state's request for rehearing. That request was denied, two months later, but nothing was done even after that, and a NAACP motion requesting remand to the lower courts received no response. In late 1959, the state attorney general asked the state supreme court to retain the mandate because the NAACP was under contempt proceedings in Montgomery County, which was the location of the original 1956 case. NAACP counsel went to federal court in mid-1960 to obtain an injunction against state officials to prevent their proceeding further against the NAACP. During arguments on this request, the state indicated that the Alabama Supreme Court had just remanded the case (finally!) to the circuit court, and the federal district judge thus denied the injunction request. But delay was still to occur, as the circuit court waited for months without doing anything to bring about hearings. Only further action before the U.S. Supreme Court—an appeal of the above-mentioned federal court action—brought about lower state court activity. After the U.S. Supreme Court, in *NAACP* v. *Gallion,* directed the federal district court to have a trial of the issues by January 2, 1962, the state circuit court held a hearing in late December. The upshot of that was a permanent injunction *against* the NAACP, rather than an order dissolving prior injunctions. The NAACP was still out of luck, and Alabama had already kept the organization out of the state for over six years at that point.

While the instances cited thus far, either from distant or recent history, are on the dramatic side, and thus may not give an adequate picture of the range of response by state judges, it is clear that far more frequently than is generally acknowledged, "the state courts either ignore the Supreme Court ruling or evade it by finding against the winner of the Supreme Court appeal on different grounds."[22] In other words, they do what Manwaring suggests the state courts did with the first Flag Salute Case: they "quarantine" it—in that instance "systematically block[ing] all attempts at further punishment of either children or parents," with some state courts eventually rebelling, holding their own state's flag-salute statutes unconstitutional."[23]

Jacob's comment suggests that the state courts do not, and do not have to, defy the Supreme Court directly; they can instead find oblique ways of managing to remove themselves from the thrust of the U.S. Supreme Court's rulings. That there are state laws and state constitutions on which they can draw allows them to do this. Thus, the Oregon Supreme Court some years ago avoided the thrust of the *Everson* and *Cochran* cases allowing benefits to parochial school students, by drawing on provisions of the Oregon constitution to invalidate, in *Dickman* v. *School District*, a statute which provided for free textbooks for parochial school students. The Oregon constitution's church-state provision was written differently from that of the First Amendment to the U.S. Constitution (as well as more precisely), and the state judges simply acted as if the U.S. Supreme Court cases didn't exist. It should be remembered here that reliance on state constitutions does not always mean evasion of the Supreme Court's decisions. A state court may rely on the state's constitution to reach the same result it would have reached using the U.S. Constitution, as has occurred with some movie censorship cases.

Distinguishing cases, noted as a response of federal courts to Supreme Court rulings, also occurs in state courts. Thus, the Texas Court of Criminal Appeals distinguished away the *Rochin* case, in which police had pumped the stomach of a man to recover heroin capsules, and upheld the admission of evidence when police executing a search warrant found the defendant attempting to swallow heroin capsules, which they made him spit out. Vanlandingham points out that most states avoided compliance with the ruling of *Tumey* v. *Ohio*, invalidating convictions before justices of the peace paid through fees collected from those they held guilty, when their courts "hold that circumstances present in such cases are unlike those of the *Tumey* case,"[24] particularly where the defendant can demand a jury trial or be tried *de novo* on appeal. However, in other situations, state judges have not made such distinctions and have used *Tumey* to invalidate justice of the peace court convictions. Thus, in Kentucky, in a case decided the same year as *Tumey*, the court of appeals reversed a justice of the peace conviction, holding itself bound by the U.S. Supreme Court's ruling. When in 1956, thirty years after the Supreme Court ruled, the Kentucky Court of Appeals held the justice courts without jurisdiction in misdemeanor cases, "[that court] perhaps has accorded the *Tumey* decision greater significance than it has heretofore received from any state supreme court."[25]

In avoiding the implications of the *Tumey* case, a number of courts relied on procedural grounds. Thus, some courts held that "even though a justice be disqualified because of financial interest, in the absence of some constitutional or statutory requirement that courts be presided over by disinterested judges, a judgment rendered by him is not void, but voidable only, and has the effect of legality until declared illegal in a proper proceeding. Such judgment cannot be attacked collaterally nor challenged on a writ of habeas corpus."[26] That the disqualification issue had been raised prior to trial in *Tumey*, rather than during or after it, was used by some courts to get rid of the precedent. This device, of using procedural grounds for denying the effect of the U.S. Supreme Court's rulings, is found elsewhere, and gives credence to Walter Murphy's suggestion that "The vague remand prescription acts as a psychological safety valve in allowing some of the pressure of resentment against reversal to be siphoned off in construing Supreme Court instructions."[27] Thus, when the U.S. Supreme Court, in *Hawk* v. *Olson*, remanded a case to the Nebraska courts on the grounds that the prisoner's allegations showed absence of effective counsel such that he should have a hearing on the matter, his attempt to obtain compliance was denied by the Nebraska Supreme Court on the grounds that he had sought relief through the wrong state remedy, which the state court claimed that the U.S. Supreme Court could not dictate to the states.

In one of the miscegenation cases discussed earlier in the volume, the state court procedure was asserted to thwart a U.S. Supreme Court remand. When the Supreme Court returned the case to the Virginia courts with instructions to remand to the trial court to make a factual determination about the residency of the parties involved before and after their out-of-state marriage, the Virginia Supreme Court of Appeals said there was no state procedure by which the record could be sent back to the trial court to be supplemented. More recently, in another situation involving Virginia, the U.S. Supreme Court had remanded a case involving refusal by a Virginia corporation running a swimming pool to allow white members to assign their membership to Negroes. After the Virginia courts had dismissed the case and Virginia court appeals had been rejected (on procedural grounds), the Supreme Court had said, in *Sullivan*

v. *Little Hunting Park,* that the Virginia courts should reconsider in light of *Jones* v. *Mayer,* the 1968 fair housing case. "On the remand, the Virgina court could not find any light in the *Jones* case," because that case did not "involve the application by a state appellate court of its rule of procedure."[28] (When the Supreme Court again heard the case, it invalidated the discriminatory practice.)

CONGRESS

The actions of Congress with respect to Supreme Court decisions have probably received more attention than the actions of other agencies of government, in part because of Congress' visibility and the greater ease of studying one legislative body than fifty (the state legislatures). Congressional reaction to Supreme Court rulings, when Congress has not simply followed or ignored the rulings, has included attempts to strip the Court of its appellate jurisdiction, questioning of prospective Justices, reluctance to pay out funds, and reversal of particular decisions by either constitutional amendment or the rewriting of statutes. It should be stressed that only a small fraction of the Court's rulings receive any such negative reaction, so that the items discussed in this chapter, as well as those mentioned earlier in the volume, are not representative of the Congress' reception of the Court.

Krislov suggests, "No study has been undertaken to estimate the number of Court decisions heavily criticized in Congress, but these would surely constitute a small fraction of the total number. Most never come to the attention of Congress at all."[29] Echoing Schubert's remark, "Decisions of the Court are themselves political data, and they provide strong ammunition for congressmen who would defend the status quo—as defined by the Court, of course—against proposals for legislative change,"[30] Krislov goes on to add, "Court standards are . . . frequently utilized in discussions in the halls of Congress as tests for prospective legislation," which he considers "a significant aspect of Court influence over the legislative process."[31]

An example of this would be the situation cited by Warren concerning the aftermath of *McCulloch,* when there was argument over the power of Congress to establish a national bank: "The binding force of the decision of the Court . . . , even upon Congress, was supported by many strong lawyers, both Democratic and Whig . . ."[32] Murphy notes, "Legislators can use court decisions as defenses against presidential pressure to pass certain legislation as well as against constituent pressure,"[33] and argues that legislators who wreck the Court's prestige by their attacks upon it lose a powerful instrument of their own. The factual assumption behind these arguments is, however, challenged by Stumpf, who finds that citation of Court decisions by Congress does not provide strong ammunition for those who would stop attempts to reverse the court.[34] He is, however, dealing only with attempts to reverse the Court, and Court decisions may be cited effectively at other times, when Court reversal is not at issue.

Attempts to remove the Court's jurisdiction have been with us almost as long as has the Court and the Constitution. Jacob tells us:

> Each time the Supreme Court has challenged congressional policy decisions, Congress has threatened to retaliate by diminishing the jurisdiction of federal courts or by changing the structure of the court. In 1802 Congress even ordered the Supreme Court not to meet again for a year, thus 'abolishing' it for fourteen months. As early as 1821 proposals were laid before Congress to restrict the Supreme Court's power to review the constitutionality of state acts.[35]

Among the attacks was a bill, favorably reported by the Senate Committee on the Judiciary in January, 1831, to repeal Section 25 of the Judiciary Act of 1789; the bill was defeated. Senators from the South and West had wanted the entire act repealed, as well as both a prohibition of decisions touching the rights of the states and unanimity by the Court when dealing with questions of constitutionality. It was also suggested that there be established a special court to handle conflicts between federal and state governments, with a judge from each state, not unlike the 1963 proposal for a "Court of the Union," composed of the chief justices of the supreme courts of each state, with power of review over Supreme Court decisions touching on states' rights.

The Reconstruction Congress made the greatest effective incursion on the Court's review power by removing a case from the Court's jurisdiction while the case was pending. This reprisal stemmed from the Supreme Court's decisions in *Ex Parte Milligan,* requiring that civilians be tried in civilian courts if they were functioning, rather than by court-martial, and the "test oath" cases (*Cummings* and *Garland*), where loyalty oaths had been required of those who had participated in the Confederacy before they could hold certain positions. Because of a fear that Reconstruction policy would be struck down by the Court, Congress repealed an 1867 statute granting the Supreme Court appellate jurisdiction over habeas corpus cases. McCardle, a Mississippi editor, had been arrested and held for trial before a military tribunal. After his case had been argued before the Court, but before it was decided, the repeal legislation was enacted, and the Court refused to make a decision, ruling that it had been deprived of jurisdiction. But this limited incursion (repeal of jurisdiction over a *single* statute) was a "high-water mark," and was not followed up with similar actions, even though the Supreme Court, in the *Yerger* case, granted habeas review of military imprisonment of another Mississippi editor under the Judiciary Act of 1789, rather than the 1867 act. This action met with proposals to strip Court jurisdiction further, but the effort was not carried through to completion. In the years which have followed, no similar action has been successful in Congress, although some have come close to victory.

"The broad historic trend has been away from bills which would remove or circumscribe a broad area of the Court's power and toward those bills which would limit a small, more specific part of the Court's functions,"[36] but there have been some recent efforts. While the reaction to the Court's striking down of economic regulation legislation during the New Deal has been seen principally in terms of President Roosevelt's efforts to "pack" the Court (to be discussed later), there were also congressional efforts to restrict the Court. Senator Wheeler, in February, 1937, suggested an amendment to permit Congress to override Court invalidations by a two-thirds vote of both houses of Congress. Senator O'Mahoney proposed another amendment the following month requiring a two-thirds vote of the Court to declare an act of Congress void, not a direct restriction of the Court's jurisdiction but clearly a limitation of its powers.

In 1958, members of the Congress, angered by Supreme Court decisions in the field of internal security, particularly those which appeared to restrict the rights of the states, joined by Southerners angered by *Brown* v. *Board,* introduced one of the broadest bills aimed at curtailment of judicial review by the Court. S. 2646 in the 85th Congress, the Jenner bill, would have denied jurisdiction in cases involving (1) contempt charges against witnesses before legislative committees; (2) any executive or administrative program adopted under congressional authority to remove individuals who might impair national security; (3) state antisubversive laws; (4) regulations by state school authorities concerning subversive activities of teachers; and (5) state bar admission regulations. Each of the provisions was aimed at a particular ruling of the Supreme Court, most of them handed down on "Red Monday" (June 17, 1957). Thus, the matter of contempt charges was directed at the case of *Watkins* v. *U.S.*, where the Court had held that questions must be made pertinent to tne purpose of the legislative committee's investigation if a person were to be held in contempt for refusal to answer. The provisions concerning internal security programs of the administration were aimed at *Service* v. *Dulles,* which Lytle says aroused ire largely by virtue of being decided on the same day as *Yates; Sweezy* v. *New Hampshire,* the basis for the attempted restriction of jurisdiction concerning state antisubversive actions; and *Watkins,* as well as following *Peters* v. *Hobby* and *Cole* v. *Young,* which had required that loyalty programs follow regulations established by the administration and be restricted to those in sensitive positions. Cases, such as *Schware,* in which the Court had required state bar qualifications committees to stay away from questions concerning candidates' political beliefs also led to provisions in the bill, as did the *Slochower* case, where the Court had reversed the firing of a college professor for his refusal (on Fifth Amendment grounds) to testify before a congressional committee.

On August 20, 1958, the Senate voted to table the bill, 49–41, with a majority of Republicans, joined by almost all the southern Democrats, favoring the bill, and all northern Democrats and the remaining Republicans opposed. Murphy justifiably calls our attention to the closeness of the vote, despite the fact that the bill failed, because those who would have limited the Court received many more votes than the Senate leadership had been able to be sure of in the Court-packing fight of 1937. Efforts were also made to enact a more generic constitutional amendment, allowing Congress, by a two-thirds vote of both houses, to limit the authority of the courts to determine the status of national acts repugnant to the Constitution. The degree of unhappiness is shown by the language of still another resolution: "The Courts of the United States and the courts of the several States shall not be bound by any decision of the Supreme Court of the United States which conflicts with the legal principles of adhering to prior decisions and which is based upon considerations other than legal."

Attacking the Court's basic power to hear cases is only one way in which the Congress strikes back at the Court. Attacks on individual Justices are also utilized. Thus, Justice Douglas' personal behavior has been attacked, both at the time of the 1967 legislation to increase Supreme Court Justices' pay, when they were given a smaller increase than were other national officials, and after Justice Fortas' resignation, when Douglas' connection with several foundations was criticized. It is not just liberal paranoia to suggest that the vehemence of the attacks on Douglas stemmed from dyspepsia over his liberal decisions, although his off-the-court activity gave critics a hook on which to hang their attacks.

When Justice Fortas' nomination to be Chief Justice was under consideration, he was attacked by several southern senators for just about every decision in which he had taken part, whether or not he had written the Court's decision in the case. Before pointing out that the Justice had participated in such 5–4 criminal procedure cases as *Miranda, Wade,* and *Gilbert,* which he found offensive, Senator Ervin (D–N.C.) remarked, "His deeds as an Associate Justice . . . make it obvious that he is one of the judicial activists now serving on the Supreme Court who toy with the Constitution as if it were their personal plaything instead of the precious inheritance of all Americans." Senator Stennis (D–Miss.) went through a number of criminal procedure cases, pointedly remarking with respect to each that Mr. Justice Fortas had sided with the majority. Senator Eastland and Senator McClellan acted particularly incensed by the Court's obscenity rulings, with the latter pointing out that Fortas had voted thirty-five times (out of a possible thirty-eight) to reverse obscenity convictions since he had come on the Court. The senator went on to add, "Since he has been an Associate Justice of the Supreme Court, Justice

Fortas has consistently voted to uphold the rights of Communists and other subversives against efforts by the State and Federal governments to proceed against these persons . . . ."

At an earlier date, southern senators had attempted to turn the hearing on Judge Potter Stewart's nomination to the Supreme Court into a debate on school desegregation. When Justice Brennan's nomination came before the Senate—after he had been a sitting Justice, because President Eisenhower had named him in a recess appointment—a number of conservative senators attempted to get him to adopt their views of the Communist "menace," clearly indicating their concern over the direction in which they felt the Supreme Court was moving with respect to internal security. "At the height of the criticism of the Court by segregationists and those who felt that the national security decisions of recent years were unfortunate, prospective justices were even asked to affirm that the Court had no right to change the Constitution and to pledge themselves to be more responsive to the intent of Congress."[37] The Senate's concern with personnel qualifications has gone beyond attempting to determine (or assure) the ideology of a prospective judge or to criticize that of a sitting one. A high proportion of bills aimed at the Court have dealt with personnel matters (29 percent), including requiring that Justices have lengthy prior judicial experience—which supposedly predisposes the individual to follow precedent—and expanding or contracting the size of the Court. This is about the same percentage as bills aimed at restricting the Court's appellate jurisdiction.

An instance which provides a crucial test of the willingness of the Congress to follow the Supreme Court is one in which the Supreme Court has said that someone should receive a sum of money. The funds must be paid from appropriations made by the Congress, and a refusal to appropriate would mean congressional noncompliance. Generally, decisions of the U.S. Court of Claims, where suits for money sought from the federal government are filed, are honored regularly, and there is no issue involved. However, sometimes the matter is far from automatic. For example, Congress almost did not appropriate money to pay back salaries to the three government employees who, Congress had earlier said, were not to be paid because of their alleged Communist affiliations. Because the initial congressional provision was in an omnibus appropriations bill and because the President could not veto individual items, there was little President Roosevelt could do about the provision. When the individuals sued for their salary in *U.S.* v. *Lovett,* the Supreme Court declared the act a bill of attainder and indicated that they were entitled to their salary. Then the question was up to Congress, which appropriated the money, but by only one vote in the House of Representatives.

A far larger compensation question faced the Congress in its early years, when the Supreme Court, in *Fletcher* v. *Peck,* ruled that under the "obligation-of-contracts" clause, Georgia's sale of the Yazoo lands was binding and that the subsequent rescinding of the grants was improper. Those who had bought the land, many of them nonresidents of Georgia, had been seeking compensation for their lands after the Georgia rescinding act. But they had trouble getting indemnification from Congress, even with the backing of *Fletcher* v. *Peck*. "*Fletcher* v. *Peck* was a major victory, but it did not provide them the dollars and cents they had been seeking for more than a decade."[38] Even though, largely because of southern opposition, Congress was slow in passing legislation to provide the funds, opposition was relatively subdued compared to that after other cases, in part because the original sale, which had been extremely controversial, had occurred some fifteen years before the Supreme Court ruled. The decision had been handed down in 1810. In 1814, a bill providing $5 million to the claimants (with the money coming from sale of acreage which Georgia and the United States had agreed to set aside for the purpose) was passed. Working in favor of passage of the act was the fact that the residents of Mississippi Territory wished to be organized as a state, and this would have been difficult with claims to the Yazoo lands unsettled, and immigration into the area would have been hindered. New England interests were in need of appeasement because of the negative impact of embargo and nonimportation policies on that area of the country, where many of the claimants resided. One New England congressman even argued that Congress, by not passing a compensation act, "would in effect annul the Supreme Court's decision, threaten the integrity of the Constitution, and strike another blow at New England's interests."[39]

The most frequent category of congressional action directed at the Court is that concerned with reversing particular decisions, particularly where statutory interpretation is involved. Thus, the Compulsory Testimony Act was passed in 1893, after the Court, in *Counselman* v. *Hitchcock,* held that immunity provided under the 1868 statute was insufficient. The Longshoremen's and Harbor Workers' Compensation Act was enacted in 1927, after earlier congressional attempts to extend state workmen's compensation statutes to longshoremen working on vessels and gangplanks between vessels and piers had been frustrated. After the Supreme Court held, in 1951, in the *Schwegmann Brothers* case that there was no antitrust immunity for nonsigner arrangements in "fair-trade" agreements, Congress passed the McGuire Fair Trade Enabling Act to exempt from antitrust laws fair-trade contracts and nonsigner clauses in states with price maintenance laws, thus reversing *Schwegmann.* After *Jencks* v. *U.S.*, the Congress partially reversed the ruling by stating, in the Jencks Act, that a judge should determine which government reports a defendant should see, where the Court had said that the defense should be allowed to inspect the reports directly. At about the same time, Congress reversed *Guss* v. *Utah Labor Relations Board,* which had applied the doctrine of federal preemption to deny a state's right to regulate interstate labor disputes even in the absence of National Labor Relations Board action.

Murphy notes in respect to the Jencks Act that almost all of the bill's supporters, even though they were modifying the Supreme Court's doctrine, "had taken great care to point out that they were not attacking the Warren Court."[40] Not only do we find this deference to the Court in some instances where the Court is being reversed, but we also find what amounts to a dialogue between Court and Congress in some instances. Thus, when the Court, in *Hill* v. *Wallace,* overturned the federal statute regulating transactions in grain futures, Justice Taft pointed out that Congress could not regulate the transactions unless Congress saw them as directly interfering with interstate commerce. Shortly thereafter, the Grain Futures Act was passed, with an explicit declaration on the point, and the statute was upheld in *Board of Trade* v. *Olsen.* This was in a sense a "reversal" of the Supreme Court, but clearly with the Supreme Court's acquiescence. We find other instances where, once the Court has held one way and Congress has reversed the Court, the latter concurs in the congressional action. The Court's upholding of the quitclaim legislation in the offshore oil cases, after the Court's earlier ruling that the land belonged to the national government, has already been discussed.

Another instance is found in the regulation of insurance. For years, insurance had not been considered part of commerce. Thus, in *U.S.* v. *South-Eastern Underwriters Association,* the Court held that insurance contracts were in fact involved in interstate commerce and were subject to the antitrust laws. Congress promptly enacted a statute to allow state insurance regulations to stay in force, and the Court accepted the statute in the *Prudential Insurance* case. More recently, the Court, in *SEC* v. *National Securities,* itself discussed the process of Court-Congress interaction in that situation. Justice Marshall, upholding a Securities and Exchange Commission regulation as not in conflict with the federal legislation, clearly pointed out, "The McCarran-Ferguson Act was passed in reaction to this Court's decision in *United States* v. *South-Eastern Underwriters Association.*" He further stated that the act had resulted from Congress' concern "about the inroads the Court's decision might make on the tradition of state regulation of insurance. . . . The McCarran-Ferguson Act was an attempt to turn back the clock, to assure that the activities of insurance companies in dealing with their policy-holders would remain subject to state regulation."

To turn from specific examples to a broader look, we find Jacob's notation that Congress reversed Supreme Court interpretations of statutes at least nineteen times between 1944 and 1957, and Krislov provides a figure of fifty occasions of *revisions* of Court action between 1944 and

1960, with thirty-four of those involving the *overturning* of some sixty decisions. In a study for the *Harvard Law Review,* instances where congressional legislation intended to reverse decisions were categorized. The analysts found that the Court twice was reversed after individual rights had been upheld against the imposition of federal power and in five instances after the Court had sustained federal jurisdiction against state claims, while such action occurred only once when the Court refused to extend federal power. On at least ten occasions, Congress modified Court actions which had favored government regulation of economic activity over self-regulation, compared with only one case ("of doubtful significance") where the Court had denied federal authority to regulate industry. While the findings concerning federal-state relations are not surprising, those concerning economic regulation run counter to a possible assumption that Congress would want to protect and extend regulation of the economy.

It has been suggested that most of the reversals by Congress have been in the economic field and that, while efforts have been made, much less success has been obtained in attempting to overrule civil liberties–civil rights decisions. However, Nagel, taking a longer historical view, suggests that "where intensely held economic interests or civil libertarian interests are involved, the likelihood of Court-curbing success is decreased" by comparison with the subjects of federal-state relations or separation of powers.[41] One might argue that the economic interests involved in the economic reversals were not "intensely held." In addition, Nagel finds economic regulation involved in some way in four of the seven high-frequency court-curbing periods, while civil liberties were involved in only two such periods—which supports Miller's earlier assertion.

Carrying their analysis further, commentators suggest that in six of the twenty-one instances they examined, Congress reversed the Court when there were policy factors the Congress could take into account which the Court could not have considered. The reaction to *Southeastern Underwriters* is an example of this type of reversal, as is the action on offshore oil. In seven other instances, the Court was held to have placed too much emphasis on a single factor involved in legislation when several were involved. Included here are a number of Fair Labor Standards Act cases, including the Portal-to-Portal Pay Case and resulting amending act. A comparable case was *Martino,* in which the Court held that services of local window-washing contractors whose customers manufactured goods for interstate commerce were "necessary" to the production and thus that the window washers were covered by the FLSA; this was changed as contrary to congressional intent. Similarly, when the Court, in *Packard Motor Car,* defined "employee" under the National Labor Relations Act to include foremen, Congress reversed when it passed the Taft-Hartley Act.

There are also instances where Congress returned the law to its original state after the Court changed existing procedure. In government contract cases, originally courts had not upheld agency decisions in disputes if there were not evidence to support them. In *U.S.* v. *Wunderlich*, the Court indicated an intent to deceive had to be shown before the agency head's decision could be set aside. Congress responded, in the Wunderlich Act, with a broader basis for judicial review than had existed before the Supreme Court's action. Other instances involve technical jurisdictional procedure in bankruptcy cases. In summarizing reasons for congressional action, the analysts note, "all the cases have one common characteristic: to a significant extent the Court's interpretation was at odds with a pre-existing 'common understanding.' The subsequent legislative reversal was largely a return to the status quo, and comparatively free from the usual political stresses involved in legislating social change."[42] They add that there was, with one exception, near unanimity in seeking reversal after the Court acted, so far from the desires of the affected interests were the Court's decisions.

It should be clear that the instances of reversal legislation, or attempts at the same, do not end with the items covered by the Harvard analysts. Mid-1969 saw the passage by the House of Representatives of two bills relating to taxation by the states which deal with problems created by the Supreme Court. One bill was H.R. 7906, the Interstate Taxation Act, passed 311–87 by the House on June 25. The Supreme Court had ruled in 1954, in the *Miller Bros.* case, that a state could not require an out-of-state business to collect sales and use taxes for the state even when the company delivered products within the state. The bill changes that result, as Representative McCulloch (R–Ohio) remarked, to "protect local retailers who now suffer from unencumbered competition from the across-the-border businessmen." Congress had already, in 1959, reacted to a related Supreme Court decision by prohibiting state income taxation of companies whose only presence in a state was solicitation of orders. Here again, the reaction of Congress may have been less reversal than part of a dialogue with the Court, for, as House Judiciary Committee Chairman Emanuel Celler pointed out, the Court had turned to Congress for guidance. The second bill related to the methods by which states could tax national banks. In 1968, the Supreme Court had said that the methods specified by Congress were exclusive, and these methods had not included sales and use taxes.[43] By a vote of 342–4 (after defeat of a recommittal motion, 123–227), the House passed H.R. 7491, which provides that national banks are to be subject to the same taxation as state banks.

We have been talking here about bills reversing the Supreme Court, but reversing particular decisions in a relatively narrow or limited fashion. Stumpf, in examining the use of Court citations in congressional debate, distinguishes between this more limited "decision reversal" and more severe, broader "Court-curbing" proposals. He finds that content analysis data do not support the hypothesis that "the higher the frequency of use of the sacrosanctity argument in Congress, the less likely is the reversal bill to pass."[44] Most of the references to the inviolable nature of the Court were found in the debates over *Jencks* and *Mallory* and in a few other cases. Stumpf does suggest, however, that when "anti-Court" rather than "decision reversal" legislation is at issue, the sacrosanctity argument does appear more frequently, although clearly it does not inhibit the passage of such legislation. Taking a broad view of Congressional action in the aftermath of Court decisions, he concludes, "Antidecision action is relatively frequent, productive of results, and is a comparatively noncontroversial method of response, whereas anti-Court action, broadly speaking, is more infrequent, highly controversial and usually unsuccessful."[45]

This is supported by Nagel, who, in examining Court-curbing, found that the types of bills with higher than average success were those "repealing jurisdiction over state supreme courts, limiting jurisdiction in regard to habeas corpus appeals, changing the rules concerning retirement and the size of the Court, restricting the Court's procedure, and limiting the Court's contempt and injunction powers."[46] While one could quarrel with Nagel's characterization of some of these, such as the limitation of jurisdiction, as "relatively milder" ways of curbing the Court, he concludes that the "substantially higher rate of success for the relatively milder bills can be explained by the fact that during all the time periods [he examined], there has been a sizeable opposition in Congress to any attempts to curb the Supreme Court." The degree of opposition may be shown by Lytle's finding that "only seven percent of some two hundred odd bills ever reached the floor of the House or the Senate," and his statement, "When proposals were offered by the more powerful conservatives, they were restricted to public condemnations of the judiciary. Thus from a Court-curbing standpoint, the legislative process was more attuned to an exercise in rhetoric than determined political action."[47]

What has affected this result? Political party is one factor. Thus, "A constitutional amendment to remedy the Knight decision [emasculating the Sherman Act] failed to receive the necessary two-thirds vote because of the Democratic Party's commitment to the principle of States' rights."[48] The Democratic and Whig support for the *McCulloch* decision was mentioned earlier. The fractionation of the political process is another variable explaining why so little reversal behavior occurs. Thus, John Roche writes, "If . . . the Court strikes down a controversial decision of the Federal Power Commission, it will be supported by a substantial bloc of congressmen; if it supports the FPC's decision, it will also receive considerable congressional support. But the important point is that *either* way it decides the case, there is no possibility that Congress will exact any vengeance on the Court for its action."[49] Disciplined majorities, cohesive majorities, are not available to hurt the Court. Then there are the usual reasons which contribute to the passage or defeat of any piece of legislation and are specific to each. Thus, Murphy points out that a crucial adjournment motion, after the failure of a motion to table a strict anti-Court substitute, was carried for a wide variety of reasons:

> Some senators supported [Senate Majority Leader] Lyndon Johnson because they were opposed to H.R. 3; some because it had been a long day and they wanted to go home; some because it was the custom to side with the Majority Leader on such questions; some because they neither understood nor cared about the issue; some because they thought that the liberals could prevent a vote on the merits anyway; but some southern senators went along because . . . they preferred limited military war against the Court to massive retaliation.[50]

Going beyond the reasons why anti-Court action is not very successful, Murphy does suggest why conflict between the Court and Congress arises. He points to four factors: the policy is based on unclear constitutional language and with respect to which public opinion is not firm; powerful groups perceive they have a vital interest involved; the Court has threatened the Congress, or congressmen have so perceived the Court's rulings; and enough legislators have thought "it was feasible as well as wise to counter that threat under existing circumstances."[51]

CHAPTER 7

Impacts in Political Arenas: B

PRESIDENT AND ADMINISTRATION

Now that we have examined the lower courts and Congress, we can turn to see what effect Supreme Court decisions have had on the President and the executive branch. We have relatively little information about impact on this aspect of government, and this is unfortunate because of the immense tasks played by administration in a large society. We know of the reactions of particular Presidents, including Jefferson and Jackson in early days and Roosevelt and Truman in the twentieth century, and we can see to some extent how Supreme Court rulings affect the process by which regulatory commissions make decisions. Yet, as the regulatory commissions have become more established and the judiciary has become less jealous of their quasi-judicial role, the Court does not often deal with the substance of the decisions of those agencies, producing few confrontations which might be expected to have an impact. Similarly, if, as Arthur Miller has argued, the executive branch deals with individuals and corporations through devices not easily subject to judicial scrutiny, the opportunities for the Supreme Court to "put down" administrators may be few and far between. In any case, we do not have a great deal of information.

Jefferson's animosity toward John Marshall undoubtedly stemmed in part from their political differences and Marshall's Federalist presence on the bench during Jefferson's administration. Marshall's *Marbury* decision, in which he roundly lectured Jefferson for failing to have Marbury's judicial commission delivered, and then held that Marbury had no remedy, thus avoiding a head-on "crunch," is thought by some to have turned Jefferson against the idea of judicial power to nullify legislation and led him to feel that it was undemocratic. When Marshall decided *Cohens* v. *Virginia,* those opposed to the idea of Supreme Court review of state court decisions solicited the assistance of ex-President Madison and President Jefferson in their attacks on the Court. While Madison would not help, "Jefferson, more hostile to Marshall, denounced the decision as another step in the scheme of the Supreme Court to destroy the federal constitutional system by consolidating all authority in the central government."[1] At the time, Jefferson wrote to Mr. Justice Johnson, "The practice of Judge Marshall of travelling out of his case to prescribe what the law would be in a moot case not before the court is very irregular and very censurable." Justice Story thought Jefferson "at the head of the enemies of the Judiciary."[2]

Andrew Jackson's distaste for Marshall is more famous and to some extent apocryphal. The remark, "Mr. Justice Marshall has made his decision; now let him enforce it!" has been quoted many times to make the point that the Court is dependent on others to see that its decisions are enforced—a valid point even if the statement was never made by Jackson. What appears to have happened over time is that people have confused Jackson's determination to be his "own man" with respect to the constitutionality of legislation, with his actions after courts decided cases. In two cases (*Cherokee Nation* and *Worcester* v. *Georgia*), Marshall held that an Indian tribe had special status, being in effect an independent nation, was entitled to the land it occupied, and that the lands were not subject to state law.

In *Worcester* v. *Georgia*, Georgia had arrested missionaries who had entered the Indian lands without a state license. When the Supreme Court decided the case, Georgia refused to respect the mandate. Jackson in fact did nothing to enforce the ruling and "rescue" the missionaries, but there is little evidence that he was deliberately defying the Court. "Jackson never asserted a right to decline to carry out a Court decision, when acting in his Executive capacity."[3] Apparently there was no statutory method by which someone could be released from *state* custody on *federal* habeas corpus and, absent some such efforts, the military force of the nation could not be brought to bear. In addition, it appears that many citizens accepted removing the Indians (Georgia's goal) as "both desirable and inevitable," which certainly would have strengthened Jackson's resolve to deal with the matter in a way other than by "rescuing" the missionaries, for example, by getting the Indians removed by treaty provision. What further suggests that Jackson's positions *on these cases* has been misrepresented is his strong stand against South Carolina's Nullification Ordinance, which included, *inter alia*, a section holding that no state court case involving congressional acts could be appealed to the Supreme Court and that, if such appeals were taken, the state courts would act as if they had not been. It was, in fact, Jackson's sponsorship of the Force bill and his willingness to implement it that caused

Georgia officials to back away from their refusal to release the missionaries, and they did so, pardoning them.

As Warren notes, "It is probable that a misconception of Jackson's exact attitude towards the Court in the *Cherokee* case arose from his known views as to Presidential authority, which he later set forth at length in his message to Congress vetoing the Bank charter . . . ."[4] Those views, in which he refused to be governed by Marshall's position that the bank was constitutionally established by Congress, were that the President could (and should) exercise independent judgment as to the constitutionality of a piece of legislation when it was before him for signature or veto. As he stated it, "The opinion of the judges has no more authority over Congress than the opinion of Congress has over the judges, and on that point the President is independent of both. The authority of the Supreme Court must not . . . be permitted to control the Congress or the Executive . . . but to have only such influence as the force of their reasoning may deserve."

In terms of action taken to reverse the decisions of the Court, perhaps the "Court-packing" attempt of Franklin Roosevelt is best known. President Lincoln had refused to honor orders of Chief Justice Taney to release a prisoner in military custody, but those orders were issued while Taney was on circuit and were not decisions of the full Supreme Court. After the landslide election of 1936, Roosevelt, presuming he had a mandate to do something about the Court, which had regularly been striking down New Deal legislation, proposed that for any Justice over age 70 who did not retire, the President could add another judge to the Court. This was proposed as a reform of Court procedure, but the effort was too obvious for people to believe it to be aimed solely at that, and Chief Justice Hughes wrote to the Senate that a Court of fifteen would be far more unwieldy than a Court of nine, thus not serving to improve what FDR was purporting to reform. And, as is broadly known, the effort failed in the Senate, with the President being unable to rally even members of his own party to support the measure with any enthusiasm.

It should be pointed out that Court-packing was not the only idea examined within the Roosevelt administration as a device to respond to the Court's decisions, although "In January 1935 [Attorney General] Homer Cummings had proposed appointing enough Justices to the Court to create a New Deal majority."[5] Nor was the Roosevelt administration totally unhappy with the Supreme Court's decisions. The invalidation of the National Industrial Recovery Act was in some sense a help to the President, because the NIRA, soon to expire, was "an outworn recovery measure" which the Court decision saved him from having to junk, as well as providing him with campaign ammunition for 1936. Thus, "A grim-lipped Chief Executive shortly told a press conference that the

Court's reasoning took the Constitution 'back to the horse and buggy days' and implied darkly that if the Court threw down the gauntlet on the issue of constitutional reform, he would gladly accept the challenge."[6]

Several responses to the *Schechter* and other decisions were made. Some suggested amending the Constitution to make clear that Congress had the powers to do that which the Court had been saying it could not do. The standard idea of limiting the Court's power of judicial review was also proposed. Senator Norris thought that the lower courts should have no say on the constitutionality of legislation and that the Supreme Court should be required to be unanimous to strike down an act as unconstitutional. One idea, "regarded with special interest by Roosevelt . . . gave a new Congress, an election having intervened, the right to re-enact a law declared unconstitutional."[7] And the Administration tossed the ball right back to the Court with respect to some of the matters declared invalid. Both the National Labor Relations (Wagner) Act (1935) and National Bituminous Coal Conservation (Guffey) Act (1935) "imposed regulations upon industry in apparent defiance of the Schechter opinion."[8] Roosevelt even wrote to a representative that Congress should pass the latter bill even if it had doubts about the constitutionality of the matter, clearly a challenge to the Court's authority.

The case of *Youngstown Sheet & Tube Co.* v. *Sawyer*, in which the Court invalidated President Truman's seizure of the steel mills, is one of the clearest examples of the Court's directly challenging a President's actions. Yet, as Krislov notes, "The most important fact about the Youngstown case is that President Truman and his administrators accepted the decision without question."[9] It is thus an example of compliance despite the high stakes involved. But it may also be an example of a case where the long-term effects, not as visible as the decision itself, turn out to be more important. If one accepts Arthur Miller's position, the executive branch learned several things from that case. One was that sanctions less than seizure, for example, directing of government purchases to certain companies, should be used, perhaps in combination, if the administration were to prevail over private industry. Another was that, whichever devices were used, those should be picked which would not end up in the courts. Miller argues that "the President, since the Steel Case, operates in the labor-management area in ways that do not present issues justiciable before the Supreme Court" and has been more "sophisticated" with respect to his stance toward collective bargaining and other economic matters.[10] One method which Miller points to by which the executive branch can operate with little challenge from the courts is to use its contracts with private business to achieve its ends, not only with respect to handling price increases but also in terms of bringing about equal employment in a racial basis.

Miller's comments suggest that administrators move away from confrontation with the Court to avoid impact, although, whatever the motivation, the result is a diminished effect of the Court on the executive branch. Schubert suggests that the decisions in which the Court tells the President not to do something, such as the Steel Seizure Case, are rare and that, in addition, such decisions do not have "the presumably salutary effect of keeping the Presidency in rein, to say nothing of rendering it mated."[11] If the President (and the Congress, he adds) are to be restrained, political forces from elsewhere in the system are needed. One reason for this may be that Supreme Court rulings affecting one part of our immense national bureaucracy, for example, a regulatory agency, do not receive much attention elsewhere within the executive branch.

Certainly, the President's war powers have not been restrained by the Court, in part because relevant decisions have been handed down at the end of wars rather than at the beginning or in the middle thereof. Rossiter has argued, "Whatever limits the Court has set upon the employment of the war powers have been largely theoretical, rarely practical," adding that comments by various judges that the war power must be exercised subordinate to the Constitution is a moral warning without much practical effect. "As in the past, so in the future," he states, "President and Congress will fight our wars with little or no thought about a reckoning with the Supreme Court."[12] However, in this connection, we must recognize that the power of the President acting alone to ignore the Court is not without limit. Given the fact that many of his subordinates may be disposed to comply with a Court ruling, the President must avoid creating conflict for them by opposing such rulings. It is also clear that the President's ability by himself to oppose the Court—although his visibility gives him a position of leadership in this respect—is far less great than if he and the Congress are acting in concert. Thus, "In the short run the President alone has great weight but must, within the clearly recognized sphere of the Court, generally follow its lead."[13]

We must recognize that the impact of decisions may be greater on the President's subordinates than on the Chief Executive himself and that he may take his lead in reacting to the Court from their reaction to or feelings about a decision. In addition, if he wishes to reduce the number of times he directly opposes the Court, he may allow his subordinates to carry the burden of reacting openly. This may have been the situation in some recent examples of administration reaction to the Court. When *Jencks* v. *U.S.* was handed down, "The executive department was thrown into an uproar,"[14] largely out of fear that the FBI would have to reveal its informers in order to win cases, a distasteful choice. United States attorneys from all over the country communicated their views about the problems created by the decision to the Department of Justice, which promptly drafted legislation, on which its staff had begun work almost as soon as the opinion was handed down. In March, 1969, when the Court ruled that defense attorneys must be able to examine the logs and transcripts of eavesdropped conversations to see whether evidence obtained had been used in trial, the Justice Department had a comparably violent reaction. The government asked for a rehearing in the case, claiming damage to national security. (The Court responded by denying the rehearing and by sending fifteen cases, including those involving James Hoffa and Mohammad Ali [Cassius Clay], back for a reopening of the record.) Included in the rehearing request was a statement by Solicitor General Griswold that the Justice Department would simply not tell the courts about "foreign intelligence surveillance" transcripts the Department itself did not consider relevant. Attorney General Mitchell, appearing at about the same time before a congressional hearing, attacked the Court's ruling, not a typical act of Attorneys General.

However, we can find instances where the reaction has been less apoplectic. Thus, the government, after *Yates,* dropped charges pending against defendants in all but one instance, clearly indicating that the government had been restricted by the decision, particularly obvious when one compares the aftermath of *Dennis.* In that situation, the Department of Justice had not instituted new prosecutions until the Court ruled, but when the Smith Act was upheld, the Department "immediately began a series of prosecutions of secondary Communist party leaders in various parts of the country."[15] The rulings concerning the government's loyalty-security programs also limited what the executive branch did. Minimally, the Court forced the government to follow its own regulations, which at times it was not inclined to do. As one observer noted, "The cumulative impact of the government's reversals in *Cole, Service, Vitarelli,* and *Greene* undoubtedly diminished the scope and curbed several excesses of the security programs."[16]

There are also instances where members of the executive branch have reinforced decisions. Thus, then Under Secretary of State (and formerly Attorney General) Katzenbach, at a National Conference on Crime Control, told police to stop complaining about Supreme Court rulings (such as *Miranda*) and to try instead to reform the American system of criminal justice. Katzenbach said that more could be accomplished to curb crime through police ability and better communications systems than through reversing Supreme Court rulings. In an earlier administration, that of President Eisenhower, the administration's opposition to legislative action which would restore state authority taken away by the Court —thus support for the Court's rulings—was criticized by an important interest-group leader. The Department of Justice was one of the few groups opposing H.R. 3, limiting the federal preemption doctrine, as well as bills asserting the principle of state control of water resources. Most recently, when the Supreme Court, in *King* v. *Smith*, invalidated some "man-in-the-house" regulations related to the Aid to Dependent Children (ADC) program, the Department of Health, Education, and Welfare reacted promptly by giving the states thirty days in which to erase their man-in-the-house rules. HEW went further by ordering the states to notify those who might have been deprived of benefits under the ruling in the prior two years. A year earlier, when the Court held, in the *Camara* and *See* cases, that search warrants were required in housing code searches by city inspectors, the Department issued a memorandum indicating proper procedures to be followed by inspectors.

It may be, as has been argued, that the Court can have little effect on the administrative establishment because of the latter's size, the earlier-mentioned lack of carry-over from one agency to another after a relevant Court decision, and the ability of administrators to cure defects to which the Court points. "If control of the bureaucracy is to be done," Miller says, "save in a few spectacular instances, judicial review is too episodic and sporadic, too dependent on the accident of litigation to permit the sustained oversight necessary."[17] But as the examples noted above indicate, there is an impact; the Court's decisions do stop certain sorts of administrative actions and, in other instances, reinforce what administrators at the national level may wish to accomplish but for which they need the support of the Court's rulings, as may have been true in the welfare cases. And we must recognize that the "accident of litigation" is also relevant in dealing with the Court's impact on other government bodies, legislative and judicial, thus not placing the administrative establishment on a different footing from them in this regard.

Even if we recognize that "a very large share of even those agency decisions that do directly affect the legal rights of individual citizens cannot be appealed to the courts, and an even larger share are not so appealed,"[18] the latter is also true even with criminal convictions. This either says that the Court has little impact or it may not say that: it may say that the number (or proportion) of instances directly touched by the courts is small, but it does not say—and we do not have evidence to prove or disprove the point—that what the Court says is not digested by the administrators directly or indirectly so that it has some effect on what they do. And while there may not be as much apparent effect with respect to actions already initiated as in the dropping of the Smith Act prosecutions post-*Yates*, future action may be affected.

As Shapiro himself concedes, "Administrative agencies are unlikely to initiate new sanctions when they feel the courts are likely to reject them. . . . Thus the courts today by their decisions largely control the decisions of the administrators tomorrow on what it is feasible to do next *in the realm of prosecution*."[19] Cardozo's statement that the power of the Court is not measured by the number of times it is exercised nowhere requires repetition more than here. We must, however, remember that while the Court may set limits to what administrative officials will find feasible, its decisions are not by themselves sufficient to stimulate executive action. While "The Court . . . by the sheer weight of its own example, . . . inspired something of a similar zeal on the part of the executive branch of government" in the 1950's with respect to desegregation, we also find the situation where, after the Court made it possible for prosecutions to be brought against state officials who excluded Negroes from juries, nothing happened "for the simple reason that U.S. Attorneys General and federal district attorneys did not prosecute offenders."[20]

One further matter bears notice in this section. The effect of the Court on the process of administrative law, particularly within the independent regulatory agencies, has been averted to. In the early years of some of the commissions, the Court severely restricted them, perhaps both because the agencies were at the heart of schemes of regulation of the economy which displeased the Justices and because they were a separate system of lawmaking in some sense competing with the judiciary. In cases in 1896 and 1897, the Supreme Court held that the ICC had no authority to prescribe reasonable rates in the course of determining whether rates proposed by the railroads were reasonable. It also undercut the clause in the Interstate Commerce Act prohibiting a railroad from charging more for a short haul than a long haul. The ICC itself admitted defeat, conceding in its 1897 report, "'By virtue of judicial decisions, it has ceased to be a body for the regulation of interstate carriers. . . . The people should no longer look to this commission for a protection which it is powerless to extend.'"[21] After 1897, Kelly and Harbison observe, the ICC could only issue "cease-and-desist" orders aimed at specific rates, orders which it found almost impossible to enforce in courts. "Since the Commission found it difficult to obtain evidence, and since the courts insisted upon a complete review of all the facts in a case, the Commission's orders were usually overturned on appeal."[22] The Commission thus became "moribund."

In its early years, the Federal Trade Commission suffered the same sort of difficulty at the hands of the Court. In the first ruling under the legislation establishing the FTC, the Court held, in the *Gratz* case, that methods of unfair competition not known before the enactment of the statute could not be dealt with by the agency; on top of that, the courts would reserve to themselves the determination of those methods. "Taken literally, the Supreme Court's words . . . would have limited the FTC to administration of pre-existing legal rules, with no authority to define and attack new practices which it found to be unfair." And, when the Supreme Court's language was applied in similar manner by the lower courts, the FTC ceased trying to move against new unfair trade practices, instead trying to deal with the limited areas still left to it. "Through the limitations set by judicial review, the Commission's principal attention was deflected away from preserving competition by attacking competition-destroying practices and into maintaining a minimum plane of honesty and fair dealing for such competition as might persist."[23] Two years later, however, the Court, in the *Winstead Hosiery* case, did allow the Commission to move against false advertising and misbranding. The Commission responded immediately, with a flurry of activity, at both the formal level (orders and stipulations) and informal level (through negotiation).

That the FTC (and other regulatory commissions) were at the mercy of the Court, even when the "green light" for commission activity seemed to have been given, is shown by the 1931 *Raladam* case, in which the Court held that false advertising, to be actionable, had to be both unfair *and* a method of competition. This hampered the Commission, because it had now to prove injury to competitors in each case, a burden from which the Wheeler-Lea Act of 1938 finally relieved it. The effect of Court decisions coupled with other actions is shown by the effect of that statute, which concentrated the FTC's actions on deceptive practices, not the protection of competition from monopolistic and anticompetitive practices. Finally, in 1934, the Court, coming around to giving greater weight to the Commission's findings, said, in the *Keppel* case, that weight would be given to the FTC's own determination of what practices were to be considered unfair, thus in effect reversing *Gratz*. The effect was substantial: instead of losing cases (until 1933, 69 won to 63 lost), the Commission began to win regularly (after 1934, 100 won to 11 lost).

The same limitations imposed on the regulatory commissions were also imposed by the Court on administrative actions within the executive branch itself. The four *Morgan* cases involving rate-setting by the Secretary of Agriculture under the Packers and Stockyards Act illustrate this well. In the first case, the Court set aside rates on the grounds that no full hearing had been held because, while the Secretary technically had made findings, another official had examined the evidence. In the second, no trial examiner's report was received by respondents as a basis for argument before the final decision. In the third, the Court said greater deference must be paid to administrators, and, in the fourth, the Court held improper an interrogation of the Secretary to determine if his examination of the record had been sufficient—in effect nullifying the first case, because, without questioning, there was little way of determining whether or not the Secretary had made the requisite findings himself.

Clearly, in these circumstances, obtaining final administrative action was close to an impossibility. This is not to say that the fault was all on the side of the Court. Difficulties in procedure within the executive branch itself clearly played a part in what happened—difficulties which were in some way remedied by the later passage of the Administrative Procedure Act (in 1946). The first two *Morgan* cases, however, did bring an examination—and reorganization—of the Department of Agriculture and several other units, as well as the selection of a Committee on Administrative Procedure to take a longer-run view. The Court, for its part, did appear to recognize that its intensive supervision (perhaps "over-supervision") of administrative agencies might cripple them—perhaps a goal desired by some earlier Justices—and the Court began to back off. Review was still there, and one can still find instances where the Court reviews a case *de novo,* as if it were being tried in the Court in the first instance, instead of simply determining whether there is "adequate evidence" or "substantial evidence" in the record to support the agency's findings.

Despite the changed position of the Court, the Justices' rulings still have an effect—and a clear one—on the work of the regulatory commissions and related agencies. An example of this occurs in the Federal Power Commission's dealing with direct sales of natural gas to major users of the gas. The FPC, which deals with such direct sales through its power to grant transportation certificates, has not been favorably disposed toward such direct sales but has not been in a position where it could outlaw them outright. The Supreme Court, in the *Transcontinental Gas Pipe Line Corp.* case, in which the Commission had said such sales were per se against the public convenience and necessity but then threw in language to suggest this was only one factor in its denial of certificate, said that the use to which the gas would be put (the purpose of the direct sale) could be taken into account as one factor in determining "convenience and necessity" in connection with the application for the certificate. This is clearly not the same as allowing the FPC *explicitly* to ban such direct sales, even if it can achieve the same end through the balancing process. But, while it can achieve the same end, the Supreme Court's ruling will have an effect. As Shapiro argues, "It would be . . . naïve . . . to assume that an agency that has to take the official position that it is weighing will not have to behave differently than an agency that can proudly proclaim that its preference for viewing one factor as decisive has now been approved by the Supreme Court and thus is part of the law of the land." Regardless of what the commissioners themselves may desire, their subordinates may take the language of the Court as the official law and take it more seriously. Thus, "the presence of the Supreme Court opinions and the need to pay lip serivce to them will reduce . . . the agency's . . . zeal and efficiency in pursuing its goals."[24]

If one does not restrict administrative law to the regulatory commissions but instead defines it to include the development of procedures in all executive branch agencies, as most scholars in the field of public administration now do, other examples of impact of the Court's rulings present themselves. The Internal Revenue Service is frequently involved in litigation, both as to substantive points of tax law and as to procedures by which they are applied. While much tax law is set out in statutes, the IRS regulations embody much supplementary law by which taxpayers are supposed to abide. Those regulations are affected by what the Court does. One example stems from the question of whether members of professions, for example, doctors and lawyers, should be able to form corporations so as to be able to utilize certain tax advantages. In a 1935 case (*Morrissey* v. *Commissioner*), the Court, interpreting the IRS provisions, set out principles for determining whether an entity was a corporation. While the particular trust in question was held to be taxable as a corporation, the case was considered a victory for the IRS, and the principles of the case were incorporated in the regulations. Whether the IRS would have so quickly incorporated the provisions of a case in which it was not victorious is, of course, another matter.

On the procedural side, the IRS found itself involved in the aftermath of *Miranda*. New internal procedures conform to *Miranda*, but the conformity was not immediate. Prior to the decision, special agents of the IRS identified themselves as such to taxpayers but did not give a warning in connection with their work or indicate they were involved in investigating a criminal matter (as opposed to a regular civil investigation). After *Miranda*, an agency directive indicated that an agent was to say that he was investigating criminal tax fraud, but the directive did not require a statement of warnings until after initial investigation had not resolved the matter about which the agents were inquiring. Only then did rights to remain silent and obtain counsel have to be stated. However, the directive was amended in November, 1968, to require warnings at the beginning, rather than in the middle, of the investigation.

The Customs Bureau provides another example of a change in internal procedures after a Supreme Court decision, in this instance *Freedman* v. *Maryland*. Six weeks after the case was handed down, the Bureau issued special instructions which served to reduce the time involved in seizure of movies. The procedures were sustained by the Court of Appeals for the Second Circuit, but a district court subsequently gave judgment to an importer for delays caused by the government in a situation where seizure had occured before *Freedman*. Three weeks later, after conferences among the Department of Justice, the Post Office Department, and the Customs Bureau, "It was decided to adopt procedures which would reduce administrative delay and avoid possible procedural conflicts which had been discussed by the Court in the *Father Silas* opinion." These new procedures were upheld shortly thereafter, leading to the comment that "The Customs Bureau has made a substantial effort to comply with the standards established in the *Freedman* decision. . . . When a court decision went against the Bureau, immediate steps were taken to comply with the Court's requirements."[25]

REACTION IN THE STATES

Unhappiness in the states over Supreme Court rulings is as old as the history of the United States. Almost as soon as the Supreme Court began to hear cases, state officials, judges and others, began to react. The reaction to *Cohens* v. *Virginia,* even though convictions under Virginia's statutes were sustained, was not one of joy, because of the Court's assertion of its right to review state court rulings. "To the Republicans, the decision as to jurisdiction and the language of Marshall's opinion came now as a climax to the continual march of encroachment by the Court on the sovereignty of the States." They "seriously believed that the fundamental doctrines on which the Union was based were in grave peril of destruction."[26]

Other examples from our earlier history are legion. The reaction was generally characterized by the assertion, on the part of those in the states, that the Supreme Court did *not* have authority to render the decisions in question. The key factor was often one of self-interest. While Virginia often reacted strongly to such rulings as *Cohens* and *Martin* v. *Hunter's Lessee,* the fact that it refused to go along with Kentucky's complaint against the Court for the land law case of *Green* v. *Biddle,* in which the Court invalidated a Kentucky statute, suggested, "State opposition to judicial action depended, not so much on the political theory held by the States, as on the particular interest aided or injured."[27]

When the Court issued a ruling which offended those who believed in states' rights but who agreed with the substance of the ruling, matters became quite confused. Such a situation was produced by *Prigg* v. *Pennsylvania.* In that case, the Court held the jurisdiction of Congress over fugitive slaves to be exclusive and held a state law invalid as in conflict with a federal statute. "The decision," Warren notes, "was equally unsatisfactory to both pro-slavery and anti-slavery men."[28] Even though there was a federal fugitive slave law on the books, the proslavery men were upset at the blow to states' rights. Because the antislavery people disliked the federal statute, they thought the Court was backing the South. This was particularly true in New York, because the New York law on the subject granted jury trials when fugitive slaves were arrested, thus assuring (through acquittals) that the federal law would be made ineffective. The Northerners did get some solace from the opinion. Justice Story had suggested that states could not only not pass laws which conflicted with federal provisions concerning fugitive slaves but that they also could not assist the national government. This meant that the federal government alone would have to handle the fugitive slave problem, and the northern states were happy not to have to assist.

Although state officials do often complain about Supreme Court rulings, it has been suggested that "the over-all movement of the modern Court has been toward increasing, not decreasing, state power." While state officials may find their situation as policy makers difficult, and while they may find the Supreme Court a convenient scapegoat, "Limitations on state power arising out of national powers have 'only a minimal effect on the capacity of states to discharge their functions.' "[29] And state officials (and other policy makers) may find it convenient to use the Court's decisions on occasion, although there are other times when they avoid introducing Supreme Court rulings into policy debate. This may be the case because of the possible complexity of the decisions and because they may wish to go further than the Court has allowed, even when the Court has legitimated some action on their part. If the feelings of the public are strong, the policy which officials propose is more likely to be in conformity with those feelings than with the Court's rulings.

While state legislatures played a strong role in the resistance to *Brown* v. *Board,* and while many called for a constitutional convention aimed at overturning *Reynolds,* they do not necessarily play a large role in the aftermath of Court rulings, at least not as large a role as they appear to have played in the earlier days of the Republic. Thus, the legislatures appeared to have played little part in the aftermath of *Miranda,* despite the importance of state statutes in the area of criminal procedure. Milner suggests that, in Wisconsin, the police chiefs association saw the legislatures as powerless to do anything about the decision, which may indicate why legislatures played little part in what happened. Not only do they not resist Court decisions (beyond the level of rhetoric), but they also do not necessarily take advantage of Court rulings making it easier for them to pass laws or legitimating policy in which they are interested. Thus, as Warren has noted, "In spite of all apprehensions and of Judge Field's foreboding, the State Legislatures refrained for many years from unduly extending their control of private business" after the *Granger* cases.[30] Similarly, in the decade after the *Beauharnais* case, which upheld "group libel" statutes, no state enacted such a law.

When a state's powers are challenged, legislative reaction is not always forthcoming. Thus, when the Supreme Court decided *Williams* v. *North Carolina,* allowing a state to look into the validity of the alleged residence of someone seeking a divorce (and thus a challenge to the granting of "full faith and credit" to the acts of other states), only ten states adopted the Uniform Divorce Recognition Act in the twenty years after its promulgation in 1948 as a reaction to the decision. When the film censorship procedures of a number of states were invalidated by the *Freedman* decision, the Maryland legislature "attempted immediately to comply with the procedural requirements,"[31] but no attempt was made to pass new laws when censorship schemes in New York, Kansas, and Virginia were invalidated, leaving Maryland the only state with a censorship board. In other situations, when state statutes are struck down, the legislatures leave them on the books, knowing that they will be enforced differently. This appears to have been the case after the invalidation of the compulsory flag salute laws.

When the legislatures do get involved, however, as they did with respect to desegregation, it complicates the question of compliance more than if lower courts were those resisting. Questions of whose authority should be followed and the origins of jurisdiction are likely to make matters less clear than otherwise. "The courts on the one hand seek to abide by the guiding principles of the judicial hierarchy. On the other hand, the legislators seek to preserve their prerogatives and what they conceive to be basic states' rights."[32]

The examples from history are, however, quite interesting. When the Court held that the state of Georgia could be sued by those outside its borders, the Georgia legislators were so incensed that the house passed a bill providing death (by hanging) without benefit of clergy to any federal marshal or anyone else who attempted to enforce writs in the aftermath of the decision. (The Eleventh Amendment did result from the decision.) We have noted Virginia's continued resistance to the Court. Also a continual opponent of the Court in the early years was Pennsylvania. Thus, when the Court decided the case of *Huidekoper's Lessees* v. *Douglass,* involving land claims by out-of-state residents, adversely to Pennsylvania's interest, the legislature passed a resolution denying the U.S. Supreme Court cognizance of the cases. This was a bit too much for the governor, even though he sympathized with the legislature's position, and he vetoed their resolution.

The state's animosity toward the Court was not, however, to end soon. In 1809, the state legislature defied a citation from the Supreme Court notifying the state to appear if she wanted to participate in a case involving conflicting federal and state claims, in a situation arising from a state court ruling against a U.S. claim for priority of payment from a debtor. The longest-term difficulty arose over claims by Olmsted that Pennsylvania was holding money due him, as a result of the seizure, by a Pennsylvania ship (in Articles of Confederation days) of a prize ship he had captured. The disputed money, for which Olmsted had continually sued, had been placed with the state treasurer.

In 1803, Olmsted revived his claims, under a ruling which gave the federal courts the power to hear cases involving orders of the Confederation courts of appeals in such matters. Federal Judge Peters agreed with Olmsted that his claim was valid, but the Pennsylvania legislature immediately passed a law defying the ruling as an improper exercise of federal court jurisdiction. Olmsted went to the U.S. Supreme Court, which ordered Judge Peters to comply, but the judge didn't wish to precipitate further difficulty between the state and the national government (as represented by his court) and he didn't carry out the U.S. Supreme Court order. Olmsted again went to the Supreme Court and won again, with the Court stating clearly that the legislature of a state could not annul federal court judgments. The governor then got into the act, indicating he would call out the militia to prevent enforcement of the decree. When Judge Peters issued papers against the holders of the money, the U.S. Marshal was blocked by the state militia and had to summon a 2,000-man posse to assist him. After a further resolution by the legislature denying the Supreme Court's power to decide matters of states' rights, state officials backed off somewhat. President Madison indicated to the governor that the federal government had to be supported; the legislature had the troops removed and began to debate a bill to appropriate the money; and the state paid the money shortly. (On the federal side, the militia general, who had been arrested for blocking the Marshal, was pardoned by Madison for acting under a mistaken sense of duty after he had been convicted for his acts.)

In the Pennsylvania situation, the legislature had been resisting a federal judge, supported by the U.S. Supreme Court. However, legislatures have attacked officials in their own states who have backed the Supreme Court. Thus, when Kentucky judges of the court of appeals (the state's supreme court) enforced the U.S. Supreme Court's rulings against Kentucky's land-law statutes, the legislature first tried to impeach the judges and, having failed that, simply abolished the court of appeals, establishing a new one in its place to which sympathetic judges were appointed by the governor.

State administrators are also involved in the reaction to Court rulings, leading to Dolbeare and Hammond's remark that differences in response to prayer decisions "were produced by systematic variations in the actions of state-level agencies and officials," who were in turn "responsive to established state statutory and constitutional requirements, and/or local practices."[33] Certainly, we carry with us images of southern governors defying school desegregation, as in Virginia's "Massive Resistance" or Louisiana's New Orleans crisis. And Frederick Bernays Wiener has recently called our attention to the substantial degree to which governors continued to invoke martial law in peaceful situations to obtain ends otherwise unobtainable, completely ignoring *Sterling* v. *Constantin*, eliminating the finality of gubernatorial determinations concerning martial law except in cases of actual violence.

But while governors are visible, it is ultimately up to many other state officials, sometimes working under the direction of the governor, sometimes not, to carry out Supreme Court rulings or to resist them. State welfare officials were the relevant officials after the Supreme Court outlawed the "man-in-the-house" rule. The director of the Michigan Department of Social Services said he would continue to deny funds to children whose mothers had extramarital sex relations. The Louisiana welfare director said that all aid to dependent children might be dispensed with, and his colleague in Georgia suggested that cuts of 50 percent in aid might result.

State legal officers are the key to the implementation of many decisions. Because of the legal form in which the decisions and resulting issues are cast, people look to the attorney general, whose reaction may either retard or facilitate compliance. Krislov, specifically examining the southern attorneys general and their reaction to desegregation, found that none had played a role in bringing about desegregation, although the first southern official to *challenge* the decision was Georgia Attorney General Eugene Cook. (On the other hand, some border state attorneys general had affirmed the decision, with Dalton of Missouri, while not suggesting immediate desegregation was required, ruling that desegregation was immediately permissive regardless of state law.) As time went on, the attorneys general, being elected officials, moved toward their constituencies' views, not away from them, and became more vehement in their opposition to the *Brown* rulings. Even the Florida attorney general, who had participated as *amicus* in the implementation decision, moved over to firm opposition. "Each has moved with, never against, the tide."[34] The reason for this, Krislov suggests, is that the attorney general's reference groups, those from whom he takes his cues, are local and his aspirations are at the state, not national, level. The National Association of Attorneys General, it can be pointed out, has generally been among the foremost defenders of the "state position" in congressional hearings, and led the way in opposing the early offshore oil rulings of the Supreme Court.

The attorney general has an impact on others in the state; the way he affects what happens to a Supreme Court ruling is through the official opinions he issues, not binding in a court of law but often followed by officials in the absence of such court rulings. Reich notes, with respect to the school prayer cases, that the official reaction within the states was often given by the attorney general in either a formal opinion or a letter to the chief educational official of the state. In four of the thirteen states requiring prayer or Bible reading at the time of the decisions, the attorney general said such exercises were not permitted, but the remaining nine said that voluntary prayer was permissible, or simply defied the Court. In other states, the officials at the state level did little, leaving matters to local officials, where the role of legal advisers (to counties and school districts) often proved determinative of the eventual outcome in those jurisdictions. The effect of this action or inaction is confirmed by Smith, who says, "Almost all the compliance occurred in those states whose attorneys general supported the Court's decisions with official opinions." He found, however, no more relation between "unofficial" action by the attorneys general and compliance than there was between no action at all and compliance. On the other hand, where the attorneys general opposed the Court, little compliance with the school prayer rulings came about.[35]

In another area of the law, we have some evidence of the "informal" role of the attorney general and its importance; at least, we find that some effort is being made to influence the activity of local officials through means other than the formal Opinion of the Attorney General. With respect to the Court's criminal procedure decisions, some attorneys general are attempting to serve as a major source of information about those decisions. A particularly well-developed system seems to exist in Wisconsin, where the attorney general set up annual meetings of law enforcement officers, wrote articles for the police chief's journal (at that group's request), and sent out memoranda about important cases. For example, with respect to *Boykin* v. *Alabama,* concerning procedure with respect to a judge's accepting a guilty plea, the memorandum related the decision to relevant Wisconsin cases and indicated items which should be reflected in the record upon a plea of guilty. The guidelines, it was asserted, "should be taken as an effective means of providing the adequate affirmative showing of voluntary and intelligent pleading required by *Boykin.*"[36] Through devices like this, Milner points out:

> The attorney general [has] attempted to improve his position as a source of information in order to get the police to adopt the new procedures. . . . The attorney general himself did attempt to minimize the extent of the possible conflict between law enforcement policy and United States Supreme Court decisions. . . . Thus attempts were made to remove some of the primary factors conducive to noncompliance or resistance.[37]

Subordinate legal advisors in other state agencies have often also played a role in the aftermath of Court rulings. Johnson points out that in the state he examined, the legal advisor to the State Superintendent of Public Instruction had written an opinion on the subject, although it was not given general distribution, being available on request (it was a pro-Court opinion). The advantage had by such a person, far from the local firing line, is that, "as a legal 'expert' and not a directly involved participant, [he] can afford to give the sort of simplistic, absolutist opinion that a more directly involved local participant would find difficult or impossible to render."[38]

The crucial nature of the part played by lower-level administrators comes from the vast number of people with whom they deal. In this sense, compliance (effective compliance) by a superintendent of schools with the school prayer rulings will mean that many more people are treated as the Court intended should be the case than if even all the legal officers of whom we have been talking should take a stand like that of the Court but find it disobeyed at lower levels. It is for this reason that we need to know about the behavior of prosecutors, who in their discretion can do so much to implement or undercut rules such as those of the *Miranda* decision.

The knowledge of the Court's obscenity rulings by Wisconsin district attorneys has been mentioned earlier. Those district attorneys who did see the Court's policy accurately—policy which served to restrict what they could do—were not critical of what the Court had done. Democrats among them gave the Court more support than did the Republicans in terms of judgments as to whether or not the Court had gone too far or not far enough in the area. What is interesting is that these officials generally do not support giving state and local governments more power in this area of policy, although here again party differences assert themselves with a slight majority of Republicans favoring greater state and local control and a large majority of Democrats opposed. We also need to know about the actions of prison administrators: in the aftermath of *Baxstrom* v. *Herold*, New York officials moved almost 1,000 former prisoners and others into civil hospitals to which they had been denied access earlier. A year after the decision, over 200 of that 1,000 had been released, and, because of the danger they might create, only 7 had been recommitted to the prison hospital.

Another category of state officials on whom Supreme Court decisions have fallen is the regulatory agency commissioner. Just as Supreme Court rulings have had an effect on administrative law at the national level, so have they had an effect at the state level. The effect at the state level was often negative, as it was at the national level. Thus, Fainsod talks of decisions posing "requirements on regulatory agencies which practically ruled out effective regulation"[39] and forced the state agencies to rely on negotiations to secure reductions in rates. The principal issue was the basis for figuring return on investment, particularly whether the costs of reproducing the facilities or the original costs were to be used. In the *Hope* case, the Court said that utility valuation was not subject to review on constitutional grounds and that the main issue involved is whether the end result of the agency decisions was just and reasonable. While perhaps quite vague and ambiguous, this ruling did give the state agencies the flexibility which some had been hoping for. The pattern of response was varied, as might be expected with no specific mandate. Some states retained their policy, from before the *Hope* decision, of using original cost or prudent investment. Others continued with the fair-value (reproduction cost) rule, while others adopted the original cost method, although seeming to adhere to fair value. A last category explicitly adopted original cost or prudential investment as the guideline after the *Hope* ruling. With four states in the first category, only nine in the second, eight in the third, and nineteen in the last, "The disintegration of the fair value formula ha[d] been rapidly accelerated by the *Hope* decision,"[40] although some of those states retaining the fair-value rule were among the most populous and contained a substantial portion of America's public utilities.

PUBLIC OPINION

Fortunately, we have more information on the effect of Supreme Court rulings on public opinion than we do concerning the effect on state officials. And some of the recent information is quite systematic. We should be careful to note, however, that what we have is information about public opinion concerning the Supreme Court and some of its opinions. It is an open question as to whether the specific opinions of the Court have produced the public opinion in the shape in which it has been discovered to exist. We must keep in mind the possibility that opinion about the Court stems from factors other than, or certainly in addition to, the Court's rulings themselves. If we find that public opinion is principally the result of the former, we would know something about how little impact the Court's rulings have—something quite important in the development of our knowledge about the scope of the Court's effect.

While concentrated attention on public opinion has come generally with the development of survey research techniques and commercial polling organizations, writers discussed the matter earlier, even without systematic data to present. The role of the media in the development of that public opinion was assumed, and what the papers said, if it were not taken to be public opinion, certainly was held to be relevant. Warren's statement about the effect of the Court is important in this connection:

> The reaction of the people to judicially declared law has been an especially important factor in the development of the country; for while the Judges' decision makes law, it is often the people's view of the decision which makes history. Hence, the effect produced upon contemporary public opinion has frequently been of more consequence than the actual decision itself; and in estimating this effect, regard must be paid to the fact that, while the law comes to lawyers through the official reports of judicial decisions, it reaches the people of the country filtered through the medium of the news-columns and editorials of the partisan newspapers and often exaggerated, distorted and colored by political comment.[41]

In the period about which Warren wrote, newspapers were more openly partisan than they are now in their reporting of the news. However, even now, in the simple factual reporting of what the Court says, distortions occur. In addition, we have come to recognize another kind of filtering, as we have discovered that many people obtain their opinions not so much directly from the media as from a combination of the media and personal interaction with "opinion leaders," who pay far more attention to the media than the average citizen and who serve as intermediaries in the path from medium to ultimate recipient. Thus, Warren's point about "filtered" material is still valid; the opinion leaders—at least those other than lawyers—are likely to find out about the Court from the media.

Whatever the process, present-day analysts of the Court agree at least implicitly with Warren that the Court's effect on public opinion is both great and significant. Recently, a group argued that tolerance for dissent over the war in Vietnam was in large measure a product of the Supreme Court's decisions in the area of freedom of speech. The American Jewish Congress, indicating that similar toleration of antiwar groups is not imaginable elsewhere, gave most of the credit to the Supreme Court. The group stressed the educational function of the decisions as well as the specific limits which those rulings placed on the actions of officials. The effect on public opinion may also be shown by recent survey findings indicating a more favorable attitude toward school desegregation than has existed in the past. While one might want to argue that not much progress has been made in actual desegregation of classrooms, and that population movements have led to retrogression in the North, the crucial symbolic—as distinguished from instrumental—effect of *Brown* v. *Board* (and subsequent reinforcing decisions) is relatively clear from these public opinion findings.

Another sort of effect in the area of public opinion is one of the second order. Matthews and Prothro find that young southern whites are more segregationist than middle-aged Southerners, a function of having been exposed to the racial vituperation which existed in the aftermath of *Brown*. Therefore, in this instance, public opinion was developed and affected by public opinion stemming directly from a ruling of the Court. The indirect development of public opinion as a result of Court rulings is also shown by the effect of certain rulings on the media themselves. The decisions in the area of libel perhaps make the point best: mass-circulation publications, sensitive to public reaction, get immediate response from their legal staff as to what is permissible and what is not under the Court's rulings. They can thus "precisely adjust verbal behavior" in order to have "relative immunity from trouble on most matters."[42] To the extent that public opinion is affected by what the mass media communicate, alteration of media behavior because of Court rulings will mean an additional effect of the rulings on public opinion.

This is an example of a situation where a decision need not be widely noticed, at least by the public, to have an effect, although it clearly would have to be noticed by key sectors of the society. Another example occurs where a prosecutor may alter his mode of operations in response to a decision, thus affecting people's behavior, before they are aware of the ruling and its possible relationship to what is occurring. To the extent that changes in the people's attitudes follow from the changes in behavior, one has an exception to the proposition that "before a decision can alter opinion, it must be widely noticed."[43]

Before turning to the more recent data, we might look at instances of effects on public opinion about which Warren writes. Some, coming from the early part of the nineteenth century, have been mentioned earlier, particularly when reaction to perceived infringements on states' rights was involved. But the reaction continued through the last half of the century as well. One instance involves the Legal Tender Cases, where the question concerned the legality of the Union Government's requiring that debts could be paid in paper money. Initially, the Court held that such a requirement could *not* be applied to debts made before the statute was enacted. A year later, an enlarged Court with some new Justices reversed the first decision. The whole sequence of events, including the appointments of Justices Strong and Bradley on the day of the first (adverse) decision, and the reopening of the case, Warren suggests, had a considerable negative effect on the public's view of the Court—and the impact of the situation was greater than the impact of the first ruling had been. He points out that the appointments did not constitute "Court-packing," because they had been under consideration for some time, and that there was consensus in the legal community that the Legal Tender Act was constitutional, regardless of the first decision. However, he states that the reopening was "a mistake which for many years impaired the people's confidence, not in the honesty, but in the impartiality and good sense of the Court."[44]

The Legal Tender Cases showed a difference in reaction between the public, on the one hand, and those more familiar with the Court's operation, on the other. Another example of this arose from cases where municipal bonds were protected against subsequent state action. Such action "had an inestimable effect upon the material and moral prosperity of the country in restoring confidence in a class of securities which were an indispensable factor in the development of municipal and industrial enterprises,"[45] but the view of the general public toward the Court was not strengthened; in fact, hostility grew as a result of them, in part because the Court was already under attack because of the controversy over Reconstruction. Thus, the "general public" and "special publics" or "attentive publics" did not always end up feeling the same way after a case. After the Slaughterhouse Cases, it was the same thing: most of the press and the bar saw the case as one in which the matter of local monopolies was for the states to decide, but others saw it as supporting monopolies and disliked the decision as a result.

That decisions do not produce uniform response among attentive publics is shown by reaction to some of the New Deal decisions. Thus, when the Court ended the life of the National Industrial Recovery Administration and National Industrial Recovery Act in the *Schechter* case, reactions varied. "The more conservative sections of the press welcomed it as putting an end to unsound experiments in government regulation of industry." Labor opposed the decision. The business community was, however, divided: some had liked the market control NRA had provided, while others disliked the "grant of anything savoring of monopolistic privilege"[46] entailed in the program. The Court's continued striking down of other New Deal legislation began to alienate more and more elements of the citizenry. "Each new adverse decision in the winter and spring of 1936 brought new bursts of hostility," Schlesinger writes.[47] The farmers were upset about *Butler,* the workers about *Carter* v. *Carter Coal,* and the minimum wage rulings "alienated nearly everybody," including those who had supported earlier decisions. Schlesinger notes that only *10* of 344 editorials approved the ruling, and some sixty papers, including a number of conservative ones, called for a constitutional amendment on the subject.

The mention of editorials brings us to two fairly systematic studies of editorial reaction to recent decisions. Nagel and Erickson examined large-circulation newspapers in a two-week period subsequent to each of four major church-state decisions. Except for reaction to the *Zorach* ruling, editorials were generally in favor of church-state separation. Few newspapers had editorials on the school transportation case (three favored, none opposed, fourteen had no editorial). On religious classes on school property, eight favored the ruling striking down the practice, and two were opposed (only seven had no editorial). All wrote editorials on the school prayer case, with thirteen favoring and nine opposed. However, with the released-time-off-school-grounds decision, none favored separation of church and state (opposed the decision), and six supported the ruling (eight had no editorial).

In trying to explain the reaction to *Zorach,* the analysts suggest that the link between church and state in that case was far milder than in the others and that attitudes toward civil liberties were far more conservative generally in 1952 than either before or after. They also point to the fact that Justice Douglas wrote the decision. They suggest that the newspapers on the whole tend to support the Court, regardless of the direction of the decision, and this "response-set" may have been operative with *Zorach.* Looking further, Nagel and Erickson found a positive correlation between the percentage of Democrats in the newspaper's city and whether it took a favorable position toward separation of church and state, a correlation which increased when the publisher's politics rather than the city's politics were examined. The publisher's religion was also relevant, with the newspaper more likely to endorse the separation decision (particularly school prayer) if the publisher were Catholic or Episcopalian.

Newland also looked at the reaction to the prayer decision, but he was more interested in coverage. He examined sixty-three papers, and found that twenty-seven had published editorials opposing the decision, while sixteen had favored it (the reverse of Nagel's finding); eleven other papers were relatively neutral. Opposition, he found, was regional, being strongest in the upper Midwest. More southern papers were neutral or favorable than opposed. Newland also looked at cartoons, finding twenty critical cartoons on the school prayer case and only a dozen favorable ones. Hostile cartoons were published by two papers which had been neutral editorially.

The first reapportionment ruling was also studied by Newland. There he found thirty-eight editorials favoring the Court's decision, and only ten opposed, with another twelve neutral or confused. Nine newspapers went so far as to publish two favoring editorials in one week. Editorial cartoons ran in the same direction: four were opposed, while sixteen were favorable. Newland thinks the mildness of the negative reaction (both in terms of numbers and even among those with negative editorials) stemmed from a conflict between a feeling that states' rights were being interfered with and a feeling that the papers' urban readers would benefit from the decisions. Newland gives us one other interesting finding: those papers supporting the Court in their editorials presented a more restrained account of the Court's rulings, in both headlines and reportage of critical reaction to the decisions, than did those papers which opposed the ruling. Our newspapers may not be as openly partisan in their news reporting as they were in the nineteenth century, but there is a notable relationship between editorial view and reportage.

Those who have been concerned about the Court's effect on, or relation to, public opinion have thought that such opinion would be related to the stake the citizen has in the opinion. Barth suggests, "The degree to which the citizen perceives the outputs of the Supreme Court is closely related to the degree to which the citizen perceives his interests to be involved in the decisions."[48] Miller and Scheflin, reinforcing the general position, hypothesize: "The prestige of the Supreme Court has little or nothing to do with its symbolic role as such . . . but rather with what it does."[49] When people agree with the results, they supposedly will have high respect for the Court.

With that as a base, what do the data tell us? Krislov, after telling us that a 1945 poll showed that only two fifths of adults knew the number of Supreme Court Justices (much less more specifics), talks of the wavering nature of public opinion about the Court, but asserts that it is "*not* dependent upon interpretation of any single case, no matter how momentous," but "is derived from the total impression made by the Court upon large numbers of people."[50] Yet we find the public differentiating in its reaction to specific decisions. A Harris Survey in November, 1966, showed the public giving the Court an overall negative rating (54 percent–48 percent), but favoring decisions on reapportionment (76 percent–24 percent) and desegregation of schools and public accommodations (both 64 percent–36 percent). Reaction to decisions forbidding the State Department to deny passports to Communists was split almost evenly, with the public disliking *Miranda* (35 percent–65 percent) and School Prayer rulings (30 percent–70 percent). Regional variations occurred, with only reapportionment receiving approval in the South, but with 44 percent of the Southerners supporting school desegregation. Other cleavages also appeared, with younger people, the better educated, and Negroes generally backing the Court, although the Negroes opposed the School Prayer ruling by roughly three to one; white Southerners, and the older and less well educated were shown to be the severest critics of the Court. A Gallup Poll in 1967 produced much the same results. In that poll, 15 percent rated the work of the Court excellent, 30 percent rated it Good, 29 percent Fair, and 17 percent Poor, thus leaving an almost perfect balance between favorable and unfavorable reactions. The changes which can occur in a short time are shown by the June, 1968, poll, in which the balance had shifted to 36 percent favorable—53 percent unfavorable, with only 8 percent rating the Court's work as excellent.

Dolbeare, recognizing the downward shifts in regard for the Court, however, says it is not clear that this is a phenomenon uniformly affecting everyone over the long term. He says some groups in the population may always be shifting toward a negative view of the Court, although overall evaluations remain fairly constant. It may also be, he says, that support is continually being revived for those for whom it has fallen off. Dolbeare's data contains a finding which should make us careful about presuming that only conservatives (for example, segregationists) are those critical of the Court. At least in Wisconsin, liberals are a substantial percentage of those unhappy about the Court, for not moving fast enough.

Among the systematic studies of public opinion available to us is one conducted by John Kessel, with a Seattle, Washington, sample in February, 1965; that by Dolbeare, using a Wisconsin adult cross section, in 1966; and the analysis by Walter Murphy and Joseph Tanenhaus of material from the Survey Research Center post–1964 and post–1966 election surveys, involving national samples. Kessel found that his respondents had relatively little information about the Court but that their attitudes were supportive of the Court's work. Those with negative views held their views somewhat more intensely than those who supported the Court. In part because relatively few cases rise to the level of visibility for the general public, he says, contrary to the Miller-Scheflin hypothesis, "How the Court reaches its decisions may be quite as important in maintaining public support as what it decides."[51] Myths about how the Court works help produce support. Dolbeare shows that those who accept the myths (that judges decide cases strictly on the basis of the Constitution, that judges as nonelected officials decide matters more fairly than elected officials) are more likely to give the Court higher ratings than others, although he says, "We cannot be certain whether the former [myth acceptance] causes the latter [higher ratings] or whether one is inclined to endorse the myths because of satisfaction with the Court."[52]

Both Dolbeare and Murphy and Tanenhaus talk about the limited awareness people had about the reapportionment decisions, even where redistricting had taken place; Murphy and Tanenhaus suggest that people cannot relate the decisions to their personal lives. Dolbeare indicates the same was true in Wisconsin for the criminal procedure cases, which had been openly attacked in the state. "Perhaps defendants' rights issues are the private preserve of policemen and editorial writers," he comments.[53] Criticizing the forced-choice questions used in such polls as the Gallup polls (where respondents may answer even without knowledge of the decision, thus leading to an overestimation of people's awareness of Court rulings), Murphy and Tanenhaus suggest that more than two thirds of the likes and dislikes about the Court in 1964 could be accounted for by civil rights and school prayer decisions; two years later, it was criminal procedure cases which were central. Kessel also suggests that "only a few cases are sufficiently dramatic to rise above the public's threshold of attention,"[54] with most of the mentions of the Court's activity falling into three or four categories (particularly civil rights and school prayer). Dolbeare remarks, "The prayer decisions have apparently been one of the most salient actions of the Court, being unknown only to the same seemingly irreducible number of persons who have managed to remain unaware of the segregation decisions."[55] Lack of awareness of the specific decisions of the Court is shown further by the inability of respondents in the Wisconsin sample to name good things (or even bad things) the Court had done and by the national sample's mention of cases (such as those dealing with Bobby Baker and Iowa child adoption) which the Court had not considered, except to deny certiorari. Only 2 percent of the Wisconsin sample had all items correct in a test of knowledge about decisions, and only 15 percent had more than half correct, with 12 percent getting every answer wrong.

The relative lack of relationship between information and ratings of the Court is suggested by Dolbeare, although he found higher knowledge correlating with greater disapproval of the Court. This is reinforced by Kessel's finding, "Critics are more likely to have paid some attention to the Court than its supporters,"[56] and by Daniels' suggestion, based on SRC data, that the more educated are "more likely to be critical of the Court." One gets disagreement here, however; Barth finds, with respect to obscenity, that disapproval is "higher among the low and medium perception groups."[57] Kessel found those with college degrees more likely to be among strong supporters *or* critics and those with little education to be weak supporters or critics or neutral, indicating that the "supporters and critics of the Court have more in common with each other than either grouping does with those who take a neutral posture." Thus, having an attitude "depends on being involved in the political culture."[58] Murphy and Tanenhaus say that those knowing more about the Supreme Court are those who know more about politics generally.

Kessel also notes the importance of prior information about the Court, which he suggests strengthens the relationships he finds between attitudes and support of the Court. He says it is even possible that favorable prior information by itself can produce a supportive attitude toward the Court. Unfavorable prior information, however, serves mainly to strengthen negative attitudes. The relationship between information and attitudes, suggesting it to be bilateral, is shown by Kessel's statement: "Having pro-Court attitudes . . . seems to explain much of what one hears and reads about the Court."[59] However, if a person agrees with what the Court has done, the influence of prior communication is reduced. If, instead, he is opposed, he gets support from that communication.

Both Kessel and Dolbeare find political party a relevant variable. The effect of respondent's attitudes is decreased, Kessel says, by political party identification, and thus the attitudes come through more clearly with independents than with party identifiers. In his Seattle sample, which Daniels points out is more favorable to the Court than is true on a national basis, Kessel finds Republican identification explaining reactions to Court decisions and Democratic identification having a clear effect on what those people hear about the Court, thus maintaining their current attitudes. Dolbeare found Republicans less favorable to the Court than were Democrats, and also found Democrats and Republicans differing more than did conservatives and liberals, not unlike Kessel's finding that belief in specific procedural rights does not affect the relationship between party identification and views of the Court. Part (but only part) of the Republicans' unhappiness with the Court had to do with the fact that the Democrats controlled the White House, although, "Approval of the President, regardless of party, correlates with approval of the Court" just as, "The party membership of the President seems to affect attitudes toward the Supreme Court."[60] Dolbeare suggests that the cleavage between parties with respect to the Court goes back all the way to the New Deal period, and particularly to the time of Roosevelt's Court-packing plan.

While they say, "Little indication is given that ideological proclivities, independent of party affiliation, exert significant influence on attitudes toward the Court,"[61] Dolbeare and Hammond also indicate that other factors emerge as correlates of attitude when the party differential is eliminated in periods of a Republican Presidency. Kessel does point to some attitudes as playing a role in one's views of the Court. For example, the relationship between agreement with Court decisions and attitude toward the Court is depressed by having less libertarian attitudes. Support for procedural rights and agreement with decisions are related. The attitudes one has may affect the communications one receives, as Kessel points out by noting, "Favorable communications about the Court are received by those who support 7 to 9 procedural rights in part because of their pro-libertarian attitude, while relatively rare unfavorable news supports and strengthens the effect of anti-libertarian attitudes."[62] These attitudinal matters may be secondary or residual, but they are relevant.

Murphy and Tanenhaus are particularly interested in the question of whether a Court decision can serve to legitimate a "regime change"—for example, a change in governmental structure or process like that required by the reapportionment decisions. It is one thing for people to say, as 71 percent of the Wisconsin sample did, that the Supreme Court can make important changes in the way people live (16 percent denied this); it is another to say that such changes made by the Court are proper. Without more evidence, "Certainly there is no reason to suppose that a judicial decision does—or does not—automatically quiet most constitutional doubts of most citizens."[63]

Murphy and Tanenhaus postulate that a Court decision could serve as a legitimator of regime changes for those who perceive the Court, recognize that it may properly interpret and apply the constitution, and feel that the court is acting in an impartial and competent manner. People can fall into this category even if they disagree with particular decisions or feel that individual judges are behaving improperly. They find that about 25 percent of the population satisfy the first two conditions, while 40 percent satisfy neither, and that only about one eighth of the sample fulfills all the criteria. Among those in the "totally inattentive public" are a majority of Negroes, despite the benefits received from the Court in recent years. "To 57 percent of the Negroes in our sample, the Supreme Court was a cipher."[64] However, among Negroes with views about the Court, 90 percent give it support. Local leaders, on the other hand, are found by Dolbeare and Hammond to be far more likely than the average citizen to satisfy criteria of the type Murphy and Tanenhaus posit. They find such leaders "much more knowledgeable" about the Court, "more likely to see [it] as an institution capable of making large-scale changes in the society, [and] more confident in it as an institution." This led them to the conclusion that "The Supreme Court is chiefly an object of leadership attention and concern."[65]

Those giving the Court diffuse support are greater in number than those giving specific support, by a 4:1 ratio, indicating that "despite the unpopularity of its decisions in recent years the Court still retains a substantial reservoir" of general support.[66] Those who give the Court diffuse support include some of those—the more articulate—who are least knowledgeable about the Court, so knowledge is not an absolute prerequisite for support. Only about 20 percent of the sample rank among those in the negative on diffuse support, but one third of the sample fall on the negative side with respect to specific support. This tends to suggest that general support may come from those opposed to particular decisions, and also that specific opposition is more intense than specific support. However, "The minority may become more highly motivated but is unlikely to become a majority."[67]

All of these data based on attitudes and views still leave us with the question of whether those opposed to the Court, whatever their numbers, will act on their opposition. Kessel suggests, "The decisions of the Supreme Court have had more effect on the reputation of the Court than the activities of its antagonists."[68] Some of Dolbeare's data do deal more directly with the matter. More than a third of his sample (36 percent) said they would do something to change a Court decision they disliked, but only a few of that number would try to develop further opposition among the public. Half would work through their congressmen, and another quarter would "act within the established legal processes."[69] As Dolbeare remarks, "This is quiescence indeed. Those who rate the Court's performance as poor are the most likely to act to change a decision, but they are neither numerous nor particularly rebelliously inclined." Most of those who said they would do nothing appeared to fit into the category of feeling powerless, a finding which tends to fit with the finding of Murphy and Tanenhaus that those who are aware of the Court are in some measure also those who do not trust government and feel it unresponsive—while the more trusting are less aware of the Court.

Drawing on the data available to him, Dolbeare argues that compliance with Court decisions has come from public acquiesence, rather than active approval, and that when people are directly affected—and have perceived that they are, as with desegregation and school prayer—compliance has been far harder to come by. When, on the other hand, public officials are able to put Court commands into effect without engaging the public in the activity, compliance is higher; reapportionment may be an example of this phenomenon, as would be criminal procedure matters (although compliance there has not been high). Dolbeare suggests that the general public is usually not relevant to most work of the Court, "either as a controlling factor or as a measure of the propriety of its decisions." As a result, "The Court can take far-reaching action . . . without ever making a dent in the public consciousness."[70]

CHAPTER 8

A Look Back and a Look Ahead—Toward Impact Theory

In the preceding chapters, drawing on the use of one aspect of the increasingly common political perspective on the Supreme Court and the judicial system, we have presented a picture of what we now know of the impact of the Supreme Court's decisions in a variety of substantive areas and in several different governmental and political arenas. We have seen that the decisions of the Court, far from producing uniform impact or automatic compliance, have varying effects—from instances in which no action follows upon them to wide degrees of compliance (usually underreported), resistance, and evasion. These varying effects include increases in the level of political activity and activity within the judicial system itself and changes in governmental structure. Widespread criticism may follow decisions, and often attempts are made to reverse the Court through enactment of statutes or constitutional amendments. Important social interests, both economic and noneconomic, may be dislocated or legitimated, and the Court's decisions also often perform an agenda-setting function for other political actors.

It is clear from this examination that we know more about what the Court has done in the field of civil liberties than in areas of economic regulation and administrative law and that we know more about impact in the lower courts, both federal and state, and Congress than we do about impact on state legislative and executive branches of government. In these terms, where we need to go is fairly clear: research must be carried out to fill in the gaps. There are, however, other types of deficiencies. We have, as noted earlier, concentrated on the ultimate *result* of Court decisions, insofar as we could determine what that ultimate result has been. The *process* by which the decisions of the Court were transmitted to the locus where the ultimate result occurred has been far less often the object of our attention. Certainly, if we are to talk about compliance by law enforcement officers with the Court's police procedure cases, we need to know whether they found out about the decisions, particularly those beyond the highly visible *Miranda* case, and we need to be aware of the form in which the cases came to them as well as the context in which they received them. So we must extend our attention back, as it were, from the result toward the source. And, in that connection, we must not lose sight of the decisions themselves—their doctrinal content and the rules of procedure utilized by the Court in arriving at its rulings.

While the overattention to doctrine of the early students of constitutional law certainly needed rectifying, shifting completely to attention to "political" matters rather than supplementing attention to doctrine with attention to impact is not healthy for a most complete understanding of the judicial process. Advocates of the systems approach to the study of the judiciary point to the feedback effect from impact on later decisions of the Court, a matter not covered here, but certainly not to be neglected. While initial studies may, for practical reasons, have to be of the effect on individual cases on environment, ultimately we should turn to studies of greater longitudinal dimension, following a case's impact back "up into" the Court's decisional process, and then "down again" into the political environment. By looking at result rather than process, we have tended to examine situations where impacts were more or less obvious, or where noncompliance was equally evident. This has meant, however, that we are not able to speak of *degrees* of impact or the *proportion* of instances in which the Court's rulings have had an effect. To be sure, the difficulty of ascertaining impact in some situations, necessary before we can talk about degree of impact, is considerable, but we seriously need the perspective of knowing *how frequently* and *to what extent* the Court's decisions do have some effect, because we often see compliance with, and resistance to, a single decision occurring concurrently.

Earlier, we explored three ways of looking at impact, three frames of reference, although our discussion of legal aspects of the problem suggests something less coherent than a "frame of reference." Those frames of reference allow us to "cut into" the process of impact from different analytical perspectives, to cast new light on the topic. Yet they are only analytical perspectives, none by itself providing a full picture, a well-developed theory. Clearly, we realize that "the law is *not* simply what the judges say it is," and that an Austinian theory of jurisprudence, while important in making us focus on what comes forth from the Court, is incomplete for our purposes. This becomes particularly clear when we realize that, on at least some occasions, judges themselves think of the impact they have, that they may be acting on a "jurisprudence of consequences," which is something of an extension of the concern of sociological jurisprudence with affected social interests.

Similarly, while it is crucial to recognize the role of groups in the aftermath of Supreme Court rulings, we also know that that frame of reference can be pushed too far and that there are many other units of analysis besides groups which need to be accounted for. The communications frame of reference, perhaps because of its high process orientation, seems most fruitful of the three frames of reference presented, and it has been used most fruitfully by some scholars examining impact. Yet, even if we must pay more attention to the way in which decisions are transmitted, and the way they are distorted (or lost) in the process of transmission, we must still determine what happens to them when, in whatever form—distorted or not—they reach their target. Thus, each is to some extent incomplete. Taken together, they give us a better picture, but there are still many nooks and crannies—and even central places—in the shadows when their spotlights are thrown on the impact process. Other perspectives are needed, and the reader is challenged to develop them.

In Chapter 2, a number of the variables which affected impact, or potentially affected it, were isolated, identified, and categorized in terms of their location in the process of impact. A number of them appeared regularly in the subsequent discussion of existing studies. The closeness of the vote in a case, the ambiguity of a decision, the way it is reported, the "follow-up" efforts of public officials and those affected—all were seen to have played a part in what happens after the Court speaks. We have seen that often these variables occur in clusters, with individual items difficult to disentangle, rather than neatly one at a time. However, we do not yet have many studies carried out with a prior specification of variables or statements of hypotheses. In other words, our identification of variables (and hypotheses) has been ex post facto. This is legitimate in exploratory stages of research, in which much of our work is located. In fact, as we have noted, a considerable portion of what we know comes from the work of those not explicitly concerned with "impact analysis" but whose descriptions of situations, particularly historical ones, give us "leads" on what has happened in the aftermath of the Court's statements. Even when political scientists became directly and openly concerned with impact, they were not sure where to start, and early work was largely descriptive and of the case-study variety. But by now we are ready, as the burgeoning impact literature suggests, to move beyond that point. The case study may, in many situations, continue to be our tool, but it must be used to illuminate theory, not for its own sake.

That leads to the question of what we can extract from the materials presented in this volume. We are not ready, it seems, for a broad "theory of impact." We can only move *toward* such a theory. A number of hypotheses have appeared, either explicitly or implicitly, in the studies discussed here. Remembering that an inventory of hypotheses, like a propositional inventory, is not a theory, we might see what some of these hypotheses are, as some indication of where we stand in terms of theoretical development. The hypotheses embody a number of the variables suggested as relevant in Chapter 2, and the order of presentation chosen parallels the order of presentation of the variables there. Perhaps in using this device, we are presenting (or developing) a new frame of reference, a map within which pieces can be fit and related to each other. Where the stated hypotheses can be so related, an effort has been made to do so, because it is this interrelatedness which makes a theory more than simply a collection of hypotheses. In any case, the hypotheses—because drawn from the studies reported and analyzed in this volume—serve in a sense to summarize the volume, something otherwise difficult to do, by extracting the theoretical essence of the studies carried out by others.

Some of the hypotheses are somewhat "soft" or not tightly operationalized. If one views hypotheses as (more general) propositions "with their necks stuck out," the necks of these hypotheses are not well developed, and lack precise delineation, to be provided by the researcher moving to apply them to a specific situation in which he might find them applicable. The reader must keep in mind the questions of measurement of impact—and related concepts—raised in Chapter 2, so as not to lose sight of the many different measurements which might be used in pursuing tests of these hypotheses. One must also remember that the hypotheses provided here are derived from existing studies, mostly after the fact, by the authors of those studies, and are meant to be suggestive, so that it is quite possible that several more specific hypotheses could be derived from a single statement provided here. These statements are cast in rough hypothesis form to make them "stand out" more.

Some of the hypotheses have already been presented, in either identical or similar language; others combine or are derived from the materials of the volume. (Where language from earlier in the volume is used, quotation marks are dispensed with.) Some of the hypotheses may appear to go beyond the discussion of the book. Here it must be remembered that they are generated from available data, not generalizations thoroughly tested. Brief references to some examples, perhaps obvious ones, are included, but the detail underlying the hypotheses is not repeated. The detailed material is, of course, available to the reader who wishes to refer to it. Some evidence of the primitive state of our theory-development is shown by the fact that competing or contradictory hypotheses can be generated from existing data, without our being able to choose one such hypothesis over the other(s) at the present time. We are, in other words, unable in many instances to specify adequately the set of conditions under which certain variables will operate in a given direction and under which conditions they will operate in another.

Characteristics of Cases. While most of our knowledge is about the effect of individual cases, we do know that cases occur in sets or "lines."

Hyp: A line of cases will have greater impact than a single case. "Elements common to the opinions . . . [tend] to reinforce each other and increase the impact of such elements in the opinions,"[1] as was noted with respect to the effect of the Supreme Court's obscenity opinions on Oregon policy making. Thus,

Hyp: One disliked opinion following on other disliked opinions will produce more noncompliance than one standing by itself.

This was the situation with respect to *Miranda* in relation to other criminal procedure decisions. It became clearer, as each subsequent decision was handed down, that the Court intended to incorporate virtually all of the Bill of Rights' protections as prohibitions against the states, even though doing it by "selective incorporation." Similarly,

Hyp: When the Court "backs off" from disliked decisions, the effect will be to reduce political controversy.

This was true in the late 1950's when the Court retreated somewhat from its internal security decisions of 1956 and 1957. However,

Hyp: A decision in which precedent is overruled will create more resistance than one in which there is no overruling.

The overruling gives those resisting a decision an additional hook on which to hang their arguments, as with *Brown's* overruling of *Plessy.* Not only do sets of cases decided with full opinion have an impact, but

Hyp: Continued denial of certiorari with respect to a given subject will decrease the number of cases filed concerning that subject.

Thus controversy over the subject involved, at least within the judicial arena, will be reduced, and those still resisting will be forced to direct their efforts elsewhere.

Hyp: Continued denial of certiorari with respect to a given subject will shift activity from the judicial system to other political arenas.

If we turn to individual decisions, which we have studied most, we find that the content and type of action taken appear to affect impact. While most of the recent decisions provoking reaction have had heavy symbolic components, over the long run,

Hyp: Noncompliance will be greater when there is an economic component to a decision than when there is not.

Of course, one can see economic ramifications in the desegregation issue and the criminal procedure decisions, and relatively few decisions are without some economic component. However, one analyst has suggested that

Hyp: Attempts to curb the Court are less likely to be successful when intensely held economic or civil liberties interests are involved then when federal-state relations or separation of powers questions are decided by the Court.

Regardless of subject matter, the breadth of a decision is an important matter affecting impact. While

quent decisions by absorbing opposition,

it is also the case that

Hyp: The broader the decision, the greater the impact and the broader the noncompliance.

Somewhat differently put,

Hyp: A ruling confined to the facts of a case will produce less noncompliance than one decided on a general principle.

However,

Hyp: The broader the scope of a holding, the more difficult evasion becomes.

That is, there is less opportunity for "escape" by those disliking the decision, and outright resistance may be the only viable alternative for them.

The type of action taken by the Court is also crucial.

Hyp: Decisions limiting government action will produce more immediate reaction than those upholding or legitimating such action.

However, it is also apparently the case that

Hyp: Permissive court decisions will be used more in support of new policies than will restrictive court decisions.

The type of government action struck down is also relevant. Thus,

Hyp: Decisions invalidating procedural defects are more frequently evaded than are decisions on substantive law.

It is unlikely that some other procedural method cannot be found to replace the one invalidated.

The basis on which the Court makes its decisions can be important in determining how people proceed after the Court has ruled. And whether or not the Court indicates a basis for its decisions is important. Thus,

Hyp: Where the basis for a decision is made clear, compliance will be greater than where it is not made clear.

The fact that the basis for the Court's ruling in *Miranda* was not made clear by the press helped limit compliance with that decision. And Peltason noted that southern federal judges helped produce the same effect after *Brown* by not making clear the basis for their decisions. Similarly, as indicated by the comparison of the reception of *Engel* and *Schempp*, where the Court provided clearer indications of the basis of its decision in the latter,

Hyp: Decisions containing "cues" as to the basis for decision will have greater acceptance than decisions not containing such cues.

By extension, because they state no basis at all, except perhaps for citation of earlier cases,

Hyp: Summary decisions of the Court are less likely to be followed than are decisions with full opinion.

However, when they come after earlier decisions with full opinion on the same subject, summary affirmances and reversals may serve the same function as that noted above for continued certiorari denial—to close off use of the courts for the development of policy.

The Court has, according to its own "rules of self-restraint," attempted to avoid constitutional issues when it can decide cases on the basis of statutory interpretation or the facts involved in a case. However,

Hyp: A Supreme Court decision based on the Constitution will receive less attack and greater compliance than a decision grounded on statute, the Court's supervisory authority, or other bases.

This hypothesis is at the heart of the argument that the Supreme Court in *Brown* should have relied more heavily on the Constitution than it did and should have avoided even footnote references to sociological material.

The Court, in addition to providing the basis for its decisions, may or may not provide guidelines as to how its rulings are to be carried out. As experience with both desegregation and reapportionment seems to make clear,

Hyp: Compliance will be more immediate when courts provide clear guidelines than when they do not.

There was much activity after *Reynolds,* but relatively few legislatures developed apportionment plans which *closely* approximated one man–one vote until some time after the ruling and until there had been much subsequent action, particularly by lower courts, with the Supreme Court still being reluctant to establish explicit guidelines. Remand orders to the lower courts once the Supreme Court has decided a case will also be of importance as guidelines. As observers of a number of remands have indicated,

Hyp: The more flexible the remand order, the greater the noncompliance.

Guidelines are future oriented; sometimes, as noted in our discussion of whether or not impacts were planned by the Justices, decisions are based in part on what the Justices anticipate reaction will be; this has an effect of its own.

Hyp: The impact of decisions based on anticipated impact will be less than the impact of decisions not so based.

This would occur because decisions based on anticipated impact would be more moderate, less forceful, and would tend to decrease the authoritativeness of the Court's action. In addition, in the area of police practices, it has been suggested that

> *Hyp:* Decisions based on anticipated impact encourage use of "questionable" practices.

While these hypotheses deal with the effect of the Court's language—for the basis of a decision and guidelines can only appear in that language—the relation between the Court's result (present in summary decisions as well as cases decided with full opinion) and its language may be relevant to how a case is greeted by those at whom it is aimed. On the basis of experience in the area of administrative law, with respect to both patent law and review of regulatory agency decisions, we can say that

> *Hyp:* The language of the Court will have a greater effect on compliance than will the results of decisions.

Similarly,

> *Hyp:* Impact will be greater where the Court's doctrine reinforces its results than where it does not do so.

That language can have an effect is shown by the unwillingness of some courts of appeals or the Patent Office to change policy in the face of changing results (higher rates of invalidation of patents) by the Court, as well as by the effect of "stray language," such as the dictum in the *Rabinowitz* search-and-seizure case or Justice Douglas' dictum in the *Zorach* case. The seeming inconsistency between Justice Black's polemic about separation of church and state in the *Everson* case and the result—to uphold payment of transportation costs to parents of parochial school children—is an illustration of the situation indicated by the latter hypothesis.

Other aspects of the Court's language have been held to be of considerable importance. For example,

> *Hyp:* The greater the technicality of the language of a decision, the smaller the impact.

But, as noted at several points earlier in the volume, ambiguity is crucial. The lesser impact of summary decisions, hypothesized above, stems from an ambiguity created because the Court sets out no explaining language. What often happens, however, is that the explaining language is itself ambiguous, or people cannot agree on a clear interpretation of it. The most basic hypothesis is simply that

> *Hyp:* Ambiguity in Supreme Court rulings decreases compliance.

Or, stated differently,

> *Hyp:* Where there is no clear agreement on the meaning of a decision, compliance is less than where there is such agreement.

Whether *Brown* required only dropping of racial lines or actual positive acts of "integration"—an oft-debated point—comes under the second form of the hypothesis. Ambiguity decreases compliance in several ways. For one thing,

Hyp: Ambiguity in a Supreme Court decision increases the divergence between the courts of appeals.

This is clear both from our information about patent law cases and from the aftermath of the Smith Act rulings. This is because, "The less clear and direct the policy communication from the Supreme Court, the more likely are the resisting circuit judges to 'misunderstand' it and continue along their own path."[2] In addition,

Hyp: Ambiguous court decisions will be used more in support of new policies than will clear decisions.

These policies will be more likely to reflect local values.

Hyp: Ambiguity in a decision increases the influence of local values in the resolution of conflict in the aftermath of a decision.

However, while such values will bulk large in the aftermath of decisions, the ambiguity may also mean greater use of the courts to resolve the conflict.

Hyp: Ambiguity in court opinions will increase use of the lower courts rather than other agencies of government.

If judges have created the ambiguity, who can better resolve it?

One other matter about cases should be mentioned briefly. The vote by which a case is decided has been alleged to have a bearing on impact. The most obvious debate on this matter concerns the even greater noncompliance which supposedly would have occurred had *Brown* not been unanimous.

Hyp: Noncompliance will be greater when dissenting and/or concurring opinions exist than in unanimous decisions.

As a corollary, with respect to effort immediately after a decision,

Hyp: The closer the vote in a Supreme Court decision, the greater the efforts to make the Court change its mind.

Communication. Because of the lengthy discussion in Chapter 3 of communication—as a frame of reference for examining impact—we need not dwell on it for long here, but we can state a limited sample of hypotheses relating to the communication of Court rulings. The first relates as much to the way the Court hands down its cases as to the way they are reported.

Hyp: Decisions released simultaneously with other decisions are less likely to have impact than decisions released separately from others.

With many decisions to report at once, the press will be selective, and some decisions will not be reported; they will be buried in the crush. When decisions are transmitted,

Hyp: The greater the number of channels through which decisions are reported, the greater the impact.

Cases which people can read about in the newspapers and/or in magazines and which they hear about from friends and co-workers will have a greater effect than those which only appear in the formal court records.

In the course of reporting cases, impact is itself reported, leading to,

Hyp: Reporting of immediate negative reaction tends to increase noncompliance.

On the other hand,

Hyp: Information about the specifics of how to comply with a decision will bring greater impact than general discussion of a case.

Police looking toward *Miranda* with a view toward complying with it need to know *how* to do so as well as *why* the Court decided as it did. Even given the fact that most newspapers receive news about the Supreme Court's cases from the same source—the wire services—what is reported will be affected by the views of newspaper publishers.

Hyp: Those papers supporting the Court's position will use more restrained reporting about the decision than will those opposing the decision.

And while we will see local officials' reactions conditioned by local political preferences, the publisher's views seem to override these.

Hyp: A publisher's political preferences will have a greater effect on his editorials about Court decisions than will the politics of the city in which the paper is published.

A possible source of information about decisions for police, and members of other organizations, is the organization itself. Milner found, contrary to what he had originally hypothesized, that

Hyp: The higher the professionalization of an affected organization, the more it will rely on internal sources of information.

Finally, we must recognize the effect of the communication of decisions not simply on particular groups but on the general public. Taking our lead from Newland's words, "Both the Court and the press need to improve their methods if essential public understanding and support of the Court and a dynamic legal system are to exist,"[3] we can state:

Hyp: Inadequate transmission of Court decisions will reduce support for and understanding of the Court.

Political Environment. The environment into which the decisions of the Court are "injected" gives rise to many of the hypotheses we have been able to generate about impact. At the most general level,

Hyp: The broader the geographical scope of potential impact, the greater the resistance to a decision.

Resistance will be less great if the affected practice occurs in only a few jurisdictions, for example, movie censorship, than if it occurs on a broad basis, for example, segregation throughout the South. However, that formal segregation was limited to the South (or seemed to be) meant far less resistance than if *Brown* had been seen as also applying to the North at the same time. Another hypothesis relating to the scope of a decision is that

Hyp: The greater the number of levels of government or the number of people affected, the greater the noncompliance.

With both school desegregation and school prayer, one was dealing with state legislatures and executives, school boards, superintendents, principals, and, ultimately (and particularly with respect to prayer), teachers, making the job of effectuating the policy of the decisions that much harder.

A set of hypotheses relates to the question of time after a decision. It should be pointed out first that

Hyp: The greater the involvement in or preoccupation with external events, the less immediate the impact of a Court decision.

This much seems clear from what we know about the first child labor case, where people were much involved in the events of World War I, and the *Olmstead* decision, where preoccupation with the stock market crash meant people deferred dealing with the problems the decision created. Presuming little involvement in other matters, we can now look at what happens after the Court hands down the decision. First of all,

Hyp: The more controversial the subject, the greater the likelihood of some action aimed at reversing the decision.

Particularly if those unhappy about a decision think the Court may change its mind, or that some way of reversing the Court is possible, they will resist compliance, as seen in the foot-dragging after *Reynolds* in some state legislatures.

Hyp: Compliance is more likely to be delayed if resisters see a chance of victory in reversing the Court than if they do not.

This is related to the earlier-stated hypothesis about the increase in resistance resulting from a close Supreme Court vote. In connection with this,

Hyp: Where it is unclear that the Supreme Court would now follow a prior decision, compliance with that decision will decrease.

That, however, is likely to be the case in the longer, rather than the shorter, run. More immediately,

Hyp: If a Supreme Court decision is seen as bringing about a crisis, reaction will be more immediate than if it is not so seen.

The immediacy of the FBI's reaction to *Jencks* is an example of this phenomenon. But this presumes that people know—or, more important, think they know—what a decision is all about.

> *Hyp:* Resistance will be greater when the significance of a decision appears clear than when it is at first unclear.

Resistance to *Marbury* v. *Madison,* for example, would have been much greater if people at the time had recognized the importance of judicial review, which was, as we know, used sparingly for many years.

The impact of cases will be greater if policy-making activity is going on at the time of the decision or commences shortly thereafter. The decision may very well bring on that activity.

> *Hyp:* Action to reverse decisions of the Court is more likely to come quickly than after a lapse of time.

and

> *Hyp:* Those opposed to a decision will act more quickly in the aftermath of a ruling than those supporting the decision.

The latter hypothesis is clearly related to the matter of "follow-up," to which we turn below. When policy-making activity is under way, a Court ruling enters a situation in which policy makers are already committed to certain goals.

> *Hyp:* "Policy proposals in conflict with court opinions seem less likely to be withdrawn from consideration if proposed before the opinions are handed down than if proposed [afterwards]."[4]

It seems clear, as a corollary of this hypothesis, that

> *Hyp:* Supreme Court decisions will have greater impact if affected jurisdictions have had no policy—or no well-developed policy—on the subject than if they have had such a policy.

It also follows that

> *Hyp:* The longer a law has been in effect, the more unwilling legislators will be to discard the practice it embodies.

Dolbeare and Hammond have shown us that existence of statutory requirements for a practice—a particular formal embodiment of a policy—will impede compliance. In hypothesis form,

> *Hyp:* Compliance is less likely when statutory requirements for a practice exist than when such requirements are absent.

Even when the thrust of policy seems to be in the same direction as what the Court commands, noncompliance—with particulars, at least—may still exist. This is one of the most important findings of Manwaring's study of the aftermath of *Mapp.*

> *Hyp:* Noncompliance with the specifics of a Court ruling may be greater on the part of those already following the general thrust of

the ruling than on the part of those not already abiding by the general principle.

But the contrary may also be true, as seems to have been the case after *Gideon's* requirement of counsel for indigents.

Hyp: Where Supreme Court rulings reinforce an existing state policy, compliance will be greater than where such reinforcement does not exist.

This is simply an example of competing hypotheses drawn from different sets of circumstances.

While the state of existing policy, and its history, is important, the contemporaneous political situation, with its majorities and coalitions, is also of key importance. Thus,

Hyp: "If the relevant social policy is backed up by a strong political majority, judicial decisions in accordance with it are readily accepted."[5]

When political interests are not in consensus, other results may occur. Based on Nagel's findings, we can hypothesize that

Hyp: Friction between parties or between factions of parties increases noncompliance and action directed at reversal of the Court's decisions.

And the same is true for interests organized other than in parties.

Hyp: A decision will be more likely to bring action if it disturbs the balance between interests than if it affects an interest without affecting others.

Stumpf, examining bills to reverse the Court, comes to the same conclusion.

Hyp: The closer to unanimity is support of politically articulate groups concerned with a reversal bill, the more likely it is to pass.

We must, however, remember Stumpf's qualification: that group unanimity is not necessary to achieve success for a reversal bill when anti-Court sentiment—not simply unhappiness with the policy of the Court's decision—is involved.

Other aspects of groups are also relevant to the impact process. A group's activation in that process is a function of the relation to the Court's decision to its interests.

Hyp: The more directly affected a group is by a Court ruling, the more likely it is to be activated by that ruling.

However, in line with our earlier hypothesis that those opposed to a ruling are more likely to react than those in favor of a decision, we might suggest:

Hyp: Rulings adverse to a group interest will be more likely to activate a group than rulings favorable to that interest.

While most interest groups are involved to one extent or another in the political arena, we recognize that involvement of most groups varies over time.

> *Hyp:* Groups with broad policy concerns are more likely to be activated by Court rulings than are groups with narrower concerns.

The way groups are structured and led was mentioned as a variable relevant to impact. Stated as an hypothesis, we have:

> *Hyp:* If an interest group is highly organized and has resources, it will be more likely to follow through to protect its interests than if it is not so organized and does not have resources.

However, organization and resources are not sufficient; internal consensus is also important. Thus,

> *Hyp:* Internal dissension in interest groups will reduce their effect on the aftermath of Court rulings.

Unity or disagreement between branches of government is apparently as relevant as the form of political majorities.

> *Hyp:* Lack of unity between branches of government at either national or state level produces more noncompliance than does unity.

However, Sigler has argued that the Court's freedom of action is greater when other branches are not divided, when they are in "stasis." Turning more specifically to some of what we know of the effect of Court rulings on Congress and the President, we find that

> *Hyp:* Attempts to reverse the Court will be more frequent when it is felt the Court has misinterpreted the intent of another branch than when this is not the case.

What happened after the Portal-to-Portal Pay decision, and after *South-Eastern Underwriters*, suggests that hypothesis. It also appears to be the case that, because of the executive's greater freedom of action,

> *Hyp:* Control of actions of the executive branch by the Court is far more difficult than is control of Congress.

However,

> *Hyp:* The President's ability to oppose the Court by himself is far less great than if he and the Congress are acting in concert.

If we are to follow Arthur Miller's analysis, the President and his subordinates can find alternative modes of action to avoid confrontation with the Court quite easily. However, as Shapiro suggests,

> *Hyp:* Court decisions have a greater effect on the executive branch where prosecution is a possibility than where other types of action are contemplated.

Some additional hypotheses concerning formal organizations, such as executive branch agencies, have been generated from what we know of police reaction to the Court's criminal procedure rulings. Getting bureaucracies to "shift gears" is often extremely difficult. Thus,

Hyp: Noncompliance will be greater when patterns of activity by bureaucracies must change than where bureaucracies are less involved.

Resistance by the juvenile court system to the procedural niceties of *Gault* suggest what is meant here. In addition, one of the difficulties of achieving compliance throughout the ranks of a police force is its extreme decentralization, as pointed out by Wilson.

Hyp: The greater the centralization in an organization, the greater the compliance with Court decisions.

In addition to the relative centralization of an organization, the norms which pervade that organization are critical to compliance, as noted by Skolnick, who wrote, "Norms located within police organization are more powerful than court decisions in shaping police behavior."[6] Thus,

Hyp: Compliance is more a function of norms in affected organizations than it is of Supreme Court rulings.

Turning from the executive to the legislative branch, specifically to Congress, we find that

Hyp: Reversal of Supreme Court rulings is more likely when additional policy factors exist which Congress can take into account than when there are not.

This is a conclusion reached by those examining reversal legislation. It is seen in a series of bills aimed at reinterpreting the Fair Labor Standards Act, as well as in insurance regulation and offshore oil quitclaim statutes. It is also the case, apparently, that

Hyp: Decision-reversal action is more likely to be successful than is Court-curbing action.

A more general proposition, more broadly applicable, is that

Hyp: Dislike of a decision will more frequently lead to evasion than to reversal, where evasion is possible or feasible.

The authority and legitimacy of the Court are such that other branches of government, as well as other individuals, will not gratuitously attack the Court, although they will still try to escape its policy.

Follow-Up. Evidence from a number of areas in which the Supreme Court has handed down rulings suggests that impact may be more greatly affected by what those outside the Court do with the decision than by the decision itself. The basic hypothesis in this regard is that

Hyp: Impact will be greater when efforts are made to follow up a decision than when such efforts are not made.

The NAACP efforts after *Brown* suggest what can happen. People may be unhappy with what they consider an unfavorable decision of the Court, and may react verbally, but their resistance will increase if efforts to enforce the disliked decision are made. A version of the above hypothesis, indicating the time sequence, is the following:

> *Hyp:* Resistance to a Supreme Court decision will be greater when efforts are started to enforce it than immediately upon the issuance of the decision itself.

The relative lack of immediate resistance to *Brown* suggests another hypothesis, relating to enforcement or "follow-up" of previous decisions.

> *Hyp:* Where past decisions have not been enforced, resistance to present decisions will be less great than where they have been enforced.

Lack of follow-up to the "but equal" part of *Plessy's* "separate but equal" led some Southerners to believe that the "with all deliberate speed" of *Brown II*—as well as the desegregation doctrine of *Brown I*—would not be particularly disturbing to their school systems. Just as past enforcement history is relevant to present reaction, the way people react to current decisions—and their ability to get them changed—will affect how they react in the future. Thus,

> *Hyp:* Failure to obtain reversal of disliked decisions will give rise to attacks on the Court for later decisions.

Phrased somewhat differently,

> *Hyp:* Those unhappy at the Court for earlier decisions will be more likely to attack current ones than will others.

Past habit, as well as unhappiness, is relevant.

> *Hyp:* Individuals are more likely to resist Court decisions when they have done so in the past than when they have not done so.

To return more directly to "follow-up," we find a number of specific hypotheses about the process. Follow-up is related to preparation by those who would be affected by a decision. If someone tries to follow up a decision and those pressured are not ready, little compliance will occur. Thus,

> *Hyp:* Noncompliance will be greater where no preparation to comply with a decision has been made than where it has been made.

Crain's discussion of resistance to school desegregation in New Orleans suggests the hypothesis. The type of follow-up is also important.

> *Hyp:* The more persistent the "enforcers" are, the greater the compliance.

Some state legislatures apparently reapportioned in line with the "one man–one vote" dictates of the Court largely because they were tired out from a constant battle with those insisting on reapportionment. A different way of putting this, with specific reference to the courts, is that

Hyp: Compliance with a ruling of the Supreme Court will be more likely when there are frequent follow-up cases than when there are not.

As Krislov put it, "If cases develop at a pace commensurate with that of the flow of events the upper court may in fact be effective."[7] The availability of courts to follow up Supreme Court rulings suggests a somewhat broader point, that

Hyp: Compliance is more likely when some reviewing body is available to those complaining of noncompliance.

Rules against unreasonable search and seizure can be more readily enforced when a case is likely to go to court, where there can be a motion to suppress evidence, than when police simply wish to harrass someone, without intent to prosecute.

Who follows up is extremely important. While we have mentioned interest groups such as the NAACP frequently, public officials may be the ones taking initial action after a Supreme Court case.

Hyp: Initial follow-up by public officials will have a greater effect than such follow-up by private individuals or interest groups.

When public officials do try to block a decision and fail, while compliance may increase, other sorts of action, more informal and more "private," may occur.

Hyp: Failure of official, public action to block the Court is more likely to result in informal, private action aimed at the same goal than where such action has not been attempted or has succeeded.

If, instead of talking of public officials, we talk of units of government, we find it alleged, in a study of the effect of lower courts, that

Hyp: Units of government are less likely to comply with court rulings than are individuals.

and that

Hyp: Government agencies are more likely to await a specific court decree before complying than are private individuals.

However, it also appears to be the case that

Hyp: When a Court decision requires action by many members of the public, compliance is far less likely than when action by government officials is all that is necessary.

This hypothesis may explain differences between police procedure cases, at least where compliance has occurred, and issues like school prayer and desegregation, where many more people, including many private citizens, are involved in the impact process.

In addition, what state courts do with Supreme Court decisions is of considerable relevance, leading to the assertion that

Hyp: A Supreme Court ruling will have greater impact on state policy if state courts utilize the ruling than if they do not.

Within the federal system, we could say that if lower federal courts utilized Supreme Court rulings, the policy of those rulings would have greater impact. This use of the Supreme Court's doctrine is affected by what goes on within the executive branch at the national level, particularly by the stance of the Department of Justice and the FBI.

Hyp: When Supreme Court decisions are followed by executive branch agencies, lower federal judges are more likely to follow the decisions than when the executive branch agencies do not do so.

"Follow-up" has generally been used here to refer to the process of obtaining enforcement of a decision. However, the negative type of follow-up, resistance, itself has some impacts worth noting. For example,

Hyp: Failure of resistance in one jurisdiction will bring quicker compliance in other jurisdictions.

Observers of the failure of "Massive Resistance" in Virginia in the aftermath of *Brown* suggest this to have been the case. It has also been suggested, by those versed in structural-functional analysis, that

Hyp: Where the Court invalidates a practice, compliance will be greater when those affected can find alternative means to replace the practice than where they cannot.

The functions performed by the practice must be carried out in some other way, in other words. It may also be the case that immediate negative reaction will give way to compliance, because of the psychological function which the resistance performs.

Hyp: An attack on the Court's rulings may bring greater subsequent compliance than where such catharsis is not possible.

Those Responding. The role of follow-up in the impact process blends in with the matter of the position of those responding to Court decisions and the effect that position has on impact. We see this, for example, in discussion of the effect of follow-up by public officials as against similar action by private individuals. In general,

Hyp: The greater the power and higher the status of those responding to a Court decision, the greater the impact of the decision.

Other sorts of distinctions can be made on the basis of what we have seen thus far. What we need to know, however, is which categories of individuals are more likely to respond or to comply. Most of what follows is based on the assumption that "Approval of a decision by other decision makers in the political process is probably more important than approval by the general public."[8]

We may start with some hypotheses about judges.

Hyp: Judges are more likely to follow Supreme Court opinions than are other government officials.

This follows from the role of judges—that they are supposed to follow both precedent and the rulings of higher courts, particularly the highest court of the land. However, state court judges have competing allegiances, and it has been hypothesized that

Hyp: Federal court judges are more likely to comply with Supreme Court rulings affecting the states than are state court judges.

Beiser, whose hypotheses take this general form, found, however, little difference between the way federal and state judges acted with respect to reapportionment. To proceed a step further, one might suggest that

Hyp: Those seeking higher office in the judicial system will be more likely to comply with Supreme Court decisions than those in other positions.

It has been alleged that fear of reversal by higher courts serves as a constraint upon lower-court judges; those seeking acceptance in "higher places" might be less inclined to invite reversal.

An extremely important offsetting phenomenon is the centrifugal pull of local values on a judge, particularly one who must campaign for re-election. If a judge's personal views and local values coincide, as they may from the process by which judges are recruited, then the judge may well turn away from, not toward, the Supreme Court.

Hyp: When local preferences reinforce a judge's personal views, he is less likely to follow the Supreme Court than when this is not the case.

Because of the great weight people tend to give to judges' statements, when judges do refuse to follow the Supreme Court, and particularly when they explicitly attack its rulings, those actions have considerable effect.

Hyp: Statements by lower-court judges will have a greater effect on impact than will the Supreme Court's decisions.

This follows from Rose's statement, "Counterstatement of constitutional principle—made by respected judicial authorities—nullify, to a certain extent, the effect on public opinion of the unanimous decisions of the Supreme Court."[9]

Turning from judges to lawyers, we might suggest that

Hyp: Lawyers are more likely to comply with Supreme Court decisions than are nonlawyers.

We have seen that the word of lawyers has considerable effect on what nonlawyers do in the aftermath of a decision.

Hyp: Statements of lawyers made after a Court ruling will have a greater effect on impact than will statements by nonlawyers.

However, lawyers are not always able to convince laymen that their word should be followed, particularly where habits of long standing must be changed. Among lawyers,

Hyp: Lawyers bringing cases in the lower courts will have a greater effect on the impact of Court decisions than other lawyers.

As comparisons between lawyers and nonlawyers imply, nonlawyers are also involved in the aftermath of Court cases. Among public officials, it has been suggested that

Hyp: The greater the range of policy matters with which an official is involved, the less likely he will be to comply with a Supreme Court decision.

The assumption here is that an official with a large number of policy matters will have to protect himself and will not be able to afford the negative effect on policies which might result from criticism of his compliance with an unpopular ruling of the Court. However, one could as well argue that single-issue policy makers, such as school boards, are in an all-or-nothing position when they comply on such matters as school prayer or desegregation, with no other policies the popularity of which might be used to offset negative views of their compliance with the Court.

A number of additional hypotheses concerning local policy makers can be suggested. One, also derived from Crain's work, is that

Hyp: Those who view compliance as an ideological matter are less likely to comply than those who view it as a pragmatic matter.

Here again, one might argue to the contrary—that an administrator might find all sorts of pragmatic reasons *not* to comply, such as the difficulties in integrating faculty or revising bus routes. However, this might be camouflage for an ideological position rather than the "real" basis for resistance. Another deals with policy makers' discretion:

Hyp: The greater the discretion of local officials, the lower the compliance with Supreme Court rulings.

Drawn from the findings of the post-*Miranda* studies concerning detectives' ability to avoid *Miranda* because of the latitude they had in questioning suspects, the hypothesis relates to other officials as well. A partial explanation for the hypothesis concerns the closeness of those officials to local values: if they have much discretion, local values can assert themselves more than if the officials were somehow compelled to take compliant action.

Hyp: The smaller the community, the more closely local officials must follow local values in reacting to Court decisions.

Size of community is related to homogeneity of values, so we can suggest:

Hyp: Noncompliance will be greater where the values of the affected area are relatively homogeneous than where they are heterogeneous.

We also see that electioneering plays a part in this process, so that

Hyp: Visibility of reaction by government officials is a function of the time until the next election.

This last hypothesis, taken alone, is, however, too simplistic. The ideology of the officials is not without its effect. Crain's examination of the desegregation process leads to the hypothesis that

Hyp: The ideology of local governing officials will be more important in bringing about compliance than will the enforcement efforts of groups.

One part of that ideology he found important was the officials' willingness to withstand some conflict, likely to arise if the officials complied.

Hyp: Compliance will be greater where local officials are willing to risk some conflict than where they are not.

One might assert that professionalization, or professional orientation, is part of an official's ideology. On the basis of Milner's study of reaction to *Miranda* in Wisconsin cities, we might say that

Hyp: The higher the degree of professionalization of a public agency, the less amenable it is to influence from outside groups with respect to compliance.

That is, it will be less subject to the influence of local values if its members are professionalized.

Beliefs and Values. A last set of hypotheses can be developed concerning the effect on the impact process of individuals' views of the Court and the relationship between the Court's rulings and the individuals' values. How closely those values are affected, what the individual expected of the Court, and the legitimacy he grants the Court are the three variables around which many of the available hypotheses cluster. It has been suggested that the individual's interests are directly related to both whether or not he reacts to the Court and the manner in which he reacts. Thus far we have presumed that the Court's decisions are perceived, but we must remember that this is not always the case.

Hyp: "The degree to which the citizen perceives the outputs of the Supreme Court is closely related to the degree to which the citizen perceives his interests to be involved in the decisions."[10]

Once the decisions are perceived, however, we find a number of phenomena. For example,

Hyp: Those affected are more likely to read decisions adverse to their positions narrowly than they are decisions favorable to their positions.

Interference with compliance is likely to occur when someone sees personal interests affected. Thus,

Hyp: When an individual sees gains in his immediate environment from noncompliance, he is more likely not to comply than if he sees no such gains.

Based on Way's findings about the effect of church attendance and maintenance of school prayers by teachers, it could be suggested that

Hyp: Compliance will be higher in the absence of personal preferences and behavior supporting an invalidated practice than where such preferences and behavior exist.

When the Court is seen as affecting matters of personal importance, the effect is not only on the aftermath of the particular case.

Hyp: Court decisions about matters perceived as personally significant will have a greater carry-over to general views about the Supreme Court than will decisions about matters not so perceived.

People's expectations about the Court are of considerable importance. Those expectations concern both the fact of the decisions and whether anything will happen after they are handed down. As to the latter,

Hyp: People will react more strongly to Court decisions if they perceive earlier decisions as having had an effect than if they do not so perceive.

In this connection, the effect of Southerners' seeing *Plessy* as not enforced has already been mentioned. As to expectations about the Court's actions,

Hyp: Resistance to disliked decisions will be less great if they are expected than if they are not; compliance with liked decisions will be greater if they are not expected than if they are.

In other words, expectation of a decision depresses reaction to it. When decisions are not anticipated, not only is reaction greater but other effects occur.

Hyp: Greater change will be perceived to result from an unanticipated decision than from an anticipated one.

This lack of anticipation or expectation we can fit into the theory of cognitive dissonance or cognitive balance, as Muir has done. It might thus be suggested that

Hyp: Compliance with Court decisions will be higher when those decisions do not upset cognitive balance than when such balance is upset.

More strongly put,

Hyp: Resistance to Court decisions will be greater when those decisions upset cognitive balance than when such balance is not upset.

If we recognize these types of effects as possible, we would want to know what might increase or decrease expectations. One item can be mentioned here:

Hyp: The higher the professionalization of a group, the greater the expectation of relevant Court decisions and the less perceived change resulting from those decisions.

We turn finally to the general views people have of the Court and the effect of those views on impact. Even when people are unhappy with specific decisions of the Court, if they hold a generally positive view of the Court, their reaction will be restrained.

Hyp: The higher the regard in which the Court is held, the less negative the reaction to its decisions.

We can see this, for example, in the response of the advocates of child labor legislation to the first child labor case. However, we are concerned not only with the general regard in which the Court is held, but also with whether people feel that the Court's authority to decide cases is legitimate.

Hyp: Those who consider the Court's authority legitimate will be more likely to comply with its rulings than those who do not.

That perceived legitimacy is by no means a constant. Thus,

Hyp: The Court's legitimacy is increased when people agree with its specific rulings.

As Johnson noted, "Those who personally agree with the substance of Supreme Court policy also acknowledge to a greater extent the Court's legitimacy and expert bases than do those who are displeased with the substantive ruling."[11] Despite this asserted connection, it has also been suggested that

Hyp: Support for the Court is as dependent on people's views of how the Court decides cases as on what the Court decides.

The "how" of Kessel's hypothesis includes the impartiality or neutrality of the judges and the belief that they only find rather than make law. Thus,

Hyp: Belief in judicial neutrality and belief that judges only find rather than make law increase acceptance of decisions.

The most broadly put proposition in this area is that propounded by Murphy and Tanenhaus in discussing the Court's role as a legitimator of regime change.

Hyp: For a Court decision to legitimate regime change, the Court must be perceived, recognized as a proper interpreter of the Constitution, and be seen as acting impartially and competently.

If we recognize that both the *how* and the *what* of Supreme Court decisions affect the legitimacy accorded the Supreme Court and, through that perceived legitimacy, the impact process, we must still ask what particular effects negative general views of the Court might produce. One, suggested by Kessel, is that

Hyp: Those with unfavorable prior views of the Court are more likely to resist decisions than those without such views.

This is reinforced by Dolbeare's suggestion that

Hyp: Those who give the Court a poor rating are more likely to act to change a decision than those who give it a good rating.

However, we must remember that just as there were few who fit Murphy and Tanenhaus's criteria, so there are relatively few who will act on their displeasure about Court decisions, and very few who would act outside of regular political channels. While the proportion of those acting on their displeasure with the Court may be relatively low,

Hyp: Greater information about Court decisions brings greater disapproval.

This relationship between greater information and level of disapproval of the Court was found by both Dolbeare and Kessel. On the other hand, it seems to be the case that

Hyp: Support of the Supreme Court is not dependent on knowledge of particular rulings of the Court.

Thus, while there is a reservoir of support for the Court independent of knowledge of the Court's decisions, such knowledge seems to have a depressing rather than positive effect on the way people view the Court and the support they give it.

* * * * *

Conclusion. The foregoing, while not complete, should give the reader some idea of where the study of impact of the Supreme Court now stands in terms of the development of theory. Filling in the holes in our inventory will lead us toward the theoretical development needed. The holes are sufficiently large that one will be making a valuable contribution by starting just about anywhere, even if this seems to reinforce the anarchic nature of the social sciences. If we had a more well-developed theory of impact, perhaps we could prescribe more specifically the exact steps to be taken to complete our task. Perhaps we have made more progress toward our real goal than we realize, but it seems, at least from where we now stand, that we have a long way to go and are not able to prescribe specific directions for other researchers.

There is another sense in which we must be concerned about theory. This comes from consideration of the relation of work on the impact of the Supreme Court to other areas of scholarly research. If we are going to give impact studies a more theoretical thrust, we can do so by attempting to apply theory developed in other areas, being constantly aware of the possible lack of applicability. Existing efforts do, however, show the promise of this approach. Two of the most sophisticated studies of impact to appear are those by Johnson and Muir, drawing on communications theory and the theory of cognitive dissonance to explain how those at the community level react to the Court's decisions. But surely there are other theories besides cognitive dissonance which are applicable, and other areas of knowledge from which we can draw. Milner's mention of hypotheses from the literature on planned social change is suggestive. He cites Zander's hypotheses[12] that change may be resisted when the nature of the change is ambiguous to the person having to make the change, when he cannot voice his views about the change, when the change is perceived as greater than it actually is, and when cross-pressure between previous values and those involved in the change occurs.

Another set of hypotheses which might also be suggestive is found in Neustadt's specification of characteristics a communication—in his frame of reference, the President's communication—must have in order to be "self-executing." In speaking of several instances of such orders, Neustadt wrote, "At least five common factors were at work. On each occasion the President's involvement was unambiguous. So were his words. His order was widely publicized. The men who received it had control of everything needed to carry it out. And they had no apparent doubt of his authority to issue it to them."[13] This statement contains some elements suggested by Suchman *et al.*, quoted earlier: "Conflict over desegregation will be minimized: (1) the more clearly, legal procedures evolve for protecting the rights of minorities; (2) the more effective, well-disciplined and impartial are the law-enforcement agencies prepared to back desegregation and the more there is public expectation that such authority will act in case of violence." Both are parallel to statements made with more specific reference to the impact of Supreme Court decisions. LaFave, in talking of the exclusionary rule, said that, for such a rule to be effective,

> (1) the requirements of the law on search and seizure and related practices must be developed in some detail and in a manner sufficiently responsive to both the practical needs of enforcement and the individual rights of privacy; (2) these requirements must be set forth in a manner that can be understood and applied by the front-line lower-echelon police officer and must be effectively communicated to him; and (3) the police desire to obtain convictions must be sufficiently great to induce them to comply with these requirements.[14]

And Krislov, drawing on similar factors, has noted:

> Compliance is at its greatest when personal advantages are highest, organizational sanctions against opposition are certain and severe, and the legitimacy of the issuing authority is acknowledged. Conversely, it will be at its minimum when the individual's utilities all point in the direction of opposition, organizational sanctions are lenient, and—most important—erratic in application, and the legitimacy of the higher authority is doubtful.[15]

The possible applicability of Zander and Neustadt and their clear parallel to some existing findings (or suggestions) in the current impact literature suggests another matter, as well: that we should move quickly to try to relate studies of the impact of the Supreme Court's rulings to the growing literature exploring the effect of law more generally, to join forces with those in the "sociology of law" rather than staying solely within the public law field. To be sure, some sociologists concerned with the effect of law and the legal order take a broader, more diffuse approach (theory in the "grand style") than do some of the political scientists who have performed impact studies, but there is no reason in principle why the two cannot assist one another. Even without linking up with the sociologists of law, we must begin to get away from concentration solely on the Supreme Court in our work on impact. We must find out whether lower-court rulings—dealt with only incidentally in Supreme Court impact studies—have the same effect as do rulings of the federal high tribunal. Of course, we do not know enough about the Supreme Court's effect to be able to afford to have everyone run off to study all these areas, and a scholar might well, for reasons related to concentrating his efforts and utilizing his time more efficiently, continue to concentrate on Supreme Court impact. But, within the rather chaotic or anarchic division of labor characterizing the social sciences, *someone* should deal with the matters here discussed.

Notes

CHAPTER 1

[1] G. Theodore Mitau, *Decade of Decision* (New York: Charles Scribner's Sons, 1967), p. 96.

[2] Charles Haar, *The Golden Age of American Law* (New York: George Braziller, Inc., 1965), p. 201.

[3] Robert G. Dixon, Jr., *Democratic Representation* (New York: Oxford University Press, Inc., 1968), p. 139.

[4] Norman Dorsen, *Discrimination and Civil Rights* (Boston: Little, Brown & Co., 1969), p. 61.

[5] Kenneth Dolbeare, *Trial Courts in Urban Politics* (New York: John Wiley & Sons, Inc., 1967), p. 110.

[6] Martin Shapiro, *The Supreme Court and Administrative Agencies* (New York: Free Press, 1968), p. 21. Copyright © 1968 by The Free Press, a Division of The Macmillan Company.

[7] James Ridella, "Miranda: One Year Later—The Effects," *Public Management*, Vol. 49 (July, 1967), p. 187.

[8] Richard Johnson, *The Dynamics of Compliance* (Evanston, Ill.: Northwestern University Press, 1967), p. 9.

[9] *Ibid.*, p. 3.

[10] Dolbeare, *op. cit.*, p. 111.

[11] Samuel Krislov, *The Supreme Court in the Political Process* (New York: Macmillan Co., 1965), p. 135. © Copyright, Samuel Krislov, 1965.

[12] Curtis, *Lions Under the Throne* (Boston: Houghton Mifflin Co., 1942), p. 45.

[13] From *Justice in America* by Herbert Jacob, p. 192. Copyright © 1965, by Little, Brown and Company (Inc.). This and subsequent quotes from the same source reprinted by permission of the publisher.

[14] Charles Warren, *The Supreme Court in United States History* (3 vols.; Boston: Little, Brown & Co., 1922), Vol. I, p. viii and Vol. III, p. 303.

[15] John Schmidhauser, *The Supreme Court as Final Arbiter in Federal-State Relations, 1789–1957* (Chapel Hill, N.C.: University of North Carolina Press, 1958), pp. 161, 183.

[16] Warren, *op. cit.*, Vol. I, p. vii.

[17] Schmidhauser, *op. cit.*, p. 212.

[18] *Ibid.*, p. 128.

[19] Shapiro, *op. cit.*, p. 64.

[20] Herbert Jacob, "Wage Garnishment and Bankruptcy Proceedings in Four Wisconsin Cities," in James G. Wilson (ed.), *City Politics and Public Policy* (New York: John Wiley & Sons, Inc., 1968), p. 199.

[21] Robert A. Dahl, "Decision-Making in a Democracy: The Role of the Supreme Court as a National Policy-Maker," *Journal of Public Law*, Vol. 6 (Fall, 1957), p. 295.

[22] Stephen L. Wasby, "The Pure and the Prurient: The Supreme Court, Obscenity, and Oregon Policy," in David Everson (ed.), *The Supreme Court as Policy-Maker: Three Studies on the Impact of Judicial Decisions* (Carbondale, Ill.: Public Affairs Research Bureau, Southern Illinois University, 1968), p. 103.

[23] Warren, *op. cit.*, Vol. I, p. vi.

[24] Jacob, "Wage Garnishment . . . ," p. 199.

[25] *Ibid.*

[26] In Lenore Cahn (ed.), *Confronting Injustice: The Edmond Cahn Reader* (Boston: Little, Brown & Co., 1966), p. 215.

[27] See Martin Shapiro, "Political Jurisprudence," *Kentucky Law Journal*, Vol. 52, No. 2 (1964), p. 295.

[28] Kenneth N. Vines, "Political Functions of a State Supreme Court," in Vines and Herbert Jacob (eds.), *Studies in Judicial Politics* (New Orleans: Tulane University Press, 1963), p. 56.

[29] Glendon A. Schubert, *Constitutional Politics* (New York: Holt, Rinehart, & Winston, Inc., 1960), p. 257.

[30] Shapiro, *Supreme Court and Administrative Agencies*, p. 58.

[31] Jack Peltason, *Federal Courts in the Judicial Process* (Garden City, N.Y.: Doubleday & Co., 1955), p. 64.

[32] Schubert, *op. cit.*, p. 257.

[33] Wasby, *op. cit.*, p. 103.

[34] Robert Dahl, *Who Governs?* (New Haven, Conn.: Yale University Press, 1961), p. 247.

[35] Philip Selznick, "The Sociology of Law," in Robert K. Merton *et al.* (eds.), *Sociology Today: Problems and Prospects* (New York: Basic Books, Inc., Publishers, 1959), p. 126.

[36] Arthur Selwyn Miller and Alan W. Scheflin, "The Power of the Supreme Court in the Age of the Positive State," *Duke Law Journal*, Vol. 1967, No. 1, p. 288; in italic in original. Copyright 1967 by the *Duke Law Journal*. Reprinted by permission of the copyright holder and authors.

[37] Glendon A. Schubert, *Judicial Policy-Making* (Glenview, Ill.: Scott, Foresman & Co., 1965), p. 66.

[38] Wasby, *op. cit.*, p. 103.

[39] Thomas E. Barth, "Perception and Acceptance of Supreme Court Decisions at the State and Local Level," *Journal of Public Law*, Vol. 17, No. 2 (1968), p. 315, note.

[40] Samuel Krislov, "The Perimeters of Power: Patterns of Compliance and Opposition to Supreme Court Decisions" (Paper presented to American Political Science Association, 1963), p. 7.

[41] Respectively, "The Impact of a Court Decision: Aftermath of the McCollum Case," *Journal of Public Law*, Vol. 6 (Fall, 1957), 455–64, and "*Zorach* v. *Clauson:* The Impact of a Supreme Court Decision," *American Political Science Review*, Vol. 53 (September, 1959), 777–91.

[42] John S. Bradway, *American Bar Association Journal*, Vol. 54 (December, 1968), p. 1212.

[43] Samuel Krislov, *The Supreme Court and Political Freedom* (New York: Free Press, 1968), p. 165. Copyright © 1968 by The Free Press, a Division of The Macmillan Company.

[44] Barth, *op. cit.*, p. 316.

[45] Johnson, *op. cit.*, p. 16.

[46] Barth, *op. cit.*, p. 313.

[47] Richard Wells and Joel Grossman, "The Concept of Judicial Policy-Making," *Journal of Public Law*, Vol. 15, No. 2 (1966), p. 287.

[48] J. Woodford Howard, "Judicial Biography and the Behavioral Persuasion" (Paper presented to American Political Science Association, 1969), pp. 17–18.

[49] Krislov, *Supreme Court and Political Freedom*, p. 166.

CHAPTER 2

[1] Johnson, *op. cit.*, p. 23.

[2] Michael J. Petrick, "The Supreme Court and Authority Acceptance," *Western Political Quarterly,* Vol. 21 (March, 1968), p. 7.

[3] Barth, *op. cit.*, p. 315.

[4] Jack P. Gibbs, "Definitions of Law and Empirical Questions," *Law & Society Review,* Vol. 2 (May, 1968), pp. 436–37.

[5] Johannes Feest, "Compliance with Legal Regulations: Observation of Stop Sign Behavior," *Law & Society Review,* Vol. 2 (May, 1968), p. 448.

[6] Petrick, *op. cit.*, p. 7.

[7] Krislov, "The Perimeters of Power . . . ," p. 11.

[8] Kenneth M. Dolbeare and Phillip E. Hammond, "Local Elites, the Impact of Judicial Decisions, and the Process of Change" (Paper presented to American Political Science Association, 1969), p. 8.

[9] Note, "*Dombrowski* v. *Eastland*–A Political Compromise and Its Impact," *Rutgers Law Review,* Vol. 22 (Fall, 1967), p. 164.

[10] Arthur S. Miller, *The Supreme Court and American Capitalism* (New York: Free Press, 1968), pp. 81, 131, 231. Copyright © 1968 by The Free Press, a Division of The Macmillan Company.

[11] Dolbeare, *Trial Courts in an Urban Setting,* p. 110.

[12] A recent study by Dolbeare and Hammond suggests the importance of visible activity, at least by comparison with survey responses. They found many school districts in which there was noncompliance with the school prayer decisions even though the districts had reported compliance in responding to surveys. *Op. cit.*, pp. 12–13.

[13] Wasby, "The Pure and the Prurient . . . ," p. 102.

[14] Nagel reminds us we should use "as a percentage base only those school districts that have some schoolage Negro children and some schoolage white children." (Stuart S. Nagel, *The Legal Process from a Behavioral Perspective* [Homewood, Ill.: Dorsey Press, 1969], p. 10.) However, if districts have been established so as to reinforce segregation, perhaps this suggestion should not be followed.

[15] Donald Reich, "The Impact of Judicial Decision-Making: The School Prayer Cases," Everson (ed.), *The Supreme Court as Policy-Maker,* p. 52.

[16] Walter Murphy, *Congress and the Court* (Chicago: University of Chicago Press, 1962), p. 238. © 1962 by The University of Chicago.

[17] Alfred H. Kelly and Winfred A. Harbison, *The American Constitution: Its Origins and Development* (rev. ed.; New York: W.W. Norton & Co., Inc., 1955), Copyright © 1955 by W.W. Norton & Co., Inc., p. 229.

[18] Krislov, *The Supreme Court in the Political Process,* p. 138.

[19] Murphy, *op. cit.*, p. 238.

[20] Warren, *op. cit.*, Vol. I, p. 269.

[21] Loren Miller, *The Petitioners: The Story of the Supreme Court of the United States and the Negro* (New York: Pantheon Books, a Division of Random House, Inc., 1966), p. 34.

[22] Wasby, "The Pure and the Prurient . . . , p. 105.

[23] Benjamin Cardozo, *The Nature of the Judicial Process* (New Haven; Conn.: Yale University Press, 1921), p. 48.

[24] Barth, *op. cit.*, p. 314.

[25] Anthony A. D'Amato, "Schools, Cemeteries and Mixed Marriages: The Supreme Court and Strategies of Desegregation" (Paper presented to Midwest Political Science Association, 1968), p. 12.

[26] Shapiro, *op. cit.*, p. 145.

[27] Wasby, *op. cit.*, p. 105.

[28] Barth, *op. cit.*, p. 314.

[29] Edward Suchman, John Dean, and Robin Williams, *Desegregation: Some Propositions and Research Suggestions* (New York: Anti-Defamation League, 1958), p. 39.

[30] Wasby, *op. cit.*, p. 105.

[31] Theodore J. Lowi, *The End of Liberalism: Ideology, Policy, and the Crisis of Public Authority* (New York: W.W. Norton & Co., Inc., 1969), p. 302. Copyright 1969 by W.W. Norton & Company, Inc.

[32] Lawrence K. Pettit, "Constitutional Ambiguity and Legislative Decision-Making: The Establishment Clause and Aid to Higher Education," in Pettit and Edward Keynes (eds.), *The Legislative Process in the U.S. Senate* (Skokie, Ill.: Rand McNally & Co., 1969), p. 271.

[33] Kelly and Harbison, *op. cit.*, pp. 391–92.

[34] Nagel, "Curbing the Court: The Politics of Congressional Reaction," *op. cit.*, p. 269.

[35] Warren, *op. cit.*, Vol. III, p. 305.

[36] Murphy, *op. cit.*, p. 88.

[37] Harry Hogan, "The Supreme Court and Natural Law," *American Bar Association Journal*, Vol. 54 (June, 1968), p. 573.

[38] Dolbeare and Hammond, *op. cit.*, p. 11.

[39] Robert K. Merton, *Social Theory and Social Structure* (Glencoe: Free Press, 1957), p. 81. © 1957 by The Free Press, a corporation.

[40] Walter F. Murphy, "The South Counterattacks: The Anti-NAACP Laws," *Western Political Quarterly*, Vol. 12 (June, 1959), p. 390.

[41] Arnold Rose, "Sociological Factors in the Effectiveness of Projected Legislative Remedies," *Journal of Legal Education*, Vol. 11 (1959), p. 477.

[42] Barth, *op. cit.*, p. 316.

[43] Krislov, *The Supreme Court in the Political Process*, p. 154.

[44] Krislov, *The Supreme Court and Political Freedom*, p. 205.

[45] Krislov, *The Supreme Court in the Political Process*, p. 147.

[46] Max Lerner, "The Constitution and the Court as Symbols," *Yale Law Journal*, Vol. 46 (June, 1937), p. 1293.

[47] Walter F. Murphy and C. Herman Pritchett, *Courts, Judges, and Politics: An Introduction to the Judicial Process* (New York: Random House, Inc., 1961), p. 161.

[48] Lerner, *op. cit.*, p. 1311.

[49] Murphy, *Congress and the Court*, p. 62.

[50] Sheldon Goldman, *American Political Science Review*, Vol. 62 (December 1968), p. 1287.

[51] Krislov, "The Perimeters of Power . . . ," p. 18.

[52] Johnson, *op. cit.*, p. 6.

[53] Albert P. Blaustein and Clarence Clyde Ferguson, *Desegregation and the Law* (New Brunswick, N.J.: Rutgers University Press, 1957), p. 216.

[54] Murphy and Pritchett, *op. cit.*, p. 159.

[55] Johnson, *op. cit.*, p. 147.

[56] Reich, *op. cit.*, p. 69.

[57] Johnson, *op. cit.*, p. 121.

[58] Sorauf, *op. cit.*, p. 791.

[59] Dan Nimmo and Clifton McCleskey, "Impact of the Poll Tax on Voter Participation: The Houston Metropolitan Area in 1966," *Journal of Politics*, Vol. 31 (August, 1969), pp. 692, 698.

[60] Krislov, *The Supreme Court in the Political Process*, p. 149.

CHAPTER 3

[1] Stuart S. Nagel has recently argued that systems analysis is less useful than the conceptual scheme supplied by stimulus-response psychology, "in which input is substituted for stimuli, output is substituted for responses, and conversion structure is substituted for organism," in part because of the emphasis on cause and effect in the S-R model. (*The Legal Process from a Behavioral Perspective* pp. 1–2.)

[2] Robert B. McKay, " 'With All Deliberate Speed': A Study of School Desegregation," *New York University Law Review*, Vol. 32 (June, 1956), p. 1039.

[3] Blaustein and Ferguson, *op. cit.*, p. 198.

[4] Robert A. Leflar, " 'Law of the Land,' " Don Shoemaker (ed.), *With All Deliberate Speed: Segregation-Desegregation in Southern Schools* (New York: Harper & Bros., 1957), pp. 5–6.

[5] A. Miller, *op. cit.*, p. 198.

[6] Henry Hart, Jr., "The Supreme Court, 1958 Term; Foreword: The Time Chart of the Justices," *Harvard Law Review*, Vol. 73 (November, 1959), p. 96. Copyright 1959 by the Harvard Law Review Association.

[7] Shapiro, *Supreme Court and Administrative Agencies*, p. 43.

[8] Jonathan D. Casper, "Lawyers before the Supreme Court in Civil Liberties and Civil Rights Cases, 1957–66: Recruitment and Goals" (Paper presented to American Political Science Association, 1969), p. 10. The article also appears in *Stanford Law Review*, Vol. 22 (February, 1970).

[9] Johnson, *op. cit.*, p. 25.

[10] Barth, *op. cit.*, p. 309.

[11] "The Acceptance of Authority," in Lewis Coser and Bernard Rosenberg (eds.), *Sociological Theory* (New York: Macmillan Co., 1957), p. 146.

[12] Blaustein and Ferguson, *op. cit.*, p. 159.

[13] D'Amato, *op. cit.*, p. 2.

[14] Glendon A. Schubert, *Quantitative Analysis of Judicial Behavior* (Glencoe, Ill.: Free Press, 1959), p. 60. Copyright © 1959 by The Board of Trustees of Michigan State University, East Lansing, Mich.

[15] Frank Remington *et al.*, *Criminal Justice Administration* (Indianapolis: Bobbs-Merrill Co., Inc., 1969), p. 46, note.

[16] Jerome Skolnick, *Justice Without Trial: Law Enforcement in Democratic Society* (New York: John Wiley & Sons, Inc., 1966), p. 224.

[17] Schubert, *op. cit.*, p. 66.

[18] Murphy, *Congress and the Court*, p. 251.

[19] *Ibid.*, p. 251.

[20] Shapiro, *op. cit.*, pp. 211, 212.

[21] Peltason, *op. cit.*, p. 55.

[22] George R. Osborne, "The NAACP in Alabama," in C. Herman Pritchett and Alan Westin (eds.), *The Third Branch of Government: 8 Cases in Constitutional Politics* (New York: Harcourt, Brace & World, Inc., 1963), p. 200.

[23] Manwaring, in Pritchett and Westin, *ibid.*, pp. 27–28.

[24] Merle Fainsod, Lincoln Gordon, and Joseph C. Palamountain, Jr., *Government and the American Economy* (3d ed.; New York: W.W. Norton, & Co., Inc., 1959), p. 135. Copyright © 1959 by W.W. Norton & Company, Inc.

[25] *Ibid.*, p. 175.

[26] Shapiro, *op. cit.*, pp. 201–2.

[27] *Ibid.*, p. 62.

[28] Warren, *op. cit.*, Vol. III, p. 424.

[29] Alan Westin, "The Supreme Court, the Populist Movement, and the Campaign of 1896," *Journal of Politics*, Vol. 15 (February, 1953), p. 40.

[30] Jeanne Hahn, "Litigation and the Political Process" (unpublished manuscript, 1968), p. 8.

[31] Donald Gregory, "Cinema Censorship and Court Compliance," (unpublished paper 1969), p. 32.

[32] Daniel M. Berman, *It Is So Ordered: The Supreme Court Rules on School Segregation* (New York: W.W. Norton & Co., Inc., 1966), p. 29. Copyright © 1966 by W.W. Norton & Company, Inc.

[33] Bob Smith, *They Closed Their Schools: Prince Edward County, Virginia, 1951–1964* (Chapel Hill, N.C.: University of North Carolina Press, 1965), p. 263.

[34] Dolbeare and Hammond, *op. cit.*, p. 9.

[35] A. Miller, *op. cit.*, p. 231.

[36] Michael Franck, "The Myth of *Spevack* v. *Klein*," *American Bar Association Journal*, Vol. 54 (October, 1968), p. 974.

[37] Murphy, *Congress and the Court*, pp. 225, 226.

[38] David Dudley Field, "The Study and Practice of the Law," *Democratic Review*, Vol. 14 (1844), pp. 345 ff.; reprinted in Haar, *op. cit.*, pp. 36–37.

[39] *American Bar Association Journal,* Vol. 54 (October, 1968), p. 1021.

[40] David L. Grey, *The Supreme Court and the News Media* (Evanston, Ill.: Northwestern University Press, 1968).

[41] Despite this statement, there are still some connections; some of the cases brought by the Legal Redress Committees of the local NAACP branches or conferences are brought under the name of the LDF, and some local (NAACP) attorneys work with the national LDF rather than national NAACP.

[42] Shapiro, *op. cit.,* p. 51.

[43] Chester Newland, "Press Coverage of the United States Supreme Court," *Western Political Quarterly,* Vol. 17 (March, 1964), p. 15. This and subsequent quotes reprinted by permission of the University of Utah, copyright owners.

[44] Johnson, *op. cit.,* p. 26.

[45] *Ibid.,* pp. 95, 62.

[46] Grey, *op. cit.,* p. 33.

[47] Warren E. Wright, "Judicial Rhetoric: A Field for Research," *Speech Monographs,* Vol. 31 (March, 1964), p. 70.

[48] Grey, *op. cit.,* p. 31.

[49] Newland, *op. cit.,* pp. 24, 26.

[50] Grey, *op. cit.,* p. 23.

[51] *Ibid.,* p. 35.

[52] *Ibid.,* p. 129.

[53] Warren, *op. cit.,* Vol. I, p. 455.

[54] Grey, *op. cit.,* p. 74.

[55] Johnson, *op. cit.,* p. 61.

[56] Barth, *op. cit.,* p. 319.

[57] Johnson, *op. cit.,* p. 62.

[58] D'Amato, *op. cit.,* p. 11.

[59] Philip Kurland, "On Misunderstanding the Supreme Court," *Law School Record,* Vol. 9 (1960), p. 13, quoted in Grey, *op. cit.,* p. 130.

[60] Neal Milner, "The Impact of the *Miranda* Decision on Four Wisconsin Cities" (Ph.D. dissertation, University of Wisconsin, 1969), p. 65. The material which follows is drawn from tables on pp. 307 ff.

[61] *Ibid.,* p. 506.

[62] Johnson, *op. cit.,* pp. 62–63.

[63] Warren, *op. cit.,* Vol. III, pp. 24–25.

[64] Compare the following: "Although Taney's assertion . . . was made as the historical assessment of a belief prevailing at the time of the adoption of the Constitution, it was, nonetheless, a definition of an existent condition, because the Chief Justice said, and the majority agreed, that the full measure of the Negro's rights was that intended by the Framers as of the time the Constitution was adopted" (Loren Miller, *op. cit.,* p. 79).

[65] Johnson, *op. cit.,* p. 55.

[66] Gilbert Cranberg, "What Did the Supreme Court Say," *Saturday Review,* April 8, 1967, p. 91, quoted in Grey, *op. cit.,* p. 100.

[67] Grey, *op. cit.,* p. 117.

[68] Lee Rainwater and William L. Yancey, *The Moynihan Report and the Politics of Controversy* (Cambridge, Mass.: M.I.T. Press, 1967), p. 154.

[69] Johnson, *op. cit.,* p. 85.

[70] *Ibid.,* pp. 26–27.

CHAPTER 4

[1] Kelly and Harbison, *op. cit.,* p. 290.

[2] Warren, *op. cit.,* Vol. II, p. 103.

[3] *Ibid.,* Vol. I, p. 537.

[4] *Ibid.,* Vol. II, p. 76.

[5] *Ibid.*

[6] Kelly and Harbison, *op. cit.,* p. 280.

[7] Stephen B. Wood, *Constitutional Politics in the Progressive Era: Child Labor and the Law* (Chicago: University of Chicago Press, 1968), p. 177.

[8] See Richard E. Morgan, "The Portal-to-Portal Pay Case," and Lucius Barker, "The Offshore Oil Cases," Pritchett and Westin, *op. cit.*, pp. 50–82 and 234–74.

[9] Morgan, *op. cit.*, p. 68.

[10] *Ibid.*, p. 77.

[11] Barker, *op. cit.*, p. 255. The cases were *U.S.* v. *Louisiana,* 339 U.S. 699, and *U.S.* v. *Texas,* 339 U.S. 707 (1950).

[12] Barker, *op. cit.*, p. 269.

[13] Fainsod *et al.*, *op. cit.*, p. 675.

[14] Shapiro, *op. cit.*, p. 169.

[15] *Ibid.*, p. 176.

[16] *Ibid.*, p. 181.

[17] *Ibid.*, p. 199.

[18] *Ibid.*

[19] *Ibid.*, p. 170.

[20] *Ibid.*, p. 215.

[21] *Ibid.*

[22] *Graham* v. *John Deere Co.*, 383 U.S. 1; *Calmar, Inc.*, v. *Cook Chemical Co.*, 383 U.S. 1; and *U.S.* v. *Adams,* 383 U.S. 39.

[23] Andrew F. Sayko, "The Impact of the Supreme Court Section 103 Cases on the Standard of Patentability in the Lower Federal Courts," *George Washington Law Review,* Vol. 35 (May, 1967), pp. 822, 824.

[24] Dixon, *Democratic Representation,* p. 113.

[25] *Ibid.*, pp. 139–40.

[26] *Ibid.*, pp. 164, 163.

[27] Edward N. Beiser, "A Comparative Analysis of State and Federal Judicial Behavior: The Reapportionment Cases," *American Political Science Review,* Vol. 62 (September, 1968), pp. 791, 793.

[28] *Ibid.*, p. 794.

[29] Dixon, *op. cit.*, pp. 378–79.

[30] *Ibid.*, p. 379.

[31] *Ibid.*, p. 299.

[32] *Ibid.*, p. 304.

[33] *Ibid.*, pp. 319–20.

[34] *Ibid.*, p. 321.

[35] *Ibid.*, p. 395.

[36] David Leuthold, *Electioneering in a Democracy* (New York: John Wiley & Sons, Inc., 1967), p. 10.

[37] Malcolm E. Jewell, "Effects of Redistricting on Metropolitan Legislative Behavior" (Paper presented at meetings of American Political Science Association, 1968), p. 5.

[38] Mitau, *op. cit.*, p. 114.

[39] Patric, *op. cit.*, pp. 457, 463.

[40] *Ibid.*, p. 463.

[41] Sorauf, *op. cit.*, p. 791.

[42] Ellis Katz, "Patterns of Compliance with the Schempp Decision," *Journal of Public Law,* Vol. 14, No. 2 (1965), p. 401.

[43] Reich, "Impact of Judicial Decision-Making . . . ," p. 45.

[44] Katz, *op. cit.*, p. 398.

[45] Johnson, *Dynamics of Compliance,* p. 108.

[46] *Ibid.*, p. 139.

[47] H. Frank Way, Jr., "Survey Research on Judicial Decisions: The Prayer and Bible Reading Cases," *Western Political Quarterly,* Vol. 21 (June, 1968), p. 191.

[48] *Ibid.*, p. 193.

[49] Reich, *op. cit.*, p. 56.

[50] *Ibid.*

[51] *Ibid.*, p. 67.

[52] *Ibid.*, p. 66.

[53] *Ibid.*, p. 67.

[54] Robert Birkby, "The Supreme Court and the Bible Belt: Tennessee Reaction to the *Schempp* Decision," p. 307. Reprinted from *Midwest Journal of Political Science*, Vol. 10, No. 3 (1966) by permission of Wayne State University Press. Copyright, 1966, by the Wayne State University Press.

[55] *Ibid.*, p. 317.

[56] Dolbeare and Hammond, *op. cit.*, p. 6.

[57] *Ibid.*, p. 7.

[58] *Ibid.*, p. 11.

[59] From Richard S. Randall, *Censorship of the Movies: The Social and Political Control of a Mass Medium* (Madison: University of Wisconsin Press; © 1968 by the Regents of the University of Wisconsin), p. 21.

[60] Ira Carmen, *Movies, Censorship and the Law* (Ann Arbor: University of Michigan Press, 1966), p. 148.

[61] *Ibid.*, p. 184.

[62] Randall, *op. cit.*, p. 32.

[63] *Ibid.*, p. 41.

[64] Carmen, *op. cit.*, p. 153.

[65] Randall, *op. cit.*, p. 91.

[66] *Ibid.*

[67] Robert James Oexeman, "Obscenity and the Law in Illinois" (Master's thesis, Department of Government, Southern Illinois University, 1965), pp. 131, 133.

[68] Wasby, "The Pure and the Prurient . . . ," p. 100.

[69] Judge Ralph Holman, *State of Oregon* v. *Childs*, 447 P. 2d 304 (1968).

[70] Barth, "Perception and Acceptance of Supreme Court Decisions . . . ," pp. 330, 332.

[71] James P. Levine, "Constitutional Law and Obscene Literature: An Investigation of Bookseller Censorship Practices," in Becker (ed.), *The Impact of Supreme Court Decisions*, p. 140.

[72] Barth, *op. cit.*, p. 347.

[73] *Ibid.*

[74] Levine, *op. cit.*, p. 147.

CHAPTER 5

[1] *The Symbols of Government* (New Haven, Conn.: Yale University Press, 1935), p. 155.

[2] James Q. Wilson, *Varieties of Police Behavior* (Cambridge, Mass.: Harvard University Press, 1968), pp. 286, 293.

[3] Dallin H. Oaks and Warren Lehman, *A Criminal Justice System and the Indigent* (Chicago: University of Chicago Press, 1968), p. 80.

[4] *Ibid.*, p. 81. Seeburger and Wettick show a higher percentage of cases disposed of through guilty plea in Pittsburgh post-*Miranda*. (Richard H. Seeburger and R. Stanton Wettick, Jr., "*Miranda* in Pittsburgh—A Statistical Study," *University of Pittsburgh Law Review*, Vol. 29 [October, 1967], pp. 1–26.)

[5] Mitau, *op. cit.*, p. 161.

[6] Peter O. Mueller, "Right to Counsel at Police Identification Proceedings: A Problem in Effective Implementation of an Expanding Constitution," *University of Pittsburgh Law Review*, Vol. 29 (October, 1965), pp. 79–80, 82.

[7] Casper, *op. cit.*, pp. 21, 26.

[8] Loren Miller, *op. cit.*, pp. 14–15.

[9] Abraham S. Blumberg, "The Practice of Law as Confidence Game: Organizational Cooptation of a Profession," *Law & Society Review*, Vol. 11 (November, 1967), pp. 36–37.

[10] *Ibid.*, p. 16.

[11] "The President's Page: *Gault* and Juvenile Justice," *American Bar Association Journal*, Vol. 55 (June, 1969), p. 503. Copyright, American Bar Association.

[12] Monrad G. Paulsen, "Juvenile Courts and the Legacy of '67," *Indiana Law Journal*, Vol. 43 (Spring, 1968), p. 531.

[13] Norman Lefstein, Vaughan Stapleton, and Lee Teitlebaum, "In Search of Juvenile Justice: *Gault* and Its Implementation," *Law & Society Review,* Vol. 3 (May, 1969), p. 509.

[14] *Ibid.,* p. 521.

[15] *Ibid.,* p. 497, note.

[16] Anthony Platt, Howard Schechter, and Phyllis Tiffany, "In Defense of Youth: A Case of the Public Defender in Juvenile Court," *Indiana Law Journal,* Vol. 43 (Spring, 1968), p. 637.

[17] Amos E. Reed, "Gault and the Juvenile Training School," *Indiana Law Journal,* Vol. 43 (Spring, 1968), p. 646.

[18] F. Thomas Schornhorst, "The Waiver of Juvenile Court Jurisdiction: Kent Revisited," *Indiana Law Journal,* Vol. 43 (Spring, 1968), p. 599.

[19] President's Commission on Law Enforcement and the Administration of Justice, *The Challenge of Crime in a Free Society* (Washington, D.C.: Government Printing Office, 1967), p. 305.

[20] Milner, *op. cit.,* p. 195.

[21] Eugene W. Linse, Jr., "Due Process in Practice: A Study of Police Procedures in Minneapolis" (Ph.D. dissertation, University of Minnesota, 1965; *Dissertation Abstracts,* Vol. 27 (October, 1966), p. 1086A.

[22] Ridella, *op. cit.,* p. 186.

[23] Matthew O. Tobriner, "Individual Rights in an Industrialized Society," *American Bar Association Journal,* Vol. 54 (January, 1968), pp. 21–23.

[24] Communication, Frank A. Day, *American Bar Association Journal,* Vol. 54 (March, 1968), p. 212. Copyright, American Bar Association.

[25] Myron L. Birnbaum, "The Effect of Recent Supreme Court Decisions on Military Law," *Fordham Law Review,* Vol. 36 (December, 1967), p. 160.

[26] *Ibid.,* p. 165.

[27] Edward J. Bellen, "The Revolution in Military Law," *American Bar Association Journal,* Vol. 54 (December, 1968), p. 1195.

[28] Michael Wald, Richard Ayres, David W. Hess, Mark Schantz, and Charles H. Whitebread II, "Interrogations in New Haven: The Impact of *Miranda,*" *Yale Law Journal,* Vol. 76 (July, 1967), p. 1534. This and the following quotes from the same source reprinted by permission of The Yale Law Journal Company and Fred B. Rothman Company.

[29] Richard J. Medalie, Leonard Zeitz, and Paul Alexander, "Custodial Police Interrogation in Our Nation's Capital: The Attempt to Implement Miranda," *Michigan Law Review,* Vol. 66 (May, 1968), p. 1363.

[30] Wald *et al., op. cit.,* p. 1574.

[31] *Ibid.,* p. 1600.

[32] Otis H. Stephens, Jr., "Police Interrogation and the Supreme Court: An Inquiry into the Limits of Judicial Policy-Making," *Journal of Public Law,* Vol. 17, No. 2 (1968), p. 255.

[33] Medalie *et al., op. cit.,* pp. 1371–72.

[34] *Ibid.,* p. 1374.

[35] Wald *et al., op. cit.,* p. 1614.

[36] John Griffiths and Richard E. Ayres, "A Postscript to the Miranda Project: Interrogation of Draft Protestors," *Yale Law Journal,* Vol. 76 (December, 1967), p. 318. This and the quotation immediately following reprinted by permission of The Yale Law Journal Company and Fred B. Rothman Company.

[37] *Ibid.,* pp. 318–19.

[38] Wayne R. LaFave, "Improving Police Performance through the Exclusionary Rule: Part II: Defining the Norms and Training the Police," *Missouri Law Review,* Vol. 30 (Fall, 1965), p. 567. Copyright 1965 by The Curators of the University of Missouri; reprinted with permission.

[39] Skolnick, *op. cit.,* p. 224.

[40] Michael J. Murphy, "The Problem of Compliance by Police Departments," *Texas Law Review,* Vol. 44 (1966), p. 940.

[41] Arlen Specter, "*Mapp* v. *Ohio:* Pandora's Problems for the Prosecutor," *University of Pennsylvania Law Review,* Vol. 111 (November, 1962), p. 4.

[42] M. Murphy, *op. cit.*, p. 941.

[43] David Manwaring, "The Impact of *Mapp* v. *Ohio*," in Everson (ed.), *The Supreme Court as Policy-Maker . . .*, p. 18.

[44] *Ibid.*, p. 20.

[45] Specter, *op. cit.*, pp. 40–41.

[46] Nagel, *op. cit.*, p. 314.

[47] *Ibid.*, p. 7.

[48] Michael Katz, "The Supreme Court and the States: An Inquiry into *Mapp* v. *Ohio* in North Carolina. The Model, the Study, and the Implications," *North Carolina Law Review*, Vol. 45 (December, 1966), p. 131.

[49] Manwaring, *op. cit.*, pp. 15, 26.

[50] *Ibid.*, pp. 10, 14.

[51] *Ibid.*, p. 11.

[52] *Ibid.*, p. 26.

[53] This account is drawn from Walter Murphy, *Wiretapping on Trial: A Case Study in the Judicial Process* (New York: Random House, Inc., 1965).

[54] *Ibid.*, p. 157.

[55] *Ibid.*, pp. 156–57.

[56] Nagel, *op. cit.*, p. 10.

[57] Anthony Lewis, "The Supreme Court and Its Critics," *Minnesota Law Review*, Vol. 45 (January, 1961), p. 307.

[58] D'Amato, *op. cit.*, p. 10.

[59] L. Miller, *op. cit.*, p. 180.

[60] *Ibid.*, p. 163.

[61] Berman, *op. cit.*, p. 5.

[62] Murphy and Pritchett, *op. cit.*, p. 591.

[63] *Ibid.*, p. 587.

[64] Blaustein and Ferguson, *Desegregation and the Law*, p. 219.

[65] Reed Sarratt, *The Ordeal of Desegregation: The First Decade* (New York: Harper & Row Publishers, 1966), p. 49.

[66] Benjamin Muse, *Ten Years of Prelude: The Story of Integration Since The Supreme Court's 1954 Decision* (New York: Viking Press, Inc., 1964), pp. 73–74. Copyright © 1961 by Indiana University Press. This and subsequent quotes from the same source reprinted by permission.

[67] Rainwater and Yancey, *op. cit.*, p. 11.

[68] David B. King, "Racial Imbalance in the Public Schools: Constitutional Dimensions and Judicial Response," *Vanderbilt Law Review*, Vol. 18 (June-October, 1965), p. 1299.

[69] *Ibid.*, p. 1312.

[70] Statement by G. W. Foster, Jr., *Congressional Record*, November 17, 1969, pp. S 14493–97.

[71] Walter Rugaber, "New Period of Tension in South as Massive Integration Begins," *St. Louis Post-Dispatch*, September 12, 1968.

[72] Sarratt, *op. cit.*, p. 1.

[73] Muse, *op. cit.*, pp. 16, 17, 27.

[74] Sarratt, *op. cit.*, p. 6.

[75] *Ibid.*, p. 6.

[76] Muse, *op. cit.*, p. 67.

[77] J. W. Peltason, *Fifty-Eight Lonely Men: Southern Federal Judges and School Desegregation* (New York: Harcourt, Brace & World, Inc., 1961), p. 244.

[78] Muse, *op. cit.*, pp. 38–39.

[79] Sarratt, *op. cit.*, p. 347.

[80] Muse, *op. cit.*, pp. 201–2.

[81] Blaustein and Ferguson, *op. cit.*, pp. 241–42.

[82] Mitau, *op. cit.*, p. 66.

[83] Muse, *Virginia's Massive Resistance*, p. 11.

[84] Robbins L. Gates, *The Making of Massive Resistance: Virginia's Politics of Public School Desegregation, 1954–1956* (Chapel Hill: University of North Carolina Press, 1962), p. 203.

[85] Muse, *Virginia's Massive Resistance,* p. 172.
[86] Smith, *They Closed Their Schools . . . ,* p. 258.
[87] Muse, *Virginia's Massive Resistance,* p. 172.
[88] Robert L. Crain, *The Politics of School Desegregation* (Chicago: Aldine Publishing Co., 1968), p. 254.
[89] Blaustein and Ferguson, *op. cit.,* p. 213.
[90] Muse, *Ten Years of Prelude,* p. 112.
[91] Sarratt, *op. cit.,* p. 76, 40–41.
[92] Blaustein and Ferguson, *op. cit.,* p. 215.
[93] *Ibid.,* pp. 223, 224.
[94] Robert Lasch, "Along the Border," in Shoemaker (ed.), *With All Deliberate Speed,* p. 64. See also, Edgar L. Jones, "City Limits," *Ibid.,* p. 80.
[95] Peltason, *op. cit.,* p. 34.
[96] Crain, *op. cit.,* pp. 304, 295.
[97] *Ibid.,* p. 309.
[98] Melvin M. Tumin *et al., Desegregation: Resistance and Readiness* (Princeton, N.J.: Princeton University Press, 1958), pp. 159–60. Copyright © by Princeton University Press.
[99] Jones, *op. cit.,* p. 76.
[100] Tumin, *op. cit.,* p. 153.
[101] Peltason, *op. cit.,* pp. 10–11.
[102] Melvin M. Tumin and Robert Rotberg, "Leaders, The Led, and the Law: A Case Study in Social Change," *Public Opinion Quarterly,* Vol. 21 (Fall, 1957), p. 361.
[103] Tumin, *op. cit.,* p. 152.
[104] *Ibid.,* p. 153.
[105] *Ibid.,* p. 154.

CHAPTER 6

[1] Paul H. Sanders, "The Warren Court and the Lower Federal Courts," in John Schmidhauser (ed.), *Constitutional Law in the Political Process* (Skokie, Ill.: Rand McNally & Co., 1963), pp. 426–27.
[2] Shapiro, *Supreme Court and Administrative Agencies,* p. 171.
[3] Krislov, *Supreme Court in the Political Process,* p. 15.
[4] Charles V. Hamilton, "Southern Judges and Negro Voting Rights: The Judicial Approach to the Solution of Controversial Social Problems," *Wisconsin Law Review,* Vol. 1965 (Winter, 1965), p. 74.
[5] *Ibid.,* p. 99.
[6] Shapiro, *op. cit.,* p. 171.
[7] Peltason, *op. cit.,* p. 246.
[8] Krislov, *Supreme Court and Political Freedom,* p. 176.
[9] Sanders, *op. cit.,* p. 430.
[10] Walter Murphy, "Lower Court Checks on Supreme Court Power," *American Political Science Review,* Vol. 53 (December, 1959), p. 1024.
[11] Sanders, *op. cit.,* p. 431.
[12] Note, "Amending the Rules of Civil Procedure after Hanna v. Plumer: Rule 3," *New York University Law Review,* Vol. 42 (December, 1967), p. 1142.
[13] Robert Mollan, "Smith Act Prosecutions: The Effect of the *Dennis* and *Yates* Decisions," *University of Pittsburgh Law Review,* Vol. 26 (June, 1965), pp. 710–11.
[14] *Ibid.,* p. 711.
[15] *Ibid.,* p. 740.
[16] *Ibid.,* pp. 735, 736.
[17] Shapiro, *op. cit.,* p. 167, note.
[18] Murphy and Pritchett, *op. cit.,* p. 588.
[19] "Arkansas School District Defends System at Rights Suit Hearing," *St. Louis Post-Dispatch,* January 9, 1969.
[20] Krislov, *Supreme Court in the Political Process,* p. 137.
[21] Warren, *op. cit.,* Vol. II, p. 530.

[22] Jacob, *Justice in America,* p. 193.

[23] Manwaring, "The Flag-Salute Case," p. 30. An interesting case of "quarantine" from the private law area is suggested in "Note: Aftermath of the Supreme Court's Stop, Look and Listen Rule," *Harvard Law Review,* Vol. 43 (April, 1930), pp. 926–32. After Justice Holmes had held, for the Court, in *B & O R.R.* v. *Goodman,* 275 U.S. 66 (1927), that it was the duty of the driver of an automobile to get out of his car and look at a railroad crossing, "the case . . . caused scarcely a ripple . . . and [gave] no appreciable impetus to the imposition of a higher standard of care." P. 931.

[24] Kenneth Vanlandingham, "Pecuniary Interest of Justices of the Peace in Kentucky: The Aftermath of *Tumey* v. *Ohio,*" *Kentucky Law Journal,* Vol. 45 (Summer, 1957), p. 609.

[25] *Ibid.,* p. 620.

[26] *Ibid.,* pp. 609–10.

[27] Murphy, *op. cit.,* p. 1018.

[28] *American Bar Association Journal,* Vol. 55 (1969), p. 178.

[29] Krislov, *Supreme Court in the Political Process,* p. 144.

[30] Schubert, *Constitutional Politics,* p. 257.

[31] Krislov, *op. cit.,* p. 144.

[32] Warren, *op. cit.,* Vol. II, p. 367.

[33] Murphy, *Congress and the Court,* p. 260.

[34] Harry Stumpf, "The Political Efficacy of Judicial Symbolism," *Western Political Quarterly,* Vol. 19 (June, 1966), p. 301.

[35] Jacob, *op. cit.,* p. 194.

[36] Nagel, *op. cit.,* p. 275.

[37] Krislov, *op. cit.,* p. 18.

[38] C. Peter Magrath, *Yazoo: Law and Politics in the New Republic* (Providence, R.I.: Brown University Press, 1966), p. 85.

[39] *Ibid.,* p. 91.

[40] Murphy, *op. cit.,* p. 53.

[41] Nagel, *op. cit.,* p. 266.

[42] Note, "Congressional Reversal of Supreme Court Decisions: 1945–1957," *Harvard Law Review,* Vol. 71 (May, 1958), p. 1336.

[43] *First Agricultural National Bank of Berkshire County* v. *State Tax Commission,* 392 U.S. 339 (1968).

[44] Harry P. Stumpf, "Congressional Response to Supreme Court Rulings: The Interaction of Law and Politics," *Journal of Public Law,* Vol. XIV (#2, 1965), p. 384.

[45] *Ibid.,* p. 394.

[46] Nagel, *op. cit.,* p. 277.

[47] Clifford M. Lytle, *The Warren Court and Its Critics* (Tucson: University of Arizona Press, 1968), p. 27. Copyright 1968.

[48] Fainsod *et al., op. cit.,* p. 453.

[49] John Roche, "Judicial Self-Restraint," *American Political Science Review,* Vol. 49 (September, 1955), p. 771.

[50] Murphy, *Congress and the Court,* pp. 260–61.

[51] *Ibid.,* p. 258.

CHAPTER 7

[1] Kelly and Harbison, *op. cit.,* p. 288.

[2] Haar, *op. cit.,* p. 121.

[3] Warren, *op. cit.,* Vol. II, p. 222.

[4] *Ibid.,* Vol. II, p. 221.

[5] Arthur M. Schlesinger, Jr., *The Politics of Upheaval* (Boston: Houghton Mifflin Co., 1960), p. 493.

[6] Kelly and Harbison, *op. cit.,* p. 737.

[7] Schlesinger, *op. cit.,* p. 491.

[8] Kelly and Harbison, *op. cit.,* p. 737.

[9] Krislov, *Supreme Court in the Political Process,* p. 135.
[10] A. Miller, *op. cit.,* pp. 101–2.
[11] Schubert, *Judicial Policy-Making,* p. 59.
[12] Clinton Rossiter, *The Supreme Court and the Commander in Chief* (Ithaca, N.Y.: Cornell University Press, 1951), pp. 127, 131.
[13] Krislov, *op. cit.,* p. 141.
[14] Murphy, *Congress and the Court,* p. 131.
[15] Mollan, *op. cit.,* pp. 708–9.
[16] Leonard G. Miller, "Subversion and the Cold War," in Pritchett and Westin (eds.), *Third Branch of Government,* p. 232.
[17] A. Miller, *op. cit.,* p. 95.
[18] Shapiro, *op. cit.,* p. 13.
[19] *Ibid.,* pp. 65–66.
[20] Loren Miller, *op. cit.,* pp. 14, 132.
[21] Fainsod *et al., op. cit.,* p. 260.
[22] Kelly and Harbison, *op. cit.,* p. 600.
[23] Fainsod *et al., op. cit.,* p. 509.
[24] Shapiro, *op. cit.,* p. 249.
[25] Gregory, "Cinema Censorship and Court Compliance," pp. 9, 10.
[26] Warren, *op. cit.,* Vol. II, p. 12.
[27] *Ibid.,* Vol. II, p. 102.
[28] *Ibid.,* Vol. II, p. 358.
[29] William Lockhart, "A Response to the Conference of State Chief Justices," *University of Pennsylvania Law Review,* Vol. 107 (April, 1959), pp. 804, 806.
[30] Warren, *op. cit.,* Vol. III, p. 316. However, compare the situation after *Berea College* v. *Kentucky*: "States and cities took the cue and tumbled over themselves to pass laws and ordinances prohibiting innocent association of Negroes and white persons in pool halls, taxicabs, restaurants . . . or in almost any conceivable place where association might occur." (L. Miller, *op. cit.,* p. 205.)
[31] Gregory, *op. cit.,* p. 10. The law was subsequently upheld.
[32] Patrick McCauley, " 'Be It Enacted,' " in Shoemaker, *op. cit.,* p. 131.
[33] Dolbeare and Hammond, *op. cit.,* p. 4.
[34] Samuel Krislov, "Constituency versus Constitutionalism: The Desegregation Issue and Tensions and Aspirations of Southern Attorneys General," *Midwest Journal of Political Science,* Vol. 3 (February, 1959), p. 79.
[35] Robert D. Smith, "Religion and the Schools: The Influence of State Attorneys General on the Implementation of *Engel* and *Schempp*" (unpublished paper, 1969).
[36] Department of Justice, State of Wisconsin, *The Prosecutor's Bulletin,* Vol. 1, No. 4 (September, 1969), p. 3.
[37] Milner, *op. cit.,* pp. 256–57.
[38] Johnson, *op. cit.,* p. 67.
[39] Fainsod *et al., op. cit.,* p. 332.
[40] Joseph R. Rose, "The *Hope* Case and Public Utility Valuation in the States," *Columbia Law Review,* Vol. 54 (February, 1954), p. 212.
[41] Warren, *op. cit.,* Vol. I, p. 3.
[42] Krislov, *Supreme Court and Political Freedom,* pp. 185–86.
[43] *Ibid.,* p. 203.
[44] Warren, *op. cit.,* Vol. III, p. 244.
[45] *Ibid.,* p. 253.
[46] Fainsod *et al., op. cit.,* pp. 540, 541.
[47] Schlesinger, *op. cit.,* p. 489.
[49] Miller and Scheflin, *op. cit.,* p. 281. In italic in original.
[49] Miller and Scheflin, *op. cit.,* p. 281.
[50] Krislov, *Supreme Court in the Political Process,* p. 153; emphasis supplied.
[51] John H. Kessel, "Public Perceptions of the Supreme Court," p. 175. This and other quotations from the same source are reprinted from *Midwest Journal of Political Science,* Vol. 10, No. 2 (1966) by permission of the Wayne State University Press. Copyright, 1966, by the Wayne State University Press.
[52] Kenneth M. Dolbeare, "The Public Views the Supreme Court," in Herbert Jacob (ed.), *Law, Politics, and the Federal Courts* (Boston: Little, Brown & Co., 1967), p. 209.

[53] *Ibid.*, p. 199.
[54] Kessel, *op. cit.*, p. 175.
[55] Dolbeare, *op. cit.*, p. 199.
[56] Kessel, *op. cit.*, p. 188.
[57] Barth, *op. cit.*, p. 340.
[58] Kessel, *op. cit.*, pp. 187, 188.
[59] *Ibid.*, p. 183.
[60] Kenneth M. Dolbeare and Phillip E. Hammond, "The Political Party Basis of Attitudes toward the Supreme Court," *Public Opinion Quarterly*, Vol. 31 (Spring, 1967), pp. 24, 23.
[61] *Ibid.*, p. 26. But see their later finding that leaders were "much more polarized politically" by the Court's decisions than was the public, with "leaders' judgments . . . based on the relation of Court decisions to their ideological and other issue-based preferences." ("Local Elites . . . ," p. 3.)
[62] Kessel, *op. cit.*, p. 182.
[63] Walter Murphy and Joseph Tanenhaus, "Public Opinion and the United States Supreme Court: Mapping of Some Prerequisites for Court Legitimation of Regime Change," in Joel B. Grossman and Joseph Tanenhaus (eds.), *Frontiers of Judicial Research* (New York: John Wiley & Sons, Inc., 1969), p. 275.
[64] *Ibid.*, p. 284.
[65] Dolbeare and Hammond, "Local Elites . . . ," pp. 3, 4.
[66] Murphy and Tanenhaus, *op. cit.*, p. 291.
[67] Kessel, *op. cit.*, p. 190.
[68] *Ibid.*, p. 191.
[69] Dolbeare, *op. cit.*, p. 208.
[70] *Ibid.*, p. 211.

CHAPTER 8

[1] Wasby, "The Pure and the Prurient . . . ," p. 105.
[2] Shapiro, *Supreme Court and Administrative Agencies*, p. 171.
[3] Newland, *op. cit.*, p. 15.
[4] Wasby, *op. cit.*, p. 106.
[5] Leflar, *op. cit.*, p. 13.
[6] Skolnick, *op. cit.*, p. 219.
[7] Krislov, *Supreme Court and Political Freedom*, p. 137.
[8] Barth, *op. cit.*, p. 316.
[9] Rose, *op. cit.*, p. 477.
[10] Barth, *op. cit.*, p. 319.
[11] Johnson, *op. cit.*, p. 139.
[12] Alvin Zander, "Resistance to Change: Its Analysis and Prevention," *Advanced Management*, Vols. 15–61 (January, 1950), pp. 9–11.
[13] Richard E. Neustadt, *Presidential Power: The Politics of Leadership* (New York: John Wiley & Sons, Inc., 1960), p. 19.
[14] LaFave, "Improving Police Performance . . . ," p. 567.
[15] Krislov, *Supreme Court in the Political Process*, p. 136.

Bibliography

Items in this bibliography are grouped by subject matter. After the initial section, which combines items discussing impact in theoretical terms with general materials, including those which are primarily historical, the headings are those of Part II of this volume. Exceptions are new headings for the substantive area of "Internal Security," the process of "Communication," and the political arena of the "Community."

The items are numbered consecutively. Where an item belongs in more than one category, the full reference appears the first time, with only the reference number repeated in subsequent sections.

Theoretical, General, and Historical

(1) Becker, Theodore L. (ed.). *The Impact of Supreme Court Decisions: Empirical Studies.* New York: Oxford University Press, Inc., 1969.

(2) Kelly, Alfred H., and Winfred A. Harbison. *The American Constitution: Its Origins and Development.* 2d ed. New York: W. W. Norton & Co., Inc., 1955. 3d ed., 1963.

(3) Krislov, Samuel. "The Perimeters of Power: Patterns of Compliance and Opposition to Supreme Court Decisions." Paper presented to American Political Science Association, 1963.

(4) ———. *The Supreme Court and Political Freedom.* New York: Free Press, 1968.

(5) ———. *The Supreme Court in the Political Process*, chap vi, "Compliance," pp. 134–55. New York: Macmillan Co., 1965.

(6) Levine, James P., and Theodore L. Becker. "Toward and Beyond a Theory of Supreme Court Impact." Paper presented to American Political Science Association, 1969.

(7) Lewis, Anthony. "The Supreme Court and Its Critics," *Minnesota Law Review,* Vol. 45 (January, 1961), pp. 305–32.

(8) Magrath, C. Peter. *Yazoo: Law and Politics in the New Republic: The Case of FLETCHER v. PECK.* Providence, R.I.: Brown University Press, 1966.

(9) Miller, Arthur S. "On the Need for 'Impact Analysis' of Supreme Court Decisions," *Georgetown Law Journal,* Vol. 53 (1965), pp. 365–401.

(10) ———, and Alan W. Scheflin. "The Power of the Supreme Court in the Age of the Positive State: A Preliminary Excursus," *Duke Law Journal,* Vol. 1967, pp. 273–320.

(11) Mitau, G. Theodore. *Decade of Decision: The Supreme Court and the Constitutional Revolution, 1954–1964.* New York: Charles Scribner's Sons, 1967.

(12) Petrick, Michael J. "The Supreme Court and Authority Acceptance," *Western Political Quarterly,* Vol. 21 (March, 1968), pp. 5–19.

(13) Pritchett, C. Herman. "Political Questions and Judicial Answers," *Western Political Quarterly,* Vol. 17 (September, 1964), Supplement, pp. 12–20.

(14) ———, and Alan Westin (eds.). *The Third Branch of Government: Eight Cases in Constitutional Politics.* New York: Harcourt, Brace & World, Inc., 1963. Case studies on Court decisions on offshore oil, portal-to-portal pay, internal security, Sunday closing laws, and flag salute.

(15) Warren, Charles. *The Supreme Court in United States History.* 3 vols. Boston: Little, Brown, 1922.

Economic Regulation and Administrative Law

(16) Comment, "Exclusivity of Prison Industries Fund: An Epilogue to *United States* v. *Muniz,*" *Catholic University of America Law Review,* Vol. 16 (November, 1966), pp. 187–200.

(17) Fainsod, Merle, Lincoln Gordon, and Joseph C. Palamountain, Jr. *Government and the American Economy.* 3d ed. New York: W. W. Norton & Co., Inc., 1959.

(18) Keating, William J. "The Supreme Court Interprets the Patent Statute: A Trilogy of Cases and Their Effect Today," *Dickinson Law Review,* Vol. 72 (Winter, 1968), pp. 244–68.

(19) Miller, Arthur Selwyn. *The Supreme Court and American Capitalism.* New York: Free Press, 1968.

(20) Rose, Joseph R. "The *Hope* Case and Public Utility Valuation in the States," *Columbia Law Review,* Vol. 54 (February, 1954), pp. 188–213.

(21) Sayko, Andrew F., "The Impact of the Supreme Court Section 103 Cases on the Standard of Patentability in the Lower Federal Courts," *George Washington Law Review,* Vol. 35 (May, 1967), pp. 818–27.

(22) Shapiro, Martin. *The Supreme Court and Administrative Agencies* New York: Macmillan Co., 1968.

(23) Wood, Stephen B. *Constitutional Politics in the Progressive Era: Child Labor and the Law.* Chicago: University of Chicago Press, 1968.

Reapportionment

(24) Beiser, Edward N. "A Comparative Analysis of State and Federal Judicial Behavior: The Reapportionment Cases," *American Political Science Review,* Vol. 62 (September, 1968), pp. 788–95.

(25) Bornhoft, Budd B., Jr. "Casenote: Reapportionment—Extension of Equal Representation to the County Level . . .," *Nebraska Law Review,* Vol. 44 (July, 1965), pp. 850–61.

(26) Dixon, Robert G., Jr. *Democratic Representation: Reapportionment in Law and Politics.* New York: Oxford University Press, Inc., 1968.

(27) Jewell, Malcolm E. "Effects of Redistricting on Metropolitan Legislative Behavior." Paper presented to American Political Science Association, 1968.

Also: (13).

Church-State Relations: School Prayer

(28) Beaney, William, and N. Edward Beiser. "Prayer and Politics: The Impact of Engel and Schempp on the Political Process," *Journal of Public Law,* Vol. 13 (1964), pp. 475–503.

(29) Birkby, Robert. "The Supreme Court and the Bible Belt: Tennessee Reaction to the *Schempp* Decision," *Midwest Journal of Political Science,* Vol. X (August, 1966), pp. 304–19.

(30) Johnson, Richard. *The Dynamics of Compliance.* Evanston, Ill.: Northwestern University Press, 1967. Some of the findings are presented in "Compliance and Supreme Court Decision-Making," *Wisconsin Law Review,* Vol. 1967 (Winter, 1967), pp. 170–85.

(31) Katz, Ellis. "Patterns of Compliance with the Schempp Decision," *Journal of Public Law,* Vol. 14 (1965), pp. 396–408.

(32) Muir, William K., Jr. *Prayer in the Public Schools: Law and Attitude Change.* Chicago: University of Chicago Press, 1967.

(33) Nagel, Stuart, and Robert Erickson. "Editorial Reaction to Supreme Court Decisions on Church and State," *Public Opinion Quarterly,* Vol. 30 (Winter, 1966–67), pp. 647–55. (Also in Nagel, *The Legal Process from a Behavioral Perspective* [Homewood: Dorsey Press, 1969], pp. 285–93.)

(34) Patric, Gordon. "The Impact of a Court Decision: Aftermath of the McCollum Case," *Journal of Public Law,* Vol. 6 (Fall, 1957), pp. 455–64.

(35) Reich, Donald. "The Impact of Judicial Decision-Making: The School Prayer Cases," in *The Supreme Court as Policy-Maker: Three Studies on the Impact of Judicial Decisions* (ed. David Everson), pp. 44–81. Carbondale, Ill.: Public Affairs Research Bureau, Southern Illinois University, 1968.

(36) Sorauf, Frank J. "*Zorach* v. *Clauson:* The Impact of a Supreme Court Decision," *American Political Science Review,* Vol. 53 (September, 1959), pp. 777–91.

(37) Way, H. Frank, Jr. "Survey Research on Judicial Decisions: The Prayer and Bible Reading Cases," *Western Political Quarterly,* Vol. 21 (June, 1968), pp. 189–205.

Free Speech: Obscene Movies and Literature

(38) Barth, Thomas E. "Perception and Acceptance of Supreme Court Decisions at the State and Local Level," *Journal of Public Law,* Vol. 17 (1968), pp. 308–50.

(39) Carmen, Ira. *Movies, Censorship and the Law.* Ann Arbor: University of Michigan Press, 1966.

(40) Randall, Richard S. *Censorship of the Movies: The Social and Political Control of a Mass Medium.* Madison: University of Wisconsin Press, 1968.

(41) Shipley, Parker. "Obscene Publication Prohibition," *Nebraska Law Review,* Vol. 40 (April, 1961), pp. 481–91.

(42) Wasby, Stephen L. "Public Law, Politics and the Local Courts: Obscene Literature in Portland," *Journal of Public Law,* Vol. 14 (Spring, 1965), pp. 105–30.

(43) ———. "The Pure and the Prurient: The Supreme Court, Obscenity and Oregon Policy," *The Supreme Court as Policy-Maker* (see [35]), pp. 82–116.

Internal Security

(44) Mollan, Robert. "Smith Act Prosecutions: The Effect of the *Dennis* and *Yates* Decisions," *University of Pittsburgh Law Review,* Vol. 26 (June, 1965), pp. 705–48.

(45) Murphy, Walter. *Congress and the Court.* Chicago: University of Chicago Press, 1962.

(46) Note, "*Dombrowski* v. *Eastland*—A Political Compromise and Its Impact," *Rutgers Law Review,* Vol. 22 (Fall, 1967), pp. 137–66.

Criminal Procedure

(47) Bellen, Edward J. "The Revolution in Military Law," *American Bar Association Journal,* Vol. 54 (December, 1968), pp. 1194–98.

(48) Birnbaum, Myron L. "The Effect of Recent Supreme Court Decisions on Military Law," *Fordham Law Review,* Vol. 36 (December, 1967), pp. 153–74.

(49) Griffiths, John, and Richard E. Ayres. "A Postscript to the Miranda Project: Interrogation of Draft Protestors," *Yale Law Journal,* Vol. 76 (December, 1967), pp. 300–319.

(50) Lefstein, Norman, Vaughan Stapleton, and Lee Teitlebaum. "In Search of Juvenile Justice: *Gault* and Its Implementation," *Law & Society Review,* Vol. 3 (May, 1969), pp. 491–562.

(51) Manwaring, David. "The Impact of *Mapp* v. *Ohio,*" *The Supreme Court as Policy-Maker* (see [35]), pp. 1–43.

(52) Medalie, Richard J., Leonard Zeitz, and Paul Alexander. "Custodial Police Interrogation in our Nation's Capital: The Attempt to Implement Miranda," *Michigan Law Review,* Vol. 66 (May, 1968), pp. 1347–1422.

(53) Mueller, Peter O. "Right to Counsel at Police Identification Proceedings: A Problem in Effective Implementation of an Expanding Constitution," *University of Pittsburgh Law Review,* Vol. 29 (October, 1965), pp. 65–88.

(54) Murphy, Michael J. "The Problem of Compliance by Police Departments," *Texas Law Review,* Vol. 44 (1966), pp. 939–46.

(55) Murphy, Walter. *Wiretapping on Trial: A Case Study in the Judicial Process.* New York: Random House, Inc., 1965.

(56) Nagel, Stuart S. "Testing the Effects of Excluding Illegally Seized Evidence," *Wisconsin Law Review,* Vol. 1965 (Spring, 1965), pp. 283–310. (Also in *The Legal Process from a Behavioral Perspective,* pp. 294–320.)

(57) Oaks, Dallin H., and Warren Lehman. *A Criminal Justice System and the Indigent.* Chicago: University of Chicago Press, 1968.

(58) Remington, Frank J., Donald J. Newman, Edward L. Kimball, Marygold Melli, and Herman Goldstein. *Criminal Justice Administration: Materials and Cases.* Indianapolis: Bobbs-Merrill Co., Inc., 1969. Both this item and (57) provide an understanding of the context into which criminal procedure decisions of the Supreme Court are injected.

(59) Reiss, Albert J., Jr., and Donald J. Black. "Interrogation and the Criminal Process," *The Annals,* Vol. 374 (November, 1967), pp. 47–57.

(60) Ridella, James. "Miranda: One Year Later—The Effects," *Public Management,* Vol. 49 (July, 1967), pp. 183–90.

(61) Seeburger, Richard H., and R. Stanton Wettick, Jr. "*Miranda* in Pittsburgh—A Statistical Study," *University of Pittsburgh Law Review,* Vol. 29 (October, 1967), pp. 1–26.

(62) Skolnick, Jerome H. *Justice Without Trial: Law Enforcement in Democratic Society.* New York: John Wiley & Sons, Inc., 1966.

(63) Specter, Arlen. "*Mapp* v. *Ohio:* Pandora's Problems for the Prosecutor," *University of Pennsylvania Law Review,* Vol. 111 (November, 1962), pp. 4–45.

(64) Stephens, Otis H., Jr. "Police Interrogation and the Supreme Court: An Inquiry into the Limits of Judicial Policy-Making," *Journal of Public Law,* Vol. 17 (1965), pp. 241–57.

(65) Symposium, "On Juvenile Problems: In Re Gault," *Indiana Law Journal,* Vol. 43 (Spring, 1968), entire issue.

(66) Wald, Michael, Richard Ayres, David W. Hess, Mark Schantz, and Charles H. Whitebread II. "Interrogations in New Haven: The Impact of *Miranda,*" *Yale Law Journal,* Vol. 76 (July, 1967), pp. 1519–1648.

Desegregation

(67) Blaustein, Albert P., and Clarence Clyde Ferguson, Jr. *Desegregation and the Law: The Meaning and Effect of the School Segregation Cases.* New Brunswick, N.J.: Rutgers University Press, 1957.

(68) Crain, Robert L., with others. *The Politics of School Desegregation: Comparative Case Studies of Community Structure and Policy-Making.* Chicago: Aldine Publishing Co., 1968.

(69) Gates, Robbins L. *The Making of Massive Resistance: Virginia's Politics of Public School Desegregation, 1954–1956.* Chapel Hill: University of North Carolina Press, 1962/1964.

(70) Graham, Hugh Davis. *Crisis In Print: Desegregation and the Press in Tennessee.* Nashville: Vanderbilt University Press, 1967.

(71) Greenberg, Jack. *Race Relations and American Law.* New York: Columbia University Press, 1959.

(72) Krislov, Samuel. "Constituency versus Constitutionalism: The Desegregation Issue and Tensions and Aspirations of Southern Attorneys General," *Midwest Journal of Political Science,* Vol. 3 (February, 1959), pp. 75–92.

(73) McKay, Robert B. "With All Deliberate Speed: Legislative Reaction and Judicial Developments, 1956–1957," *Virginia Law Review,* Vol. 43 (December, 1957), pp. 1205–45.

(74) ———. "'With All Deliberate Speed': A Study of School Desegregation," *New York University Law Review*, Vol. 31 (June, 1956), pp. 991–1090.

(75) Murphy, Walter. "The South Counterattacks: The Anti-NAACP Laws," *Western Political Quarterly*, Vol. 12 (June, 1959), pp. 371–90.

(76) Muse, Benjamin. *Ten Years of Prelude: The Story of Integration Since The Supreme Court's 1954 Decision.* New York: Viking Press, Inc., 1964.

(77) ———. *Virginia's Massive Resistance.* Bloomington: Indiana University Press, 1961.

(78) Note, "Implementation of Desegregation by the Lower Courts," *Harvard Law Review*, Vol. 71 (1957–58), pp. 486–502.

(79) Peltason, J. W. *Fifty-Eight Lonely Men: Southern Federal Judges and School Desegregation.* New York: Harcourt, Brace & World, Inc., 1961.

(80) Sarratt, Reed. *The Ordeal of Desegregation: The First Decade.* New York: Harper & Row, Publishers, 1966.

(81) Shoemaker, Don (ed.). *With All Deliberate Speed: Segregation-Desegregation in Southern Schools.* New York: Harper & Bros., 1957.

(82) Smith, Bob. *They Closed Their Schools: Prince Edward County, Virginia, 1951–1964.* Chapel Hill: University of North Carolina Press, 1965.

(83) Tumin, Melvin M., *et al. Desegregation: Resistance and Readiness.* Princeton, N.J.: Princeton University Press, 1958.

(84) ———, and Robert Rotberg. "Leaders, the Led, and the Law: A Case Study in Social Change," *Public Opinion Quarterly*, Vol. 21 (Fall, 1957), pp. 355–70.

Communication

(85) Clayton, James E. "News from the Supreme Court and the Justice Department," *The Press in Washington* (ed. Ray Eldon Hiebert), pp. 182–96. New York: Dodd Mead & Co., 1966.

(86) Grey, David L. *The Supreme Court and the News Media.* Evanston, Ill.: Northwestern University Press, 1968.

(87) Newland, Chester. "Press Coverage of the United States Supreme Court," *Western Political Quarterly*, Vol. 17 (March, 1964), pp. 15–36.

Also: (30), (32), (33), (70).

Lower Courts

(88) Murphy, Walter. "Lower Court Checks on Supreme Court Power," *American Political Science Review,* Vol. 53 (December, 1959), pp. 1017–31.

(89) Note, "Amending the Rules of Civil Procedure after Hanna v. Plumer: Rule 3," *New York University Law Review,* Vol. 42 (December, 1967), pp. 1139–54.

(90) Note, "State Court Evasion of United States Supreme Court Mandates," *Yale Law Journal,* Vol. 36 (1947), pp. 574–83.

(91) Sanders, Paul H. "The Warren Court and the Lower Federal Courts." Paper presented to American Political Science Association, 1959. Reprinted in *Constitutional Law in the Political Process* (ed. John Schmidhauser), pp. 423–35. Skokie, Ill.: Rand McNally & Co., 1963.

(92) Schmidhauser, John. "The Tensions of Federalism: The Case of Judge Peters," *Constitutional Law in the Political Process,* pp. 36–41.

(93) Vanlandingham, Kenneth. "Pecuniary Interest of Justices of the Peace in Kentucky: The Aftermath of *Tumey* v. *Ohio,*" *Kentucky Law Journal,* Vol. 45 (Summer, 1957), pp. 607–25.

Also: (16), (21), (24), (25), (41), (42), (44), (51), (78), (79).

Congress

(94) Elliot, Shelden D. "Court-Curbing Proposals in Congress," *Notre Dame Lawyer,* Vol. 33 (1957–58), pp. 597–616.

(95) Lytle, Clifford M. *The Warren Court and Its Critics.* Tucson: University of Arizona Press, 1968. Some of the same material is in "Congressional Response to Supreme Court Decisions in the Aftermath of the School Segregation Cases," *Journal of Public Law,* Vol. 12 (1963), pp. 290–312.

(96) Nagel, Stuart S. "Court-Curbing Periods in American History," *Vanderbilt Law Review,* Vol. 18 (June, 1965), pp. 925–44. (Also in *The Legal Process from a Behavioral Perspective,* pp. 260–79.)

(97) Noone, Michael F. "Federal Medical Care Recovery Act," *American Bar Association Journal,* Vol. 55 (March, 1969), pp. 259–61.

(98) Note, "Congressional Reversal of Supreme Court Decisions: 1945–1957," *Harvard Law Review,* Vol. 71 (May, 1958), pp. 1324–36.

(99) Stumpf, Harry P. "Congressional Response to Supreme Court Rulings: The Interaction of Law and Politics," *Journal of Public Law,* Vol. 14 (1965), pp. 376–95.

(100) ———. "The Political Efficacy of Judicial Symbolism," *Western Political Quarterly,* Vol. 19 (June, 1966), pp. 293–303.

Also: (8), (45), (46).

President and Administration

See: (22), (44).

State Officials: Executive and Legislative

(101) McKay, Robert B., "Georgia Versus the U.S. Supreme Court," *Journal of Public Law,* Vol. 4 (1955), pp. 285–98.

Also: (20), (26), (35), (39), (43), (69), (72), (75), (77).

Community

See: (29), (30), (31), (32), (34), (37), (38), (39), (40), (42), (50), (52), (53), (54), (57), (60), (61), (62), (66), (68), (81), (83).

Public Opinion

(102) Dolbeare, Kenneth M. "The Public Views the Supreme Court," in *Law, Politics, and the Federal Courts* (ed. Herbert Jacob), pp. 194–212. Boston: Little, Brown & Co., 1967.

(103) ———, and Phillip Hammond. "The Political Party Basis of Attitudes toward the Supreme Court," *Public Opinion Quarterly,* Vol. 31 (Spring 1967), pp. 16–30.

(104) Hirsch, Herbert, and Lewis Donohew. "A Note on Negro-White Differences in Attitudes Toward the Supreme Court," *Social Science Quarterly,* Vol. 49 (December, 1968), pp. 557–62.

(105) Kessel, John H. "Public Perceptions of the Supreme Court," *Midwest Journal of Political Science,* Vol. 10 (May, 1966), pp. 167–91.

(106) Murphy, Walter F., and Joseph Tanenhaus. "Public Opinion and the United States Supreme Court: Mapping of Some Prerequisites for Court Legitimation of Regime Changes," in *Frontiers of Judicial Research* (eds. Joel Grossman and Joseph Tanenhaus), pp. 273–303. New York: John Wiley & Sons, Inc., 1969.

Table of Cases

Index

D

J

K

L

This book has been set in 10 and 9 point Caledonia, leaded 2 points. Part numbers and titles and chapter numbers and titles are in Craw Modern. The size of the type page is 27 by 45½ picas.